P9-BJU-488

STUDIES IN THE HISTORY
OF CHRISTIAN MISSIONS

R. E. Frykenberg
Brian Stanley
General Editors

STUDIES IN THE HISTORY
OF CHRISTIAN MISSIONS

CHRISTIANITY REBORN

*The Global Expansion of Evangelicalism
in the Twentieth Century*

Edited by

Donald M. Lewis

WILLIAM B. EERDMANS PUBLISHING COMPANY
GRAND RAPIDS, MICHIGAN / CAMBRIDGE, U.K.

© 2004 Wm. B. Eerdmans Publishing Co.
All rights reserved

Wm. B. Eerdmans Publishing Co.
255 Jefferson Ave. S.E., Grand Rapids, Michigan 49503 /
P.O. Box 163, Cambridge CB3 9PU U.K.

Printed in the United States of America

08 07 06 05 04   5 4 3 2 1

Library of Congress Cataloging-in-Publication Data

Christianity reborn: the global expansion of evangelicalism in the twentieth century /
edited by Donald M. Lewis.
    p.   cm.   — (Studies in the history of Christian missions)
Includes bibliographical references and index.
ISBN 0-8028-2483-8 (pbk.: alk. paper)
1. Evangelicalism — History — 20th century.
2. Missions History — 20th century.
I. Lewis, Donald M.   II. Series.

BR1640.C49   2004
270.8′2 — dc22

2003068576

www.eerdmans.com

Contents

SECTION II

SECTION III

SECTION IV

SECTION V

General Editors' Preface

The majority of the chapters in this volume were originally delivered at a consultation of the Currents in World Christianity Project that took place at St. Catherine's College, Oxford, in July 1999. Thanks are due to The Pew Charitable Trusts of Philadelphia, who funded the Project, to Professor Donald M. Lewis of Regent College, Vancouver, who has edited the papers for publication, and to Liesl Amos, who provided invaluable editorial assistance in the final stages. The opinions expressed in this volume are those of the authors, and do not necessarily represent the views of The Pew Charitable Trusts. The Currents in World Christianity Project was coordinated by the University of Cambridge and directed by Dr. Brian Stanley. The Project, which ran from 1999 to 2001, was concerned with the twentieth-century transformation of Christianity, particularly in its evangelical Protestant forms, into a global religion. The principal publications of the Project, and its predecessor, the North Atlantic Missiology Project (NAMP), are being published in the Studies in the History of Christian Missions series.

ROBERT ERIC FRYKENBERG
BRIAN STANLEY

Contributors

Donald M. Lewis is Professor of Church History at Regent College, Vancouver. A specialist in Victorian evangelicalism, he is the editor of the *Blackwell Dictionary of Evangelical Biography: 1730-1860* (2 vols., 1995) and the author of *Lighten Their Darkness: The Evangelical Mission to Working-Class London* (1986). He is currently working on a book dealing with Evangelicals and Jews in the nineteenth century.

W. R. Ward is Emeritus Professor of Modern History at the University of Durham. A past president of the Ecclesiastical History Society, his many publications include *The Protestant Evangelical Awakening* (1992), *Faith and Faction* (1993), and *Christianity under the Ancien Régime, 1648-1789* (1999).

Mark A. Noll is McManis Professor of Christian Thought at Wheaton College, Illinois, and the author of many books on American religious history and Evangelicalism, including *A History of Christianity in the United States and Canada* (1992), *The Scandal of the Evangelical Mind* (1994), and *The Rise of Evangelicalism: The Age of Edwards, Whitefield, and the Wesleys* (2004).

Brian Stanley is Director of the Henry Martyn Centre for the Study of Mission and World Christianity and a Fellow of St. Edmund's College, University of Cambridge. He was formerly the Director of the Currents in World Christianity Project, under whose auspices this volume was produced. His publications include *The Bible and the Flag* (1990), *The History of the Baptist Missionary Society, 1792-1992* (1992), and *Christian Missions and the Enlightenment* (2001).

Philip Yuen-sang Leung is Professor of History at the Chinese University of Hong Kong. His research specializations include Confucianism and Christianity in contemporary China. He is author of *The Shanghai Taotai: Linkage Man in a Changing Society, 1843-90* (1990), *Confucianism and the Singapore Chinese Community: Historical Documents* (1995), and co-editor of *Modern China in Transition* (1995).

Robert Eric Frykenberg is Emeritus Professor of History and South Asian Studies at the University of Wisconsin-Madison and joint editor of Studies in the History of Christian Missions. His books include *Guntur District, 1784-1848: A History of Local Influence and Central Authority* (1965), *History and Belief: The Foundations of Historical Understanding* (1996), *Christians, Cultural Interactions, and India's Religious Traditions* (edited with Judith M. Brown, 2002), and *Christians and Missionaries in India* (2002).

Allan K. Davidson is Lecturer in Church History at St. John's College, Auckland, and Director of Postgraduate Studies in the School of Theology, University of Auckland. His publications include *Selwyn's Legacy* (1993), *Aotearoa New Zealand: Defining Moments in the Gospel-Culture Encounter* (1996), *Semisi Nau: The Story of My Life* (1996), and (editor) *Tongan Anglicans* (2002).

Jehu J. Hanciles is Associate Professor of History of Mission at Fuller Theological Seminary. A Sierra Leonean, he holds a Ph.D. from the University of Edinburgh. He has a forthcoming book from Greenwood Press on the outworking in Sierra Leone of Henry Venn's ideal of a three-self church.

Marthinus L. Daneel has developed contextualized ecumenical ministries in theological education, community development, and earthkeeping for and with the African Independent Churches in Zimbabwe. His books include *Fambidzano: Ecumenical Movement of Zimbabwean Independent Churches* (1989) and *African Earthkeepers* (2 vols., 1998-99). He serves part-time as Professor of Missiology at Boston University School of Theology.

Paul Freston is Professor of Sociology on the post-graduate programme in Social Science at the Federal University of São Carlos, Brazil. Since 2003 he has also held the Byker Chair of Christian Perspectives on Political, Social, and Economic Thought at Calvin College, Grand Rapids, Michigan. He has published in Portuguese, Spanish, and English on the sociology of Protestantism in Brazil and Latin America, and is the author of *Evangelicals and Politics* *in Asia, Africa and Latin America* (2001) and of *Protestant Political Parties: A Global Survey* (2004).

David Martin is Emeritus Professor of Sociology at the London School of Economics and Honorary Professor in the Department of Religious Studies at Lancaster University. His recent books include *Tongues of Fire: The Explosion of Protestantism in Latin America* (1990), *Does Christianity Cause War?* (1997), and *Pentecostalism: The World Their Parish* (2002).

Introduction

DONALD M. LEWIS

Three religious movements in the world today can claim to be global faiths: Roman Catholicism, Islam, and evangelicalism. Of these three, it is perhaps surprising that the evangelical movement is so little studied and poorly understood. Though the corpus of material on its history in the West has been growing, evangelicalism still remains relatively unexamined for being such an influential religious and social phenomenon. If our knowledge of evangelicalism in the West is limited, our knowledge of how it has fared in the non-Western world is, by comparison, far weaker; there still is very little available to scholars and serious readers on the nature and growth of evangelicalism beyond the English-speaking world.

Several reasons may be advanced for this neglect. Many Western historians and social scientists view evangelicalism as a spent force, more a movement of the past than the wave of the future. This assumption leads many to conclude that there is little need to treat evangelicalism seriously as an object of academic study. On an ideological level, an overriding assumption among many academics is the notion that "modernization" inevitably produces secularization. This view has led many toward the expectation that religion in general would become increasingly marginalized and moribund; evangelicalism would thus, in turn, cease to be a lively option for people in the modern world. This view was undoubtedly confirmed and strengthened in the minds of many in the English-speaking world by the apparent decline of evangelicalism in Britain and America during the interwar period.[1]

1. Joel Carpenter has argued that this "decline" in America, at least, was perhaps more apparent than real. Joel A. Carpenter, *Revive Us Again: The Reawakening of American Fundamentalism* (New York, 1997).

A second reason that could be advanced for the scholarly neglect of evangelicalism is not entirely unrelated to the first. With the dismantling of colonial empires after World War II, there was a widespread assumption that Christianity would dwindle and die in Africa, India, and Southeast Asia. It has been assumed — both by Westerners and by some non-Westerners — that Christianity's presence and prestige were integrally related to its perceived association with the colonial enterprise. Remove colonialism and the props of Christian presence would fall away, leaving Christianity to dwindle and die. This was the thrust of the argument advanced by the Indian diplomat and historian, K. M. Panikkar, in his widely read work *Asia and Western Dominance,* published in 1953. The persuasiveness of this line of reasoning is apparent when one talks with many academics who are genuinely surprised to learn of the remarkable appeal which evangelicalism still has in many areas of the non-Western world.

Reality has unfolded in unexpected ways. Evangelicalism, while sidelined in comparison to its influence in nineteenth-century Britain and America, has managed to compete rather well in pluralistic settings in the non-Western world and remains a dynamic force even in the United States. Martin Marty of the University of Chicago has suggested that there is a symbiotic relationship between how evangelicalism has developed and how modernity has unfolded, even suggesting that "Evangelicalism is the characteristic Protestant way of relating to modernity."[2] If Marty is correct in this, then the study of evangelicalism's development in the non-Western world becomes all the more important, for as the non-Western world encounters "modernity," evangelicalism's influence may well grow and expand. Certainly the record of its growth in the non-Western world in the twentieth century would lend credence to this view.

This concern to understand better the circumstances and growth of evangelical faith in the non-Western world brought together some six historians in a consultation in 1996: Mark Hutchinson, then Director of the Centre for the Study of Australian Christianity in Sydney, Australia; Mark Noll, Professor of Christian Thought at Wheaton College, Illinois; J. W. Hofmeyr, Professor of Theology at the University of South Africa; John Wolffe, Chair of the Religious Studies Department of the Open University in England; Richard Pierard, then Professor of History at Indiana State University; and myself. Together we developed what we conceived of as a focus on "Evangelicalism and

---

2. Martin E. Marty, "The Revival of Evangelicalism and Southern Religion," in David E. Harrell, Jr., ed., *Varieties of Southern Evangelicalism* (Macon, Ga., 1981), p. 9. Quoted in Carpenter, *Revive Us Again,* p. 235.

Globalization," and an outcome of our planning was an international symposium on this theme, held in Sydney, Australia, in August 1997. The papers from this gathering were subsequently published under the title *A Global Faith: Essays on Evangelicalism and Globalization.*[3] The Sydney consultation elucidated three rubrics under which our concern for "Evangelicalism and Globalization" might be pursued: Evangelicalism and Power, Evangelicalism and Culture, and evangelicalism and Identity. (Readers will notice that these themes are reflected in several of the articles incorporated in this book.) In 1999 our "project" was incorporated into the "Currents in World Christianity Project" (CWC) centered in the Divinity Faculty of the University of Cambridge and funded by The Pew Charitable Trusts of Philadelphia. The essays included in this book were written by participants in a conference sponsored by the CWC Project and held at St. Catherine's College, Oxford. The theme of the conference was "Christian Expansion in the Twentieth-Century Non-Western World," with a particular focus on the growth of evangelicalism.

The essays in this collection do not address in detail the vexed question of defining the term "evangelicalism." Professor Ward begins his chapter by noting the widespread acceptance of David Bebbington's fourfold definition of evangelicalism (focusing on "conversionism," "activism," "biblicism," and "crucicentrism"), but Ward seeks to understand evangelicalism through its inner religious content rather than by outward, observable criteria. There is, of course, no single "evangelicalism" but a multiplicity of evangelicalisms, and the articles in this volume demonstrate how difficult it is to establish a unified field of vision for such an amorphous movement. If anything, this work illustrates how amazingly diverse this expression of traditional Christianity became as it moved out of its North Atlantic context and became indigenized in the bewildering array of cultures, subcultures, and tribal and ethnic groups which it encountered in the nineteenth and twentieth centuries. Evangelical Christianity took root in these cultures, as its message was appropriated and inculturated by local people.

The active initiative of indigenous Christians was crucial to evangelicalism's success, and as local Christians appropriated evangelical Christianity for themselves, it became fully indigenized and was thereby transformed. This appropriation was not, of course, immediate and was often hampered by attitudes of paternalism and assumptions of cultural and sometimes racial superiority on the part of the messengers. The reluctance, even unwillingness, of some evangelicals to hand over power and responsibility to native Christians is

---

3. Mark Hutchinson and Ogbu Kalu, eds., *A Global Faith: Essays on Evangelicalism and Globalization* (Sydney, 1998).

part of the twentieth-century story of international evangelicalism. It was not, for instance, until the 1950s that the Church Missionary Society began appointing natives as diocesan bishops overseas, and it did not become commonplace until the 1960s.[4] Perhaps the greatest strength of evangelicalism, especially manifested in its Pentecostal expression, is its ability to adapt to local cultural expressions once it is freed from the tethers of missionary control and intrusive forms of foreign influence — in effect, to radicalize Christianity in the process of fully indigenizing it. Certainly it has resulted in a remarkable diversity of evangelical expression throughout the world. The local adaptability of what is now a global movement and its capacity both to radicalize and to indigenize evangelicalism are themes that recur throughout the contributions in this book. In the long run, the result of evangelicalism's success beyond the North Atlantic world has been a massive shift in the center of Protestantism from its historic locus in northern Europe to the non-Western world. Many will be surprised to read in Paul Freston's contribution that Brazil now has the world's second largest community of practicing Protestants. This shift only became obvious to some in the late 1990s. The change was perhaps most evident in the discussions of the bishops of the Anglican Communion, when they met for the Lambeth 1998 conference, a gathering of Anglican bishops which occurs every ten years. Commentators were especially surprised by the dominance of the agenda of Lambeth 1998 by non-Western bishops. But in retrospect it is clear that the Lambeth gathering merely reflected an ecclesiological reality of which many Westerners were unaware: the growth of conservative, often evangelical forms of Anglicanism in the non-Western world, while Anglicanism's fortunes seemed to be in rapid decline in many areas of the West where Anglicanism once enjoyed a privileged position.

Such dramatic changes challenge peoples' understandings of religious boundaries. We are used to thinking of the "West" as "Christian" and associating the term "Protestant" with Britain and America; we are being challenged to rethink where the center of gravity of world Christianity is located. Many areas once regarded as on Christianity's periphery — sections of Africa and the whole of Oceania, for instance — have far higher levels of practicing Christians than do Western European "Christian" nations. Areas such as Latin America which were once regarded as strongholds of Roman Catholicism are now arguably more Protestant than Catholic. These are some of the issues that this book raises.

4. Kevin Ward, "'Taking Stock': The Church Missionary Society and Its Historians," in Kevin Ward and Brian Stanley, eds., *The Church Mission Society and World Christianity, 1799-1999* (Richmond, Surrey, and Grand Rapids, 2000), p. 29.

Introduction

The chapters are arranged in five sections. Section One explores the historical background of the rise of evangelicalism. W. R. Ward, one of the leading authorities on eighteenth-century evangelicalism, examines the nature of the movement at its origin, and the particular contributions of German Pietism and forms of Christian mysticism to its subsequent development as a globalizing religious force. The international networks that nurtured the movement in its infancy and the indebtedness of the English-speaking evangelical world to German-speaking Lutheran Pietism are common themes in many of Professor Ward's works. From its beginning the movement has been internationally focused, and the German Pietist missionary example served to expand the horizons of late-eighteenth-century English-speaking evangelicals beyond their North Atlantic networks.

Mark Noll looks at the worldwide expansion of English-speaking evangelicalism in the period from the founding of the Baptist Missionary Society in 1792 through to the Edinburgh Missionary Conference of 1910. It was during this period that the foundations for the global expansion of evangelical forms of Christianity were laid: mission societies were founded; missionaries recruited and sent; and Bible translation work begun. Professor Noll examines how evangelicalism changed internally as it moved out in mission. Again the question of evangelical self-identity and the changing content of that identity are key questions that Professor Noll addresses.

In the third chapter of this section, Dr. Brian Stanley uses the Edinburgh Missionary Conference of 1910 as a device to examine the assumptions of Protestant missions thinkers at that time about the course that they expected Christian missions to follow in the twentieth century. Providing his own summary analysis of the actual directions of Christian missions, he then evaluates the expectations and assumptions of those who gathered at Edinburgh. His essay is rich in terms of raising interpretive questions that will undoubtedly help to chart the future agenda for scholars as they write the history of the expansion of twentieth-century evangelicalism.

Section Two looks at the growth of evangelicalism in several areas of Asia and in Oceania in the twentieth century. Professor Philip Leung's contribution focuses on the spectacular growth of the underground church in China since the Communist Revolution of 1949, and seeks to explain its origins and account for its success. In world-historical terms, the indigenization of evangelicalism in the Chinese countryside may in the long term be one of the most important religious developments of the twentieth century. In the history of Christianity in China, it is a breakthrough that has been fourteen centuries in coming.

In his contribution, Professor Robert Frykenberg examines the meaning of the terms "Hindu" and "Hinduism" both for the peoples of India and for non-Indians. He discusses the history of Christianity in India, the concept of conversion in the Indian context, and the challenge of globalizing tendencies. Professor Frykenberg's essay, like Professor Leung's, is extremely important for those who seek to understand the paradox of Christianity's growth in highly pluralistic settings where Christians face powerful forces hostile to their religious message and anxious about Christianity's impact upon political and social realities.

Dr. Davidson's chapter examines the experience of Oceania where evangelical missionaries experienced some of their most successful advances in the early nineteenth century. Today the long-established Protestant churches are being challenged by new, indigenous, evangelical movements that often regard traditional Protestant church members as objects for proselytization. The impact of globalization on these traditional Christian societies is particularly acute, and Dr. Davidson enumerates the challenges faced by Pacific islanders in this "globalized" environment.

A word of apology must be sounded in that there is no essay here on South Korea, a country that has proved to be so very fertile for evangelicalism. Indeed, Korea is arguably evangelicalism's greatest success story in the century in question. Nor is there a contribution on the success of evangelicalism among the Chinese diaspora (particularly in Singapore and Malaysia); nor on the remarkable success that evangelicalism has enjoyed with certain tribal peoples in parts of Southeast Asia. All of these are important areas of research that might have been included.

Section Three examines the continent where evangelicalism has been growing the most rapidly: Africa. Dr. Hanciles discusses the debate over the concept of "conversion" in the West African context in which tribal societies have suffered profound disturbance. Access to the advantages and benefits of Western education and technology and the appeal of a global faith over against a local belief system have played a role in the changes which have occurred, and have provided an impetus for the restructuring of indigenous religion. Dr. Hanciles discusses as well the rise of "Ethiopianism" and the emergence of the spectacularly successful prophet-healing movements in that region at the beginning of the twentieth century and the much more recent success of the charismatic "Third Wave" of Pentecostal expansion.

Professor Daneel's chapter considers a very different aspect of African Christian expression in his study of the characteristics of those movements variously described as "African Initiated" or "African Independent" churches. Unlike Dr. Hanciles's essay, Daneel focuses on southern Africa, with particular reference to such groups in Zimbabwe. He evaluates their relationship to mainstream Protestantism and classical Pentecostalism, arguing for a clear distinction between the latter and the African Initiated Churches. The remainder of his chapter is devoted to the peculiar characteristics of these churches and their highly creative approaches to mission in the southern Africa context.

Section Four consists of a single chapter. Dr. Paul Freston provides English-speaking readers with a helpful survey of the most recent scholarship on Latin American Pentecostalism, much of which is inaccessible to many scholars as the sources are available only in Spanish or Portuguese. It has not only been language, of course, which has obscured the view of English-speaking scholars wanting to observe Latin American Protestantism. Two other factors need to be considered. First, the fact that the explosion of Protestantism in Latin America has been Pentecostal in orientation has had an effect. Scholarship on Pentecostalism, a relatively new movement in world Christianity, is beginning to develop in the English-speaking world. However, there is little historical consciousness among non-English-speaking Pentecostals and little concern to record the movement's history — much less to interpret and explain it in academic terms. Second, the growth of Latin American Pentecostalism has occurred so rapidly — it began to grow rapidly only in the 1950s — and the movement is so new that there has been little time to gather data and to perform serious scholarly analysis and assessment. All of these factors have helped to obscure the significance and impact of non-English-speaking Pentecostalism.

The fifth and final section contains again a single chapter: David Martin's contribution provides a sociological analysis of the global spread of evangelical Christianity, accounting for its ability to create a multiplicity of faith communities suited to very different ethnic, racial, and geographical locations. He provides a sketch of how evangelical, and particularly Pentecostal, forms of Christianity have grown and expanded in the North Atlantic region, Eastern Europe, Latin and South America, as well as in Asia and Africa.

The exponential growth of evangelical Christianity in the non-Western world has produced a Christianity of amazing cultural diversity but one which is largely hidden from the purview of Western scholars. Andrew Walls has suggested that in its encounter with new forms of thought and new networks of relationship, Christianity itself is being translated and shaped in ways which may be as determinative of its future as was its encounter with the Hellenistic world.[5] Perhaps such revolutions usually occur largely unnoticed

---

5. Andrew F. Walls, "Introduction," in *The Missionary Movement in Christian History: Studies in the Transmission of the Faith* (Maryknoll, N.Y., 1996), p. xviii.

by contemporary intellectuals; however, it is not necessary that this be the case. While Christianity is today becoming increasingly marginal to Western intellectual discourse, it is both possible and necessary that such discourse come to terms with Christianity as a non-Western religion; necessary if we are to understand the modern world and necessary if we are to understand Christianity as a world-shaping religion. I thus share with the contributors to this volume the hope that these essays will provide a much-needed scholarly reappraisal of evangelicalism as the non-Western face of contemporary Protestantism.

SECTION I

CHAPTER ONE

Evangelical Identity in the Eighteenth Century

W. R. WARD

The title which I have been given might well be thought otiose, for it is an orthodoxy among many of us that the whole matter was clarified long ago by
our good friend David Bebbington; indeed the famous Bebbington Quadrilateral has become the most quoted sentence in the whole literature and was
for long virtually the only beacon the suffering student had to distinguish
men walking like trees in the gloom (Mark 8:24). The beacon illuminated the
four marks of evangelical religion: "*conversionism,* the belief that lives needed
to be changed; *activism,* the expression of the gospel in effort; *biblicism,* a particular regard for the Bible; and what may be called *crucicentrism,* a stress on
the sacrifice of Christ on the Cross."[1] None of these marks would in itself distinguish an evangelical from a great range of other Christians, but where all
four were found together in one time and place a new religious movement or
party might be identified; and conveniently enough that was in the 1730s, precisely when Lewis's *Dictionary of Evangelical Biography*[2] was to begin. My
thankless assignment is to have another look at a guide to the undergrowth
that has served so many so well. Unlike David Bebbington I want to elicit not
the continuities but some of the discontinuities in evangelical history, ways in
which the marks of evangelical identity opened the door to globalization but
laid up problems for the future.

Look first at the dates. When Donald Lewis and I were discussing the

1. D. W. Bebbington, *Evangelicalism in Modern Britain: A History from the 1730s to
the 1980s* (London, 1989), p. 3.
2. Donald M. Lewis, ed., *Blackwell Dictionary of Evangelical Biography,* 2 vols. (Oxford, 1995).

planning of the dictionary, we were in agreement that its scope would have to be limited to the English-speaking enterprise if it was to be feasible at all; there was no suggestion that evangelicalism was defined by this consideration of feasibility. Moreover, even if the definition is to be an Anglophone one, the 1730s are the time when revivalism does not indeed begin, but commences a continuous history. But no one, I think, would wish to equate revivalism and evangelicalism. Finally we want if we can to get a definition of evangelicalism in terms of its inner religious content rather than from the outside; the Bebbington Quadrilateral approaches mostly from the outside. Thus the New Birth was one of the standard counters of the mystics among the contemporaries of the early evangelicals, and it was not respect for the Bible *per se* which was peculiar to the evangelicals, but their determination to put a copy in the hands of every literate Christian. It is said that the original Luther Bible cost the equivalent of half a cow and was clearly not meant for the masses; even in the eighteenth century only 300,000 Bibles and parts of Bibles were printed at Wittenberg, while three million were produced at Halle;[3] and even before the Halle presses began to roll Spener had established a distinguishing mark of the stiffer sort of evangelicals, that they brought their Bibles to meetings in order to follow the readings and check the texts.[4] This quirk of evangelical correctness lasted until the Fall of Man in the last generation, when some evangelicals developed a postmodern conviction that it was utterly *passé* to expect even students to hold a book of any kind when the bright light of the overhead projector was at hand. Moreover, if Spener, having proposed "to spread word of God more richly among us," did not go into the publishing business, he did get around the limitations of the Lutheran lectionary readings by pressing daily Bible readings for the heads of families, by establishing public Bible reading classes for those not able to read, and, most dramatic of all, by establishing class meetings after the pattern of 1 Corinthians 14, where members of the congregation, under the direction of the preacher, should read and expound the Scriptures in public.[5] Finally, if a definition of evangelicalism from the outside were wanted, it would be simpler and more inclusive to replace the Bebbington Quadrilateral with a Ward Watchtower and define eighteenth-century evangelicals as those who felt spiritually

3. P. R. Ackroyd et al., eds., *Cambridge History of the Bible* (Cambridge, 1963-70), vol. 3, p. 478.

4. Kaspar Hermann Sandhagen, indeed, got the Stern press at Lüneburg to facilitate the whole process by producing a pocket Bible. See Markus Mathias, *Johann Wilhelm und Johanna Eleonora Petersen* (Göttingen, 1993), p. 194.

5. Johannes Wallmann, *Theologie und Frömmigkeit im Zeitalter des Barock* (Tübingen, 1995), pp. 228-29.

bound to create Orphan Houses. But it is not external definitions that we need, and here the difficulties arise.

The result of exhaustive and often acrimonious discussions in Germany has been to leave no doubt that what became the Pietist party derived from Lutheran Orthodoxy, or at any rate that wing of it known as the "movement for piety" whose fountain-head was Arndt. Our definition of evangelical identity has somehow to embrace this party, if only because eighteenth-century evangelicals did so in a way that the modern commentators have not. Whether it is Jonathan Edwards including them as pioneers of the final consummation,[6] or Wesley declaring himself "thoroughly convinced it might be of more service to the cause of religion were I barely to translate his *Gnomon Novi Testamenti* [of "that great light of the Christian world" Bengel] than to write many volumes upon it,"[7] or even Bengel himself acclaiming Arndt and Spener as the first and second angels of the Apocalypse (he himself being the third),[8] there is no mistaking the sense of international kinship among the innovators in the evangelical world for some two generations before the conventional dates of the beginning of the revival. The differences between Spener and the Orthodox milieu from which he sprang amount to two, one internal and one external: the internal factor was his eschatology, succinctly portrayed as his "hope of better times," and his patronage of informal, small-group religion, the *collegium pietatis* or class meeting, which had hitherto been taboo in the Lutheran tradition but henceforth was perhaps the most enduring external mark of the whole evangelical tradition. There was a degree of paradox in all this. Spener was aiming at a program for the renewal of a decayed church establishment, and had rather wearied of his class meetings before he went to Berlin at the end of his career; but the essence of what he wanted was stumbled upon almost of necessity by heads of families in the Protestant farm kitchens of Silesia, Austria, and Salzburg where there was now no Protestant church to revive; and it caught on too in some of the Reformed churches, especially in Germany, where a variety of small meetings had existed, usually for purposes other than the mutual edification and conversion envisaged by Spener. Moreover, Spener's gatherings marked a new turn in religious strategy. What had always been understood by reform had

6. S. E. Dwight and E. Hickman, eds., *The Works of Jonathan Edwards* (repr. Edinburgh, 1974), vol. 1, p. 600.

7. John Wesley, *Explanatory Notes on the New Testament*, new ed. (London, 1958), p. 7.

8. Gottfried Mälzer, *Johann Albrecht Bengel: Leben und Werk* (Stuttgart, 1970), p. 248; Friedhelm Groth, *Die "Wiederbringung aller Dinge" im Württembergische Pietismus* (Göttingen, 1984), pp. 30-31.

been action from above by the state; and although Spener was not under the extreme pressure to get results quickly experienced by those who became re-vivalists, he knew he could no longer wait for state action. Reform as tradi-tionally understood had involved the public disciplining of the irreligious; Spener's scheme was to improve those who were religious *virtuosi* in the sense that they were prepared to do more than their churches required as a mini-mum, and to do it not for their own sake but for the well-being of the estab-lishment as a whole.[9] There was indeed rather less ambiguity about whether holiness was a public or a private virtue in the Spenerite *collegium pietatis* than there was about the Wesleyan class meeting. And it is significant that when the revivalists came along, they everywhere made a beeline for the little groups of religious *virtuosi* who, though excluded from traditional ecclesias-tical history by virtue of their informality, acted as the sort of leaven Spener had envisaged.

As Davidson pointed out years ago, the inflation which had overtaken millennial logic in America by the time of the War of Independence simply eliminated the problem of state which Spener was trying to circumvent, by assuming (for example) that there would be no need for standing armies when regenerate kings put aside their dreams of aggrandisement.[10] There was, therefore, a fitness in the fact that Spener was distinguished doctrinally from the Lutheran Orthodox by a turn in eschatology. At the end of his life Luther had lived in the expectation of an imminent Last Judgment that would be ushered in by the fall of Rome and the defeat of the Turks, and in radical Protestantism the expectation of an earthly millennial kingdom remained vigorous. This notion was rejected for Lutheran Orthodoxy by Article 17 of the Confession of Augsburg, and the Münster troubles of 1535 had given no inducement to change that view. By the later-seventeenth century the Lu-theran Orthodox were trying to sustain a belief in the imminence of the end, and to use it as a scourge of conscience; they disappointed many by perpetu-ally deferring the end, and especially the radicals whose hopes of imminent earthly fulfillment had revived during the Thirty Years War. In the mid-seventies, however, Spener adopted what became famously known as "the hope of better times." In this view the end would not come until all God's promises to the church had been fulfilled. The scourge to conscience now was not that repentance tomorrow might be too late, but that it was possible in the power of the Spirit to make a real improvement in the state of the church;

9. Wallmann, *Theologie und Frömmigkeit*, pp. 23-24.
10. J. W. Davidson, *The Logic of Millennial Thought: Eighteenth-Century New En-gland* (New Haven, 1977), pp. 228-29.

and the millennial question gave particular urgency to one special field of study. One of the signs of the end according to Romans 11 was to be the conversion of the Jews, and one of the extraordinary features of the history of seventeenth-century Lutheran Orthodoxy was that it gave itself to rabbinic studies with an intensity paralleled at no other time.[11] Spener followed a train of other Lutheran theologians over to the Reformed world at Basel to improve his expertise in Hebrew and Hebraic studies. And, as Senior of Frankfurt with a major Jewish ghetto on his doorstep, he concluded that the great obstacle to the conversion of the Jews was the decayed state of the church. Here the exercise of the general spiritual priesthood, the deferment of the Last Days, and the cultivation of the largest domestic mission field of the church hung rationally together.

So far, so good. But to postpone the Last Day did not solve for Spener a problem which Christian orthodoxy had long carried within itself, and which was pointed out almost at once by the Petersens, husband and wife, whom Spener married, and supported against church hostility; it was also explored by the little group of English Behmenists led by Pordage, Bromley, and Jane Leade. One side of Christian doctrine had generally maintained an original sympathy between man and the universe: man was the microcosm as well as the image of God, and it was the sin of man which destroyed this harmony and left the whole creation groaning after redemption. When therefore God's purposes were accomplished among men, there should also be a "restoration of all things" to their original sympathy. The Western churches, however, had always fought against this conclusion in the interests of legal justice. At the consummation of all things not only should there not be a general restoration of sympathy, but even the race of men should be finally and eternally divided into the redeemed devoted to the adoration of God, and the damned sentenced to eternal punishment. But this involved a logical problem which orthodoxy and in the end much of evangelicalism expended considerable energy in ignoring. What were the relations of these two kingdoms of men? Either they knew nothing of each other or they knew something of each other. The first assumption would imply that the redeemed would know God only as eternal love, and not as justice. The damned would know God solely as justice. But the story of Dives and Lazarus (Luke 16:19-31) suggested that the damned had some perception of the kingdom of bliss, and the Latin fathers heavily worked the idea that this was an essential part of their punishment. To make this more bearable it was suggested that the saved were spared the view. In short in the end the tri-

11. H. J. Schoeps, *Philosemitism im Barock. Religions- und geistesgeschichtliche Untersuchungen* (Tübingen, 1952), p. 134.

umph of justice in Western theology destroyed the humanity of men; even the redeemed were robbed of obligation to love their enemies and to have sympathy with them, let alone the rest of creation.[12] When Petersen and his wife embarked on questions of this kind, the church speedily got rid of them. But Spener's eschatology and Petersen's restorationism had a deep influence in Württemberg. Bengel put the one on a sounder biblical basis, and it came home to roost in John Wesley; Oetinger endeavored to solve the problems of the other with a large dose of mysticism and created a map of knowledge which was very inaccessible but was not rivaled by any later evangelical.[13]

Meanwhile, were the Last Days nearer or farther away in the Reformed tradition? The Reformed tradition had been vexed by a curious mixture of vagueness and precision. Calvin had been embarrassed by the speculative use made of eschatology by the Catholics, and by the apocalyptic use of it by the radicals; indeed, he went so far as to say that even if Paul had known by special revelation the date of the Last Day, he would still have had to affirm to his flock human ignorance of it, to guard them from a sense of false security and unholy curiosity.[14] J. H. Olsted (1588-1638) defended the premillennialism of the Early Church Fathers and looked forward to the binding of Satan; this would allow the Church peace for a thousand years, and permit the conversion of multitudes. There would be a victorious struggle with Gog and Magog, and the millennium could be expected in 1694. Later in the century many of the northern Reformed churches went over to the federal doctrines of Coccejus which were the real domain of eschatology.[15] He divided the history of the Kingdom of God since the ascension into seven periods. The sixth would be a period of judgment and purification of the people of God during the Thirty Years War, and the seventh, heralded by the imminent seventh trumpet, would see the general conversion of the peoples, and would wind up with the return of Christ in glory and the general resurrection and judgment. (Coccejus was not interested in the restoration of all things.)

12. On all this see Ernst Benz, "Der Mensch und die Sympathie aller Dinge am Ende der Zeiten (nach Jakob Boehme und seiner Schule)," *Eranos-Jahrbuch* 24 (1955): 133-97.

13. On this story see the works of Mälzer, Mathias, and Groth, cited above; also M. Brecht and K. Deppermann, eds., *Geschichte des Pietismus* (Göttingen, 1995), vol. 2, pp. 269-78; and Hartmut Lehmann, *Pietismus und weltliche Ordnung in Württemberg* (Stuttgart, 1969), ch. 2. Friedrich Christoph Oetinger's *Selbst-Biographie* (Stuttgart, 1845) was edited long afterward by Julius Hamberger as an anti-rationalist and anti-materialist tract. See also Rainer Piepmeier, "Theologie des Lebens und Neuzeitprozesse: Fr. Chr. Oetinger," *Pietismus und Neuzeit* 5 (1979): 184-217.

14. Heinrich Quistorp, *Calvin's Doctrine of the Last Things* (London, 1955), p. 110.

15. W. Nordmann, "Im Widerstreit von Mystik und Föderalismus," *Zeitschrift für Kirchengeschichte* 50 (1931): 163.

So much ink has been spilt in the study of the eschatological ideas of Puritans on both sides of the Atlantic that it is not necessary to repeat much here. The Westminster Confession maintained the usual Orthodox stance of keeping a grip upon conscience by insisting that the time of the end was unknown but might be imminent, and Cotton Mather, believing to the end that the Second Coming was imminent, postponed it continually but always to a date just around the corner. What he would not have was Mede's belief that Gog and Magog, who would harass the saints in the end, would originate in America.[16] Baxter too spent the last years of his life trying to resolve the question whether Christ would return to inaugurate the millennial rule of his saints in the imminent future.[17] And even the famous statement in the Savoy Declaration of the Congregational churches (1658), which was not reticent as to the amount that needed to happen before the end — with the "Anti-Christ being destroyed, the Jews called, and the adversaries of his dear Son broken, the churches of Christ being enlarged and edified through a free and plentiful communication of light and grace," the saints should enjoy a more peaceable and glorious condition than hitherto — expected the whole to take place soon.

This point is indeed more important than much of the discussion about pre- and postmillennialism. Jonathan Edwards has been credited with being the first American to teach that the final consummation would come not after a cosmic cataclysm, but after a period of prosperity for the Church brought about by men prepared to do the work of the Spirit.[18] Certainly after spending twenty years on his grand map of history, *A History of the Work of Redemption,* he failed to finish it, perhaps not only because of a miscarried smallpox vaccination. He failed to get to the point of suggesting when the end of this present age was likely to occur, but was able to defend himself against Chauncy with some effect; he had indeed been excited by the First Great Awakening, but he had not said that it would bring on the latter-day glory.[19] There would be dark times to come, but the Scripture gave no countenance to any view other than that the work would "be accomplished by *means,* by the

16. Cotton Mather, *Magnalia Christi Americana* (London, 1702; repr. Edinburgh, 1979), vol. 1, p. 46. In the end he fell back upon the position of the Westminster Confession (vol. 2, p. 207); see Robert Middlekauf, *The Mathers: Three Generations of Puritan Intellectuals, 1596-1728* (New York, 1971), p. 342.

17. William M. Lamont, *Richard Baxter and the Millennium* (London, 1979), p. 11.

18. This issue raised in C. C. Goen, "Jonathan Edwards: A New Departure in Eschatology," *Church History* 28 (1959): 25-40, is discussed by John F. Wilson, "History, Redemption and the Millennium," in Nathan O. Hatch and Harry S. Stout, eds., *Jonathan Edwards and the American Experience* (Oxford, 1988), pp. 131-41.

19. Jonathan Edwards, *Works*, vol. 1, p. lxxix.

preaching of the gospel, and the use of the ordinary means of grace, and so shall be *gradually* brought to pass."[20] It was not Edwards's fault if others grafted a secular millennialism upon what he insisted was a work of the Holy Spirit, nor if De Jong, in a thoroughly one-sided book, were to trace his Reformed version of Spener's "hope of better times" back almost to the beginning of the Reformed movement.[21]

Pierre Poiret, the universal salesman of mysticism, whose works and reprints had a powerful influence on the first generation of evangelicals, also found his own means of escape from the historical structure worked out by Coccejus. He would not have his federalism, and insisted that prophecy might have historical, mystical, and prophetic fulfillment. Not surprisingly in his case mysticism provided the way out, in the shape of a pneumatic theory of the Second Coming which he took over from Antoinette Bourignon, the Belgian mystic.[22]

The principal exception to the picture of evangelical willingness to break with the eschatology of the old Orthodox parties is provided by the English evangelicals, and here the exception is rather that of the Church of England itself. The Church of England had no formal Orthodox party and turned a blind eye to the millennial question. Bengel himself had noted that "when Christianity had received the upper hand in the world through Constantine the Great, its hope in the future was much weakened by its enjoyment of the present";[23] and the Church of England having survived the assaults of millennialists was sufficiently sure of its loaves and fishes even to dabble in Jacobitism. Daniel Whitby is supposed to have given vent to optimistic postmillenarian views, but how defunct the issue had become is well illustrated by the winsome naïveté of Wesley's introduction to his *Notes* on Revelation: "It is scarce possible for any that either love or fear God not to feel their hearts extremely affected in seriously reading either the beginning or the latter part of the Revelation . . . but the intermediate parts I did not study at all for many years, as utterly despairing of understanding them, after the fruitless attempts of so many wise and good men; and perhaps I should have

20. Edwards's italics (*Works*, vol. 1, p. 605). Since at one stage there was a suggestion that I should deal (inter alia) with the growth of evangelical interest in the Southern hemisphere, it is notable that Edwards looked to the evangelization in "the next whole century" of Africa and Terra Australis (*Works*, vol. 2, p. 306).

21. James A. De Jong, *As the Waters Cover the Sea: Millennial Expectations in the Rise of Anglo-American Missions, 1640-1810* (Kampen, 1970).

22. Nordmann, "Im Widerstreit von Mystik und Föderalismus," p. 154; P. Poiret, *The Divine Oeconomy* (London, 1713), vol. 4, part iii, pp. 248-63.

23. J. A. Bengel, *Erklärte Offenbarung*, 2nd ed. (Stuttgart, 1746), p. 1103.

lived and died in this sentiment, had I not seen the works of the great Bengelius. But these revived my hopes of understanding even the prophecies of this book; at least many of them in some good degree."[24] He paid him the ultimate accolade of bowdlerizing him for the faithful, and, without committing himself to every detail, defending his views to the end of his life.[25] It is also true that some of the familiar trappings of the European millennium are missing in Wesley; there were not enough Jews in England or America to make their conversion as significant a signpost as that of the American Indians,[26] and an obscure passage in one of the letters suggests that Wesley objected to a printer who attributed to him views on the restoration of all things.[27] But both in the middle and at the end of his life, when Wesley became excited about the progress of the revival, he would use the conventional postmillennial language about the latter-day glory with all the optimism of Jonathan Edwards;[28] and he perceived the downfall of the papacy more than a decade before it became a standby of millennial commentators on the French Revolution.[29] Whitefield, too, though prepared to conclude his will with the prayer, "Come, Lord Jesus, come quickly,"[30] was, especially for a voluble man and a Calvinist to boot, remarkably silent about the whole issue of the end time.

Zinzendorf can be relied on to be a difficult case. In his "twenties a chiliast, but not for long,"[31] he found the apocalyptic imagery turned against himself; that brave but difficult character, Christian David, moved out of Herrnhut in 1727 and took to describing Zinzendorf as the beast out of the

24. Wesley, *Notes on the New Testament*, p. 932.

25. J. Telford, ed., *Letters of John Wesley* (London, 1931), vol. 8, pp. 63, 67.

26. But cf. John Wesley, *Sermons* (London, 1872), vol. 2, pp. 325-26.

27. Wesley, *Letters*, vol. 8, p. 153.

28. *Wesley, Letters*, vol. 8, pp. 199, 204; *Sermons*, vol. 2, esp. nos. 58 and 66. In Sermon 4 (*Sermons*, vol. 1, pp. 40-58) preached before the University of Oxford in 1744, Wesley had incorporated a three-stage historical scheme in which the Kingdom of God was first established by the apostles in Palestine, then developed into Christendom, and was now entering its final stage, "when Christianity will prevail over all, and cover the earth." I am grateful to Professor John C. English for drawing my attention to this in an unpublished paper "John Wesley's Politics in the Light of His Realized Eschatology." Perhaps not surprisingly Fletcher, Wesley's Swiss sidekick and expected successor, gave much more attention to continental prophecies of an imminent and catastrophic end. See P. P. Streiff, *Jean Guillaume de la Fléchère: Ein Beitrag zur Geschichte des Methodismus* (Frankfurt am Main, 1984), pp. 108-19.

29. Wesley, *Letters*, vol. 6, p. 291.

30. L. Tyerman, *Life of the Rev. George Whitefield*, 2nd ed. (London, 1890), vol. 2, p. 610.

31. O. Uttendörfer, *Zinzendorf und die Mystik* (Berlin, 1950), pp. 46, 54.

pit, and Rothe, the parish minister, as the false prophet![32] Zinzendorf himself had a horror of mass conversions, and in millenarian terms believed that the time of the heathen had not yet come.[33] Yet the famous picture in the settlement at Zeist, depicting Christ surrounded by the converts of the Moravian mission field, is entitled (after Rev. 14:4) "The First-fruits";[34] he believed that the American Indians were the lost tribe of Israel, but did not regard Indian missions as missions to Jews.[35] In a celebrated first meeting with Bengel he fell out badly with that character and was relentlessly pursued by him in the press thereafter.[36] In his general attitude toward the Last Things, Zinzendorf was characterized by an optimistic caginess: he did not accept the eternity of the pains of hell; he did not reject the restoration of all things, but thought it on the whole none of his business; and since the technical millenarian questions formed no part of the original apostolic preaching, he thought that Moravian preaching should follow suit.[37] Thus Zinzendorf, too, in the convoluted way that was all his own, sought to escape the constrictions and certainties of the Orthodox eschatologies, and to channel the release of energies into mission. In this he embodied the second distinguishing mark of evangelical identity. And this liberation from Orthodox ideas of time carried with it a liberation from Orthodox constraints of space;[38] if the gospel had to follow the flag, the missions which were launched from Halle, Herrnhut, and Basel would never have issued forth at all.

It is, however, the third mark of the original evangelical identity that presents the most difficulty. All the original evangelicals were more or less deeply involved with mystical literature, and it is important to form an estimate of where they stood in the mystical spectrum. Here the discouragements are almost overwhelming. Andrew Louth commences his article on "Mysticism" in the *Theologische Realenzyklopaedie* with the proposition that there is no agreement as to what it is, and no one apart from the Catholic systematizers will say him nay. Evelyn Underhill and her army of admirers insist that mysti-

32. Brecht and Deppermann, *Geschichte des Pietismus*, vol. 2, p. 25.

33. J. C. S. Mason, "The Role of the Moravian Church during the Missionary Awakening in England, 1760-1800," Ph.D. thesis, University of London, 1998, p. 170.

34. Reproduced in Brecht and Deppermann, *Geschichte des Pietismus*, vol. 2, p. 72.

35. Erich Beyreuther, "Zinzendorf und das Judentum," repr. in *Zinzendorf Werke*, Reihe 2, Bd. XII, p. 724.

36. G. Mälzer, *Bengel und Zinzendorf* (Witten, 1968).

37. A. G. Spangenberg, *Apologetische Schluss-Schrift* (1752), repr. in *Zinzendorf Werke*, Ergänzungsband 3 (Hildesheim, 1964), pp. 167-68, 554-57.

38. Hartmut Lehmann, *Protestantische Weltsichten: Transformationen seit dem 17. Jahrhundert* (Göttingen, 1998), pp. 14-18; idem, "'Absonderung' und 'Gemeinschaft' in frühen Pietismus," *Pietismus und Neuzeit* 4 (1977-78): 54-82.

cism has no history, only a succession of better and worse mystics. Finally, it is clear that in the immediate European background to evangelicalism there was much dabbling in Jewish mysticism, and the Christian kabbala has suffered the same fate as this year's Tesco hot cross buns, which bore the cross on one side and the Star of David on the other, that of being denounced by the Orthodox on both sides as a nonsense. Even supposing this to be so, the poor historian has his classification to attempt.

The involvement of the original evangelicals with mysticism, though neglected in the literature, is so obvious as to need little laboring. There had always been an undercurrent of mysticism in the Christian world, and when existing systems of thought and belief began to look fragile, it generated a sudden and extraordinary outpouring of influence.[39] The whole Pietist enterprise was an offshoot of the seventeenth-century "movement for piety" at the fountain-head of which stood Arndt's *True Christianity* which was a great compendium of excerpts from medieval mystics subject to Lutheran editing. Everybody read it, and, from our point of view, it is significant that the great posthumous *Blütezeit* of Arndt publishing was the Bebbington decade, 1730-40.[40] Every Pietist leader except Francke wrote prefaces to part of the Arndt corpus, Spener's *Pia Desideria*, originally a preface to Arndt's lectionary sermons, being the most celebrated programmatic writing of the whole movement. Like Wesley later, he always had an eye to sources of religious vitality, and his sympathetic view of "the mystical theology" (the nature of which is to be encountered below) did him no good at all with the Lutheran Orthodox.[41] Francke translated Molinos into Latin for academic purposes, and Molinos and Arndt between them played a significant part in his conversion.[42] Makarius the Egyptian was not just one of the more implausible pieces of baggage taken by Wesley to Georgia, but was as great a cliché of spirituality right through the evangelical world as being converted "while one was reading Luther's *Preface* to the Romans"; it was a major item in the Protestant rediscovery of Christian mysticism in the seventeenth and eighteenth centuries.[43] Much the same can be said of the *Lives* of Gregory Lopez and M. de

39. Ernst Schering, "Mystik als Erkenntnis: Motive und Aspekte der mystischen Theologie Fénelons," *Pietismus und Neuzeit* 5 (1979): 164-83.

40. Wilhelm Koepp, *Johann Arndt: Eine Untersuchung über die Mystik im Luthertum* (Berlin, 1912), p. 151.

41. Brecht, *Geschichte des Pietismus*, vol. 1, pp. 314, 372.

42. Erhard Peschke, "Die Bedeutung der Mystik für die Bekehrung August Hermann Franckes," *Theologische Literaturzeitung* 91 (1966): 881-92. Repr. in M. Greschat, ed., *Zur neueren Pietismusforschung* (Darmstadt, 1977), pp. 294-316.

43. Ernst Benz, *Die protestantische Thebais: Zur Nachwirkung Makarios des Ägypters*

Renty[44] and versions of which Wesley published, and to which he was deeply indebted. Of course a comprehensive common pool of mystical materials had been assembled by Pierre Poiret, the émigré pastor from the Palatinate, later skillfully exploited by Tersteegen, but an asset on which others could draw.[45]

Wesley, as we shall see, could never quite swallow the Mystic Way whole, but he could certainly never spit it out, and from the beginning he needed something of this kind to support his heavy stress on sanctification. So of course did the odd little knot of Scots Episcopalians who paid court to Mme. Guyon.[46] In the early 1730s Wesley went through a sort of mystical crisis and was sustained by John Byrom, who was seeking to propagate Poiret's edition of the mystics and put him on to Antoinette Bourignon and Mme. Guyon. And at this early stage in their careers both the Wesley brothers were deeply influenced by William Law and his ideal of Christian Perfection.[47] At this stage Whitefield was also deeply indebted to Law, though the latter turned against him in 1739;[48] and he had the later satisfaction of quoting the mystical canon from Scougal to Arndt against Wesley.[49] Mystical phrases about Christ being formed in our hearts tripped off his pen.[50] And in company with the whole evangelical army he beat the drum about the New Birth,[51] and must have known that this term was part of the mystics' technical vocabulary.

The case of Jonathan Edwards is less straightforward partly because his lifelong effort was to harmonize the Bible with a doctrinal scheme, and partly, no doubt, because the great fund of European mystical literature was less readily available in New England except in so far as it appeared second-hand

im Protestantismus des 17. und 18. Jahrhunderts (Wiesbaden, 1963); cf. Gottfried Arnold, *Historie und Beschreibung der mystischen Theologie oder geheimen Gottes Gelehrtheit wie auch derer alten und neuen Mysticorum* (Frankfurt, 1703), p. 157, and his *Vertheidigung der mystischen Theologie* (n.d.), §16-17.

44. On the general diffusion of this work see Martin Schmidt, "Die Biographie des französischen Grafen Gaston Jean-Baptiste de Renty (1611-1649) und ihre Aufnahme im 18. Jahrhundert," in *Wiedergeburt und neuer Mensch* (Witten, 1969), pp. 390-439.

45. For these two and the literature on them see my essay "Mysticism and Revival: The Case of Gerhard Tersteegen," in Jane Garnett and Colin Matthew, eds., *Revival and Religion since 1700: Essays for John Walsh* (London, 1993), pp. 41-58.

46. On whom see W. R. Ward, "Anglicanism and Assimilation; or Mysticism and Mayhem in the Eighteenth Century," in *Faith and Faction* (London, 1993).

47. J. Brazier Green, *John Wesley and William Law* (London, 1945); Eric W. Baker, *A Herald of the Evangelical Revival* (London, 1948).

48. Tyerman, *Life of the Rev. George Whitefield,* vol. 1, p. 281.

49. *Works of the Rev. George Whitefield* (London, 1771), vol. 4, pp. 60, 66.

50. *George Whitefield's Journals* (Edinburgh, 1960), p. 205. Cf. *Letters of George Whitefield* (repr. Edinburgh, 1976), vol. 1, p. 340.

51. Whitefield, *Works,* vol. 4, p. 457.

in Puritan dress. But that Edwards had a powerful streak of mysticism in him personally is borne out by his vivid personal response to the divine beauty. The saints, he declared, with doubtless himself in mind, "do not see first that God loves *them,* and then see that he is lovely; but they first see that God is lovely, and that Christ is excellent and glorious; their hearts are first captivated with this view"; indeed, the great difference between gracious affections and those which are false and untrue is that they have "beautiful symmetry and proportion."[52] This was what he found embodied in David Brainerd, and this was what he impressed on Americans as the nature of the New Birth.[53]

All this is obvious and does not take us far toward a profile of evangelicalism, except to emphasize the warning that it does not constitute the evangelicals as the middle term between Catholicism and Protestantism, which has often been claimed. It is now quite clear that the Protestant churches had never produced enough devotional literature to meet the demand, and that the faithful had stayed themselves throughout a century of terrible trials not on Protestant Orthodoxy but on a diet of medieval mysticism received sometimes directly through writers like Thomas à Kempis, sometimes indirectly through Arndt or the much translated Puritan writers. The evangelicals were not only appealing to this market; they were certainly middlemen between it and a popular milieu. But what was happening to mysticism as a whole, and where does evangelical mysticism fit into its picture? It is convenient to begin in this way, though the question contains ecclesiastical presumptions of a very constricting kind.

The short history of official mysticism seems to be this. By the end of the Middle Ages the school of *Devotio Moderna* had developed a method for mental prayer which carried that practice into lay circles, and by that very fact created a presumption that among professionals something more was required. Xavier was suspected of illuminism because he instructed laymen in his exercises, but the desire to further and, in particular, to explore the processes of contemplation and meditation led to the extraordinary flowering of mysticism in the sixteenth century. In this work, women, less corseted by scholastic education than the men, took the lead, though St. John of the Cross eventually got into the canon with his concept of the two dark nights of the soul. But St. Teresa of Avila, who was able to analyze her personal experience with remarkable lucidity, if with imperfect consistency, set the pattern with her description of the seven steps of the soul to ultimate spiritual marriage

---

52. Edwards, *Works,* vol. 1, pp. 276, 309.

53. A. Heimert, *Religion and the American Mind from the Great Awakening to the Revolution,* 2nd ed. (Cambridge, 1968), pp. 42-43.

with God. The other pattern, that mystical creativity moved south, was also sustained, and the hold of northern mystics was supported mainly by burgeoning reprints of their works. Only in the seventeenth century did mysticism in a creative sense return to France. The great flowering of French mysticism was, however, cut short by a catastrophe from the outside and a development from within. At the end of the seventeenth and the beginning of the eighteenth centuries there were papal condemnations of Molinos, the Jansenists, and Fénelon, and the severe trials that befell Mme. Guyon and the Quietists dealt a serious blow to the mystical tradition in its Catholic heartlands. Mme. Guyon artlessly maintained that "the establishment of all those ends [the conversion of sinners, etc.] which [Christ] proposed in coming into the world, is effected by the apparent overthrow in that very structure which in reality he would erect: for by means which seem to destroy his church, he establishes it."[54] What was more apparent to Church authority was that Quietism offered a route to circumvent rather than to shore up ecclesiastical power. Dale van Kley has shown how greatly the anti-Jansenist measures undermined the *ancien régime* in France, and the anti-Quietist campaign made mysticism a politically trickier option than it had been. But the type of literature produced in quantity by a movement past its best years is also indicative of a change. There were no longer durable accounts of religious experience; encyclopedias, treatises, manuals, précis, and directories were given a scientific character by appearing in Latin; there were "vocabularies" of mystical theology; a declining field was propped up by the creation of chairs in Carmelite colleges, and the chairs generated an output of *summas*; and in the eighteenth century Maurists and Bollandists applied a historical critique. But mystical literature went into a decline from which even intense scholarly application in the present century has hardly rescued it.[55] Thus the evangelicals, especially the Western ones, who drew heavily on the more recent, and especially the Quietist, literature, were deriving nourishment from a movement in

54. *The Exemplary Life of the pious Lady Guion* (Dublin, 1775), p. 27.

55. For a swashbuckling compendium of information on all this, see the article "Mystique," in M. Villier, ed., *Dictionnaire de Spiritualité* (in progress), vol. 10, part 2, pp. 1889-1984. In the article *Lumen Gentium* the Second Vatican Council affirmed the call of all Christians to sanctity without reference to the mystical life, identifying sanctity with the perfection of charity. In view of the comments, well up in the Premier League of female felinity, of Evelyn Underhill on Mme. Guyon, as not ranking high among the mystics, the subject of "some unfortunate incidents," as "unbalanced, diffuse and sentimental," "marred by a terrible and unctuous interest in the peculiar graces vouchsafed to her," and basking "like a pious tabby cat in the beams of uncreated light," this may have been as well. See E. Underhill, *Mysticism: The Development of Humankind's Spiritual Consciousness,* 14th ed. (London, 1995), pp. 66, 182, 247.

decay, a movement which was being subjected to so thorough a process of "textbookization" as to lose its earlier appeal as a refuge from the constrictions of scholastic theology, systematic rationalism in the style of Descartes, mechanistic views of the universe, or even male domination.

There was, however, a major Protestant mystic to be taken into account, Jakob Böhme, and he illustrates the fact that Protestant ecclesiastical mysticism had always been flanked by two other things that were different but not entirely unrelated, illuminism and magic. It was not just polemical convenience which led the Lutheran Orthodox Ehregott Daniel Colberg to produce a vast treatise[56] on *Platonic-Hermetic Christianity comprising the historical account of the origin and manifold sects of modern fanatical theology, under the names of Paracelsists, Weigelians, Rosicrucians, Quakers, Behmenists, Anabaptists, Bourignists, Labadists and Quietists,* for there was indeed a considerable spectrum of opinion which rebelled against the certainties of Protestant Orthodoxies. One of the clear signs of weariness with the various baroque systems was that this critical world was characterized by eclecticism and syncretism, and, barred from university and church, it thrived in informal gatherings of its own, class meetings, lodges, Temples of Wisdom Not all the menu was available to all the customers all the time; the extreme emphasis in church mysticism on the passivity of the subject made combination with magic, the object of which was to secure a result, good or bad, very difficult — but up to the time of the prohibition of the French Masonic lodges in 1737, they were said to be "assemblies of Quietists and Molinists," and certainly their chancellor, the Chevalier Ramsay, had been a confidant of Fénelon and Mme. Guyon. Moreover, to this whole milieu there was a revelation of some kind in nature as well as in Scripture. Gottfried Arnold provided a historical pedigree for the true understanding of the latter; Jakob Böhme provided a powerful exposition of the former, making use of ideas which had been in circulation since the Renaissance.[57] On the side of nature the other great authority was Paracelsus, and Paracelsus interpreted in the light of the Jewish mystical tradition, the Kabbala. Whether this could have anything to do with Christianity

---

56. Leipzig, 1709.

57. For this background see R. C. Zimmermann, *Das Weltbild des jungen Goethe* (Munich, 1969), pp. 22-36, 98; and the comprehensive work of Will-Erich Peuckert, *Pansophie,* 3 vols. (Berlin, 1956-73). One of the less incomprehensible expositions of Böhme is J. J. Stoudt, *Sunrise to Eternity: A Study in Jacob Boehme's Life and Thought* (Philadelphia, 1957). How the confusion of this rich menu has persisted is illustrated by the fact that Evelyn Underhill (*Mysticism,* pp. 121, 473) took her mystical definition of that evangelical cliché, the New Birth, from the illuminist Eckhartshausen (on whom see Antoine Faivre, *Eckartshausen et la Théosophie Chrétienne* [Paris, 1969]).

(or even Paracelsus) was perhaps over-zealously denied in the last generation by Barthians, and also by Orthodox Jews; but it appeared to many in the late seventeenth and early eighteenth centuries that the kabbalistic idea of the divine emanations could be used to promote a trinitarian understanding of nature, and an interpretation of the mysteries of the world as a reflection of the mysteries of the divine life.[58] At any rate before long anything the least occult from astrology to alchemy and nature-magic became "kabbala." Part of the attraction of this style of thought to Spener and his followers was that chiliastic hopes had been cherished by disciples of Paracelsus[59] who might therefore be won to Spener's "hope of better times"; again, with the Frankfurt ghetto on the doorstep, to preach in this milieu was a pastoral obligation. It was to this ghetto that Oetinger came in 1729 to learn the Christian and the Jewish kabbala in the same house. One of his mentors, Knorr von Rosenroth, had written (for missionary purposes) a celebrated book, *Cabbala Denudata*, which was admired all over Europe, and not least by Spener, Francke, and Leibnitz. Of course Oetinger himself came from a Württemberg that was full of mystics, enthusiasts, and chiliasts. He believed that the Bible contained (typologically) all the events of the past, present, and future, and that Bengel had the key to them. He made it his life's work to combine Böhme, the kabbalists, and Bengel in a new map of knowledge. And it was this strand of evangelicalism which was most ready to ally with other kinds of mysticism and anti-intellectual elements of the Enlightenment to make a new conservative prefiguring of romanticism before the end of the eighteenth century.[60]

It is remarkable that English Behmenism did not work out in this way at all. There were early English translations of Böhme which had an impact upon the Neo-Platonists; Jane Leade, Pordage, and the English Philadelphians had a considerable importance in the Netherlands and Germany, if only because they were so much more lucid than Böhme himself, and had a posthumous influence even on Zinzendorf; but the German separatists who took up with Behmenism did not become evangelicals in either Germany or America.[61] Of the influential English mystics, John Byrom turned rather to

---

58. This subject is impressively treated by Gershom Scholem, *Alchemie und Kabbala: Ein Kapitel aus der Mystik* (n.p., n.d. [Berlin, 1927]) and *On the Kabbalah and Its Symbolism* (London, 1965); and Ernst Benz, *Die Christliche Kabbala: Ein Stiefkind der Theologie* (Zurich, 1958).

59. Wallmann, *Theologie und Frömmigkeit*, p. 106.

60. Hans-Martin Kirn, *Deutsche Spätaufklärung und Pietismus* (Göttingen, 1998), pp. 15, 36.

61. Elizabeth W. Fisher, "'Prophecies and Revelations': German Cabbalists in Early Pennsylvania," *Pennsylvania Magazine for History and Biography* 109 (1985): 299-333.

Poiret and the Quietists, while William Law seems to have intensified the feuds which destroyed his early influence on the evangelicals by becoming an English spokesman for Böhme. Note also Warburton's intemperate inquiry of Doddridge in 1738:[62] "Pray, what think you of our new Cabalists, are they more rational than the Jewish? Is not Hutchinson's method as much a disgrace to human reason as that of the Talmud? What think you too of the Methodists? You are nearer to Oxford; we have strange accounts of their freaks. The books of Madame Bourignon, the french *visionnaire*, are, I hear, much inquired after by them." Here the anti-Methodist charge is of Quietism not Behmenism. Through Law, Böhme's literary influence persisted into the nineteenth century, but the Enlightenment had struck home too hard on the main English evangelicals for them to experience the impact he had had on the Neo-Platonists and the Philadelphians. Neither Wesley nor Jonathan Edwards could say what he wanted to say without the Lockean psychology, and, whatever his merits, Böhme could never satisfy the Lockean criteria of clarity and simplicity. Much of the time Wesley gunned for Böhme and the "mystical theology" in the Lutheran Orthodox style, with the criticism that they boldly speculated where Scripture feared to tread,[63] but in 1780 it only needed his old friend Francis Okeley (by then a rather off-beat Moravian) to publish some of Böhme's autobiographical tracts[64] to spur him into one of his most virulent and uncomprehending polemics.[65] It was a similar story with the Swedish visionary Swedenborg, who struggled to produce a sort of engineer's mysticism free from the mechanical constraints of engineering. Some of his English followers clung round the fringes of Methodism, but, though attracted at first by evidence of spiritual vitality, Wesley himself almost instantly lost patience, concluded that a fever in mid-life had "introduced [Swedenborg] into the society of lunatics," and denounced him at length in the *Arminian Magazine*.[66] Yet at this point David Bebbington's "Biblicism" and "crucicentrism" come home to roost. Behind the discomfort with Böhme's cosmogony there lurked the feeling that it distracted attention from the need for atonement, and by the later years of the century this had become a knee-jerk reaction among

---

62. G. F. Nuttall, ed., *Calendar of the Correspondence of Philip Doddridge* (London, 1979), no. 505.

63. Wesley, *Letters*, vol. 3, pp. 107-8.

64. *Memoirs of the Life of Jacob Behmen* (Northampton, 1780).

65. *Thoughts upon Jacob Behmen* (1780), repr. in *Works of the Rev. John Wesley,* 3rd ed. (London, 1830), vol. 9, pp. 509-18.

66. *Works of John Wesley* (Bicentennial ed.), vols. 22, 23; *Journal and Diaries,* edited by W. R. Ward and R. P. Heitzenrater, vol. 5, pp. 216-17, 301; vol. 6, pp. 126-28; *Arminian Magazine* 1783 passim.

evangelicals. No man was more deeply indebted to Law than the young Henry Venn, and "he read till he came to a passage wherein Mr. Law seemed to represent the blood of Christ as of no more avail in procuring our salvation than the excellence of his moral character. 'What!' he exclaimed, 'does Mr. Law thus degrade the death of Christ, which the Apostles represent as a sacrifice for sins, and to which *they* ascribe the highest efficacy in procuring our salvation! Then farewell such a guide. Henceforth I will call no man master.'"[67] Here is perfectly expressed the disappointment that Behmenite mysticism had liberated men from the systematic Protestant Orthodoxies only at an unacceptable price.[68]

In much the same spirit Wesley at the end of his life was purging "mysticism" from his brother's hymns,[69] but the extraordinary thing is that he could never quite bring himself to do the same with Quietism. Orcibal maintained that Wesley was particularly open to mystical influence before 1738 and after 1765;[70] what is perhaps more striking is the way right to the end of his life he was recommending the Quietist writers and warning against their dangers in almost the same breath.[71] Fletcher, his intended successor in the Methodist leadership, was less reserved in his enthusiasm.

Behind Wesley's hesitations and inconsistencies there were of course other difficulties. The optimistic eschatology of the evangelical movement,

67. John Venn, *The Life and a Selection from the Letters of the Late Henry Venn,* edited by H. Venn (London, 1834), p. 18. Venn also turned against Swedenborg (p. 43).

68. How this happened more generally in the Anglo-Saxon world is faithfully reflected in Thomas Haweis, *An Impartial and Succinct History of the Rise, Declension and Revival of the Church of Christ* (London, 1800), vol. 3, p. 75.

69. Wesley, *Letters,* vol. 8, p. 122. He missed at least one, "Happy the man that finds the grace," clearly a hymn to the Divine Sophia, still in the current hymnbook, *Hymns and Psalms,* no. 674.

70. Jean Orcibal, "The Theological Originality of John Wesley and Continental Spirituality," in R. Davies and G. Rupp, eds., *A History of the Methodist Church in Great Britain* (London, 1965), vol. 1, p. 109. Despite its title, this useful paper is almost exclusively Franco-centric.

71. See, e.g., in the case of Antoinette Bourignon, Wesley, *Letters,* vol. 6, pp. 66, 126-27. For sterner warnings based on the fact that the Quietists could not be content to describe their religious experience in biblical language, see Wesley, *Letters,* vol. 5, p. 313; vol. 6, pp. 39, 43-44, 115. It is notable that much of Wesley's correspondence on this theme is with ladies. Alexander Knox acutely noted that "Mr Wesley had a predilection for the female character . . . partly from his generally finding in females a quicker and fuller responsiveness to his own ideas of interior piety and affectionate devotion." See R. Southey, *Life of Wesley* (London, 1925), vol. 2, p. 339. The tenor of his advice is very similar to that on novels (also given to a lady): "I would recommend very few novels to young persons for fear they should be too desirous of more" (*Letters,* vol. 7, p. 228).

which underlay their activism, could not in the long run be combined with the heavy emphasis on passivity in the Catholic mystical tradition. If Edwards came to insist that holiness "consists not only in contemplation, and a mere passive enjoyment, but very much in action,"[72] so did they all. There were, moreover, pastoral considerations that pointed the same way. All the Anglo-Saxon evangelicals were familiar with good men who had had a vivid initial religious experience and had fallen into perplexity or despair at their inability to repeat it. The truth was that the mystical experience of union with God was the fruit of a leisure industry and was not indefinitely replicable by those who had not undergone the strenuous discipline described by the great mystics. A post-conversion diet of endless "dark nights of the soul" did no one any good. Above all, as the evangelicals could not know, and historians have been unwilling to say, they had here hitched their wagon to a declining source of religious vitality. Persecuted by authority and textbookized out of its spontaneity by its friends, the mystical tradition was not going to recover. The Catholic Church would have to change, and the evangelical world would have to find a way out from the blind alley it had entered. In Germany it attempted this with the minimum of change by entering into an alliance with the Orthodoxy from which it had once escaped,[73] and by seeking support in romanticism and political conservatism. In the Anglo-Saxon world it was possible to fall back on empiricism at the price of future difficulties with the doctrine of the Holy Spirit. There was one other possibility announced from within the tradition of evangelical mysticism in Germany by Jung-Stilling of which much was to be heard in the Anglo-Saxon world, and that was to surrender the mystical aim of union with God, to recognize that God was always other, and to trace his guidance within.[74] This edifying retrospect was not, however, a basis for policy, and when given a public reference it was easily transfigured into a deplorable political messianism.[75]

It is bound to seem paradoxical to seek the marks of evangelicalism at the moment when it was about to enter upon its most dramatic successes in the blind alleys it had entered at the beginning. But the fact is that it had sought escape from systems, whether Orthodox or Cartesian, and had been only partially successful; it did not have the millennium in its grasp as in its wilder moments it had hoped; its hopes of propagating a transplanted mysticism

---

72. Edwards, *Works,* vol. 2, p. 31.

73. Cf. M. C. F. Duttenhofer, *Freymüthige Untersuchungen über Pietismus und Orthodoxie* (Halle, 1787), Preface, p. iv.

74. M. Hirzel, *Lebensgeschichte als Verkündigung* (Göttingen, 1998), pp. 70, 74-75.

75. On this see W. R. Hutchinson and Hartmut Lehmann, eds., *Many Are Chosen: Divine Election and Western Nationalism* (Minneapolis, 1994).

had failed. What enabled the evangelical movements to take opportunities which now came their way, and to take the first steps toward globalization, was their empiricism; and their internal history turned largely on the questions of whether empiricism was enough, whether the eighteenth-century blind alleys were in truth blind alleys, and, if they were, what means could be found for escaping them. This is a theme for a book, not an essay.

CHAPTER TWO

Evangelical Identity, Power, and Culture in the "Great" Nineteenth Century

MARK A. NOLL

For a history of evangelical Christianity that takes the entire world as its domain, "the nineteenth century" may be considered as stretching from 1792 to 1910 — from, that is, the publication of William Carey's *Enquiry into the Obligations of Christians to Use Means for the Conversion of the Heathens* to the convening of the World Missionary Conference at the Assembly Hall of the United Free Church of Scotland in Edinburgh.[1] During that long century, the shape of world Christianity was altered decisively. Although Roman Catholics, Orthodox, and nonevangelical Protestants certainly played large parts in that alteration, the driving forces for change were primarily evangelical. The well-considered judgments of Kenneth Scott Latourette, whose multi-volume *History of the Expansion of Christianity* is today even more relevant for world-historical concerns than when it was published over fifty years ago, are worth repeating:

> 1. Solo efforts to tackle huge topics like all evangelicals in the entire nineteenth century are foolish in principle. They are even more foolish if done without acknowledging the disciplined, hard-won labor of others who have paved the way and who let some of the rest of us think that we too could and should take on such foolish tasks. In my case, this means offering a public word of thanks to Reginald Ward for his pioneering work opening up the international character of eighteenth-century evangelicalism, to Andrew Walls for luminous writing on world Christian history, to Robert Frykenberg for introducing me to the complex history of Christianity in India, and to Mark Hutchinson, Ogbu Kalu, and the colleagues who gathered with them at Sydney in 1997, and then produced the path-breaking book, *A Global Faith: Essays on Evangelicalism and Globalization* (Sydney, 1998), which has served as a beacon to guide many of us in our thoughts on the subject.

Nothing to equal [the nineteenth-century dissemination of Christian-
ity] had been seen in the history of the faith. Nothing remotely approaching it could be recorded of any other religion at any time in the
human scene. . . . [T]he nineteenth-century expansion of Christianity
would not have occurred had the faith not displayed striking inward vitality. That vitality expressed itself in part through . . . revivals. . . .
[These revivals] were particularly marked in Protestantism. Indeed, in
some respects the nineteenth century was preeminently the Protestant
century.[2]

The dimensions of nineteenth-century Christian expansion, often evangelical Christian expansion, are daunting in their breadth, complexity, and
depth. In 1800, there were, according to David Barrett, a total of one hundred
Protestant foreign missionaries in the entire world.[3] For the 1910 Edinburgh
Conference, the Student Volunteer Movement for Foreign Missions compiled
extensive statistics covering "all existing foreign missionary effort which is
evangelical in aim." Their survey recorded thirty-three separate regions or
countries in the world where at least one hundred evangelical Protestant missionaries were at work.[4] Again according to Barrett, the proportion of the
world's population that was Christian grew from about 23 percent in 1800 to
almost 35 percent in 1914, which represented the fastest proportional growth
of the Church since its earliest centuries — and over a period in which world
population grew more rapidly than it ever had before. In addition, Barrett's
figures suggest that the proportion of "nonwhite" adherents increased from
slightly more than one-eighth of the Christian total in 1800 to nearly one-
fourth in 1914. The combination of rapid rise in general population, propor-
tionate expansion of Christianity, and accelerating Christian growth outside
of Europe and North America meant that in 1914 the number of nonwhite
Christians in the world was rapidly nearing the number of all Christians who
were alive in 1800. What these gross numbers hide are dramatic changes in
many individual locations. For example, in 1910 evangelical Protestant communities of some strength existed in many parts of the world where there had

2. Kenneth Scott Latourette, *A History of the Expansion of Christianity*, vol. 6: *The
Great Century in Northern Africa and Asia, 1800-1914* (New York, 1944), pp. 442, 448.

3. David Barrett, ed., *World Christian Encyclopedia* (New York, 1982), p. 28. All other
references to Barrett are from this volume. Information on world population in general is
from Colin McEvedy and Richard Jones, *Atlas of World Population History* (New York,
1978).

4. James S. Dennis, Harlan P. Beach, and Charles H. Fahs, eds., *World Atlas of Christian Missions* (New York, 1911), pp. 9, 83.

been no, or virtually no, Protestant presence in 1792. These places included, as a very partial list: Japan, Korea, China, the Dutch East Indies, Melanesia, Polynesia, Australia, New Zealand, many parts of India, many regions of West Africa, East Africa, and South Africa, Madagascar and Mauritius, Greenland, the United States west of the Appalachians, Canada west of Quebec, Brazil, the Lesser Antilles, and Jamaica.

From 1914 the absolute expansion of Christianity, including evangelical Christianity, has continued, although throughout the course of the twentieth century that expansion paralleled rather than outstripped the general growth in world population. In the twentieth century the course of evangelical Christianity was accelerated and complicated by two notable developments: the rise of Pentecostal or charismatic expressions of the faith and the rise of indigenous Christian churches which might have had some vestigial connections with traditional forms of Protestantism but which were essentially independent. Fueled especially by Pentecostal and independent movements, Christians with more-or-less evangelical commitments were to be found almost everywhere on the globe by the end of the millennium. Evangelicalism, in these terms, had become a world religion of great consequence.

Study of the nineteenth century is important for understanding the present character of world evangelicalism because it was during these years that the outward movement of evangelicalism began. At the risk of oversimplification, it is useful to remember that evangelicalism began as a series of interconnected renewal movements within state-church European Protestant regimes with leaders who saw themselves as direct descendants of the Protestant Reformation and who manifested that Reformation heritage in their sharp opposition to the Roman Catholic Church. Early evangelicals, in addition, were also shaped significantly by their adaptation to the main cultural currents of the eighteenth-century West. That adaptation included, among others, an innovative willingness to use the techniques of entrepreneurial market capitalism for spreading the gospel, an eagerness to move Christian proclamation into the public spaces created by new forms of commerce and entertainment, an assumption that the West's historic institutions of higher education could be easily and naturally exploited for evangelical purposes, a felt need to defend the faith in terms of scientific rationality, a countervailing concern for making the gospel relevant for an Enlightenment sense of the self, and at least the beginnings of a movement toward regarding civil society as made up of self-created and self-regulating voluntary associations. These circumstances in which evangelical movements began were, in other words, marked by their embeddedness in the scientism, the commerce, the psychology, the Enlightenment, the education, the democratizing forces, and the still dynamic Reformation consciousness of the eighteenth-century West.

It is much more difficult to generalize responsibly about the nature of worldwide evangelicalism at the beginning of the twenty-first century. Using conditions of the eighteenth century for comparison, however, it might be possible to hazard the following tentative generalizations.

(a) Worldwide evangelical movements today are much less self-conscious about the Reformation origins of Protestantism than were evangelicals in the eighteenth century. For different sets of reasons in the West and non-West, consciousness of links to figures like Luther, Calvin, Tyndale, Ridley, and Latimer is slight. Similarly, the once fixed attitude toward Roman Catholicism has fragmented — among worldwide evangelicals today can be found some continuing hostility toward the Catholic Church, much indifference, and some cooperation. Indeed, unlike the situation in the eighteenth century, some today who call themselves evangelicals and who are recognized as such by others *are* Roman Catholics.

(b) For the most part, state-church consciousness among evangelicals at the beginning of the twenty-first century has nearly vanished. Ironically, contemporary evangelicals in the United States, who in the late eighteenth century led the drive against establishment, probably look to their government for more establishment-like services today than do evangelicals in most other parts of the world.

(c) For the practice of education, modern evangelicals worldwide are probably more alienated from the mainstreams of Western university life than were their predecessors in the eighteenth century. In the West, the general secularization of modern higher education has left evangelicals with a number of intellectual uncertainties, including efforts to promote an alternative science of human origins. Outside of the West the progress of the gospel has far outstripped the progress of Western higher education. The result may be that evangelicals today have more dilemmas with respect to worldly standards of knowledge than was the case two hundred years ago, but also that they possess more opportunities for educational innovation that is both truly Christian and truly intellectual.

(d) The connections between modern evangelicals and modern commerce have become much more complicated than was the case in the eighteenth century. In general, many evangelicals today resemble their ancestors in the faith by being flexibly entrepreneurial in using the various communication media that have grown up as part of the modern expansion of capitalism. Evangelical attitudes toward market capitalism, as opposed to capitalism's advanced forms of communication, however, are now widely divergent.

Some modern evangelicals are textbook exemplars of the Weber Thesis, some have been decimated by expanding markets, many are trying to gain the advantages of membership among the petite bourgeoisie, a few are leaders of world business, and some are vocal opponents of international free-market economics. The feature of modern worldwide evangelicalism that most resembles eighteenth-century evangelicalism is that evangelicals are more inclined to *action* in market relationships than they are to thought about the *theological meaning* of markets and their effects.

(e) If evangelicalism was characterized at its origins by adaptation to the modernism of eighteenth-century Enlightenment rationalism, worldwide evangelicalism today is radically divided among modern, postmodern, and premodern sensibilities. Early evangelicalism featured a full measure of premodern practices — seen most clearly in Methodist exploitation of dreams, portents, and special revelations. Yet the drift among Western evangelicals in the late eighteenth and early nineteenth centuries was toward modern rationalism, logocentricism, and linear thought. Today, with the prominence among evangelicals of power encounters, charismatic gifts, talismanic use of Scripture, prophecy, and affectional song, the premodern and the postmodern are probably more important in worldwide evangelicalism than the modern. In today's evangelical world there are many Jabez Buntings eager to rationalize and dignify evangelical life and worship, but not nearly so many as there are Lorenzo Dows and Hugh Bournes to promote the direct supernaturalism of Primitive Methodism.

Even this inadequate glance at the journey undertaken by evangelical movements from their origins in eighteenth-century Europe and North America to their places throughout the world today should indicate why attention to the nineteenth century is important. The period when William Carey and the Baptist Missionary Society, the London Missionary Society and the Church Missionary Society, the American Board of Commissioners for Foreign Missions and the American Bible Society began to open up Western evangelicals to the possibilities of a world Christianity was, that is, precisely when the transition began from what evangelicalism was to what it has become.

The interrelated themes of identity, power, and culture, which several scholars have helped to define as essential for studying evangelicalism as a world phenomenon, are propitious for examining that transition. In particular, the opening of evangelicalism to the world offers a good opportunity for enriching the most serviceable general definition of evangelicalism we currently have. That definition is David Bebbington's identification of the four key marks of evangelicalism as biblicism (a reliance on the Bible as ultimate

35

religious authority), conversionism (a stress on the New Birth), activism (an energetic, individualistic approach to religious duties and social involvement), and crucicentrism (a focus on Christ's redeeming work as the heart of essential Christianity). A contribution to the recent volume marking the 150th anniversary of the British Evangelical Alliance allowed Bebbington to restate that definition in a form useful for considering the world phenomenon: "The evangelicals across these [many] denominations are all united in the bonds of the gospel. As many of them discover, through joint expressions of their activism, . . . they all try to be obedient to the Bible and therefore faithful to the cross, and eager for conversion."[5] Again, the theme of power is especially appropriate since the nineteenth century witnessed the developments that moved evangelicals from their Western location — where they were either the disadvantaged struggling against the powers that be or negotiators for power as it was defined by interaction among social forces of relatively equal weight — out into the broader world. In that broader world evangelicals experienced power quite differently — on the one hand, missionary evangelicals were allied or at least associated with the dominant forces of imperialistic power; on the other hand, new evangelicals in emerging churches were usually dependent in significant ways on the missionaries and were often also numbered among the least powerful in their own societies. Culture is the most complicated of these three themes, but in terms explicated by Andrew Walls — where the incarnation of Christianity in new cultural settings may be said to display the essential character of the Christian faith itself[6] — perhaps also the most important theme in any examination of the evangelical nineteenth century.

A single essay, especially a single essay by a historian, can only make a start on these weighty themes. But a historian can offer significant — and perhaps indicative — incidents where, in the outward journey of evangelicalism, issues of identity, power, and cultural adaptation came to the fore. In what follows I offer only two incidents, out of an untold number of possibilities, for

5. David W. Bebbington, "Towards an Evangelical Identity," in Steve Brady and Harold Rowdon, eds., *For Such a Time as This: Perspectives on Evangelicalism, Past, Present and Future* (London, 1996), p. 46. See Bebbington, *Evangelicalism in Modern Britain: A History from the 1730s to the 1980s* (London, 1989), pp. 2-17; and, for another recent restatement especially relevant to the themes of this chapter, Bebbington, "Of This Train, England Is the Engine: British Evangelicalism and Globalization in the Long Nineteenth Century," in Mark Hutchinson and Ogbu Kalu, eds., *A Global Faith: Essays on Evangelicalism and Globalization* (Sydney, 1998), pp. 122-39.

6. See especially Andrew F. Walls, *The Missionary Movement in Christian History* (Maryknoll, N.Y., 1996), part I, "The Transmission of Christian Faith."

each of the themes of identity, power, and culture, as a way of assessing some of the important transitions of the nineteenth century.

Evangelical Identity

First, then, two incidents for focusing the question of evangelical identity. In 1797 an extraordinary debate took place in Sierra Leone between two exemplary evangelicals. The precipitator and recorder of the debate was Zachary Macaulay, at that time the twenty-nine-year-old governor of the colony. Macaulay was the son of a Church of Scotland minister who, after clerking in the office of a Glasgow merchant, had discovered his vocation while working as a bookkeeper on an estate in Jamaica. What Macaulay saw of slavery in Jamaica appalled him, and that disgust eventually brought him into contact with the Clapham Sect and William Wilberforce, who immediately recognized his rare combination of evangelical and abolitionist zeal. From 1793 Macaulay had been serving as the assistant, and then the governor, of Sierra Leone, itself a grand experiment in evangelical philanthropy. The other participant, who had traversed an even more remarkable road to this encounter, was David George, in 1797 aged fifty-four. George was one of the founders of the black Baptist church in Silver Bluff, South Carolina, which when constituted in the early 1770s may have been the first African-American church on the North American mainland. He was converted and instructed by Particular Baptist preachers, black and white, whose view of salvation included the conservative Calvinist conviction that Christ died only — or *particularly* — for the elect. George himself began to exhort before he had learned to read, a skill he acquired as an adult in order to study the Scriptures. During the American Revolutionary War, George joined the liberating British forces and continued to preach in nearby Savannah, Georgia.[7] But when his liberators were defeated by the Americans, he accepted transportation to Loyalist Nova Scotia, where he founded the second black church to be established in that colony. While in Nova Scotia, George seems to have been touched by the radical evangelicalism flowing from the ministry of Henry Alline, which combined mystical theo-centricity with ardent defense of human free will.[8] In 1792, after a decade in Nova Scotia, George removed to Sierra Leone with part

7. On George's place in the political, racial, and religious history of the British occupation, see Sylvia R. Frey, *Water from the Rock: Black Resistance in a Revolutionary Age* (Princeton, 1991), pp. 37-39.

8. See for introduction and examples, George A. Rawlyk, ed., *Henry Alline: Selected Writings* (New York, 1987).

of his congregation and became the leading black minister in that African-American African colony.

It was on April 25, 1797, that the governor, Zachary Macaulay, called George to his residence for "a free and full conversation." The result was twelve hours of talk, the gist of which Macaulay recorded in his journal. Macaulay had initiated the meeting in order to warn George away from the error of antinomianism and to convince him that holiness of life was essential for all individuals who had been truly born again by the Spirit. The conversation showed the independence of George's theology — only reluctantly did he cave in to Macaulay's barrage of Scripture texts and concede that occasional acts of drunkenness or theft were as important as Macaulay took them to be.[9] George's response to Macaulay's worry was to pose the question, "But is not God unchangeable, how then can he withdraw his love from his children?"[10] To defend his understanding of proper Christian life, George also relied much more on his own personal experiences of grace than Macaulay thought he should.

What is most interesting about Macaulay's record of the conversation, however, is his conclusion that George belonged with what he called "those high Calvinists"[11] because of George's unshakeable commitment to the doctrine of the perseverance of the saints, a commitment that Macaulay felt could lead only to antinomianism. Four years earlier, Macaulay recorded another incident with a similar conclusion. When a white chaplain taught that Christ's death availed for all humanity, George had rebuked him with the traditional Calvinist view that this death was intended only for the elect.[12] The intriguing thing about this debate is how difficult it was for these seasoned evangelicals to find common ground. In a faith compounded of Particular Baptist preaching, New Light experientialism, and perhaps elements of African ritual, George also incorporated elements of strongly traditional Calvinist theology. In Macaulay's moderate Calvinism, notions of civilized propriety were mingled with what he regarded as a consistent biblical ethic. George

9. The conversation is summarized and excerpted in Grant Gordon, *From Slavery to Freedom: The Life of David George, Pioneer Black Baptist Minister*, Baptist Heritage in Atlantic Canada Series (Hantsport, N.S., 1992), pp. 142-50. Gordon draws upon the manuscript journal and letters of Macaulay that are housed in the Huntington Library, California, and the account in Viscountess Knutsford (= M. J. Holland), *Life and Letters of Zachary Macaulay* (London, 1900).

10. Gordon, *From Slavery to Freedom*, p. 145.

11. Gordon, *From Slavery to Freedom*, p. 146.

12. Macaulay's journal, October 30, 1793, in Knutsford, *Life and Letters of Zachary Macaulay*, p. 340, n. 219.

could not be convinced that Macaulay grasped the nature of Christianity as that faith had redeemed and nurtured him. Macaulay could not grasp the independent theological agency that a first-generation convert from paganism had come to exercise.

Only a few years after this debate in Sierra Leone, a series of theological disputes over a wide range of subjects took place on the American frontier. One of the main factions stimulating those debates was made up of individuals who concluded that the move into the frontier had rendered the churches' traditions virtually meaningless. Many of them came to be known as Restorationists.[13] This movement sought, in effect, to begin Christianity over again by stripping away the accumulated baggage of the centuries. Its name came from the effort to "restore" Christianity to the purity of the New Testament. Its leaders included a father and son who immigrated from Scotland by way of Ireland, Thomas (1763-1845) and Alexander (1788-1866) Campbell. They were joined by Barton W. Stone (1772-1844), a plain-speaking Marylander who participated in the great western migration into Kentucky of the 1790s. The Campbells and Stone shared a disillusionment with traditional churches, which they felt were too much constrained by stale European traditions. After affiliating for brief periods with existing denominations, they eventually broke away and set about recovering the primitive Christianity they thought they could see in the New Testament's Book of Acts. Alexander Campbell and Barton Stone created separate movements called "Christians only" (Stone) and "Disciples of Christ" (the Campbells). The names were deliberately chosen to emphasize liberation from the historic denominations. The parallel movements were also alike in seeking to follow the New Testament literally, in practicing baptism by immersion for adult converts, and in stressing the autonomy of local congregations. In the early 1830s, the churches inspired by Stone's and the Campbells' ideals joined together as the Christian Church (Disciples of Christ).

An exchange that symbolized the Restorationist disdain for tradition took place in 1811. Two of Barton Stone's associates were engaged in literary polemics with more traditional evangelicals. They were active in Kentucky, a state that in the preceding twenty years had seen its population mushroom from well under 100,000 to now over 400,000. Their work was published in Cincinnati, a city on the Ohio River that had only recently sprung up out of nowhere. When Robert Marshall and J. Thompson took up their pens, they

13. See Richard T. Hughes, *Reviving the Ancient Faith: The Story of the Churches of Christ in America* (Grand Rapids, 1996); and David Edwin Harrell, *Quest for a Christian America: The Disciples of Christ and American Society to 1866* (Nashville, 1966).

left no doubt about their disdain for Protestant Christian traditions: "We are not personally acquainted with the writings of John Calvin, nor are we certain how nearly we agree with his views of divine truth; neither do we care."[14]

These incidents both draw attention to questions of essential Christian identity even more than to the issue of evangelical identity. Yet in broader perspective, George and Macaulay, the Restorationists and their opponents, were clearly part of evangelical movements. Each incident, therefore, illustrates something that happened often in the outward journey of evangelicalism over the course of the nineteenth century. Entrance into virgin territory like the American frontier, where no Christian institutions were in place to channel the energies of converts or immigrants, was often the occasion for disposing of much Christian tradition that leaders of the earliest evangelical movements had simply taken for granted. In addition, a convert like David George, who came to faith from an environment substantially devoid of prior Christian structures, did not wait to act as a Christian until he had mastered the theological environment of the already existing evangelical world. Rather, he began his labor as a Christian thinker — as a preacher and theologian — almost as soon as he was converted. That activity as thinker, preacher, and theologian was aimed, moreover, at bringing Christian resources to bear on the circumstances of the life he was living rather than at qualifying him to enter the recognized circle of theological authorities in the established evangelical world.

Such activity, by "new" Christians — whether Restorationists, Africans, or African-Americans — suggests that they were accentuating a quality present among eighteenth-century evangelicals, but a quality not highlighted in standard definitions like David Bebbington's. That quality was a willingness to set aside the authority of tradition, even evangelical tradition, in appropriating the faith for oneself. Even more than a willingness to sit lightly to tradition, it was an assumption that authoritative Christianity *must* set aside the baggage of its history if it was to thrive in the new environments lying beyond historic Christian regions.

Early evangelicals leaned against Christian traditions. Many later evangelicals did away with them almost entirely. In place of traditional authority many evangelicals in the West, and increasing numbers outside the West, have relied upon the authority of self-created civil society — what Jürgen

---

14. For this incident, I rely on Nathan O. Hatch, *The Democratization of American Christianity* (New Haven, 1989), p. 174. The work of Marshall and Thompson was *A Brief Historical Account of Sundry Things in the Doctrines and State of the Christian, or, as It Is Historically Called, the Newlight Church* (Cincinnati, 1811), p. 17.

Habermas in another context has called "the sphere of private people come together as public," or "bourgeois society."[15] Alternatively, many evangelicals in the West, and perhaps even more outside the West, have looked to the authority of charismatically endorsed leaders. In this situation, embracing evangelical Christianity is not so much a democratic move as it is a determination to follow leaders who are recognized exclusively for their own ability to demonstrate effective leadership in the here and now. In both cases, to join the stream of evangelical Christian movements is to leave traditional authorities behind, including the authority of evangelical tradition. During the nineteenth century, worldwide evangelicalism seems to have moved steadily, and in some cases rapidly, to this understanding of self-created evangelical authority.

Evangelicals and Power

For approaching multi-dimensional questions of power, two incidents from later in the century may be relevant: first, the struggle for unity at the 1846 London Conference of the Evangelical Alliance, and, second, the stripping away of Samuel Ajayi Crowther's episcopal powers in the 1880s.

The 1846 London Conference of the Evangelical Alliance, which met from August 19 to September 2, was convened for the purpose of giving expression to the unity of the Church.[16] Participants came to the meeting in their capacity as individual believers, but they represented more than fifty denomina-

15. Jürgen Habermas, *The Structural Transformation of the Public Sphere: An Inquiry into a Category of Bourgeois Society,* trans. Thomas Berger (Cambridge, 1989 [orig. 1962]), pp. 27-29. I thank Frank Turner for drawing this work to my attention and for indicating how its analysis might fit the situation of evangelicals.

16. For research assistance on the Evangelical Alliance and on Bishop Crowther, I am pleased to thank Rachel Maxson. This account of the 1846 meeting relies upon *Report of the Proceedings of the Conference, Held at Freemasons' Hall, London, From August 19th to September 2nd Inclusive, 1846. Published by Order of the Conference* (London, 1847); J. W. Massie, *The Evangelical Alliance; Its Origin and Development. Containing Personal Notices of Its Distinguished Friends in Europe and America* (London, 1847); Robert Baird, *The Progress and Prospects of Christianity in the United States of America; With Remarks on the Subject of Slavery in America; and on the Intercourse Between British and American Churches* (London, 1851); J. B. A. Kessler, Jr., *A Study of the Evangelical Alliance in Great Britain* (Goes, Netherlands, 1968); Philip D. Jordan, *The Evangelical Alliance for the United States of America, 1847-1900: Ecumenism, Identity and the Religion of the Republic* (New York, 1982); and Clive Calver, "The Rise and Fall of the Evangelical Alliance: 1835-1905," in Steve Brady and Harold Rowdon, eds., *For Such a Time as This: Perspectives on Evangelicalism, Past, Present and Future* (London, 1996).

tions. A resolution passed on the second day put the desire for unity with forceful clarity:

> This Conference, composed of professing Christians of many different Denominations, all exercising the right of private judgment . . . re-joice[s] in making their unanimous avowal of the glorious truth, that the Church of the Living God . . . is One Church, never having lost, and being incapable of losing, its essential unity. Not, therefore, to create that unity, but to confess it, is the design of their assembling together.[17]

In accord with this emphasis on unity and mutual Christian love, participants labored to avoid divisive issues like whether there should be Church establish-ments and what kind of support to give temperance movements. Delegates suc-ceeded in formulating a nine-point basis of faith that affirmed common evan-gelical convictions like "(1) The Divine Inspiration, Authority, and Sufficiency of the Holy Scriptures. . . . (5) The incarnation of the Son of God, His work of Atonement for sinners of mankind, and His Mediatorial Intercession and Reign. (6) The Justification of the sinner by Faith alone." As it would turn out, the statement's second point posed the greatest practical difficulty: "The Right and Duty of Private Judgment in the Interpretation of the Holy Scriptures."

The one divisive issue participants could not avoid surfaced when they turned to developing the organizational structure of the proposed alliance. It was the question of slavery. The difficulty arose over a stipulation, included at the urging of American delegates, that membership in any national branch of the Alliance would be automatically transferable to any other branch. British anti-slavery delegates feared that this stipulation would obligate them to en-ter fellowship with slaveholders since the American delegation included some who owned slaves and more who were in churches that tolerated slavery.

The debate that ensued featured Britain versus the United States. The British anti-slavery movement, which in 1833 had secured the liberation of slaves in the British West Indies, was sympathetic to the radical wing of American abolitionism. The Rev. J. Howard Hinton of London expressed grave doubts that a man could be both a slaveholder and a Christian, since he took the biblical prohibition of "man-stealing" to make all slaveholding a sin. Many of the American evangelicals were themselves personally opposed to slavery and considered it a grave evil that should be eradicated, but they did not necessarily support the demands for immediate emancipation. They pled, rather, for understanding of those slaveholders who had not chosen their sit-

17. *Report*, p. 44.

uation and for whom immediate emancipation was not a viable option. The Americans were also offended by what seemed to them foreign meddling in a complex domestic situation from a nation with which they had so lately fought two destructive wars of independence. Americans also wondered why their particular problems were being singled out for attention when other matters embarrassing to the British — like the civil disabilities of evangelical Nonconformists in England — were left untouched.

The five days of debate, and the 180 pages in the official report, on this issue revealed unanticipated antitheses lurking in the common affirmation concerning "The Right and Duty of Private Judgment in the Interpretation of the Holy Scriptures."[18] Participants debated St. Paul's relationship to the slave owner Philemon. Others asked to add intemperance, the exploitation of children in factories, and other social problems to the agenda. A member from the United States tried to define slavery as a moral issue excluded from the doctrinal basis upon which the alliance was to rest. Dr. Thomas Smyth, an Irish-born Presbyterian minister from Charleston, South Carolina, quoted the conference's affirmation of the right of private judgment as solving the whole problem. Failing to reach an acceptable compromise on the admission of slaveholders into the alliance, the members finally decided to delay working out the details of the international organization until a future general conference — a conference that has never yet been held.

Several years after the event, Robert Baird, who spent most of his adult life in Europe as an agent for American evangelical voluntary societies, summarized American sentiments:

> The brethren from America, who were at London in 1846, returned home with heavy hearts. Some of them had been among the first, if they were not the very first, to propose the movement. They had written much about it; they had prayed much for it, and over it. . . . They had supposed that all who were members, in good standing, of the several Evangelical branches of the one true Church of God might be received as members of this holy Alliance, with the confidence that if there were evils with which any of them were for a time entangled, and which might seem, or be under certain circumstances, inconsistent with true religion, they would be better looked after, and more certainly removed, by the proper ecclesiastical organizations, than by such an alliance as was proposed.[19]

18. This summary of the debate is from Kessler, *Evangelical Alliance*, p. 44.
19. Baird, *Christianity in the United States*, pp. 42-43.

The Americans' hopes were dashed. British evangelicals considered slavery more than a minor entangling evil. Concern for control over individual national destinies turned out to be stronger than shared evangelical principles.

A generation after aspirations for an international evangelical association were subverted by British and American differences, an even more severe case of international tension within Evangelicalism played itself out in the West of Africa. Samuel Ajayi Crowther was ordained to the Anglican ministry in 1843 and through the efforts of the Church Missionary Society's Henry Venn was in 1864 appointed "Bishop of the countries of Western Africa beyond the Queen's dominion."[20] Both appointments were landmark events aimed at fulfilling Venn's vision of self-governing, self-supporting, and self-propagating African churches. Crowther's Niger Mission attempted a daunting series of tasks: Bible translation, church planting, coordination of advice and funds from England, creative interaction with Muslims, and recruitment of African fellow laborers. Into the 1870s Crowther seemed to be managing this backbreaking range of duties better than any could have hoped.

But then a new generation of missionaries during a period of renewed European expansion began to express their doubts. Once begun, the expressions of doubt rolled down like thunder — in 1878, controversy between Crowther and a steamer captain sent out by the Church Missionary Society to assist the work; in 1879, an audit of the Niger Mission that charged fifteen of Crowther's twenty-five managers with corruption; in 1881, a conscious decision by the Church Missionary Society to extend European involvement in the mission; in 1882 and 1883, resignations and recriminations among Europeans appointed to assist Crowther; in 1883, damaging publicity in London about the murder of an African girl by two of Crowther's agents several years before; in 1886, the creation of the Royal Niger Company that set up British colonial protectorates over much of Crowther's jurisdiction that had previously lain "beyond the Queen's dominions"; in 1889, the transfer of much of Crowther's

---

20. I was introduced to Crowther by writing from Andrew Walls, "Samuel Adjai (or Ajayi) Crowther," in Gerald H. Anderson, ed., *Biographical Dictionary of Christian Missions* (New York, 1998), pp. 160-61; and "Samuel Ajayi Crowther, c. 1807-1891: Foremost African Christian of the Nineteenth Century," in Gerald H. Anderson et al., eds., *Mission Legacies* (Maryknoll, N.Y., 1994), pp. 132-39. These paragraphs also draw on Jesse Page, *The Black Bishop: Samuel Adjai Crowther* (London, 1908); E. A. Ayandele, *The Missionary Impact on Modern Nigeria, 1842-1914: A Political and Social Analysis* (New York, 1966); J. F. Ade Ajayi, *Christian Missions in Nigeria, 1841-1891: The Making of a New Elite* (Evanston, Ill., 1969); G. O. M. Tasie, *Christian Missionary Enterprise in the Niger Delta, 1864-1918* (Leiden, 1978); and M. O. Owandayo, "Bishop Samuel Ajayi Crowther (1810-1891)," in J. A. Omoyajowo, ed., *Makers of the Church in Nigeria* (Lagos, Nigeria, 1995).

remaining authority to a new "Sudan Party" of young English missionaries; in 1890, the wholesale suspension of African agents, including the Bishop's son, D. C. Crowther, for various reasons involving funds and factional loyalties; in 1891, upon the death of Bishop Crowther, the appointment of an Englishman as his successor.

Details of Crowther's interaction with Church Missionary Society missionaries from England are probably not the key to this incident. In world-historical perspective, Crowther's Niger Mission along with Venn's three-self principles were swept away by an avalanche, the European scramble for Africa. If that avalanche was not enough, other bombardments out of Europe would have done the job — for example, the intensification of racialist understandings of history and the rise of Social Darwinism (whereby Crowther, as an African sold into slavery as a youth, represented a very weak member of the least fit race).

Even in the face of these tectonic shifts, however, the development of local fault lines still deserves attention. Of those local faults, one of the most pertinent for evangelical history was the theological character of the young English missionaries who from the mid-1800s did so much to undermine Crowther's work. That theological character was formed, at least in part, by the newer Keswick emphasis on the Higher Life and by the growing influence of a kind of pietism that rejected Christian engagement with culture. Against Crowther's strategy of using schools and other structures borrowed from Western societies, the new missionaries pursued a "more individualistic and more otherworldly" plan. In the words of J. F. A. Ajayi, the new missionaries "itched to go into the villages and live like the 'natives' they despised, in the belief that by 'reasoning of the Gospel and righteousness' they would sweep them out of their old ways into a pure, simple, primitive Christianity."[21] Evangelical currents that were doubtless producing a quickening effect in the West worked with quite different results along the Niger.

What can the stories of the 1846 London conference and of changes in Samuel Crowther's Niger Mission tell us about evangelicals and power? At the very least, these accounts show that evangelical spirituality, which has such great potential for quickening individual Christian life, also bears a number of chronic perils. As illustrated by the failure of the Evangelical Alliance, these perils include a naïve reluctance to acknowledge differences between the power of Scripture to speak in every conceivable human situation and the interpretations of the Bible produced by particular social or historical loca-

---

21. Ajayi, *Christian Missions*, p. 50. For "individualistic" and "otherworldly," see Walls, "Crowther," in *Mission Legacies*, p. 137.

tions. They include as well an Edenic, if also self-delusionary, innocence about the despotic dangers as well as the liberating potential of "the Right and Duty of Private Judgment in the Interpretation of the Holy Scriptures." As illustrated by the experience of Samuel Crowther, these perils include the capacity of Higher Life theologies to mask the continuation of Lower Life self-aggrandizement, even among the converted. They include as well a tendency to personalize and spiritualize the gospel to such an extent that the influence of world-historical forces drops beneath the horizon of conscious thought.

These incidents do testify to the power of the gospel interpreted in evangelical terms: there would have been no attempt at an international Evangelical Alliance if multitudes in several continents had not been called to God by similar messages about the saving power of the cross; there would not have been a Niger Mission to undermine if the message of redemption in Christ had not miraculously altered the life course of many Englishmen and women and many more in West Africa. Both incidents also testify, however, to the propensity of evangelicalism, which promotes an intensely personal faith, to obscure broader dimensions of the gospel. Participants at the Evangelical Alliance Conference confessed their belief in "The utter Depravity of Human Nature, in consequence of the Fall." Keswick-trained missionaries testified by their protracted individual struggles for personal holiness that they knew sin was not easily extirpated. But when it came time to understand how the interpretation of Scripture can reflect as well as reveal power relationships, to remember that the gospel spoke to human structures as well as to human hearts, they forgot. Nineteenth-century evangelicals made a drastic difference in the world because they believed the death of Christ had conquered the oppressive powers of sin, death, hell, and the devil. They opened themselves to docetic cheap grace when they looked upon the atonement of Christ as exempting themselves from the universal human tendency to act as oppressors.

Evangelicals and Culture

Evangelical engagement during the nineteenth century with a multiplying range of societies led to a spectacular kaleidoscope of cultural permutations, adaptations, disruptions, and transformations. Full attention to the cultural history of evangelical movements — which would take in narratives for older Christian regions, for missionary efforts, for the process of indigenization, and for the maturing of new Christian communities — is a great desideratum. What brief attention to only two nineteenth-century incidents can suggest, however, is that study of the evangelical past could be dramatically useful for understanding activity in the evangelical present.

From insights contributed mostly by Ogbu Kalu, Brian Stanley, Andrew Walls, and Andrew Porter, I would like to draw attention to what strikes me as one of the nineteenth-century events that is most pertinent for Christian contemplation at the beginning of the twenty-first century. It is the Niger Expedition of Thomas Fowell Buxton in 1841.[22] That expedition, which Buxton undertook in order to extend the evangelical battle against slavery, is widely perceived as a failure — "brief and disastrous," in Kenneth Scott Latourette's words, a "panacea," according to Livingstone biographer Tim Jeal, that resulted only in "heavy loss of life and little or no achievement."[23] Recent studies, as by C. C. Ifemesia, may be successfully revising judgments about the nature and extent of Buxton's failure, but they do not alter the conclusion that his expensive and highly publicized expedition did not succeed in setting up the farms, trading networks, and churches that he hoped would both drive slavery out of the Niger River Valley and, as a by-product, turn a profit for all concerned.

It is not the record of this mission, and not necessarily the detailed shape of Buxton's hopes, that strikes me as so prescient. It is, rather, his wisdom in drawing into a common analysis Christianity, commerce, and civilization. At the end of his lengthy appeal from 1840, *The African Slave Trade and Its Remedy*, Buxton waxed euphoric about the benefits he saw arising on every side from the replacement of slavery with scientific agriculture as the backbone of West African economy. As he did so, however, he paused to insist that links between a successful commercial agriculture and the advancement of civilization had to rest on the Christian faith: "THIS alone can penetrate to the root of evil, can teach [the African] to love and to befriend his neighbor, and cause him to act as a *candidate* for a higher and holier state of being." Buxton continued to rhapsodize, but his rhapsody had a particularistic religious anchor: "Let missionaries and schoolmasters, the plough and the spade, go together,

---

22. This brief treatment relies especially upon Andrew F. Walls, "Thomas Fowell Buxton, 1786-1844: Missions and the Remedy for African Slavery," in *Mission Legacies*, pp. 11-17; Brian Stanley, *The Bible and the Flag: Protestant Missions and British Imperialism in the Nineteenth and Twentieth Centuries* (Leicester, 1990), pp. 70-74 and passim; and C. C. Ifemesia, "The 'Civilising' Mission of 1841: Aspects of an Episode in Anglo-Nigerian Relations," in O. U. Kalu, ed., *The History of Christianity in West Africa* (London, 1980), pp. 81-102.

23. Kenneth Scott Latourette, *A History of the Expansion of Christianity*, vol. 5: *The Great Century in the Americas, Australia, and Africa* (New York, 1943), p. 436; Tim Jeal, *Livingstone* (New York, 1973), p. 41.

and agriculture will flourish; the avenues to legitimate commerce will be opened; confidence between man and man will be inspired; whilst civilization will advance as the natural effect, and Christianity operate as the proximate cause of this happy change."[24]

What makes Buxton relevant for later evangelical history is that the triangle of forces he identified as centrally important in the 1830s reemerged in the second half of the twentieth century as the critical elements of globalization, whether understood economically, politically, or religiously. In our day, evangelical Protestantism joins Roman Catholicism and Islam as the major global religions; modern electronic communications are creating global cultures; and economic exchange that respects no borders defines what globalization means for most ordinary people. Buxton may have been romantic in his own aspirations. Yet his attention to commerce, civilization, and Christianity — and particularly his insistence that trade without Christianity will never produce "a higher and holier state of being" — represents for evangelical Christians a challenge of extraordinary contemporary relevance. If evangelicals in the twenty-first century are ever to be a religion of hope for the whole world, they will do so by, in effect, rethinking, reevaluating, but also revisiting the Niger Valley with Thomas Fowell Buxton.

Buxton's notion of "civilization" involved in a simplified form what is frequently referred to now as the domains of culture. For the potential of evangelicals to communicate the gospel message into the extraordinary diversity of human cultures on the planet, no practice has more potential than the work of translation. And so my last incident concerns a small part of what went on when evangelicals began to translate the Bible into Korean.

Christian contact with Korea occurred as early as the sixteenth century. It was not, however, until the late eighteenth century that Catholic missionaries were able to bring a sustained Christian witness. Although Catholic converts were persecuted mercilessly, the fortitude of converts and missionaries, supported by some Christian influence seeping in from China and then Japan, sustained a Christian presence in Korea throughout the first three-fourths of the nineteenth century. The modern phase of Christian expansion in Korea began in 1876 when Japan pulled Korea out of its historic dependency upon China into its own expanding imperial orbit. After the Japanese imposed a law guaranteeing religious freedom and Korea in 1882 signed a treaty with the United States, Protestant missionaries from Canada, Australia, and the United States soon followed. From the 1880s, Christianity expanded rapidly

---

24. Thomas Fowell Buxton, *The African Slave Trade and Its Remedy* (London, 1967 [orig. 1840]), p. 511.

until at the present about two-fifths of the South Korean population identifies with Christian churches, with Protestants of one sort or another accounting for about four-fifths of that total.[25]

The rapid advance of Protestantism in Korea is regularly associated with a number of structural factors beyond the religious zeal with which many Koreans have practiced the Christian faith. From the first the indigenizing principles of John Nevius, who visited Korea in 1890, provided the standard for Protestant missionary efforts. With their emphasis on small group Bible study, the spiritual self-discipline of converts, and the missionary as itinerant facilitator, the Nevius principles formalized for mission purposes what was, in effect, the general shape of early Methodist practices in Britain and North America. More importantly, Protestants entered Korea during a period of manifest social and political crisis. From a long period of domination by China, Korea was being pulled violently into the Japanese empire. Many historians of Korea have, thus, described Christianity as a religion offering a powerful message of hope for a desperately beleaguered people at an especially critical time. Also factoring into the rapid Christian expansion, however, was a critical decision with respect to Bible translation. This decision can serve as a representative example of the kind of evangelical-cultural interaction that occurred almost everywhere in the world where Western evangelical missionaries went over the course of the long nineteenth century.[26]

Portions of the Scriptures were available in Korean from the late eighteenth century through the work of Catholic translators working out of China. As a result of protracted Catholic debate over the best Chinese word to use when translating the biblical "God" (the famous "term question"), Roman Catholics working in China at the end of the eighteenth century were following papal instruction by using the Chinese word *T'ien-Chu*. When Catholic translators adapted this Chinese usage for Korea, they transliterated the Chinese word into the Korean *Ch'onju*. When, however, the Protestant

---

25. For current figures, see Georg Evers, "Asia," in *The Encyclopedia of Christianity*, vol. 1 (Grand Rapids, 1999), p. 137. See also David Barrett, *World Christian Encyclopedia* (New York, 1982), s.v. "Korea, South."

26. My attention was drawn to this subject by a student paper from Sang Hun Roh in fall 1997. The following paragraphs rely upon Sek-Keun O, "Der Volksglaube und das Christentum in Korea," Ph.D. dissertation, Free University of Berlin, 1979 (Munich, 1979); Jeong Man Choi, "Historical Development of the Indigenization Movement in the Korean Protestant Church: With Special Reference to Bible Translation," D.Miss. dissertation, Fuller Theological Seminary, 1985; Ki Jong So, "The Translation of the Bible into Korean: Its History and Significance," Ph.D. dissertation, Drew University, 1993; and the wise personal counsel of Professor Steven Kang.

missionaries arrived, they agreed upon a missionary strategy (finalized at a meeting in 1893) aimed at the ordinary people, many of whom did not read the formal language that closely followed Chinese. A critical part of this strategy was to undertake a Bible translation that used ordinary Korean (the *Hangul*) rather than a Chinese-based language. This determination led to the translation of "God" into Korean as *Hananim*, a word that was associated in time-honored Korean history with a more personal deity. Popular Korean resonance with the word *Hananim* was one of the reasons Christianity in Protestant dress appealed to Koreans.

The use of an indigenous Korean word instead of a borrowed Chinese term for God could, thus, be seen as a noteworthy instance of the sort of incarnated indigenization of the gospel described in broader terms by Lamin Sanneh.[27] A 1979 dissertation by Sek-Keun O raises the possibility, however, that this indigenization might have been more effective than anyone at the time realized. O suggests, that is, that Koreans were comfortable with the word *Hananim* for "God" because it was a word that had factored large in Korea's historic shamanistic religion — or, to put it more accurately, the shamanistic shape that Confucianism, Buddhism, and a wide variety of animistic religions had assumed in Korea. In his interpretation, shamanism is a form of religious practice in which the shaman functions as a mediating adept who is able by contact with the *Hananim* to offer multiple services to ordinary believers. Those services include priestly mediation with the divine, healing of bodily ills, and prophetic interpretation of events. O argues that shamanistic associations with the worship of *Hananim* reappeared in Korea with a vengeance after the end of Japanese occupation in 1945 and the traumas of migration necessitated by the Korean War. In his reading, these events effectively removed the control of external influences (both Japanese and American) and allowed Korean religion to develop along Korean lines. O suggests that an obvious effect of this development was the emergence of syncretistic religions like Sun-Myung Moon's Unification Church, which he characterizes as "a mixture of Christianity with oriental religions, Confucianism, Taoism, Buddhism, and above all shamanism." At the same time, O thinks that more orthodox Protestant groups also displayed "shamanistic peculiarities."[28] He bases this conclusion on the radically schismatic character of postwar Korean

27. Lamin Sanneh, *Translating the Message: The Missionary Impact on Culture* (Maryknoll, N.Y., 1989); and "Gospel and Culture: Ramifying Effects of Scriptural Translation," in Philip C. Stine, ed., *Bible Translation and the Spread of the Church* (Leiden, 1990). See also Andrew Walls, "The Translation Principle in Christian History," in Stine, *Bible Translation.*

28. O, *Volksglaube*, pp. 212, 201 ("schamanistische Eigenheiten").

Protestantism, where dozens, if not hundreds, of individual Protestant sects have been created out of the relative handful of denominations that existed before 1945. As O describes the Korean situation, when leaders of Protestant denominations treat themselves as extraordinary channels of divine revelation, special instruments of divine healing, and uniquely inspired interpreters of obscure yet determinative texts of Scripture, they are acting in a shamanistic way.

If O is correct, use of the term *Hananim* may have facilitated early Korean acceptance of a Protestant Christianity that missionaries regarded as traditional, even traditionally Western. At the same time, that very translation usage may also have helped make it possible for the habits of traditional Korean shamanism to be incorporated within the new framework of Protestant Christianity. The process of indigenizing Protestant Christianity in Korea, in other words, may have meant both more and less than the missionaries anticipated: more, because it preserved within the new Christian faith elements of Korean culture that the missionaries thought had been discarded; less, because a successfully transplanted Christianity that moved rapidly to maturity did not necessarily lead to forms of the faith that missionaries recognized as Christian maturity.

Conclusion

In grand historical terms, the nineteenth century opened Western evangelicals and evangelical movements to the world. That opening broadened and refined what it meant to be an evangelical. It multiplied occasions for redeeming power and for obfuscating power. It transformed evangelical engagements with culture from a fairly narrow range of interactions with Western European, British, and North American social and linguistic structures into a bewildering variety of associations with local societies on every continent in the world. The nineteenth century was "great" for evangelicals because it fulfilled the aspiration of John Wesley who claimed the world for his parish. It was equally "great" because of the challenges it posed. During the nineteenth century a renewed old religion was carried around the world. In the twentieth century that religion continued to be presented afresh in many more corners of the globe. In the twenty-first century, the character of evangelical identity will depend, in no small part, on the ability of evangelical movements to Christianize the use of power and to promote the cultural incarnation of the gospel.

CHAPTER THREE

Twentieth-Century World Christianity:
A Perspective from the History of Missions

BRIAN STANLEY

The Prophetic View from Edinburgh, 1910

On June 14, 1910, Randall Davidson, archbishop of Canterbury, concluded his address to the opening evening session of the World Missionary Conference in Edinburgh with a prophecy. It was a conditional prophecy, whose fulfillment was made dependent on the willingness of the Western churches to give foreign missions the central place which they deserved. If that condition were met, asserted Davidson with an appropriately Anglican lack of total certainty, "*it may well be that* 'there be some standing here tonight who shall not taste of death till they see' — here on earth, in a way we know not now — 'the Kingdom of God come with power.'"[1] It was that closing sentence, recalled Temple Gairdner, coming as it did from "a Scots statesman-ecclesiastic with a merited reputation for sobriety of thought and word," that "gave the unforgettable thrill."[2] Here was one of the most notable (and problematic) eschatological statements of the Gospels reinterpreted and appropriated for the current generation. Qualified though it was, Davidson's prophecy appeared to give the highest ecclesiastical sanction to a sentiment which was in the hearts of the great majority of the 1,216 delegates at Edinburgh — the anticipation that,

1. World Missionary Conference, 1910, vol. 9, *The History and Records of the Conference* (Edinburgh and London, n.d.), p. 150, italics mine. A slightly shorter version of Davidson's words is found in W. H. T. Gairdner, *"Edinburgh 1910": An Account and Interpretation of the World Missionary Conference* (Edinburgh and London, 1910), p. 43.
2. Gairdner, *"Edinburgh 1910,"* p. 43.

through the redoubled missionary endeavors of the churches of the West, the world was on the eve of a new transfiguration destined to inaugurate the kingdom of God in its fullness.

A distinctly eschatological tone permeated the text of the reports presented at Edinburgh, particularly of the report of Commission 1 on "Carrying the Gospel to All the Non-Christian World." "Never before," proclaimed the opening paragraph, "has there been such a conjunction of crises and of opening of doors in all parts of the world as that which characterizes the present decade."[3] Appeal was made to what we might term "globalization" as evidence for the feasibility of attaining the goal of world evangelization: the rapid expansion of railway networks was affording missionaries ready access to millions of people; and the fact that "the vast majority" of non-Christian peoples were now under the sway either of "Christian" (that is, Western colonial) governments or of governments not antagonistic to Christian missions was identified as of peculiarly hopeful significance.[4] More disconcerting still to our ears was the confident assertion that "the money power in the hands of believing Christians of our generation is enormous."[5] In country after country the report discerned signs that the world stood at the fulcrum of major religious change. The premise of the argument was, however, not the inevitability but the realistic possibility and indeed urgent necessity of imminent Christian triumph. As Davidson implied, everything depended on the willingness and ability of the Church to grasp the providential moment. Non-Christian nations were in an unusually "plastic" condition, ready to be molded by any religion or ideology that seized the chance. The door for Christian missions was open, but it might not be so for long.[6]

China, after thousands of years of "self-centeredness and self-satisfaction," was turning her face from the past and had "begun to go to school to the world." But in China, as also in Korea, Japan, Turkey, and Persia, the question was whether the Church would be able to channel the strengthening currents of political, educational, and religious reform in the direction of Christianity: ". . . if the tide is not set toward Christianity during the next decade both in the Far East and the Near East, it may be turned against us in the decade following."[7] India also stood at the parting of the religious ways, but here the report contrived to interpret the ambiguous signs of the times in

3. World Missionary Conference, 1910, vol. 1, *Carrying the Gospel to All the Non-Christian World* (Edinburgh and London, n.d.), p. 1.
4. World Missionary Conference, 1910, vol. 1, pp. 5-6.
5. World Missionary Conference, 1910, vol. 1, p. 10.
6. World Missionary Conference, 1910, vol. 1, pp. 25, 27, 49.
7. World Missionary Conference, 1910, vol. 1, pp. 25-30 (quotation from p. 29).

a more consistently optimistic light. The educated were turning to various forms of "neo-Hinduism" through such movements as the Arya and Brahmo Samaj, which, for all their outward antagonism to Christianity, should be seen as "preparing the way of the Lord." Even the revival in certain parts of India of "orthodox Hinduism" was properly to be understood as a reaction to Christian advance and hence as a desirable development which "will in the end hasten the progress of Christianity, as was the case in the Roman Empire."[8] The outcastes and depressed castes were more responsive than ever before to Christianity, but equally to Islam, which had gained six million converts in the ten years preceding the last Indian census: Christians and Muslims were engaged in a race for the soul of the outcaste.[9] The Muslim world as a whole constituted both opportunity and threat: Islam was thought to be losing its grip on the educated and disintegrating philosophically into new sects and parties; yet its aggressive expansion among the uneducated posed the greatest of all challenges to Christian missions, above all in sub-Saharan Africa. "If things continue as they are now tending," warned the report, "Africa may become a Mohammedan continent." Missionary enterprise in Africa was likely to become ever more difficult in the face of the southward Islamic advance. "Paganism" was "doomed" to crumble away before "higher and more dogmatic" religions. As with the tribals and outcastes in India, the only question was whether Christianity or Islam should prevail.[10]

Edinburgh 1910 thus spoke with two intermingled voices. The voice most audible in the public sessions of the conference was one of boundless optimism and unsullied confidence in the ideological and financial power of Western Christendom. A more muted and discerning voice, heard periodically throughout the text of the Commission reports, and deriving from the more astute serving missionaries whose questionnaire replies formed the raw material for the reports, spoke of crisis and opportunity, challenge and competition. The former voice, of course, was soon to be rendered hollow and ultimately silent by the First World War and its aftermath. Despite its obvious historical significance, it need not occupy too much of our attention in this discussion. The muted voice, however, is worth listening to: its predictions have proved partly right and partly wrong, but they form an appropriate introduction to the themes of this chapter. We will discuss seven anticipated trends in the future global expansion of Christianity based on the various ex-

8. World Missionary Conference, 1910, vol. 1, pp. 12, 16-18. The revival of Buddhism in Japan, Burma, and Ceylon, unlike the Hindu revival, was not given an optimistic gloss but was presented simply as a call for more effective Christian effort (pp. 14-15).

9. World Missionary Conference, 1910, vol. 1, pp. 8, 18-19.

10. World Missionary Conference, 1910, vol. 1, pp. 12-13, 18-21.

plicit predictions or implicit assumptions made by the reports presented to the World Missionary Conference.

The first of these assumptions we shall simply note at this point in view of the fact that this volume contains a chapter on Christian conversion in India from the expert hand of Professor Frykenberg. Edinburgh 1910 anticipated that the Indian subcontinent would see a continuation of the Christian growth of the preceding half-century, particularly through mass movements among the fifty million of the "depressed classes," a category which was deemed to include non-Hinduized tribal peoples as well as those now known as Dalits or scheduled castes.[11] As far as caste Hindus were concerned, the Commission 1 report anticipated that education would exert a growing solvent effect on orthodox Hinduism, and that the widespread Hindu respect for the person of Jesus Christ would issue ultimately in an accelerating rate of actual conversions.[12]

A second assumption of the Edinburgh conference which can be no more than touched on from time to time in the course of this chapter was the dismissal by default of any possibility that the Roman Catholic, Orthodox, and other ancient churches might be expected to make any significant contribution to the evangelization of the world. This should not surprise us, and the ecclesiological reasons for the decision to exclude Latin America (with the exception of animist Indian tribal peoples and "Orientals") from the conference's terms of reference are well known.[13] The Commission 1 report noted that, on account of the monopolistic position enjoyed by the Roman Catholic Church, South America was still "the Neglected Continent" of Christian (i.e., Protestant) missions,[14] but Edinburgh perpetuated the neglect; there was not the slightest anticipation of the pivotal role that Latin America would play in both Catholic and Protestant religious history in the later years of the twentieth century.

In the remainder of this chapter, we shall examine in turn the remaining five predictions or assumptions as a device to facilitate a summary analysis of actual trends since 1910 and to indicate profitable directions of future research into the various fortunes of both Western and non-Western mission agency in the twentieth century.

11. World Missionary Conference, 1910, vol. 1, pp. 38-39, 147-50.

12. World Missionary Conference, 1910, vol. 1, pp. 12, 17, 39-40, 151.

13. It was a condition of the participation in the conference of leading Anglo-Catholics (notably Bishops Charles Gore, Edward Talbot, and H. H. Montgomery) that the conference and its preparatory commissions should be concerned only with missionary efforts among non-Christians, and not with Protestant missions in Roman Catholic territories such as Latin America.

14. World Missionary Conference, 1910, vol. 1, p. 249.

Missions and Modernization in East Asia

As has been seen, the World Missionary Conference anticipated that in most of the Far East, as also in parts of the Near East, Christian missions must within the next decade either capture the forces of reform and modernization or be swept aside by them.[15] On one level, this prophecy proved remarkably accurate. The Republican revolution in China in 1911-12 was hailed by missionaries with wild enthusiasm as a sign that the greatest nation on earth had, once and for all, embarked on the pathway of pro-Western reconstruction. The mission boards, especially American ones, began a massive program of investment in educational and medical institutions calculated to shape the new China in a modern and Christian image. The message promulgated by the YMCA and the Christian Literature Society for China that Christianity held the key to scientific and educational progress began to receive a warm welcome from sections of the educated elite. Until 1919 mission and modernization in China appeared to be proceeding on sweetly parallel tracks. Then came the May Fourth Movement of 1919, the formation of the Chinese Communist Party in 1920-21, the anti-foreign riots of 1922 and 1925, and the seizure of power by the Kuomintang in 1927. The alliance of missions and modernity had been rudely severed, and Christianity was increasingly portrayed as a reactionary force, wedded to both imperialism and prescientific irrationality. After 1927 there was no prospect of Christianity in urban China making further headway hitched to the cart of modernity; if it was to make progress at all, it had to be, as perhaps it already was in the countryside, in radical dissociation from Western power and ideology.

In Japan, similarly, a heavy Protestant emphasis on Western education during the Meiji period attracted support for a time from elite groups, and missions made substantial contributions to the modernization of medicine and social welfare. By the 1930s, however, strengthening nationalism was eroding the appeal of Protestantism. The modernizing imperative had proved to have only a temporary and superficial effect on adherence to the churches.[16]

Much of the heady expectation focused on East Asia at the Edinburgh conference derived from the extraordinary progress of Protestantism in Korea. The first two Protestant missionaries had arrived in the country as recently as 1884, when Christianity was still illegal and Korea seemed as resolutely anti-foreign as China. Yet since 1895 the Protestant churches in Korea

15. See n. 7 above.
16. R. G. Tiedemann, "China and Its Neighbours," in Adrian Hastings, ed., *A World History of Christianity* (London, 1999), pp. 400-401.

had grown with apostolic rapidity, fortified by the "Great Revival" movement of 1907. By 1910 there were 200,000 Protestant adherents in the country: Korea, commented the Commission 1 report, "presents the most striking example of a whole nation being moved by the Holy Spirit."[17] Yet American missions in Korea, no less than those in China and Japan, promoted education, social welfare and modernization. The difference, of course, was that Korea was under informal Japanese control from 1895, and under formal Japanese rule from 1910 to 1945. Although the significance of the 1907 revival was that it substantially indigenized the Church, a Christianity oriented toward Western modernity was able in Korea to establish its credentials as an ally, rather than as an enemy, of developing national consciousness.[18]

The divergent fortunes of Protestant mission Christianity in China, Japan, and Korea in the period up to 1945 might, therefore, appear broadly to confirm the accuracy of the predictions made at Edinburgh. Much depended on whether the force of nationalism reinforced or undermined the marriage of missions and modernity. Yet questions remain. Did Edinburgh greatly overestimate the importance of riding the wave of modernizing enthusiasm? Is there not evidence that Christianity in rural China continued to grow even during the 1920s and 1930s, though often quite independently of missionary aid and beyond the boundaries of the mission churches?[19] Was Korean church growth purely the product of pro-Western national sentiment, or in fact more deeply influenced by the popular revivalistic currents first apparent in 1907 which were less directly related to nationalist politics? What are we to make of the fact that the 1990s, which saw the bursting of the bubble of East Asian economic expansion, also apparently witnessed the end of Protestant church growth in Korea?

Missions, Empire, and Nationalism

The Commission 1 report devoted just four pages to a consideration of the growing spirit of nationalism and the desire to be free of European or American influence or control. In India, China, and Japan, it was observed that such sentiment was generating resentment against what was felt to be missionary domination. Chinese officials in particular were laboring under the miscon-

---

17. World Missionary Conference, 1910, vol. 1, p. 36.

18. Kenneth M. Wells, *New God, New Nation: Protestants and Self-Reconstruction: Nationalism in Korea, 1896-1937* (Honolulu, 1991).

19. Tiedemann, "China and Its Neighbours," p. 398; Daniel H. Bays, "The Growth of Independent Christianity in China, 1900-1937," in Daniel H. Bays, ed., *Christianity in China from the Eighteenth Century to the Present* (Stanford, 1996), pp. 307-16.

ception that "the missionary movement is after all only another form of political activity."[20] There was, however, no expectation that such anti-missionary feeling would become widespread. Indeed, the report forecast that nationalism in the Indian subcontinent would be a modernizing and unifying influence which would eventually abolish caste and hence "prepare India for a more rapid and thorough spread of Christianity."[21] In so far as nationalism was part of modernity, Edinburgh assumed that its effect would prove conducive to the missionary advance; nevertheless, without proper Christian direction and "purification," national sentiment had the power to hinder rather than promote the kingdom of God. The Edinburgh conference was assured that relations between missions and colonial governments were increasingly cordial, even though reports from missionaries on the field suggested a more diverse picture.[22]

It would be easy enough to point out the lacunae in Edinburgh's prophetic vision on this subject. It was not in Asia alone that missionaries were perceived to be linked to Western colonial power, and the matter was too complex to be remedied by simple appeals for non-Westerners to rectify their misunderstanding of missionary motives. Indian nationalism would turn out to be much more tightly wedded to Hindu identity than could have been anticipated in 1910. The assumption (extraordinarily enduring in the minds of political scientists and modern historians) that nationalism is a post-Enlightenment product propelling tradition-bound societies into the modern world has recently been effectively undermined by Adrian Hastings.[23] The literature on missions, colonialism, and nationalism in the twentieth century is, of course, immense, and this chapter can do no more than select a few relevant themes for emphasis and as signposts for further exploration. This section of the chapter will concentrate on Africa, because scholarly debates on the relationship of conversion and colonialism have focused more on Africa than anywhere else, but it will also urge the importance of setting the African story in a broader comparative context.

In the first place, it could be said that the 1910 conference failed to recognize the extent to which the open door for missions that so excited its enthusi-

---

20. World Missionary Conference, 1910, vol. 1, p. 33.

21. World Missionary Conference, 1910, vol. 1, pp. 34-35.

22. See Brian Stanley, "Church, State, and the Hierarchy of 'Civilization': The Making of the Commission VII Report, 'Missions and Governments,' Edinburgh 1910," in Andrew Porter, ed., *The Imperial Horizons of British Protestant Missions, 1880-1914* (Grand Rapids, 2003).

23. Adrian Hastings, *The Construction of Nationhood: Ethnicity, Religion and Nationalism* (Cambridge, 1997).

asm was indebted to the increasing impact of European colonialism. Colonial governments were seen as a good thing for missions on account of their supposed respect for freedom of religion, Christian morality, and law and order, but there was little emphasis on the degree to which indigenous responses to Christianity might be shaped by the new colonial order: Edinburgh thought mostly in terms of Western opportunity to evangelize, and only rarely in terms of incentives or disincentives for non-Westerners to convert. It remains the case, as will be stressed below, that the conference anticipated plentiful conversions in Africa with a confidence that contrasts markedly with the low estimation of Africa's prospects that obtained in British missionary circles fifty years previously, before the European partition of Africa and consequent missionary penetration of the interior. The Liverpool missionary conference in 1860 made only occasional reference to Africa.[24] A new missionary of the United Methodist Free Church who left for East Africa in 1861 was told repeatedly by his friends that he was wasting his time on those who lacked the moral and intellectual capacity to respond to the gospel.[25]

By 1910, the missionary enterprise in Africa stood on the threshold of a very different era. In much of the continent church growth became significant only after colonial rule attained stability and seeming permanence after the First World War (though it should be pointed out that in east and central Africa mission penetration itself became substantial only after 1918). In Kikuyuland, for example, adherence to the CMS mission rose dramatically after 1918: mission education offered access to the "white man's magic" of literacy, and the Christian doctrine of the one sovereign God made better sense of the newly expanded world opened up to the Kikuyu by war-time experience than did traditional beliefs.[26] Most Kenya missions doubled the number of their adherents every three years in the interwar period.[27] The phenomenon, it should be noted, was as much a Catholic as a Protestant one. The Roman

24. *Conference on Missions Held in 1860 at Liverpool* (London, 1860), pp. 29-31, 39-40, 51, 55, 189-90, 213-15, 333.

25. *Ecumenical Missionary Conference (New York, 1900)*, 2 vols. (London and New York, 1900), vol. 1, p. 462.

26. John Karanja, "The Role of Kikuyu Christians in Developing a Self-Consciously African Anglicanism," in Kevin Ward and Brian Stanley, eds., *The Church Mission Society and World Christianity, 1799-1999* (Grand Rapids, Cambridge, and Richmond, 2000), pp. 254-82. Karanja's oral research confirmed the validity in the Kikuyu case of Robin Horton's famous theory of African conversion, first outlined in his "African Conversion," *Africa* 41 (April 1971): 85-108.

27. David B. Barrett et al., eds., *Kenya Churches Handbook* (Kisumu, 1973), pp. 158, 169, cited in John Lonsdale, "Mission Christianity and Settler Colonialism in Eastern Africa," unpublished paper, 1999.

Catholic population of East Africa increased from some 300,000 in 1914 to 1.7 million by 1946.[28] In South Africa in the period from 1911 to 1960, much of the most spectacular Church growth was recorded by the Roman Catholic Church, which expanded its membership tenfold in this period, a much higher rate than that recorded by any of the other mission churches or the African independent churches.[29]

In Africa, more than anywhere else, the evidence for some form of connection between the phasing of conversion to Christianity and the transformative impact of the consolidated colonial order is undeniable.[30] Even if the Horton thesis of a primarily spatial movement from "tribal" microcosm to imperial macrocosm is deemed generally inadequate as an explanation of accelerated rates of African conversion under colonial rule, one of the most generally accepted alternative theories — J. D. Y. Peel's argument on the basis of Yoruba experience that the narrative of Christian salvation presented a new and linear form of temporality, congruent with the progressive assumptions of colonial modernization — still reaches the same conclusion that mass adhesion to Christianity came only after the colonial order had begun to impact substantially the patterns of everyday African life.[31]

However, a project such as Currents in World Christianity offers a distinctive opportunity to pose some questions to the historical orthodoxy on the relationship of conversion and colonialism. It enables us, first, to compare African experience with the patterns of religious change that obtained elsewhere, for example, in the South Pacific or in South Asia. Broadly speaking, it may be suggested that, in the nineteenth century, South Pacific conversion to Christianity proceeded rather faster than it did in Africa without the aid of formal European control; nevertheless, accessions to Christianity took place, as in early-twentieth-century Africa, in the context of the influx of European ideas, trade, technology, and disease; in both spheres, literacy beckoned as the way both to understand and master the encroaching new world.[32] In India,

---

28. Roland Oliver, *The Missionary Factor in East Africa*, 2nd ed. (London, 1965), pp. 235-36.

29. David Goodhew, "A Different Kind of *Kairos:* Church Growth and Decline in South Africa, 1960-91," CWC Position Paper 105, now published as "Growth and Decline in South Africa's Churches, 1960-91," *Journal of Religion in Africa* 30.3 (2000): 344-69.

30. See Adrian Hastings, *The Church in Africa: 1450-1950* (Oxford, 1994), pp. 404-5.

31. J. D. Y. Peel, "For Who Hath Despised the Day of Small Things? Missionary Narratives and Historical Anthropology," *Comparative Studies in Society and History* 37.3 (July 1995): 581-607.

32. See David Hilliard, "Australasia and the Pacific," in Hastings, *A World History of Christianity*, p. 513.

whereas the conversion of tribals to Christianity can often plausibly be explained in similar terms to those advanced by Horton for African societies,[33] the behavior of low-caste Hindu populations is, as Professor Frykenberg's chapter suggests, more complex. Mass movements to Christianity were not simply a product of the heyday of the Raj, but first appeared beyond the boundaries of direct East India Company influence among the Shānars of Tirunelveli at the close of the eighteenth century.[34] Conversely, British power in India, despite being much longer lasting and more intrusive than in Africa, proved far less conducive to the progress of Christianity. Second, the scope of the Currents in World Christianity project permits us to take a longer historical view than is normal by reflecting on the continuation, and indeed acceleration, of conversion to Christianity in postcolonial Africa. As Paul Gifford has noted, the assumption widely made at the time of independence that Christianity would dwindle now that its colonial props had been kicked away has proved spectacularly wide of the mark.[35] More than a decade ago Terence Ranger uttered a weighty protest against the tendency to assume that "everything that happened under colonialism was in some way a result of it." Whether his warning against the distorting effect of what he termed the "dichotomy" (surely "trichotomy") of "pre-colonial/colonial/post-colonial" on conceptions of religious change has yet been adequately heeded is open to debate.[36] On the one hand, we may take heart from what Leon De Kock has called "a gathering swell of reaction against binary models which assume that Christianity was little more than a tool of imperialism, and that it is best analyzed within the context of colonial imposition or capitalist machination."[37] On the other hand, the current fashion for defining one's ideological perspective as "postcolonial" tends to isolate the colonial era (which in much of Africa lasted for scarcely more than a life-time) as a period of privileged historical status that can be understood only by the deployment of postcolonial historiographical devices devised to unpick the supposedly unique structures of colonial economy and mentality. Part of the problem may be that the literature on conversion and colonialism is dominated by studies of nineteenth-

---

33. Geoffrey A. Oddie, "Introduction," in Geoffrey A. Oddie, ed., *Religious Conversion Movements in South Asia: Continuities and Change, 1800-1900* (London, 1997), pp. 7-9.

34. R. E. Frykenberg, "India," in Hastings, *A World History of Christianity,* p. 177.

35. Paul Gifford, *African Christianity: Its Public Role* (London, 1998), pp. 21-22.

36. Terence O. Ranger, "Religious Movements and Politics in Sub-Saharan Africa," *African Studies Review* 29.2 (June 1986): 49-51.

37. Leon De Kock, *Civilising Barbarians: Missionary Narrative and African Textual Response in Nineteenth-Century South Africa* (Johannesburg, 1996), p. 14. De Kock notes the work of Sanneh, Gray, Elphick, Elbourne, Landau, Etherington, and Ranger.

century southern Africa, where colonial rule arrived earlier than elsewhere on the continent, and where Christianity was irredeemably associated with a uniquely powerful white settler presence. The leading figures in that literature, Jean and John Comaroff, dissect the "long conversation" between missionaries and the Tswana, not out of any interest in the size and character of the Tswana church which resulted, but simply because they judge the conversation to have proved ultimately effective in making them into colonial subjects.[38] Even if their interpretation is deemed substantially valid for the nineteenth-century Tswana kingdoms, it is not clear that it can be universalized as a sufficient framework of explanation for the African churches established by the subsequent and rather shorter conversation between missionaries and Africans in other parts of the continent. This is particularly the case in relation to the sub-Saharan belt where so much of the twentieth-century growth in evangelical Protestantism has been concentrated, for here conversion to Christianity threatened to destabilize the fragile equilibrium between Christianity and Islam. Students of African religious and colonial history need to pay heed to the recent argument of Gauri Viswanathan that, in a context in which religious minorities challenge majority rights and identity, religious conversion operates as a profoundly destabilizing force, imperiling colonial objectives.[39]

Adopting a wider comparative perspective would suggest that what was crucial in creating the conditions for Christian growth in twentieth-century Africa was neither the presence of formal colonial rule nor even of less formal devices of European hegemony, but rather the convergence of a variety of forces of social and economic change, not all of which were unique to the colonial period, but most of which clearly related to the incorporation of African societies in wider economic networks. Stating the issue in this way permits us to place conversion to Christianity in colonial Africa within a longer story of processes of African religious change that both antedated the European colonial interlude and, as we are now well aware, followed it.

If the 1910 conference said less than might have been expected about empire, the fact that it said anything favorable at all about nationalism may surprise us. At the heart of the four pages in the Commission 1 report on the growing spirit of nationalism was the lofty verdict that "Christ never by teaching or example resisted or withstood the spirit of true nationalism."[40]

38. Jean and John Comaroff, *Of Revelation and Revolution*, vol. 1: *Christianity, Colonialism and Consciousness in South Africa* (Chicago, 1991), p. 200.

39. Gauri Viswanathan, *Outside the Fold: Conversion, Modernity, and Belief* (Princeton, 1998).

40. World Missionary Conference, 1910, vol. 1, p. 33.

However, as Hastings points out, this was a characteristic statement of Protestant confidence that God's workings with humanity dealt primarily in national units.[41] It certainly did not imply that the missionary response over the coming decades to burgeoning nationalist or anti-colonial movements in Asia, and later in Africa, would be uniformly favorable. Missionary critics of the *conduct* of empire were, of course, legion; some of those critics, such as C. F. Andrews in India or W. E. Owen in Kenya, were radical enough to identify themselves with political movements of a nationalist hue; but very few indeed went as far as Arthur Shearley Cripps in Rhodesia in disputing the central moral legitimacy of empire.[42] Neither did Edinburgh's apparent endorsement of nationalism imply any presentiment of the extent to which missions in the twentieth century would lay the foundations for resistance to colonialism through their educational endeavors and commitment to translating the Bible, hymns, and (in Protestantism) liturgies into local vernaculars — a priority which Hastings has identified as crucial for the metamorphosis of ethnicities into nations.[43]

Four questions arise under this broad theme that, it may be suggested, are especially worthy of further investigation in the light of the issues raised in this volume.

First, what significance do we attach to the fact, noted by K. S. Latourette with some perplexity in 1938,[44] that the interwar period witnessed *both* a marked acceleration of the rate of conversion to Christianity in Africa and elsewhere (for example, South India, parts of China, the Philippines) *and* the intensification of political crises fueled by anti-foreign or anti-colonial sentiment? Should we postulate a separation between the two trends along the lines of a rural and apolitical populace becoming increasingly responsive through mass movements to the Christian message, particularly as mediated through indigenous evangelists, and an urban educated elite becoming increasingly dissatisfied with the constraints placed upon them in both church and state? Or are the two apparently divergent trends in fact much more closely related, and does the new attraction of literacy in the colonial order provide the key for relating the two?

Second, if Andrew Walls, Lamin Sanneh, Adrian Hastings, and others are right, as surely they are, to pinpoint the importance of vernacular translation

41. Hastings, *The Construction of Nationhood*, p. 204.
42. On Cripps see Hastings, *The Church in Africa: 1450-1950*, pp. 433, 558-59; also Lonsdale, "Mission Christianity and Settler Colonialism in Eastern Africa."
43. Hastings, *The Construction of Nationhood*, passim.
44. K. S. Latourette, "The Church on the Field," in J. I. Parker, ed., *Interpretative Statistical Survey of the World Mission of the Christian Church* (London, 1938), p. 240.

for cultural and political identity, what patterns of relationship can be discerned in the period from about 1914 to 1960 between the completion in this period of many of the missionaries' goals of Bible translation, production of dictionaries, grammars, vernacular hymnbooks, and liturgies, and the growth of various forms of "modern" political consciousness? Work by John Karanja and Derek Peterson offers a valuable signpost here. Karanja has shown how the Kikuyu New Testament (1926) and, even more, Old Testament (1951) provided the Kikuyu with new narrative and linguistic resources for the articulation of tribal identity, as traditional vocabulary such as *muthamaki* (a spokesman for the council of elders) acquired new political resonance by being affixed to the kings of ancient Israel.[45] Peterson's comparison of two Kikuyu dictionaries published in 1904 and 1914 has taken the argument further by showing that crucial lexicographical decisions could not, in the nature of the case, be driven by the "linguistic colonialism" of which the Comaroffs have accused missionaries: dictionaries and, by extension, all acts of translation, are of value only in so far as they reflect genuine, open, and egalitarian dialogue between representatives of the two linguistic groups.[46] However blatant the cultural follies of some missionaries, the charge of cultural imperialism founders at the most crucial point of intersection between an alien religion and indigenous culture — the incarnation of doctrine in vernacular and "uncontrollable" texts.[47] Thus, even if missionaries continued to dominate the leadership structures of the Church (as they did in Africa until the 1950s and 1960s), the growing body of vernacular literature which nourished both ethnic consciousness and Christian devotion was weaving a different pattern. As translation processes came to fruition, a people's sense of ownership of the Christianity represented by these texts was necessarily greatly enhanced. What the connections were between this progressive sense of appropriation and, for example, the explosion of Church membership experienced by most of the mission churches in the 1950s[48] requires subtle elucidation of a kind that has not yet been attempted.

45. John Karanja, "Athamaki for Kings: The Bible and Kikuyu Political Thought," NAMP Position Paper 41 (Cambridge, 1997).

46. Derek Peterson, "Translating the Word: Dialogism and Debate in Two Gikuyu Dictionaries," *Journal of Religious History* 23.1 (February 1999): 31-50. Contrast Jean and John Comaroff, *Of Revelation and Revolution*, vol. 1, pp. 213-30.

47. See Andrew Porter, "'Cultural imperialism' and Protestant Missionary Enterprise, 1780-1914," NAMP Position Paper 7, now published in *Journal of Imperial and Commonwealth History* 25.3 (September 1997): 377-79.

48. See Adrian Hastings, *A History of African Christianity, 1950-1975* (Cambridge, 1979), p. 108.

Third, what was the significance for the appeal and influence of the churches of the varying roles played by the missions in colonial education in different geographical contexts? In Africa the two reports of the Phelps-Stokes Commission published in 1922 and 1925 introduced an era of remarkably close educational cooperation between missions and colonial governments (particularly in British territories).[49] At the start of this era, the missions supplied between 90 and 100 percent of all schools in British colonies in Africa.[50] The proportion had doubtless dropped somewhat by independence, but the significant points remained the general lack of competition faced by the mission schools and the extent of the subsidy they received from the colonial state. In 1949 both Protestant and Catholic missions in East Africa received substantially more in government grants than they did from domestic supporters and local contributions combined.[51] In the Pacific, the missions exercised a similar virtual monopoly of education until the end of the Second World War.[52] In Asia, on the other hand, missions rarely wielded such unrivalled power, though their influence was greatest at the highest levels of education. Government grants-in-aid had been a feature of British India since 1854, but even where the missions dominated the private sector of education, as in Madras presidency, their control of education was never total: in 1912 the missions controlled all of the girls' high schools in the presidency, but only 179 out of 311 of the boys' secondary schools, and half of the primary schools.[53] After the Government of India Act of 1919 placed education under the control of the new elected provincial governments, the influence of the missions declined further as the provincial governments introduced compulsory primary education in government schools, and mission schools often had to accept a conscience clause as the price of continuing grant aid.[54] In China, mission schools were responsible for an even smaller proportion of total educational provision: Protestant schools accounted for just 214,000,

49. *Education in Africa* (New York, 1922) and *Education in East Africa* (New York and London, n.d. [1925]); see Oliver, *The Missionary Factor in East Africa*, pp. 263-84.

50. *Christian Education in Africa and the East* (London, 1924), pp. 4, 87.

51. Oliver, *The Missionary Factor in East Africa*, p. 277.

52. John Barker, "Long God Yumi Stanap: Repositioning the Anthropology of Oceanic Christianity," unpublished paper presented at the Roundtable on Christianization in Oceania, École des Hautes Études en Sciences Sociales, Paris, May 1999, p. 15.

53. Aparnu Basu, *The Growth of Education and Political Development in India, 1898-1920* (Delhi, 1974), pp. 126-27.

54. Syed Nurallah and J. P. Naik, *A History of Education in India* (London, 1951), pp. 661-64; *Village Education in India: The Report of a Commission on Inquiry* (London, 1920), pp. 171-75.

and Catholic schools, 145,000, of a total of 5.7 million pupils in Chinese schools in 1922.[55]

Fourth, what were the short- and medium-term effects of decolonization on the growth of different sections of the Church? Did the mission churches benefit immediately from the removal of the stigma of adherence to a colonial religion; or, did they continue to labor under that stigma until well after independence; or, was that stigma never in fact as widespread at popular level as the writings of the educated elites who have created the non-Western theologies of the last four decades would suggest? Certainly it appears that only in a minority of African states did the political elite in independent Africa gravitate toward African-instituted churches rather than mission-instituted churches.[56] Did independence affect Protestant and Catholic churches differently? Did the latter benefit from retaining control of mission schools for much longer, as seems to have been the case in South Africa?[57] Whilst decolonization gave an immediate and long overdue boost to the devolution of power from mission to church, experience from other mission fields, such as India after 1947, would suggest that the mission churches derived no *necessary* immediate benefit in terms of growth rates from the transfer of power. In India national independence brought a marked intensification of the restrictions imposed on the churches' freedom of evangelistic operation, while the sudden accession into national hands of large amounts of mission property could function as a diversionary influence, encouraging factionalism within the churches.[58] In parts of Africa where colonial states bestowed independence with haste and inadequate preparation, as in the former Belgian Congo, the churches often had to construct national structures of ecclesiastical decision making where only regional or ethnic structures had existed previously, and all within a context of the political chaos resulting from the absence of any genuine "nation."[59]

Christianity, Islam, and the Race for the Animist

The Edinburgh conference was told of the substantial progress of Christian missions within the last two decades among the animistic peoples of sub-

---

55. *Christian Education in Africa and the East*, p. 40, citing the report *Christian Education in China* (New York, 1922).

56. Hastings, *A History of African Christianity, 1950-1975*, pp. 95-96.

57. Goodhew, "A Different Kind of *Kairos*."

58. For example, in the Baptist churches of Bengal and north India; see Brian Stanley, *The History of the Baptist Missionary Society, 1792-1992* (Edinburgh, 1992), p. 420.

59. See Stanley, *History of the Baptist Missionary Society*, pp. 439-50.

Saharan Africa, Sumatra, Java, Borneo, Celebes, and New Guinea.[60] In comparison to East or South Asia, very little was said at Edinburgh about the Dutch East Indies (where the Anglo-American missions which dominated the conference were poorly represented), and relatively little about Africa. As has been observed by Professor Walls, there was not one black African delegate at Edinburgh; there was a small, but apparently silent, African-American presence, including an African-American from Liberia whose "immense size" impressed Temple Gairdner.[61] The Commission 1 report referred to India and China as "the two great mission fields of the world"; Africa did not merit such status on the grounds of its sparse and "primitive" population. Nevertheless, because the "primitive" religion of animism was considered to offer such weak opposition to Christianity, "rapid and widespread triumphs of the Gospel" in Africa were possible.[62] The problem worrying missionary minds in 1910 was not, as Kwame Bediako has suggested,[63] whether the animist could be converted, but rather what he or she would be converted to. Edinburgh considered that animistic heathenism "inevitably goes down before the sustained attack of Christian missionary effort," and hence anticipated the possibility of "an early and abundant harvest" for missions in Africa. However, as has already been stressed, this was a provisional expectation. The question in Africa, as also in the East Indies, was whether Islam or Christianity would get to the ripening harvest first.[64]

In the pronouncements made on Islam in 1910, the note of urgency so characteristic of the Edinburgh conference became edgy in the extreme. These statements were consistent with a tradition of concern about the threat posed by Islam discernible in evangelical circles from the 1870s onward, in response particularly to the extension of British imperial control over Muslim Africa.[65] The public admissions of the apparently superior appeal of Islam to animistic peoples made in the 1880s by Christian spokesmen such as Edward Blyden and Isaac Taylor had evidently had their ef-

60. World Missionary Conference, 1910, vol. 1, pp. 40-41.

61. A. F. Walls, "The Significance of Christianity in Africa," Friends of St. Colm's Public Lecture, 1989, p. 2, and "African Christianity in the History of Religions," in C. Fyfe and A. F. Walls, eds., *Christianity in Africa in the 1990s* (Edinburgh, 1996), p. 2; cf. Gairdner, "Edinburgh 1910," p. 58; see n. 107 below.

62. World Missionary Conference, 1910, vol. 1, pp. 204, 207-8.

63. Kwame Bediako, *Christianity in Africa: The Renewal of a Non-Western Religion* (Edinburgh, 1995), pp. 192-93.

64. World Missionary Conference, 1910, vol. 4: *The Missionary Message in Relation to Non-Christian Religions* (Edinburgh and London, n.d.), p. 36; vol. 1, pp. 20-21, 40-41.

65. Andrew Porter, "Evangelicalism, Islam, and Millennial Expectation in the Nineteenth Century," NAMP Position Paper 76 (Cambridge, 1998), p. 18.

fect.[66] The paradigm of religious competition that was so unquestioned at Edinburgh is, of course, widely repudiated on theological grounds today, but historical analysis of the twentieth-century growth of Islam and Christianity at the expense of animistic religion cannot avoid the issue of whether their respective progress has in fact conformed to a competitive mode, and, if so, what the decisive terms of the competition have been. The Horton thesis of African conversion assumes that Islam and Christianity have functioned as alternative and competing versions of the monotheism held to be a suitable catalyst for the easing of the transition from a traditional to a modernizing world.[67]

Edinburgh's predictions of the progressive transformation of the animistic sections of the non-Western world into a Christian or Muslim image have proved broadly correct, but important questions remain unanswered. If the metaphor of the race implied in the Edinburgh reports is pursued to its logical conclusion, the issue becomes simply one of the comparative speed and efficiency with which Christian or Muslim missionary resources were mobilized, and indigenous people are denied any independent agency in the making of religious choices. But how far were Africans on the religious frontier in, for example, the Sudan or Nigeria actually confronted with two discrete options, one bearing the label "Christianity," and the other the label "Islam"?

Note must be taken here of the warnings uttered by the Comaroffs and now more fully by Paul Landau against the imposition on indigenous experience of a typically modern and Western reification of "religion." The Comaroffs protest that the use of the noun "conversion" leads to the reification and abstraction of religious belief, thus making "spiritual commitment into a choice among competing faiths, and 'belief systems' into doctrines torn free of all cultural embeddedness."[68] Landau, arguing cogently that the very concept of "religion" was a construct borne out of the Western encounter with alterity, pleads that we should attempt to understand African responses to mission Christianity in terms congruent with Africans' own perceptions, without the distortions created by Western notions of what constitutes "Christianity" or the anthropological construct of "African traditional religion."[69] The point is well made, though exactly what Landau means by advo-

66. See Lamin Sanneh, *Piety and Power: Muslims and Christians in West Africa* (Maryknoll, N.Y., 1996), pp. 70-81.

67. Horton, "African Conversion," pp. 104-5.

68. Jean and John Comaroff, *Of Revelation and Revolution,* vol. 1, p. 251.

69. Paul Landau, "'Religion' and Christian Conversion in African History: A New Model," *Journal of Religious History* 23.1 (February 1999): 8-30.

cating an alternative approach based on acceptance of the principle that "all people act and react in the landscape of the real" is not entirely clear.[70] What it may mean, however, is that adequate recognition should be given to the truism that Africans responded not so much to "Christianity" or "Islam" as to the particular individuals or groups who represented the new message: in Yorubaland, for example, Christianity was branded as the religion of the *Oyinbo* (Europeans), just as the earlier arrival, Islam, had been given the label of the *Imale*, the men from Mali who introduced it to the Yoruba.[71] From this recognition it follows that Africans who were deemed by the missionaries to have been "converted" to Christianity did not so much accept a unitary package of doctrine and practice as expand and reorder their existing world of concept and ritual in response to those whose union of word and life seemed to make new and better sense of the transformed "landscape of the real" presented by the colonial era. This reordering might mean the radical and absolute repudiation of aspects of existing practice that were losing credibility — such as the use of charms or witch-finders — but it might equally mean reorienting the old toward a relationship to the new in ways that defied missionary criteria of orthodoxy. Such alignments are most clearly observable in what we term African independent or African-instituted churches, but are clearly present in mission churches also. To that extent, the boundary between the two categories is not a rigid or particularly helpful one. The currency in modern Africa of the phenomenon of multiple religious adherences, in which a person may oscillate between mainstream and independent churches, and also resort on occasion to traditional healers, offers confirmation of this open-ended understanding of Christian conversion in twentieth-century Africa.

What Landau's thesis, along with other similar recent interpretations of the African encounter with mission Christianity, does not attempt to address is the degree of success experienced in Africa and other "primal" societies by Islam. On account of its self-definition in terms of a fixed body of divine law contained in the Qur'an and Hadith, Islam does not lend itself so readily to postmodern deconstruction as an "invention" of the Western mind. One of the few sophisticated studies we possess of the comparative appeal of Islam and Christianity in an African context — John Peel's study of Muslim and Christian evangelism in nineteenth-century Yorubaland — locates the appeal of the former in the spiritual realm and that of the latter more in the

---

70. Landau, "'Religion' and Christian Conversion in African History," p. 21.
71. J. D. Y. Peel, *Religious Encounter and the Making of the Yoruba* (Bloomington, Ind., 2000), pp. 129, 140, 190, 215.

material. The *alufa* (Muslim clerics) appeared to offer tangible spiritual power in the form of amulets containing prayers and invocations and the offering of sacrificial alms — *saraa* — whose appeal derived from their assimilation to traditional sacrifices (a salutary reminder that Islam, for all of its untranslatability at the level of language, often made less onerous demands on converts than did Christianity). Muslims also, as James Johnson observed in 1875, were zealous evangelists who associated freely with pagans, unlike the Christians who kept themselves separate and were identified with foreigners.[72] Christianity, on the other hand, gained much of its immediate credibility from its association with the manifestly superior power of European technology.[73] Despite this apparent contrast, the dominant impression made by Peel's account is of the way in which the Yoruba responded to Christianity and Islam as alternative variants of the same phenomenon, to be assessed by a common criterion of their effectiveness in mediating between God and man. In this respect, Christian evangelism possessed the potentially decisive advantage of being able to present Christ as a mediator of more elevated status and powers than Mohammed. It also, contrary to the rhetoric purveyed in 1910, derived significant benefit from the fact that Islam arrived in Yorubaland first, so that Christians were able to appropriate Muslim theological terminology for Christian use: Samuel Crowther, for instance, adopted the Islamic term *alufa* rather than the traditional *aworo* (the possession priests of the Yoruba deities) to translate the word "priest" throughout the Yoruba Bible.[74]

The Yoruba case might suggest that what has been decisive in determining the respective fortunes of Christian and Islamic expansion among "primal" peoples in the twentieth century has been not so much which religion got there first, but rather which was more successful in presenting its message in terms which combined "material" benefits in this life with the promise of assured mediatorial benefits in the world to come. Thus Okorocha's study of conversion in early twentieth-century Igboland concludes that Christians were much more successful than Muslims in presenting their faith as a source of spiritual power capable of effecting salvation — *Ezi-Ndu* — understood as a holistic enhancement of life in all its facets both this side of the grave and beyond it.[75] In other contexts, of course, the outcome of the competition was different. To what extent this was so, and why it was so, are questions for fu-

72. Peel, *Religious Encounter*, pp. 200-205.
73. Peel, *Religious Encounter*, pp. 213-14.
74. Peel, *Religious Encounter*, p. 195.
75. Cyril C. Okorocha, *The Meaning of Religious Conversion in Africa: The Case of the Igbo of Nigeria* (Aldershot, 1987), ch. 7.

ture exploration. In the Tengger highlands of eastern Java, for example, the Christian missionary effort initiated in the 1880s ultimately failed to win more than a handful of converts in a context where national and Islamic identity were closely linked and where Islam proved flexible enough to tolerate aspects of traditional religious practice.[76] Christianity in both its evangelical and Catholic forms could be variously adept or inept in accommodating itself to an understanding of religion in terms of spiritual power rather than of credal orthodoxy. However, such accommodation was intrinsically easier for Roman Catholicism, grounded as it was in a medieval tradition that valued mystery and miracle more highly than cognition, than for word-centered Protestantism, particularly in its post-Enlightenment form. The hypothesis may be advanced that evangelical forms of Christianity have achieved lasting and substantial conversionist success among traditional religionists only to the extent that they have succeeded in shedding the casing in which they have been housed in Western Christian history, namely, the Reformed antipathy to the exercise of supernatural power and the Enlightenment preference for rational thinking over felt experience.

Indigenous Agency and the Transfer of Power to Indigenous Churches

Although the Edinburgh conference paid due homage to the necessity of raising up an adequately trained indigenous evangelistic agency,[77] the underlying assumption of the commission reports was that the white European and North American agency held the key which would unlock the singular opportunities of the present age. Part of the advantage held by Islam in Africa, for example, was held to be that it was being spread "by those who do not differ essentially from the natives in their ideas and emotions, whereas Christianity, until a force of native workers can be prepared, must be spread by Europeans who differ greatly from the natives."[78] This comment reveals scant awareness of what was already the reality of the missionary movement. In most of the areas of notable Church growth, such as Uganda or Yorubaland, the overwhelming majority of

76. Robert W. Hefner, "Of Faith and Commitment: Christian Conversion in Muslim Java," in Robert W. Hefner, ed., *Conversion to Christianity: Historical and Anthropological Perspectives on a Great Transformation* (Berkeley, Los Angeles, and Oxford, 1993), pp. 110-13.

77. World Missionary Conference, 1910, vol. 1, p. 241; vol. 2: *The Church in the Mission Field* (Edinburgh and London, n.d.), ch. 5.

78. World Missionary Conference, 1910, vol. 1, pp. 20-21.

missionary faces were black. The largest British Protestant mission agency — the Church Missionary Society — had in 1906 8,850 accredited "native agents" compared with 975 European missionaries.[79] Yet the comment was an accurate reflection of the slow progress made by Protestant missions up to 1910 in developing and giving proper recognition to trained indigenous agency. A similar observation had been made in 1908 by George Adam Smith, when preaching on "Mohammedanism and Christianity" before the Baptist Missionary Society: "When we compete with Islam for the conversion of the heathen," commented Smith, "it has these advantages over us. Its creed is simple, and not expressed, like our own, in the forms of a Western theology, nor commended by Western missionaries. Its missionaries are Asiatic or African."[80]

There is considerable evidence that Protestant missions as a whole had by 1910 fallen away in practice, though not in theory, from the determination of mid-Victorian theorists such as Henry Venn and Rufus Anderson to make rapid progress toward a self-governing, self-financing, and self-propagating church. Recent writing suggests that the reasons for such failure should be sought not so much in the influence of late Victorian racism (though that was clearly a factor) as in the institutional dynamics of missionary societies that had become large, sophisticated, and partly self-absorbed institutions. The CMS by this time, writes Peter Williams, "was a mini-empire and in truth no more disposed to grant real independence to its satellites than the Colonial Office."[81] There was also a feeling that rapid devolution of authority to indigenous leaders had been tried and found theologically or morally wanting. In Jamaica, where the BMS, CMS, and LMS had relinquished control to the churches as early (in the case of the first two societies) as the 1840s, the societies were by the early twentieth century inclined to blame their premature withdrawal for the poor quality of church leadership and declining membership.[82] In China, Karl Gützlaff's Chinese Union had contrived during its brief history from 1844 to 1851 to give indigenous agents a bad name, even though there is evidence that Chinese Union evangelists contributed to some of the

79. Cited in C. Peter Williams, *The Ideal of the Self-Governing Church: A Study in Victorian Missionary Strategy* (Leiden, 1990), p. 262.

80. George Adam Smith, *Mohammedanism and Christianity: A Sermon Preached on September 30th, 1908, at the Autumn Session of the Baptist Missionary Society, Held in Bradford* (London, n.d.), p. 18.

81. Williams, *The Ideal of the Self-Governing Church*, p. 262.

82. Stanley, *History of the Baptist Missionary Society*, pp. 240-44; Eugene Stock, *The History of the Church Missionary Society*, 4 vols. (London, 1899-1916), vol. 2, p. 424; Norman Goodall, *A History of the London Missionary Society 1895-1945* (London, 1954), pp. 443-46. The London Missionary Society withdrew from Jamaica from the 1860s onward.

most successful church-planting endeavors of Protestant missions in nineteenth-century China, such as the Basel Mission's work among the Hakka of Guangdong province.[83] In South Africa, the missions were by 1910 conscious that native evangelists had been at the roots of most of the Ethiopian or other independent secessions from the mission churches: Christianity, write the Comaroffs in a vein that undermines their own thesis of how missionaries "colonized" the mind, was "sowing itself with vigor . . . in a hardy, hybrid strain propagated some way off from the closely tended mission garden."[84] Most notorious of all, Samuel Crowther's episcopate on the Niger was remembered "as a symbol not only of African leadership but also of the supposed failure of African leadership."[85]

Such bad memories lingering in the missionary mind help to explain the missions' notable failure to recognize the First World War as an opportunity for accelerating the devolution of power to the indigenous churches. With few exceptions, the societies sought after 1918 to restore the structures of missionary control that had obtained before the hiatus of the war. The interwar years in East Africa, notes Pirouet, witnessed numerous baptisms and the establishment of the schools and hospitals characteristic of the missionary movement at its peak, but no significant progress in the transfer of power into African hands.[86] Part of the difficulty lay in the financial differential that opened up between the Christian ministry and the teaching profession once government grants became available for teacher training and salaries. Wherever, as in the Anglican Church in Uganda, missions insisted on the ostensibly noble principle of the indigenous church being wholly self-supporting, ministerial stipends were depressed to levels far below those available to teachers and government employees, resulting in a dearth of gifted candidates for ordination and hence the retarded development of a self-governing church. For all the advantages that accrued to the missions from the colonial era, they eventually had to come to terms with what J. V. Taylor in 1968 called "the harsh economic fact that the ministry was the only modern profession in the developing countries which was not artificially subsidised by local governments and international aid."[87]

83. Jessie G. Lutz and R. Ray Lutz, "Karl Gützlaff's Approach to Indigenization: The Chinese Union," in Bays, *Christianity in China*, pp. 269-91.

84. John L. and Jean Comaroff, *Of Revelation and Revolution*, vol. 2: *The Dialectics of Modernity on a South African Frontier* (Chicago and London, 1997), p. 85.

85. Bengt Sundkler, *The Christian Ministry in Africa* (Uppsala, 1960), p. 44.

86. M. Louise Pirouet, "East African Christians and World War I," *Journal of African History* 19.1 (1978): 129.

87. Gordon Hewitt, *The Problems of Success: A History of the Church Missionary Soci-*

Nevertheless, the relations between Protestant missions and indigenous churches began to change in the wake of the Jerusalem meeting of the International Missionary Council in 1928. Influenced by recent "dramatic and swift-moving social and political changes" (notably the anti-Christian movement in China from 1925 to 1927), the Council issued a strong statement urging the necessity of adopting a "church-centric" approach to mission in which "the indigenous church will become the centre from which the whole missionary enterprise of the area will be directed."[88] Delegates at Jerusalem returned to their fields fired with new zeal for devolution. In Asia especially, the next decade witnessed substantial transfers of power from mission to church, but the crucial impetus may have been less idealistic than financial. C. E. Wilson, foreign secretary of the BMS, found it necessary during a tour of the society's India missions in 1931-32 to explain that the society's determination to devolve power to the Indian and Ceylonese churches was "not merely the present result of our reduced income and a hasty desire to cast the burdens of the BMS upon other shoulders"; yet in domestic committees, the connection between financial crisis and devolution was quite explicit.[89] Other sections of the British missionary movement experienced similar or worse difficulties: the CMS recorded a deficit in every year from 1910 to 1941.[90] The trend was in fact global: the enormous expansion in both personnel and institutional commitments undertaken by Protestant missions since the late 1880s imploded in the interwar period in a series of protracted financial crises. The American mission boards were hit particularly hard after 1929 by the Depression, coming as it did on top of the splintering of their funding base by the fundamentalist controversies initiated in the 1920s and an accelerating decline in the numbers of student volunteers from the peak attained in 1920.[91] The aggregate expenditure of all North American Protestant missions in the Indian subcontinent fell from $6.9 million in 1929 to $4.5 million in

---

ety, 1910-1942, 2 vols. (London, 1971), vol. 1, p. 253; see also Oliver, *The Missionary Factor in East Africa*, pp. 282-83; Kevin Ward, "Africa," in Hastings, *A World History of Christianity*, p. 227.

88. *The Relations between the Younger and Older Churches: Report of the Jerusalem Meeting of the International Missionary Council, March 24th–April 8th 1928* (London, 1928), vol. 3, pp. 207, 209.

89. Stanley, *History of the Baptist Missionary Society*, pp. 292, 383-85.

90. Hewitt, *The Problems of Success*, vol. 1, pp. 430-31; see also Goodall, *History of the London Missionary Society*, pp. 549-52.

91. New volunteers enlisting for the Student Volunteer Movement declined from 2,783 in 1920 to 1,471 in 1923 and 465 in 1930; see Nathan D. Showalter, *The End of a Crusade: The Student Volunteer Movement for Foreign Missions and the Great War* (Lanham, Md., and London, 1998), p. 161.

1936.[92] In Japan and Korea the number of Protestant missionaries fell sharply from the late 1920s; in China, the total number of Protestant missionaries by 1929 was some 40 percent below the peak of 8,325 attained in 1926; the waning of the anti-foreign movement produced a limited recovery after 1929, but in 1938 the total was still only 5,747.[93]

The consequences of these structural crises in the missionary movement deserve much fuller investigation than has yet been attempted. We have suggested that they may have been the most important engine driving the transfer of power from mission to church in Asia during the late 1920s and 1930s. Since 1910 the missionary hopes of American Protestantism had been heavily concentrated on the Christian awakening of the Orient. Now that goal was fast receding in the face of political and economic reality. When coupled with the questioning of the theological legitimacy of converting those of other faiths posed by the Laymen's Foreign Missions Inquiry report of 1932, the crisis dealt American denominational missions a blow from which they never recovered. The initiative in American Protestant missions passed to nondenominational, conservative evangelical or fundamentalist mission agencies. These have focused their goals not on the structural and educational refashioning of Asia into the image of Christian civilization but on pioneer evangelism among tribal peoples in Southeast Asia, Papua New Guinea, Africa, and Latin America. British denominational missions experienced a less drastic decline, but they too began to redirect their efforts away from the priorities that had dominated horizons in 1910. The CMS provides an extreme example of a more general trend in that between 1910 and 1942 Asia and Africa changed places in the league table of missionary personnel: of the 1,360 CMS missionaries in 1910, 479 were in India and Ceylon, 302 in China, and only 253 in Africa; by 1942, there were only 259 in India and Ceylon, 158 in China, but 450 in Africa.[94] In Protestant missions as a whole, the number of overseas personnel serving in Asia decreased from 16,663 in 1925 to 14,318 in 1938, whereas those serving in Africa increased from 6,289 to 8,447.[95] Many of those Africa missionaries were supported in part or whole by government grants-in-aid of mission education. The switch to Africa doubtless reflected awareness of the rapid advances that the churches had made on the continent in the interwar period, but it also made economic sense, as has already been

92. K. S. Latourette, *A History of the Expansion of Christianity*, vol. 7 (London, 1947), p. 289.

93. Parker, *Interpretative Statistical Survey of the World Mission of the Christian Church*, pp. 245, 271, 277.

94. Hewitt, *The Problems of Success*, vol. 1, p. xiv.

95. Parker, *Statistical Survey of the World Mission of the Christian Church*, p. 243.

pointed out. Subsidies in Africa helped to conceal from the Western churches the truth that the age of Anglo-American dominance in the world church was already passing.

The structural realignment of the missionary movement between the world wars opened up the spaces in which the postwar configuration of world Protestantism could develop. As missionary numbers and budgets declined, the Asian churches were finally granted their autonomy. A generation of Christian leaders shaped by the high-quality and predominantly liberal theological education which the missions supplied in Asia, and by the parallel influence of the YMCA in the universities and colleges, assumed control. From their ranks, and the ranks of their pupils, emerged the architects of the Asian theologies of the 1960s and beyond: Asian theology was, for all of its desire to distance itself from Western models, the heir to the investment in Christian higher education made from the 1830s by Protestant missions captivated by the vision of modernizing and regenerating Asia from the top down. Yet, at the same time, the scaling down of the missionary presence in the Asian churches also enhanced the visibility of alternative currents of popular Christian piety, expressed in the mass movements or revivals already flowing beneath the surface or beyond the reach of the mission churches. Just as Macaulay's vision of downward educational filtration in India has resulted today in a divorce between a highly educated Anglophone minority and a poorly educated mass rural population,[96] so Christianity in much of Asia suffers from a polarity between a theological elite oriented toward the conciliar movement borne of Protestant missionary parentage and a poorly educated mass constituency whose international links are often with more recently established evangelical or fundamentalist networks.

Africa, meanwhile, witnessed a continuing escalation of the missionary presence. In contrast to the East and South Asian fields that preoccupied missionary attention in the earlier decades of the century, the number of Western missionaries in most African countries has continued to rise to the present day; what has, of course, changed radically since the Second World War is the proportion between those supplied by older "mainline" societies and those from the new evangelical or fundamentalist missions.[97] Relative to total population, the Christian community in Africa has been much larger than in most of Asia. Compared with the Asian churches, African Christianity had the benefit until the 1960s of a broader base of heavily subsidized mission ed-

---

96. Tapan Raychaudhuri, "British Rule in India: An Assessment," in P. J. Marshall, ed., *The Cambridge Illustrated History of the British Empire* (Cambridge, 1996), p. 369.

97. Gifford, *African Christianity,* pp. 44-47.

ucation at primary and secondary levels, but had very few institutions of advanced theological or secular education and a marked shortage of indigenous clergy.[98] Mission agencies retained power until at least a generation later than in the historic Asian fields. It may be suggested that this pattern has contributed to the markedly lay and populist character of modern African Christianity that is simultaneously its strength and its weakness, helping to explain both its spontaneity of initiative and its apparent vulnerability to noncontextual external theological influences. John Mbiti's remark in 1967 that the Church in Africa was "a Church without a theology, without theologians, and without theological concern" was an overstated but entirely understandable verdict from one of the handful of African Protestant clergy at that time who had received a theological education commensurate with that received by Christian leaders in the Indian subcontinent.[99]

"Alternative" Christianities[100]

An implicit presupposition made consistently throughout the 1910 reports was that sectors of Christianity not under white missionary control would have little or no part to play in the anticipated transfiguration of the non-Western world. The Commission 1 report did make brief reference to the potential of popular revival movements to create, in the case of Korea, the prospect of "the first non-Christian nation evangelized in the history of modern missions." The impact of such movements on the uneducated was also noted in Japan, China, Siam, Laos, and the Malay Peninsula. Although the rather faint-hearted opinion of two Laos missionaries was cited that, as a result, the country could become "nominally Christian" within their lifetime, the report appears to have perceived no particular significance in such movements other than the fact that they were representative of a "rising spiritual tide" in many fields.[101] There was no sense that movements of popular conversion or indigenous renewal possessed an autonomy of character and momentum that

98. See Hastings, *The Church in Africa: 1450-1950*, pp. 553-56; Parker, *Interpretative Statistical Survey of the World Mission of the Christian Church*, pp. 195-211.

99. J. S. Mbiti, "Some African Concepts of Christology," in G. F. Vicedom, ed., *Christ and the Younger Churches* (London, 1972), p. 51, cited in Hastings, *A History of African Christianity*, p. 165.

100. This phrase is meant to convey the most favorable construction that was put on such expressions of Christianity by Western observers in 1910. Arguably, over ninety years later, the "alternative" has become the norm.

101. World Missionary Conference, 1910, vol. 1, pp. 36-38.

would challenge missionary preconceptions as much as uplift missionary hearts.

In point of fact, however, in numerous contexts over the next few decades, movements of this kind were to contribute substantially to the numerical growth and reshaping of non-Western Christianity. Bays estimates that by the 1940s various independent groups may have accounted for some 20-25 percent of all Protestants in mainland China, despite being largely ignored by the mission establishment. Many of these groups were broadly "Pentecostal" in character.[102] In India the mass movements among those now termed *dālits* and other low-castes continued to be a major feature of the Christian landscape until at least the 1930s. These movements were neither sought by missionaries nor led by them. Today, as a result of these independent movements of group conversion, between two-thirds and three-quarters of Indian Christians are *dālits*.[103] Within a few years of the Edinburgh conference, Christianity in West Africa was to be profoundly affected by conversion movements led by William Wadé Harris, Garrick Braide, and other prophet figures. These were autonomous of missionary control, yet rarely anti-missionary, supplying thousands of converts to the mission churches, both Protestant and Catholic, as well as leading to the founding of new independent churches.[104] Twenty years later East Africa experienced a similar phenomenon in the shape of the *balokole* revival which began in Rwanda in 1933, transforming mission-dominated Anglican and Protestant churches into a genuinely indigenous though strongly anti-traditionalist movement. If financial crisis was one crucial stimulant provoking the missions' withdrawal from direct control from the 1930s onward, the other was the appearance of movements such as the *balokole* which subverted the established criteria of spiritual maturity and hence challenged missionary notions of who was and who was not "converted." The two stimuli may even have been indirectly related in so far as the East African revival has been interpreted as in part a Christian response to the crisis in the colonial economy in the 1930s.[105] Perhaps more plausibly, it may be suggested that such twentieth-century movements represent a recalling of evangelicalism to its eighteenth-

---

102. Bays, "The Growth of Independent Christianity," pp. 310-13. Note should, however, be taken of Dana Robert's recent warning against the unreflective application of the term "Pentecostal" to current movements in non-Western Christianity; see Dana Robert, "Shifting Southward: Global Christianity since 1945," *International Bulletin of Missionary Research* 24.2 (April 2000): 57.

103. J. C. B. Webster, *A History of the Dalit Christians in India* (San Francisco, 1992), pp. i, 37, 66.

104. See Hastings, *The Church in Africa*, pp. 443-53.

105. John Iliffe, *A Modern History of Tanganyika* (Cambridge, 1979), pp. 342, 363-65.

century roots in lay religion, challenging the tendencies of bureaucratization and organizational control that characterized Protestant missions in their early-twentieth-century heyday.

Even more telling than the scant attention paid in 1910 to movements of indigenous conversion to Christianity was the fact that Ethiopianism in South Africa, which had drawn some thousands of adherents from the mission churches in the two decades before 1910, was dismissed in the Commission 1 report as "spreading through the country a superficial and largely emotional form of Christianity, unable to resist the disintegrating and corrupting influences of surrounding heathenism."[106] Nevertheless, the numbers concerned were significant enough for the *Statistical Atlas of Christian Missions,* published alongside the conference, to draw attention to the fact that Ethiopian adherents were not included in its statistics for the African Christian community.[107] No voice was heard at Edinburgh 1910 urging the necessity for missions to respond to the Ethiopian movement in a self-critical spirit. In contrast, the Ecumenical Missionary Conference at New York in 1900 had heard a forthright address from Charles Morris, a missionary of the (black) National Baptist Convention, warning that the Ethiopian movement was "not simply a blind rebellion on the part of the natives to get out from under European control," but the product of the infection of the younger missionary generation in South Africa with racial prejudice. In terms that were typical of the African American missionary movement at the time, Morris identified the black Christian population of the southern United States, with their supposed double immunity from racial prejudice and malaria, as the best hope for the evangelization of both South and West Africa.[108]

In significant contrast to the records of the New York conference in 1900, the Edinburgh reports made no mention of the foreign missions of African American or Afro-Caribbean churches, which, though poor in financial terms, were already by 1910 of major importance for Christianity in both western and southern Africa. African-American mission societies were represented only minimally among the delegates at Edinburgh, being largely excluded by the financial basis of representation.[109] African-

106. World Missionary Conference, 1910, vol. 1, p. 229.

107. *Statistical Atlas of Christian Missions* (Edinburgh, 1910), p. 61.

108. *Ecumenical Missionary Conference (New York, 1900),* vol. 1, pp. 469-71. See also the remarks of H. B. Parks, of the African Methodist Episcopal Church on pp. 471-72.

109. Two representatives of the Foreign Mission Board of the National Baptist Convention of the United States of America and two representatives of the African Methodist Episcopal Foreign Missionary Society were among the official delegates. See World Missionary Conference, 1910, vol. 9, pp. 52, 58.

Americans and Afro-Caribbeans were deemed to be part of Christendom rather than the non-Christian world in so far as their churches did not figure in the statistical tables published at Edinburgh (only the churches of "Asiatic immigrants" to the West Indies or North America, and, in the latter case, those of Native Americans and Eskimos, did so).[110] Yet the African-American and Afro-Caribbean church population *was* taken into account in the *Statistical Atlas*'s computation of the total "fruitage" of modern Christian missions, with the happy and probably misleading result that Protestant "fruitage" ended up well in excess of the results of Roman Catholic and Russian Orthodox missions.[111] Nevertheless, African diaspora Christians were almost entirely excluded in practice from any consideration of the missionary resources of Christendom. The Christian tradition which has contributed more than any other to the shaping of Pentecostalism — the most rapidly expanding sector of contemporary Christianity — thus simply dropped out of view at Edinburgh.

The marked seepage in many parts of the contemporary world from older churches, whether Catholic, Protestant, or "independent," to forms of charismatic and "prosperity" Christianity has implications for some of the theories of conversion in the colonial period which we have examined earlier in the chapter. Paul Gifford concludes that such an overtly trans-cultural, and apparently anti-contextual imported "religion" as American-style charismatic fundamentalism appeals to Africans precisely because it enables some sort of religious sense to be made of an impoverished and politically fragile "landscape of the real" in which the dominant manipulative forces are the external ones of American capitalism.[112] If Gifford is correct in his judgment that today "the growth areas of Christianity are those that demonise African traditions and culture,"[113] then sophisticated theories of African conversion (such as Landau's) which insist on the irrelevance of externally constructed notions of "religion" to African perceptions of reality become not simply of decreasing usefulness in the explanation of *current* religious change but may also come under increasing scrutiny as explanations of why Africans became Christians in the colonial era. Gifford points out that under colonialism many West Africans chose to become Muslims rather than Christians, attracted by much the same combination of magico-

110. World Missionary Conference, 1910, vol. 9, p. 63.

111. World Missionary Conference, 1910, vol. 9, p. 61. It was estimated that, out of a total "fruitage" of 21 million, only 5.7 million converts were the result of Roman Catholic and Orthodox missions.

112. Gifford, *African Christianity,* pp. 308-25.

113. Gifford, *African Christianity,* p. 324.

spiritual power, zealous proselytism, and incorporation into a manifestly trans-local, even global, network as is offered by the new charismatic churches of Africa today.[114]

However, what may appear to be quintessentially American or "capitalist" expressions of religious culture may turn out to have deeper roots in non-Western tradition and experience than is often appreciated. Church growth theory, for example, may have been packaged for the American market at Fuller Theological Seminary but its origins lie in Donald McGavran's observation as a Disciples of Christ missionary of the patterns of Indian conversion to Christianity displayed in the mass movements. Furthermore, it must be stressed that there is nothing new about the challenge posed to Western Christianity in the Enlightenment tradition by forms of indigenous Christian faith that place a premium on spiritual power rather than orthodoxy. Such tensions were integral to the process whereby the religion of the Great Awakening was received and reinterpreted by African-American slaves from as early as the 1740s. From about 1800 this movement of "double conversion" became profoundly significant in the American South, as the slave population increasingly converted to, and in so doing transformed, evangelical Christianity. These new African-American versions of evangelicalism passed from the southern states to the Caribbean, and from both regions in due course back to Africa.[115] In the Caribbean, where black evangelicalism flourished for two decades or more with little or no white missionary influence, the issues of how to define evangelical conversion and spirituality in relation to African cosmology became sharper still. In Jamaica the conversion of several thousand slaves after the implantation of Baptist Christianity from Georgia after 1787 raised searching questions of ecclesiological control that led its early black leaders to appeal to British Baptists for aid. The BMS missionaries who arrived to help from 1814 were, however, soon out of their depth in a religious environment that was inclined to make ecstatic seizure by the Spirit and ability to see visions a prerequisite for baptism and church membership. In Jamaica popular evangelical religion and myalism shaded into each other, and in the intersection salvation was reconceived as power and protection against the material and spiritual evils attributed to the sorcery of the obeahman, including, significantly, the oppression of the slave system itself. This was essentially black Pentecostalism a century before

114. Gifford, *African Christianity,* pp. 322-23. Gifford is drawing on Peel, "Engaging with Islam," especially pp. 29-30.

115. See especially Sylvia R. Frey and Betty Wood, *Come Shouting to Zion: African American Protestantism in the American South and British Caribbean to 1830* (Chapel Hill, N.C., and London, 1998).

Azusa Street — and a far cry from the missionary Christianity of an expanding Europe.[116]

The redefinition of Christianity in terms of the promise of not merely spiritual but also physical well-being, material prosperity, and power to combat evil may, therefore, have less to do with the globalization of white American culture and capital than with the congruence of neo-Pentecostal religion with patterns of cosmological understanding deeply embedded in the consciousness of many non-Western peoples.[117] To what extent this redefinition should be construed as a syncretistic distortion, and to what extent (*pace* Gifford) as an astonishingly successful example of inculturation, is the key issue which the theologians must address. The appropriation of evangelical religion by Afro-Caribbean and African-American people from the eighteenth century onward has much more to contribute to an understanding of current global religious trends than most interpretations allow. That is one reason among several why it is essential that scholarly inquiry into the current growth of non-Western Christianity should maintain a long historical perspective.

All this, of course, was almost entirely hidden from the gaze of those who gathered on the Mound in Edinburgh in 1910. The missionary statesmen (and a few stateswomen) who filled the Assembly Hall of the United Free Church of Scotland in June that year were, no less than those who now occupy those premises for a different purpose,[118] people of idealism but inevitably partial vision. There is much about the course of world Christianity over the next ninety years that they failed to see. But we should not be too hard on them. There were times when the prophetic voice at Edinburgh spoke with discernment and accuracy, and perhaps it is appropriate to conclude this chapter with one such utterance:

116. Frey and Wood, *Come Shouting to Zion*, pp. 131-32; Winston Arthur Lawson, *Religion and Race: African and European Roots in Conflict: A Jamaican Testament* (New York, 1996), pp. 25-31; Horace O. Russell, *The Missionary Outreach of the West Indian Church: Jamaican Baptist Missions to West Africa in the Nineteenth Century* (New York and Washington, D.C., 2000), pp. 25-27, 41; Stanley, *History of the Baptist Missionary Society*, ch. 3.

117. For two interpretations of current charismatic Christianity in terms of congruence with indigenous culture, see Murray A. Rubinstein, "Holy Spirit Taiwan: Pentecostal and Charismatic Christianity in the Republic of China," in Bays, *Christianity in China*, pp. 353-66; and Ruth Marshall, "'Power in the Name of Jesus': Social Transformation and Pentecostalism in Western Nigeria 'Revisited,'" in Terence Ranger and Olufemi Vaughan, eds., *Legitimacy and the State in Twentieth-Century Africa: Essays in Honour of A. H. M. Kirk-Greene* (Basingstoke and London, 1993), pp. 213-46.

118. The Hall is the temporary meeting place of the Scottish Parliament.

Informed, transformed, enlightened, enlivened by the reception of Christ and the indwelling of the Holy Spirit, Asia, Africa, and Oceania will surely exercise a profound influence upon the western Church and help greatly to enlarge and enrich its conception of Christ and His Kingdom.[119]

This volume is itself evidence that this particular prophecy has been amply fulfilled.

119. World Missionary Conference, 1910, vol. 1, p. 47.

SECTION II

CHAPTER FOUR

Conversion, Commitment, and Culture: Christian Experience in China, 1949-99

PHILIP YUEN-SANG LEUNG

Prologue

In the New Testament there was a man called Lazarus. The following is his story as told in John 11:

> There was a man named Lazarus. He was from Bethany and he was sick. He had two sisters, Martha and Mary. And they all loved Jesus. When Jesus heard of Lazarus' illness, he said, "This sickness will not end in death. No, it is for God's glory so that God's son may be glorified through it."
>
> On his arrival, Jesus found that Lazarus had already been in the tomb for four days. Many Jews had come to Martha and Mary to comfort them in the loss of their brother. Jesus came to see the sisters. When he saw Mary weeping, and the Jews who came with her also weeping, he was deeply moved. . . . He came to the tomb, and said, "Take away the stone." So they took away the stone. Then, Jesus looked up and said, "Father, I thank you that you have heard me."
>
> When he had said this, Jesus called in a loud voice, "Lazarus, come out!" The dead man came out, his hands and feet wrapped with strips of linen, and a cloth around his face. Jesus said to them, "Take off the grave clothes, and let him go."

According to the Scripture:

Lazarus was sick;
Lazarus was dead;
Lazarus was revived;
Lazarus walked again and lived a vigorous Christian life.
Lazarus's life is a story of resurrection.

The story of the Chinese Christian church after 1949 is quite similar to Lazarus's:

The Chinese Christian church was sick in the early period of the People's Republic;
The Chinese Christian church was practically dead during the decade of the Great Proletarian Cultural Revolution;
The Chinese Christian church was revived in the Reform Era of the late seventies and early eighties;
The Chinese Christian church has been growing rapidly and vigorously in the recent years of the eighties and nineties.

The story of Christianity in China in the last half-century is a Lazarus story that this chapter will address. However, in considering Lazarus, we must also tell the stories of his two sisters, Martha and Mary.

Nationalization, Unification, and Dissension as Illnesses: The Three-self Patriotic Church and Its Challengers, 1949-65

"Master, Lazarus is ill; he is dying."

In 1949 when the Communists came to power on the Chinese mainland, most Chinese people, including Christians, faced a difficult dilemma: whether to flee with the Nationalists to Taiwan or to stay home under the rule of the Communists. For the majority of Chinese Christians the fear of atheistic Communism was real even if they were not pro-Nationalist in political orientation. Many Christians were simply apolitical, and whether the ruler was Chiang Kai-shek, Mao Zedong, or some other warlord, it was of little concern to them. As Christians they identified the things of the spiritual realm as priorities in their lives: evangelism, spiritual growth, and church work. The things in the secular world — social, political, and cultural activities — were thought of as secondary, if not totally insignificant. However, not all Christians were apolitical. A number of them, especially those from bourgeoisie or mercantile-comprador backgrounds and with an education obtained in Christian universities in China or overseas, consciously chose to support Chiang Kai-shek and the Nationalist government whose key members had close ties with the Christian circle. A large number of these Chinese Christians later followed the Nationalists to Taiwan. However, there were some socially conscious and politically active Christians who chose a different path by following the Communists and working arduously for the socialist transformation of China.

The politically indifferent majority of Christians in China could be called the "Marys" for they were God-centered and Scripture-oriented and emphasized prayer rather than social action; they were more interested in the spiritual life than in social engagement. Most of them were the followers of John Sung, Watchman Nee, Andrew Gee, Wang Mingdao, and many other Evangelists and fundamentalist "Gospellers." They were the "Marys" in China who concentrated their attention and energy on spiritual learning rather than on secular affairs, and this "Marian Model" is representative of mainstream Chinese Christianity in China before the Communist revolution. Most of the small, independent, and indigenized local churches in the rural regions shared this spiritual inclination: preaching, evangelism, scriptural study, and prayer were their salient characteristics. On the other hand, there were some Chinese Christians, particularly those who lived in urban areas and who were better educated, who were prone to become "Marthas." They included the Christian intellectuals who advocated social and political reform at the national level, and who thought Christianity was highly relevant to social change and to the political transformation of the Chinese society. They included many of the YMCA workers, the Christian industrial and agrarian reformers, and the socially conscious and politically active Christians eager to apply Christian ethics in areas of moral and social reform. Some were associated with the Nationalist government such as Yu Rizhang (David Yui), Xu Qian, and Liu Tingfang (Timothy T. Lew); but some, Zhang Zhijiang and Chen Chonggui (Marcus Cheng), for example, also worked for warlords such as Feng Yuxiang and Sun Quanfang. Others, still, worked for the Communists: people like Wu Yaozong (Y. T. Wu), Deng Yuzhi (Cora Teng), and Ding Guangxun (Bishop K. H. Ting). Despite their political loyalties, they shared one common concern, that is, they were working for the transformation of their society and nation from a Christian standpoint. But most of the time they showed greater interest in social and political movements than in the expansion of the Church. They were more interested in working arduously for what they termed "national salvation" rather than for "individual salvation." Significantly, there were Christian social and political activists on both the right and the left. Despite their political loyalties, theologically many of them were indebted to the Social Gospel and the "modernist" theology so popular in many Western seminaries in the early twentieth century.

In the post-1949 period, the story of Christianity in China is one of tension and conflict between the Chinese "Marys" and the left-wing Chinese "Marthas."

The "Marthas" of the left after 1949 in China were represented by Wu Yaozong, Liu Liangmo, Ding Guangxun, Deng Yuzhi, and other leaders of the "Three-Self Patriotic Movement" (TSPM). Believing in Christian participation in the socialist reconstruction of China and Christian responsibility for social betterment and nation building, they were willing to cooperate with the Chinese Communist Party's programs of social and political reform. They were united in their support of Premier Zhou Enlai when he offered them and other Chinese Christian leaders a role (albeit a subordinate and rather insignificant one) in government and the freedom to continue in their faith commitment. In 1954, after several national meetings and consultations with Premier Zhou Enlai, Wu Yaozong presented a public statement to the country and the government on behalf of Chinese Christians. The so-called "Chinese Christian Manifesto" of 1954 echoed the Communist principles of anti-imperialism, anti-feudalism, and anti-bureaucratic capitalism, and rallied Chinese Christian support for the new regime. This "Manifesto," signed by 138 Christian leaders, was published in the September 22, 1954 issue of the *Renmin Ribao (The People's Daily)*. A propaganda movement followed, and by 1957 the Chinese authorities claimed that the overwhelming majority of Chinese Christians had joined the TSPM.[1]

In the first five years after the founding of the People's Republic, the TSPM Chinese Christians were fully engaged in the social and political movements organized and led by the Chinese Communist Party such as the "Anti-American and Support North Korea" campaign in 1950-52, the "Three-anti" and "Five-anti" campaigns in 1952-53, and other "patriotic activities" related to the "Three-Self" (self-governing, self-supporting, and self-propagating) movement. The slogan often used by Wu Yaozong and Liu Liangmo during these years — "Love your country, love your church" — seemed to suggest that there was not only a close relationship between state and church, but more importantly, there was an order of priority in the slogan.

---

1. For more historical background on and development of the "Three-Self Patriotic Movement," please see Xing Fuzeng (Ying Fu Tsang) and Liang Jialin (Leung Ka Lun), *Wushi niandai sanzi yundong di yanjiu* (The Three-Self Patriotic Movement in the 1950s) (Hong Kong, 1996).

The TSPM was engineered by Chinese Christians who supported the Communist government. However, the origin of the "three-self" formula was not directly related to the Communist movement. As Bishop K. H. Ting pointed out in 1984: "It wasn't the Communists who imposed this movement on the Chinese Christians. Long before there were Communist(s) in China, certain missionary authorities, such as Henry Venn, the Chief Secretary of the Church Missionary Society in London in the 1850s, had already put together these three words as the ideal for missionary work in Africa, Asia and Latin America." Richard X. Y. Zhang has also traced the foreign roots of the "three-self" concept to Rufus Anderson,[2] while Paul Lee emphasizes the application of the "three-self" principle in China by C. Y. Cheng in the early twentieth century.[3] It is not my intention here to analyze the origins of the "Three-Self Movement" in China. Suffice it to say that the leaders of the "Three-Self Patriotic Movement" in the 1950s were eager to use the concepts of "self-government," "self-support," and "self-propagation" as counter-imperialist and anti-foreign tools. In other words, the movement hoped to unite Chinese Christians, but it also served a political purpose, which was to arouse nationalism and patriotism among the Chinese Christians. Its political nature made the "Three-Self Movement" different from the previous Christian efforts to promote self-reliance and the independence of the Chinese church. The illness of the Chinese church under TSPM leaders was not because they were socially conscious and politically active, but because they had given politics a higher priority than religious faith.

As a result of this politicization, the differentiation and separation between Chinese Christianity and world Christianity became the dominant mode of thinking in the minds of Chinese Christians. Chinese isolationism was accepted as a healthy development while internationalization or external linkage was not desirable. For the political activists, the Chinese "Marthas," the TSPM seemed to be the only way forward for Chinese Christianity. Even for the spiritual-minded "Marys," the link with Christians in other parts of the world was not considered necessary. Their focus was on "spiritual growth" or their "vertical relationship," that is, learning directly from Jesus Christ, praying directly to God, and relying only on the Holy Spirit, rather than depending on missionaries or foreign friends.

The cooperation between TSPM Christians and the Chinese Communist Party in the early fifties resulted in a "nationalization" of churches similar to the nationalization of private industries and educational institutions.

2. Richard X. Y. Zhang, "The Origin of the 'Three-Self,'" *Jian Dao*, vol. 4 (Hong Kong, 1996), pp. 179-80.
3. Paul Lee's idea, cited in Zhang, "The Origin of the 'Three-Self,'" p. 198.

Through the reorganization or merging of almost all private Christian enterprises in China, formerly Christian colleges and universities became public or government institutions. So, too, did the churches. Independent churches were asked to join the TSPM, and churches which had maintained ties with foreign missions were forced to sever their links or drop their denominational affiliations altogether. For example, there were over sixty Christian churches and organizations of various denominational backgrounds in the city of Beijing before 1949 including the YMCA and YWCA, the Salvation Army, the Chinese Church for Christ, the Chinese Anglican Church, the Methodist Church, the Congregational Church, the Assembly of God churches (Norway, United States, Sweden), the Presbyterian Church, the Seventh-Day Adventist Church, the Union Church, the Oriental Mission of America, and the Bible Society. In addition, there were many other self-supporting, self-governing independent churches such as the True Jesus Church (founded by Paul Wei in 1915), the New Holy City Church (founded by Sun Yongnian in 1926), the Dong-da-di Church (founded by Peng Hongliang in 1947), the Fu-nei-da-jie Church (founded by Yuan Xiangshen in 1946), the Christian Tabernacle (founded by Wang Mingdao in 1925) and the Christian Meeting Place (founded by Meng Xiangzhao in 1936).[4] By the end of the 1950s, after almost a decade of "nationalization," there were no more denominational churches or foreign missions, and the sixty-odd churches were reduced to only four official "Three-Self" churches. In Shanghai, about two thousand churches of different backgrounds were reorganized and forced to merge, thereby reducing the number to fifteen "Three-Self" churches.[5] Stressing unity and patriotism, the "nationalization movement" sought to unite all Christian churches under the leadership of the TSPM, which was in turn directed and controlled by the Religious Affairs Bureau (RAB) of the Communist Party. Power over and control of the TSPM churches was centralized in the hands of the officials at the RAB. Initially there was opposition from some independent evangelical churches; pastors such as Wang Mingdao of the Christian Tabernacle refused to cooperate with the government and adamantly resisted joining the TSPM. Wang, however, was no internationalist, nor was his congregation a foreign mission outpost. The church was independent, self-supporting and self-governing. Wang maintained that he and his followers should follow the will of God and not the instructions of man, emphasizing the spiritual and not the secular value and functions of the

4. Yang Zhouhuai, "Beijing jidujiao lishi he xianchuang tubiao" (Graphic Charts and Tables on Beijing's Christian Churches: Past and Present), *Ming Pao Monthly* 12 (1994): 56-57.

5. Jonathan Chao, "Dalu jidujiao ri di quzhe jiqi qianzhan" (The Origins and Prospects of Christianity Fever in Mainland China), *Ming Pao Monthly* 12 (1994): 45.

church. Accordingly, Wang and his wife, along with eighteen members of his church, were arrested and imprisoned in August 1955; the arrests ushered in a period of bitter tension and conflict between the politicized TSPM and the spiritually oriented evangelicals and fundamentalists, a split that continued into the Reform Era with the "house churches" following the anti-TSPM line.[6] The power struggle between the political activists and the "spiritually minded," however, did not occur on a level playing field, with the TSPM and Chinese "Marthas" enjoying government support and the "Marys" suffering suppression and persecution.

If politicization, forced unification, and nationalization — characteristics that were primarily associated with the TSPM — were illnesses affecting the health of the Chinese church of the fifties, it should not be construed that the elixir of health was in the hands of the evangelicals and fundamentalists. Their uncompromising and unyielding attitude toward the TSPM and their "salvationist orthodoxy"[7] also exacerbated the split and contributed to dissension within the Chinese church. In the documents of the early fifties, we see a conciliatory tone on the part of the TSPM Christian leaders (perhaps because they wanted to achieve the aim of a united front) but an intolerant and sometimes self-righteous attitude in the essays of the fundamentalists such as Wang Mingdao. While Wang should have been allowed to continue his preaching and practice, his militancy only aggravated the split in Chinese Christianity in the first decade of the PRC.

The honeymoon period between the TSPM Christians and the Chinese Communist Party came to an end as leftist extremism began to rise after 1957. An anti-rightist movement was launched after the "Hundred Flowers Campaign" of 1958 during which persecution began of all people formerly affiliated with the Nationalists, of church workers, and even of students who had studied abroad. They were accused of assisting the "reactionaries" (Nationalists) and of helping the "imperialists" (the Americans). Even the TSPM Christian leaders were considered "bad elements" because of their religious pronouncements and their past connections with foreign missions.

In conclusion, the sickness of the Chinese church during the 1950s was not strictly related to theology. The Christian theological circle has never been monolithic and uniform, and debates on theological issues and sociopolitical positions always occur in an open democratic society. The different opinions

6. For Wang Mingdao's anti-TSPM stance, see Xing Fuzeng and Liang Jialin, *Weshi niandai sanzi yundong di yanjiu* (The Three-Self Patriotic Movement in the 1950s) (Hong Kong, 1996), pp. 92-97.

7. Jane Schneider and Shirley Lindenbaum, *Frontiers of Christian Evangelism* (Washington, DC, 1987), p. 4.

and approaches taken by the modernist theologians and the social and political Chinese Christian activists, on the one hand, and those of the Chinese fundamentalists and evangelicals, on the other, should not be considered unique to the Chinese situation. Debates and differences are common within the Christian community; some will always be uncomfortable with the interpretations of others. The problem causing the ill health of the Chinese church in the 1950s came from two sources, one external and one internal.

The external factor was the demand of the Communist government to create a uniform socialist culture that allowed little or no room for different points of view, hence the standardization, centralization, and nationalization policies in industry, agriculture and education, as well as in religion. This led to the shutting down of denominations, the expulsion of missionaries and foreign organizations, and the suppression of independent churches. The government supported the unified church, that is, the TSPM, at the expense of small independent churches, and unification, not unity, was the foundation of a politicized religious policy. Gao Wangzhi observes,

> Unification meant the wholesale abandonment of ritual differences between the denominations and the curtailment of many activities. Unification on these terms was especially detrimental to the evangelical churches. In a sense, the government purposely took the opportunity of the unification to subjugate the evangelicals.[8]

As a result of unification, centralization, and nationalization, all Christian churches and sects were required to belong to the TSPM or face persecution. Consequently, Wang Mingdao's independent church, the Christian Tabernacle, was closed down; the "Little Flock" of Watchman Nee was condemned; the Salvation Army abandoned its activities; the Seventh-Day Adventists changed their rituals and practices. As Gao has observed, "After the unification of 1958, all the different Protestant churches in China became in fact Three-self churches, although this has not been an official name for them."[9]

The internal factor was the bitter struggle and intolerance between the two camps within the Chinese church: the liberal TSPM leaders versus Wang Mingdao and other conservatives.

It was no surprise that the Communists who publicly denounced religion

---

8. Gao Wangzhi, "Y. T. Wu: A Christian Leader Under Communism," in Daniel H. Bays, ed., *Christianity in China: From the Eighteenth Century to the Present* (Stanford, 1996), p. 347.

9. Gao, "Y. T. Wu," p. 347.

as "the opiate of the people" and proclaimed themselves atheists would turn against Christianity in China. But the purge and persecution of the TSPM leaders by their Communist comrades deserves more investigation and analysis. Were the TSPM leaders sincere Christians as they believed themselves to be? Were they Communist agents whose united goal was to destroy the Chinese church and get rid of Christianity in China? Were they forced to cooperate with the Communist government or were they willing partners of the repressive policy?

Wang Weifan, Qin Mu, Chui Xianxiang, Ding Guangxun, and other TSPM leaders defended themselves in *Tian Feng,* arguing that it was the Chinese Christian's duty to stand up against enslavement and exploitation by foreign "imperialists" and to make a clear distinction between the agencies of foreign missions as the willing servants of "imperialist" governments, and authentic Christianity, which was a revolutionary religion. In other words, they did not see Christianity as an antagonist of Communism, and they insisted that their collaboration with the Communists was not an act of betrayal of the Christian church. Rather, they believed the TSPM would liberate the Chinese church from foreign control both in mind as well as in finance. They thought that the fundamentalist and conservative Christians such as Wang Mingdao were narrow-minded and intolerant.[10] Some contemporary scholars hold that the TSPM leaders were sincere Christians who mistakenly trusted the Communists, naively thinking that such a cooperative partnership was possible. Their mistake became evident when the Communist movement moved to the extreme left, demanding singular loyalty to atheistic Maoism and persecuting these Christian apologists for Communism. According to this line of interpretation, the TSPM leadership may have been mistaken in their judgment of the Communist movement, but they were nevertheless sincere members of the Chinese church.[11]

However, scholars such as Jonathan Chao and Joseph Lam and the members of the "house churches" do not view the TSPM leaders in such a benevolent light. They were not "Marthas" but "Judases."[12] Like Judas, who betrayed Jesus Christ, they betrayed the Chinese church by working for the Communist Party that not only wanted to inflict great harm upon Chinese Christians but actually aimed at destroying the very foundations of Christianity in China.

10. Wang Changxin, *You Sishi nian* (Scarborough, Ont., 1997).

11. Wang Weifan and Ji Fengwen, "Forty Years of Chinese Christianity," in *Chinese Theological Review* 8 (1990): 44-62.

12. Jonathan Chao, *The China Mission Handbook: A Portrait of China and Its Church* (Hong Kong, 1989), p. 25. Cf. Joseph Lam, *China: The Last Superpower* (Green Forest, Ark., 1997).

They were "nonbelievers," "false prophets," and "Satan's helpers." The debate between the TSPM and Wang Mingdao was no "family feud" but a life-and-death struggle between light and darkness, and between God and Satan. This infighting has greatly damaged the Chinese church and created a seemingly unbridgeable gap between the official Three-Self Church and the house churches.

Anti-Religious Maoism, and Atheism as Religion: The "Death" of the Chinese Church During the Turbulent Decade, 1966-76

"Master, you should have come earlier. It's too late. He is dead."

The decade 1966-76, known as the years of Cultural Revolution, was the most tumultuous and chaotic period in modern Chinese history. During these years mob violence, massive killing, and unrelenting persecution were carried out in the name of extreme patriotism, class struggle, and permanent revolution. Supported by Chairman Mao and planned by the "Gang of Four" (leaders of the Maoist radicals: Jiang Qing, Zhang Chunqiao, Yao Wenyuan, and Wang Hongwen), the movement was carried out by young radical Maoists known as the Red Guards. They attacked all whom they deemed as "reactionaries" and "revisionists" within the Communist Party and harassed and persecuted intellectuals, professionals, Christians, Buddhists, and any other group that did not conform to their Maoist extremism. In the years of the Cultural Revolution all religions were considered "subjectivistic" and "feudalistic," hence targets of the "Anti–Four Olds Movement" (*fan sijiu,* i.e., anti–old customs, anti–old culture, anti–old habits, and anti–old thoughts). Christianity, because of its historical ties with the West, was considered the lackey of Western imperialism and branded with other labels as well. The Christian church in China suffered tremendously during the entire period of the Cultural Revolution. All the churches (including the TSPM churches) were closed and many church buildings were transformed into facilities for political and social activities. The Red Guard declared openly that there was no room for any religion in China, insisting that "religion has now been moved into a historical museum." They burned all the Bibles and hymnbooks that they could find; they terrorized, purged, and killed many Christians, whether associated with the TSPM or the independent churches. The only Christian seminary allowed to operate in the late 1950s, the Ginling Theological Seminary of which Ding Guangxun was president, was dismantled. Even the Religious Affairs Bureau and the United Front Bureau of the Chinese Communist Party, which handled religious affairs, were closed down.

We know few details of Christian life and experience during this chaotic decade. Officially the Christian church during these years was "dead" because the TSPM was in a state of dormancy and its leaders were persecuted; all churches were closed and all Christian activities were prohibited. Wang Mingdao and other evangelicals had been arrested and imprisoned before the Cultural Revolution. This may have been a blessing in disguise for during the years of the Cultural Revolution others were purged and tortured by a variety of means, inflicting severe physical and psychological harm upon the victims. For example, Zhao Zizhen (T. C. Chao), a prominent theologian and TSPM leader who supported the Communist government and the church unification movement of the 1950s, was criticized, tortured, imprisoned, and then sent to hard labor camp. His house and properties were confiscated; his son-in-law, poet and architect Chen Mengjia, was driven to commit suicide. For a long period, Zhao Zizhen, by then a man in his eighties, was seen sweeping the streets and pasting paper boxes for the neighborhood community organizations.[13]

The period of the Cultural Revolution involved great suffering for Chinese Christians and for most Chinese people. Some of the tragic stories of imprisonment, beatings, killings, and suicides have been recorded in the works of Jonathan Chao,[14] Richard Bush,[15] G. N. Patterson,[16] L. T. Lyall[17] and in Wang Changxin's new biography of Wang Mingdao.[18] But the full story of their sufferings will probably never be known. When Martha and Mary came to tell Jesus about the death of their brother, they wept. Jesus also wept, and the Jews said, "See how he loved him." Jesus would have wept, too, over the great suffering of the Chinese church in the period of the Cultural Revolution.

Officially the church was "dead" (even Ding Guangxun, leader of the TSPM, openly said so) because all religions were considered illegal and all church activities were suppressed. No evangelism was allowed, no public worship was permitted, and no singing of hymns was tolerated. There was no more Three-Self Patriotic Movement or Religious Affairs Bureau, no clergy, no religious officials.

---

13. Lam Wing-hung, *The Life and Thought of Chao Tzu-chen* (Hong Kong, 1994), pp. 302-3.

14. Chao, *The China Mission Handbook*, p. 26. Also Jonathan Chao and Richard Van Houten, eds., *Wise as Serpents, Harmless as Doves: Christians in China Tell Their Story* (Pasadena, Calif., 1988), pp. 23-77.

15. Richard Bush, *Religion in Communist China* (Nashville, Tenn., 1970).

16. George N. Patterson, *Christianity in Communist China* (Waco, Tex., 1969).

17. Leslie T. Lyall, *New Springs in China* (London, 1979), and *God Reigns in China* (London, 1983).

18. Wang Changxin, *You Sishi nian* (Scarborough, Ont., 1997).

During the Cultural Revolution, one of the Maoist radicals claimed that "there is no more religion in China."[19] When he uttered these words he and many like-minded Maoists were being driven by a kind of religious freneticism in their battle against religion. The Maoist radicals or extremists claimed that they believed in materialism, evolution, and science. They criticized all religions as deceptive, irrational, and superstitious. In short, they were uncompromisingly anti-religion and atheistic. Radical Maoism during the Cultural Revolution turned out to be a mass movement with many salient religious characteristics: "god" worship, sacred texts, sacraments, rites and rituals, and religious behavior.

For the radical Maoists, especially the young Red Guards, Mao Zedong had become their "god." The effective "deification" of Mao began in the early sixties, then intensified in the mid sixties, probably engineered by Lin Biao and the "Gang of Four." They wanted to elevate Mao to be a "demigod" or religious figure. The ubiquitous larger-than-life image of Mao served as a national symbol that transcended politics, and Mao emerged among his fellow "Long Marchers" and long-time colleagues as almost a semidivine "super hero." This in turn became a powerful tool to crush potential opponents within the Chinese Communist Party such as Liu Shaoqi and Deng Xiaoping.

The quasi-religious character of the Red Guard Movement was seen in their routine study sessions, their pilgrimages to Beijing, and their belief in Mao's magical powers. During the Cultural Revolution, there was no normal education; schools were used for the purposes of political meetings and rallies. The young Red Guards organized themselves into study groups and devoted a great deal of time to the study of Mao's writings. The "Little Red Book" (of Mao's sayings) became the Bible of Maoism. The Red Guards committed most of the Red Book to memory and used his sayings on almost all occasions for guidance, for teaching others, and for self-protection. They chanted songs that expressed their affection and loyalty toward Chairman Mao as the greatest leader, the greatest teacher, and the greatest helmsman. During the study sessions, they praised Mao, discussed Maoist ideas, and sometimes criticized others and themselves. The parallels between these study groups and Christian conventicles involving Scripture study, hymn singing, and confession are striking. Only the aspect of prayer was less evident. But when these youngsters went on the *da-chuan-lian* (great link), joining other groups in the "long march" to Beijing to pay homage to Mao, their religious fervor was no less than the zeal of Muslim pilgrims to Mecca or that

19. Jonathan Chao, *Zhongguo dui jidujiao di zhengce* (China's Policy toward Christianity) (Hong Kong, 1983), p. 125.

of Christians motivated by revival meetings. They converged on the capital from all parts of China. To do so they went through a variety of obstacles and difficulties; they often waited for days, even weeks, just to take part in the parades in Tiananmen Square, hoping that Mao himself might appear atop the city wall to wave his hand, as if blessing them. They would respond by chanting "Long Live Chairman Mao," while raising their heads and hands and waving their "Little Red Books." One participant recalled her experience at one of the parades thus: "Most of us shouted 'Long Live Chairman Mao' until our voices became hoarse, our energy exhausted, and our faces covered with tears."[20]

The radical Maoists mounted an anti-religion campaign during the Cultural Revolution full of religious fervor and replete with religious symbols; paradoxically this amounted to a "religious war" on religion. They sought to eliminate all rivals in the struggle for the hearts and minds of the Chinese people. In doing so they tried to create a Maoist orthodoxy that was exclusivist, self-righteous, and intolerant. As a result of this religious persecution, Christianity suffered the darkest period of its history in China since the seventh century.

Resurrection and Revival: Church Growth and the "Christianity Fever" in Recent Years, 1977-99

"Master, he is out of the grave; he is walking."

Following the tumultuous time of the Cultural Revolution, a new era dawned with the coming to power of Deng Xiaoping in 1978. He and his reformers introduced "Special Economic Zones" and led China toward the development of a market economy. Under Deng, China also improved its relations with Western countries. All the while, the ideals of Marxism, Leninism, and Mao Zedong thought and the leadership of the Chinese Communist Party were reiterated time and again. With the opening of China to foreign investors, travelers, and professionals, there came more personal freedom in lifestyle, career choice, research and teaching, and religious orientation, if not in political expression and action. These were the forces that helped move away the tombstone and open the cave.

During the late 1970s, the first phase of the Reform Era, there were "great leaps" in economic progress, and some signs of more religious freedom. First,

---

20. Chang Jung, *Wild Swans: Three Daughters of China* (New York, 1991), p. 5.

some of the churches that had been closed or used for other purposes during the Cultural Revolution were permitted to reopen for worship services. The earliest reopened churches included Mi Shi Da Jie Church in Beijing, the Moore Memorial Church, the Pure Heart Church and the Trinity Church in Shanghai, the Dongshan Church in Guangzhou, and others. In the years which followed, more churches were reopened, and thus there were twenty-one churches open for services in 1980 in the following cities: Beijing (1), Tianjin (1), Shenyang (1), Nanjing (1), Shanghai (5), Hangzhou (2), Ningbo (1), Wenzhou (1), Fuzhou (1), Xiamen (1), Shantou (1), Guangzhou (3), Chengdu (1), and Chongqing (1).[21] The growth continued rapidly in the 1980s. If the first decade of the history of the PRC was characterized by the decline and deterioration in the health of the Chinese church, and the second decade by death and dormancy, then the two decades of the Reform Era under Deng and his successors could be described as a period of recuperation, rapid expansion, and record growth.

Conversions, and More Conversions: The Jidujiao Re

In 1949 the number of Christian communicants in China was estimated at about a million. According to Jonathan Chao, there were 834,000 communicants, 5,000 missionaries, 8,500 unordained preachers, 3,500 women preachers, 2,150 ordained pastors, and over 2,000 churches. All other historians seem to agree with the estimate of around one million Protestant Christians in China before the Communist Revolution of 1949.[22] But the statistics concerning the Chinese Christian population in recent years have produced more controversy than consensus. The general agreement among scholars of Chinese Christianity is that there was rapid growth in the number of churches and Christians in China after the difficult and chaotic years of the sixties and early seventies. Following a period of political relaxation after the death of Mao, the two decades since 1979 recorded marked growth and rapid expansion in church activities. A few TSPM churches were reopened in 1978 and 1979 in Beijing, Shanghai, and Guangzhou, which were then followed by doz-

21. Information from *Pray for China* (Hong Kong, 1980), p. 5.
22. Zhong Min and Chan Kim-Kwong, "The 'Apostolic Church': A Case Study of a House Church in Rural China," in Beatrice Leung and John Young, eds., *Christianity and Confucianism: Foundations for Dialogue* (Hong Kong, 1993), p. 251; Liang Jialin (Leung Ka Lun), *Wu Yaozong sanlun* (Three Essays on Wu Yaozong) (Hong Kong, 1998); and Alan Hunter and Kim-Kwong Chan, *Protestantism in Contemporary China* (Cambridge, 1993), p. 66.

ens, then by hundreds, in other cities in the early eighties. In 1986, less than a decade after the official reopening of the churches, statistics concerning Chinese Christianity compiled by the government showed the following:[23]

Churches	4,044
Family Meeting Points	16,868
Baptisms in 1986	151,062
Number of Protestants	3,386,611

In 1992, Chen Zimin estimated that there were 6.5 million Christians in China;[24] in 1994, official statistics showed that there were 7 million churchgoers; and, according to Jonathan Chao, the Three-Self Patriotic Church in China admitted in 1998 that there were over 10 million Christians in China.[25] But many other sources indicate that the number of Christians in China was far greater than the official figure. In 1992, one scholar estimated the number of Chinese Protestant Christians at 63 million, with an additional 12.3 million Catholics.[26] Scholars who have been following the development of the "house churches" tend to give high figures for the Chinese Christian population, which range from 50 to 65 million. One observer has even given an estimate of 85 million, but this claim lacks substantial evidence.[27] Zhong Min and Chan Kim-Kwong hold that the correct estimate of the number of Chinese Christians is somewhere between the official government figure and those given by the scholars of the "house churches." In 1992 they set the figure at about 20 million, arguing that if they are correct, then "the Christian population has increased twenty times since 1949 while the general population had only increased threefold."[28] Leung Ka Lun, in his 1998 book on the development of the Christian churches in rural China in the last two decades, agrees that 20 million is a fairly accurate estimate.[29] He argues that the greatest growth has occurred in the rural areas and in the inner provinces such as

23. This information was published in *Bridge* 25 (September-October 1987): 16. *Bridge* was a periodical published by the Christian Study Centre on Chinese Religion and Culture in Hong Kong, and ceased publication in 1997.

24. Zhong and Chan, "The 'Apostolic Church,'" p. 250.

25. Jonathan Chao, "The Church in China Today," in *Ershiyi shiji huaren fuyin shigong xin celue* (Argyle, Tex., 1998), p. 135.

26. Chao, "Dalu jidujiao ri di quzhe jiqi qianzhan," p. 44.

27. Liang Jialin (Leung Ka Lun), *Gaige kaifang yilai di Zhongguo nongcun jiaohui* (The Christian Church in Rural China since the Reform Era) (Hong Kong, 1998), p. 34. Hereafter referred as Leung, *The Christian Church in Rural China*.

28. Zhong and Chan, "The 'Apostolic Church,'" p. 250.

29. Leung, *The Christian Church in Rural China*, p. 35.

Henan, Anhui, and the mountainous southwestern region, rather than in the coastal cities.[30]

The rapid growth of Christianity in China, a post-Mao phenomenon, is referred to by the Chinese as *jidujiao re* (Christianity craze). Cultural historians and China specialists have attempted to explain it as an integral part of the Cultural Fever *(wenhua re)* phenomenon of the 1980s. "Cultural Fever" denotes the upsurge of intellectual interest in Western culture in China due to widespread disillusionment with Communism among Chinese intellectuals. The feeling of general letdown or disappointment is referred to by the Chinese as involving a "crisis of confidence" in regards to Communism, which in turn led many intellectuals to search for new alternatives. Led by Jin Guangtao, Gan Yang, Bao Zunxin, and others, a generation of young Chinese scholars (most of whom are junior professors at China's top universities and research institutes) have openly expressed dissatisfaction with the orthodox political culture of China — Marxism, Leninism, and Maoism — and they have encouraged fellow Chinese to seek new ideas and models in the West. They have translated into Chinese various Western works of social theory, political thought, and representative volumes in philosophy and cultural studies (in series such as *March toward the Future* edited by Bao and Jin). They have organized public forums[31] and published journals and magazines promoting their ideas and interests. The focus of "Cultural Fever" has mainly been on Western political thought, social theory, and all kinds of cultural expressions ranging from classical to postmodern culture. However, it has also included an interest in both the Protestant and Catholic traditions: their religious and ethical values have been studied by some Chinese intellectuals who are aware of their integral role in shaping Western culture. This perspective is very different from that of the May Fourth generation. The May Fourth period (1917-27) was also a period of intellectual ferment during which Westernizers in China such as Hu Shi turned to Western science and democracy for the solution to China's ills. Influenced by Enlightenment philosophy and evolutionary theories, this generation of Westernizers in China made a clear distinction between modern and premodern cultures in the West. They saw the Enlightenment as a watershed separating the two periods. Modern Western culture, they believed, was grounded on reason, science and democracy, whereas premodern culture was steeped in superstition and religious values. Traditional Western culture, they argued, was dominated by the

30. Leung, *The Christian Church in Rural China*, p. 23.

31. New forums emerged such as the "Cultural Saloon" *(Wenhua salong)* in Beijing and similar groups in Shanghai.

Christian church, and it was against this tradition that Voltaire, Rousseau, Locke, Mill, Darwin, Marx, and other modern thinkers of the West had fought and earned their reputation. In other words, the May Fourth Chinese intellectuals had rejected Christianity and what it represented as part of the Western past, and accepted only Western Enlightenment culture as they defined it (reason, progress, science, democracy, and, for some, materialism). The young intellectuals of China in the 1980s, however, did not see modernity and tradition in Western culture in dichotomous or contradictory terms. They were aware that many "modern" Enlightenment concepts were in fact rooted in medieval or ancient ideas, and were derived from Greek and Christian thought. Further, they were cognizant of the fact that contemporary Western society is not totally disconnected from its Christian roots, and that Christianity still continues to influence Western democracies. Their view of the interrelationship between tradition and modernity was much influenced by Western sociologists (particularly Weber) and modernization theorists.

This perspective has enabled young Chinese scholars to look at Christian influence as part of a developing continuum rather than viewing it as the antithesis of progress and modernity. Christianity therefore became a potentially valuable contributor to national reconstruction and intellectual pursuit. Many young intellectuals in the universities and in urban centers set out to explore Christianity because of their initial interest in Western culture. Many of the so-called "Cultural Christians" *(wenhua jidutu)* such as Liu Xiaofeng traveled the same route. Li Qiuling, He Guanghu, and Jiang Zhen all became interested in Christianity as an expression of Western culture, and then began researching Christian history and theology.

The cultural interpretation, however, does not fully explain the *jidujiao re,* which was as much a cultural, as it was a religious, phenomenon. Many turned to Christianity not because it is an important aspect of Western culture, but because it satisfied their religious and spiritual needs. Even Communist scholars have conceded that Christianity became popular in the post-Mao period because the youth had lost faith in Communism and because Christianity appeared able to fill the vacuum in their hearts. Their search for something more intrinsically satisfying and transcendent came at a time when market capitalism and naked materialism were replacing puritanical Communist ethics and the Maoist philosophy of class struggle as common features of Chinese life. While most Chinese were becoming money-minded and materialistic, there was a minority that pursued spiritual fulfillment.

The upsurge of Chinese interest in Christianity, as some of the religionists have suggested, was in part due to the long-term suppression of religion that had preceded it. Suppression had created a strong desire for spiritual exploration. Christians attributed it to divine causality: the prayers of the long-suffering Chinese Christians were finally being answered. For example, Paul E. Kauffman explained the phenomenal growth of Chinese interest in Christianity in terms of the following: (1) it was a demonstration of the power of the Almighty God; (2) it was the result of the long period of suffering by Chinese Christians; (3) it was due to the Chinese awakening from the illusion of Maoism, and the conclusion that they had been deceived by the Communists; (4) it grew out of the dedicated commitment of the Christians who survived the Cultural Revolution; (5) it involved the adoption of a Sinicized model of church planting; and (6) it was the end product of the untiring prayer effort of many Chinese Christians.[32] Similarly Tony Lambert and Leslie Lyall have insisted that the tremendous growth of the Chinese church in the eighties was related to the power of prayer and the sufferings of the Chinese Christians during the Cultural Revolution.[33]

The TSPM attributed the rapid growth to their own leadership, arguing that the unification forced by the TSPM and the elimination of denominational differences and foreign reliance had indigenized the Chinese church, thereby making it more attractive to the Chinese people. "House church" sympathizers, of course, disagreed and argued in the opposite direction, maintaining that real church growth occurred in their constituency because of their strong faith commitment and vigorous efforts in evangelization.

All of these perspectives have sought to explain one obvious phenomenon: the dynamic growth of Chinese Christianity in recent years. But they provide only partial analysis and are of limited usefulness when one is attempting to understand the whole picture. The cultural perspective and the TSPM argument may help to explain Christian growth in urban centers and among young intellectuals; the religious perspective is more relevant to Christian growth in rural areas, and to understanding the "house church" phenomenon.

Faith, Culture, and Commitments: Chinese Christians in Contemporary China

Studies of contemporary Chinese Christianity have often focused on the division and differences between the TSPM and the underground "house churches." TSPM supporters like Philip Wickeri have accused the house

---

32. For a summary of Paul E. Kauffman's ideas, see Leung, *The Christian Church in Rural China*, p. 27.

33. See Tony Lambert, *The Resurrection of the Chinese Church* (London, 1991), and Lyall, *God Reigns in China*.

churches of a fundamentalist approach and an unwillingness to cooperate. House church champions like Jonathan Chao regard the TSPM leaders as government agents who seek to control the church and minimize, if not eliminate, its influence in Chinese society. Given these perspectives, it is no surprise that rivalry and confrontation have long characterized Chinese church life.

Leung Ka Lun's 1998 study of the Chinese church suggests a new approach. Although aware of the organizational differences between the TSPM and the house churches, he suggests another way of analyzing the divisions and differences. He proposes an analysis that stresses the distinctive forms of Christianity in urban and rural China. The Christians of the countryside are from both TSPM and house church backgrounds and constitute more than 80 percent of the Chinese Christian population; this is the mainstream of the Christian movement in contemporary China. Past scholarship has paid little attention to geographical differences; sporadic and unsystematic reports have created the impression that rural churches have been dominated by house churches composed of fundamentalists and evangelicals.

Contemporary Chinese Christianity, however, is far more complex, and the dichotomies of "official versus unofficial," "legal versus illegal," TSPM versus house church, urban versus rural, or "culture versus religion" are less than helpful. We need to move beyond these themes and examine the interrelation and interaction between institutional churches and unregistered Christian communities, the congruence of cultural and religious commitments. We need more cooperation, collaboration, mutual concern, and mutual respect between the "Marthas" and the "Marys."

A real faith commitment is a major distinguishing characteristic of the urban Christians and the vast majority of the TSPM Christians. Many TSPM Christians, particularly those who have joined the church in the last few years, are motivated by a deep religious concern, are focused on eternal rewards, desire spiritual fulfillment, and embrace a personal salvation. A 1994 survey by a researcher at the Chinese Academy of Social Sciences in Beijing confirms that the central issue among the Beijing TSPM churchgoers was personal faith:[34] that is, these Christians care more about salvation, hope, redemption, judgment, love, and conviction, all matters pertaining to their faith commitment, and are not motivated primarily by social concern and/or cultural development.[35] Even many of the Cultural Christians whose initial

---

34. The researcher interviewed some fifty Christians from all the official churches in the city of Beijing.

35. Wu Ying, "Jidujiao zai dalu chengxiang di chuanbo yu fazhan," in *Ming Pao Monthly* 12 (1994): 51-52.

interest was in Christianity as a cultural tradition later became drawn to its specifically religious aspects and to theological issues. Their intellectual endeavor led them to a religious path and eventually even to a "leap of faith," whereby they became committed Christians rather than dilettantes with only a scholarly or a research interest in Christian studies. Many became Christian converts following a long period of intellectual inquiry and cultural research.

On the other hand, rural Chinese churches are full of spiritually minded believers, faith healers, evangelists, and devoutly praying Christians. Their faith commitment seems much stronger than their commitment to the cultural implications of Christianity. However, it is also clear that traditional Chinese culture has profoundly influenced and shaped the Christian movements of rural China. As Leung Ka Lun has persuasively argued, Christianity in rural China has incorporated more traditional cultural elements than have the urban TSPM churches. This has occurred in part because of inadequate training in systematic theology and a lack of knowledge of basic Christian doctrines. Given this situation, the influence of traditional Chinese culture has been proportionally greater in rural churches and can be seen in the following areas: millennialism and charismatic tendencies (often influenced by Chinese folk religions); a pragmatic and utilitarian orientation (conversion for practical purposes like healing and peace); superstitious and cultic practices (rites and rituals which resemble those of popular folk religions); and an often uncritical emphasis on miracles and even magic.[36] Clearly some of the distinctive features of the rural churches were inherited from the popular evangelists and Bible preachers of the past such as John Sung and Wang Mingdao; yet it is also clear that the Christian movement in the countryside has absorbed numerous elements from Chinese traditional culture and folk religions. The rural church may emphasize "faith," but the whole movement, including its religious practices, organizational structure, and values, can be properly understood only in the context of traditional Chinese culture.

Conclusion

We return to the story of Lazarus and his two sisters at the end of this chapter. There has been always inner conflict within the Chinese Christian community. In the Republican period there was great tension between the itinerant evangelists and Bible preachers, on the one hand, and the Social Gospellers and modern theologians, on the other. In the early years of the PRC, there

36. Leung, *The Christian Church in Rural China*, pp. 408-27.

were conflict and rivalry between the TSPM and the nonconformists, and in recent years there have been conflict and confrontation between the "official" churches and the "underground" churches. Differences and debates between different groups of Chinese Christians should not be viewed as entirely negative. Arguments and differences are natural and sometimes necessary in a vibrant, creative, and energetic culture or faith system. Many Chinese Christians in the past as well as in contemporary China have seen such differences as dangerous and even heretical and therefore have developed an intolerant attitude toward those in the opposite camp. They treat the others as enemies rather than looking at them as members of one big family. I prefer to view them as "Marthas" and "Marys" and to consider them members of the same family with some notable differences, particularly in their social and political orientations and in their spiritual emphases. Inclusion, not exclusion, cooperation rather than confrontation, should characterize Chinese Christianity. Debate and dialogue should replace persecution and purge; Martha should embrace Mary. Indigenization should parallel globalization. Chinese Christianity should take its distinctive place in world Christianity. The fundamental problem of Chinese Christianity both past and present is an overwhelming desire for cultural legitimacy and for a strict, unbending orthodoxy. This is a cultural trait perhaps more indebted to China's Confucian heritage than to its Christian one.

CHAPTER FIVE

Gospel, Globalization, and Hindutva: The Politics of "Conversion" in India

ROBERT ERIC FRYKENBERG

The Hindu world is the most perverted, most monstrous, most implaca-
ble, demonic-invaded part of this planet. There is just no question about
it. . . . The greatest, biggest, blackest, most hopeless mass of confusion,
perversion, deception and oppression is this massive Hindu bloc. . . . The
perversion of Satan in this part of the world is just absolutely legendary.

Ralph Winter, *Mission Frontiers Bulletin*
(November-December 1994): 16-18

These words, in the February 22, 1999 issue of India's widely popular magazine, *Outlook,* can be found on the web site of the Hindu Vivek Kendra
(HVK).[1] The HVK and agencies spawned by the Rashtriya Swayamsevak
Sangh (RSS), such as the Vishwa Hindu Parishad (VHP), the Bajrang Dal, the
Bharatia Janata Party (BJP), which has ruled India since 1999,[2] together with
the Shiv Sena, make up an alliance known as the Sangh Parivar. Together they
stand for the enhancement of *Hindutva* or "Hinduness" in India, and are seen
as "Hindu fundamentalists" at least by the press and the public. That the
HVK should uncover, acquire, and distribute words put forth by a missionary
arm of American evangelicalism, which it sees as fundamentalist, can be
viewed as but one more dramatic manifestation of current globalization.

1. http://www.hvk.org/articles/articles/0299/0056.html
2. The BJP, which lost a confidence vote by 269 to 270, on April 18, 1999, remained as
caretaker government until elections were held later that year.

Winter's words appeared in India exactly one month after Australian missionary Graham Stewart Staines (fifty-eight) and his two young sons (Philip, nine, and Timothy, six) were burned alive by a mob of *Hindutva* activists.[3] The arrival of these words occurred in the wake of a year of increasing and widespread violence over scores of incidents which had brought death and destruction to India's Christians and their institutions.[4] The words came at a time when India was convulsing in controversy over Christian "conversions" (as also the issues of "forced conversion" and "reconversion"). Week by week, heated rhetoric had become more strident — the backward, the poor, and the weak of India were being exploited by Christian missionaries; *adivāsis* (aboriginals or "tribals") and *dalits* ("oppressed" or "untouchable," "outcaste" peoples)[5] were being pressured and proselytized by "foreign elements." National opinion, rocked by the Staineses' slayings, recoiled in dismay, shock, and shame. Atal Behari Vajpayee, India's *Hindutva* (BJP) Prime Minister, announced a day-long, personal fast — held on the anniversary of Gandhi's assassination by an RSS sympathizer (Nathuram Godse) in 1948 (January 30). At the same time, he also called for a national debate on the "problem of conversion."

I

But exactly what does the term "Hindu" mean, especially for peoples of India? Did Winter know what it means? Did he understand how complex and problematic such rhetoric might be? (He is reported to have retreated from, if not rescinded, his words.)[6] No understanding of the impact of globalization with respect to India is possible without a more discriminating definition of "Hindu" and "Hinduism." Nor can one understand the character and place of

---

3. Incited by the Bajrang Dal, they doused oil on the jeep in which they were sleeping, and set it ablaze.

4. Manini Chatterjee, "Persecution of Christians in India," *Asian Age* (July 11, 1998): INS Release 10th.

5. M. K. Gandhi wooed such peoples, calling them *harijans* (children of Hari or Krishna); but he also castigated Bishop V. S. Azariah for his evangelizing of Madigas and Malas in Dornakal; and he clashed with B. R. Ambedkar over the political mobilization of those now known as *dalits*. Cf. Susan B. Harper, *In the Shadow of the Mahatma: Bishop V. S. Azariah and the Travails of Christianity in British India* (London and Grand Rapids, 2000); and *Dalit International Newsletter*, vols. 1-4, edited by John C. B. Webster (Waterford, Conn., 1996-99).

6. Stan Guthrie, "Sticks and Stones: Global Report on India," *Evangelical Missions Quarterly* 35.4 (October 1999): 471.

the gospel in India, or of "conversion," without appreciating and refining distinctions between the terms "Hindu," "Hinduism," and "Hindu World." Even in the simplest senses, these terms possess varied meanings — three of which need to be distinguished.

In current and popular perspective, in our day and in the West, if not also among many of the modern, secularized, and Westernized elites of India, the terms "Hindu" and "Hinduism," as also "Hindu World," assume the existence of some clearly identifiable, discrete, and monolithic religion (or religious system) — something, moreover, which originated in India. Many who think this, and have done so for a century, see "Hinduism" as a "World Religion."[7] Yet, in a strictly technical sense, before modern times there had never been such a thing as "Hinduism." Nothing so clear or discrete had ever existed with defined boundaries or circumscribed edges. In a continent where, by literary conventions, "thirty-three crores" (330 million) of deities dwell and receive worship, whether in some family house, village shrine, or huge temple; where many forms of belief, ritual, and worship coexist; and where followers of such diverse religious traditions as Buddhism, Jainism, Judaism, Christianity, Zoroastrianism, and Islam, in combination, have made up one third of the total population, it makes as much sense to think of Hinduism as having constituted one single and overarching religious monolith as to think that all forms of religious expression which existed in the Mediterranean Basin during the hegemony of imperial Rome, from Britain to Egypt and Babylon, were one single, overarching religious system.

Strictly speaking, peoples of India have never possessed even a word for "religion" as such. *Dharma,* the Sanskrit term for "duty," "law," "order," or "rightness," whether cosmic or particular, is too exclusively Brahmanical and too profoundly philosophical. Even modifying it with prefixes, such as *Sanatana Dharma,* meaning "cosmic or eternal order," does not suffice. Each living thing, every single thing that breathes (or does not breathe, for that matter) has its own particular and peculiar nature, its own inherent and unique properties, its own genetic code or cosmic structure *(dharma).* *Karma,* the Sanskrit term for "causal consequences," for strictly fulfilling or not fulfilling (or for breaking) *dharma,* is no better. It is just the flip side of *dharma.* Philosophical principles which describe the properties and functions of entities, one by one or in aggregate, do not constitute a "religion." No metaphysical principle, by itself, is equivalent to, or a substitute for, the term "religion." Among life forms belonging to the category called "mankind"

7. Having done so ever since the World Parliament of Religions convened at Chicago in 1892.

(manusha), over three thousand separate "castes" (*jatis* or "birth species") have been identified — each with its own unique *dharma/karma*. Each has a generic identity, each belongs within its own ethnic "birth" group, and each is seen or perceived to be a distinct and separate species of people. Under such circumstances, inter-dining (ingesting of common substances) or intermarriage (mingling of different substances: e.g., genes) between genetic entities is unthinkable. Such behavior profoundly violates the biological and cosmic order. Violation of *dharma* and/or *karma* brings chaos. This is the Brahmanical (or *Vedic*) perspective. Whether derived from systematic empirical observation or "invented" as a rationalization for hegemonic domination, this perspective has had an enormous influence over ruling communities and elites, and has done so for millennia. As recently summarized by Gail Omvedt:

> Brahmanism had been given shape as the ideology of the ruling class in the middle of the first millennium BC, with an exclusive intelligentsia claiming cultural purity and sacredness. This ideology and the caste hierarchy it was linked to gained hegemony over its greatest rival, Buddhism, about a thousand years later. It succeeded in maintaining its dominance under vastly changed material conditions even during the colonial period and the 50 years of Independence, with the Congress representing the "moderate" and the Jan Sangh (now BJP) the "extremist" form of the Brahmanic ideology. One aspect of its success was the ability of the elite to define the 'Indian' identity in its own terms, claiming that the core of Indian culture lay in Sanskrit, the Vedic tradition and the Vedanta. Since the 19th century this has been projected as "Hinduism." This was the "Great Tradition," the national tradition. All other challenging cultural traditions, whether based on the masses of the Bahujans and the Dalits, or among the Adivasis or in linguistic-national identities, were relegated to regional or local "Little Traditions."[8]

Furthermore, ethnically distinct castes falling within the three uppermost stratas (*varnas* or "colors") of "Hindu" society, making up roughly 15 percent of India's population, still see themselves as "twice-born" *(dvīja)* or "clean" peoples. Ethnically distinct *jatis* inhabiting the lowermost strata, which constitute the bottom 20 percent of the population, have been seen as the "polluted" and "untouchable" peoples. These, seeing themselves as the "broken" or "oppressed" *(dālit)* peoples, have long seen themselves as "outside" the fold

8. Gail Omvedt, "The Dravidian Movement — II," *The Hindu* (June 22, 1999): http://www.the-hindu.com/

of Hindu society.[9] Such self-definitions are based upon long and hard experience. In short, there are no peoples in India who have not seen themselves, in some degree, as ethnically and cultural distinct from one another or who have not been obliged, sometimes on pain of death, to follow the rules of ethnic and cultural apartheid.

This too is the "Hindu World" which Winter castigated. It contains, at least in any simple sense, no single religion. "Hinduism" of this sort is also a name for the cultural environment and for the political economy. It is within this world that those who claim the gospel as their own must reside and to which they, like everyone else in India, are subject. The same kinds of ethnocentric consciousness and culture, deeply rooted in birth and caste, have long been conditions in which virtually every one of the distinct, ethnocentric, and endogamous communities, in one way or another, still lives. In a very profound and inescapable sense, therefore, all "Indian" Christians and Christian Indians may be described as "Hindu." They are, in that sense, part and parcel of "Hinduism" and of the "Hindu World."

The term "Hindu," in other words, refers to more than religion. It relates to anything that is "native" to India. "Hinduism," in this sense, is a distinctive form of "Nativism" and/or, in more recent times, of "National Consciousness." In modern times, this outlook has come to encompass patriotic fervor and loyalty to the "Fatherland" — or even, to be more accurate, to the "Motherland" — to *Bandé Mataram*.

Finally, there is the rise of yet another discrete and modern form of Hinduism, "neo-Hinduism," which Professor Romila Thapar has labeled "Syndicated Hinduism." This kind of Hinduism is a by-product of the Indian Empire. It was formed under the heavily Brahman influence of the Raj. As such, it is a composite of ideological and institutional structures that arose as part of the logic of imperial policy. It provided some of the infrastructure for national integration (something which I have described in previous articles).[10]

---

9. Categorized by Brahmans as polluting or "untouchable," *varna* or "without color," as *panchamas* or "fifth"-strata peoples, and, if tribal peoples, as polluting *adivāsis* or "aboriginals."

10. Romila Thapar, "The Emergence of Modern 'Hinduism' as a Concept and as an Institution: A Reappraisal with Special Reference to South India," in Gunther Sontheimer and Hermann Kulke, eds., *Hinduism Reconsidered* (Heidelberg, 1989, 1997), pp. 1-29; "Hindu Fundamentalism and the Structural Stability of India," in Martin Marty and Scott Appleby, eds., *The Fundamentalism Project*, vol. 2: *Fundamentalisms and the State: Remaking Polities, Economies, and Militance* (Chicago, 1993), pp. 233-55; and "Constructions of Hinduism at the Nexus of History and Religion," *Journal of Interdisciplinary History* 23.3 (Winter 1993): 523-50.

It was (and still is) a kind of institutionalized Hinduism which, with its heavily Brahmanized overtones, possessed two faces. One virtually became the implicit or unofficial ideology of the state. Beginning in the eighteenth century, this ideology emphasized pluralism, religious "neutrality," "secularism," syncretism, and tolerance. It epitomized, as essential features, those kinds of "Hinduism" that have always been necessary for the survival of India as a unified political system. Its principles, generated as part of the constitutional development of India since the 1770s, are enshrined within India's 1950 Constitution. From this perspective, the terms "Hindu" and "India" have been twins: Both were born in the eighteenth century and both have grown together. Under this kind of regime, "Hindu" or "Indian" so-called "secularism" differed from that of the West — calling not for a separation of the sacred from the nonsacred but for state sponsorship and support for all forms of religious life. Secularism consisted of state support within a matrix of a strictly observed official impartiality and neutrality.

Another, and opposite, face of modern Hinduism grew up at the very same time. Initially provoked into reaction as a consequence of large-scale mass movements of conversion to Christianity that had begun in Tirunelveli during the 1790s, this kind of Hinduism is the progenitor of the nationalistic religion of "Hindutva." As this grew and gained momentum in the early nineteenth century, this kind of movement was and still is reactionary and revivalistic. In many respects copying from and being modeled after the great, globalizing forms of monotheism (which are the seed of Abraham), these movements invariably became chauvinistic, defensive, and exclusivistic in their "nativism." They placed emphasis upon the eternal verities of "sacred birth" and "sacred earth" as epitomized by the concepts of *Sanātana Dharma*. Each such movement, beginning with the Vibuthi Sangam, Dharma Sabha, and Chaturvedi Siddhantha in the 1820s, 1830s, and 1840s, became successively more militant and strident than its predecessor. Carried forward into the late nineteenth century by Arya Samaj and Nagari Pracharini Sabha, such movements found their culminating apotheosis in the formation of the Hindu Mahasabha (1916) and the Rashriya Swayamsevak Sangh (in 1924).

Agencies of Hindutva, especially the VHP (Vishwa Hindu Parishad) and the Bajrang Dal, as branches of the RSS (Rashtriya Swayamsevak Sangh) have always reacted violently when whole families and villages of low-caste people have forsaken "proper place" (of thraldom) and when, by becoming literate and educated, they have then set in motion a social revolution. Hindu reaction to anything that disturbs the status quo of *sanā tanadharma* and *varnā shramadharma* has also become militant, and sometimes violent. Whatever may be the immediate objects of animus and fear, militant Hindu reactionaries have become most alarmed at the prospect of seeing whole communities of low-caste, untouchable, and tribal peoples changing their religious identity and becoming upwardly mobile. Many such "converts" were peoples who had either never submitted to the Brahmanical "Hindu" yoke of caste thraldom in the first place; or they were peoples who had never become acculturated "into the fold" of subjugation and thraldom by processes of Sanskritization. These were peoples whose customs and deities had never been fully or successfully absorbed, or digested and incorporated into Brahmanical systems of rationalizing, systematizing, and legitimizing dominance. Most of all, these were peoples who, having had little or no prior attachment to the "Hindu World," might never have been willing to submit to any form of "Hindu Nation," "Hindu Raj" or "Ram Rashtriya."[11] It is from among "true believers" in the ideology of "Hindutva" that, on January 30, 1948, a zealot arose and assassinated that false "Mahatma," Mohandas Karamchand Gandhi. Gandhi, he felt, had compromised the "sacred blood" and "sacred earth" of India.

II

Globalization, as a process, is not new. What is new is the scale and speed, the accelerating momentum and the encompassing intrusiveness, of the current process. But both past and present forms of this process need to be understood if one is to appreciate the significance of what is happening to the gospel in India. To understand the impact of globalization and the cohorts marching under this banner, it is important to comprehend and compare ancient with modern forms of this phenomenon. From the perspective of the gospel, what James Kurth has recently labeled "one of the most profound revolutions the world has ever known"[12] was never, even from its very earliest beginnings, something optional. The injunctions of the Great Commission and Pentecost were, from the very outset, mandatory.[13] It should hardly be surprising, there-

11. Bent G. Karlsson, "Entering into Dharma: Contemporary Rabha Conversions to Christianity," paper presented at the Conference on Cultural Interactions in India, Oxford University, September 22-25, 1999, published in J. M. Brown and R. E. Frykenberg, eds., *Christians, Cultural Interactions, and India's Religious Traditions* (Grand Rapids and London, 2002), pp. 119-32.

12. James Kurth, "Religion and Globalization," The 1998 Templeton Lecture on Religion and World Affairs, *Foreign Policy Research Institute WIRE* 7.7 (May 28, 1999). Email address: fpri@aol.com (*Orbis* 42.2 [Spring 1998]).

13. "Go forth to every part of the world and proclaim the Good News [Gospel] to the whole of creation" (Mark 16:15); and ". . . Bear witness of me in . . . to the ends of the earth" (Acts 1:8).

fore, that the Good News has always possessed radically disruptive and revolutionary qualities and implications: new ways disturb and threaten the status quo; old ways of doing things are turned upside down. The sense of safety and security, if not the very identity, of people touched by the gospel becomes altered. Peoples so touched have reacted, often with unpredictable consequences. In its impact, the gospel has always been, by its very nature, disturbing, transcultural, and globalizing. Its universalizing claims, however, have also found concrete expression and specificity in flesh and blood. Its ethos has consisted in the particularities of ethno-local cultures. That being so, the nature of the gospel itself has been altered and remolded with each wave of expansion. No concrete or earthly manifestation of the gospel, after all, has ever existed in the abstract: such a thing is a contradiction in terms. What was "turned" or "transformed" through conversion to the gospel has never been without local roots. Roots of the gospel have always had to sink deep into the cultural soil of some particular living people whose feet were planted in some specific place, at some specific time — at some place and "time on earth."

The initial matrix of Jerusalem was profoundly altered, if not crushed and ultimately destroyed. Subsequent interactions with cultures of the Greco-Roman World followed. Later encounters with Celtic, Germanic, and Slavic peoples altered its cultural properties. Farther east were encounters with peoples and cultures of Armenia, Ethiopia, India, Persia, and China. Each encounter led to local challenges and modifications. Each also led to some local kind of manifestation of the gospel. During medieval and then modern times also, expansions of the gospel brought still further unexpected and unforeseeable mutations with distinctive adaptations and nuancings in ceremonial and doctrinal emphases, altered institutions and ideals, and new qualities and styles. Variations in the content evolved and brought about many localized forms of gospel expression (many have yet to be studied or understood).

The gospel in India is not just something new, or freshly arrived, although it is certainly also that. Its history goes back nearly two thousand years. In heuristic terms, its "arrivals" can be seen as having gone through successive phases: premodern, modern, and postmodern.[14] Despite periods of dormancy and quiescence, there never has been a time, especially after 1500, in which one cannot find trace elements of an evangelizing gospel in India. Nor can one find a time when this evangelizing process has not been accelerating.

The process begins, of course, with the Thomas Tradition. Belief that the

---

14. Kurth ("Religion and Globalization") describes "three paradigms or perspectives" from which to view the role of religion in the globalization process: (1) the modernist, (2) the postmodernist, and (3) the premodernist.

Apostle brought the gospel to India in 52 A.D. and that he later suffered martyrdom in what is now Mylapore remains strong. Whatever its historicity, in metaphorical terms this tradition retains a canonical status.[15] Multiple arrivals thereafter, stretching over many centuries, also cannot be denied — refugees fleeing from persecution by Zoroastrian, Islamic, and other oppressors. This process of arrivals continued for a thousand years. Each new group became all but completely cut off from contacts to the West — from the Orthodox and, even more, from the Catholic communions of Europe. The gospel in India remained linked only to the Church of the East.

Christians of Malabar became "Hindu." They were Hindu in culture, Christian in faith, and Syrian in doctrine, liturgy, and polity. Their ritual purity and social rank among high-caste aristocracy became fixed. Due to self-insulating defensive strategies, the vitality of their gospel eventually went into hibernation. Locked within local cultures, as if hermetically sealed, their gospel remained dormant, not to awaken for nearly a thousand years. Within the Brahmanical ranking of social order *(varnāshramadharma),* most Christian communities can be seen as having fallen somewhere between the "color" *(varna)* categories of Kshatriya and Vaishiya. Not all were of the same birth *(jati)* or lineage *(vamsha),* but all possessed distinctly "Hindu" features. Husbands tied the *thāli* around the necks of their brides, bestowed the "marriage cloth," and took part in ceremonial investitures marking stages *(ashrams)* of life. Malankara Nazaranis, especially, wore tonsure with tuft; and, like Nayars and Brahmans, they lived in *tharavad* dwellings. They followed Brahmanical rituals for removing pollution and were especially strict in matters of inter-dining, intermarriage, and disposing of dead bodies. Many were warriors and some were rulers. Family claims of seventy, eighty, and ninety successive generations of pastors *(kattanars)* and bishops *(metrans)* were not uncommon, and the learned maintained Syriac libraries and schools. (At least six communities still lay claim to the apostolic tradition of St. Thomas.)[16] Within Indo-Islamicate regimes of India, Armenian Christians settled in commercial centers, often as servants of Muslim or Hindu rulers, looking to Armenia for inspiration and pastoral support.

With the coming of the Portuguese in 1498 and the establishment of their

15. Thomas Christians remark that they have as much evidence for Thomas coming to India as there is for Peter going to Rome. The gospel in India antedated the Canons, Creeds, or Councils in the West.

16. Namely, the Orthodox Syrian Church (in two branches), the Independent Syrian Church of Malabar (Kunnamkulam), the Mar Thoma Church, the Malankara (Syrian Rite) Catholic Church, the (Chaldean) Church of the East, and St. Thomas Evangelical Church (in factions). Virtually all have Roman Catholic branches.

Estado da India the process of globalizing expansion began to reawaken and gain momentum. Catholic orders, under the *Padroado* of Goa and Lisbon, enjoyed considerable autonomy from Rome. From monastic redoubts and collegial citadels, missionaries sallied forth into the countryside, winning converts and expanding clerical domains. Inspired by Francis Xavier, whole communities of fisher folk along the coasts came into the fold, some in order to gain protection from predatory Muslim and Hindu rulers. "Roman Brahmans," such as Roberto de Nobili and Giuseppe Beschi, won converts and established a tradition blending Catholic piety and Sanskrit scholarship. Attempts to impose a Roman Catholic hegemony upon the ancient communities of Thomas Christians backfired, especially after the 1599 Edict of Diamper (Udayampur), when the resilience and resourcefulness of indigenous Mar Thoma communities enabled them to endure, resist, and survive cultural domination.

Globalizing of conversion took another quantum leap forward in 1706 with the arrival in Tranquebar of the Pietist (Evangelical) German missionaries Ziegenbalg and Plütschau. Like a cloud no bigger than a hand, this event was but a first glimmer, a harbinger of much more radical cultural transformation. The Halle dictum of A. H. Francke — that true evangelization would never encompass the whole world until every single man, woman, and child was literate, able to read the Word of God in his or her own mother tongue[17] — set in motion nothing less than the first truly global "information revolution." (Accelerating developments since Gutenberg, including the cybernetic revolutions of our own day, can be seen as stemming from the impetus and momentum of this process.) Nowhere did the ideal of universal literacy envisioned by Francke seem more promising than in India. Within twenty-five years of its initial arrival, technologies of modern education and printing had become so well rooted that, under the royal patronage from Hindu princes, Tamil Christians were establishing schools in the Kingdom of Thanjāvur. By the 1790s, scores of such schools were functioning, not only in Thanjāvur, but also in Tiruchirappalli and Tirunelveli, and in Ramnad and Sivaganga. Serfojee Rajah of Thanjāvur, inspired by his missionary Raja-Guru Christian Friedrich Schwartz, even constructed a modern scientific laboratory, fully equipped with the latest modern instruments (e.g., microscopes, telescopes, and test tubes). Also housed in his new palace, the "Saraswat Mahal" (or "Palace of Wisdom"), was a modern library with its own archival collections and its own "Cabinet of Wonders" *(Wunder Kammer* or *Kunst und Naturalien*

---

17. Francke's corollary dictum making mathematical, practical, scientific, and technical knowledge no less imperative, as a way of "reading" God's World (Creation), brought the Enlightenment to India.

Zimmer). By then, William Carey was initiating in Serampore (Srirampur) what would eventually spread into Bengal and North India. The Enlightenment, with its new forms of transcultural interaction, then brought a further explosion in various forms of path-breaking scholarship, translation, printing, and scientific inquiry. That reactions to the impact of this process would later be accompanied, both in Hindu and in Muslim cultures, by revivalist and sometimes violent forms of what became modern or "syndicated" Hinduism and rejuvenated Islam is hardly surprising.

The emergence of the modern epoch in India, therefore, can be seen as beginning with this cultural transformation. This emergence was also marked by a decline of Indo-Islamic sway and a rise of European power. It was also accompanied, increasingly, by other more confused and varied forms of globalization. These new forms were sometimes malevolent. Too often the term "Christian" became confused with what was European *(Farangi)* or American. Out of the turmoil of the eighteenth century, an all-embracing Indian empire eventually emerged. When this modern construction was eventually also challenged, in the name of an emerging and prospectively all-encompassing nation-state, rivalry between the Indian National Congress (led by Gandhi and Nehru) and the Muslim League (led by Jinnah) led to the breakup of India. The Partition of the Old Raj, in 1947, into the successor states of India and Pakistan also brought a simultaneous end to many forms of Euro-Christian dominance. Thereafter, despite the gradual decline and disappearance of almost all Western missionaries,[18] various radical movements of conversion and cross-cultural transformations within a multiplicity of local "Hindu-Muslim" (or "Indian") environments, both urban and rural, continued to accelerate. These sometimes radical transformations, in turn, have been accompanied and succeeded by a welter of competitive, evangelizing or proselytizing, fundamentalist and revivalist movements (Buddhist, Christian, Hindu, Muslim and Sikh), among which various forms of Marxist socialism and secular humanism have also become globalizing movements of radical conversion.

18. But what has yet to be fully appreciated, or thoroughly studied, was the dramatic rise in the number of Indian Christian missionaries, under both indigenous agencies (e.g., Indian Missionary Society, National Missionary Society, etc.) and foreign agencies, so that the overall amount of missionary activity seems to have increased in each decade.

III

Conversion, understandably, has become a bone of contention in India.[19] For many Hindus, it is a "bogey" — a cause for "national" concern and a fear or threat.[20] It represents something alien and hostile: a malignant and polluting virus from "outside" India; a "foreign hand" disrupting and destroying the achievements and benefits refined by a great and ancient civilization. It is a blow to "Hindu" pride: against family and against hearth and home. For many Hindus, conversion is seen only as "forced": as a result of coercion, enticement, intimidation, and proselytization.[21] If conversion is indeed a consequence of neo-colonial globalization, Hindu concerns are understandable. One has but to look at and measure the accelerating velocity and increasing volume of conversions in each decade, marking its rise over the past two centuries but especially during the past fifty years since India attained Independence, to see why some are anxious.

For many peoples in India, on the other hand, conversion is also a form of social or political protest. It is a means of escape from caste domination and the thraldom of untold centuries. Many followers of Christ see conversion only in theological terms: a result of a divine intervention, redemption. For them, "conversion" involves an inner or spiritual, even mystical, transformation of the human heart. For them conversion can only be an act of God, accomplished by the Spirit of God. For them, conversion represents a divine promise and assurance of eternal, everlasting life, life beyond death, and joining one's self and one's family identity with the identity of a community of fellow believers which is global and universal. Many others, however, see conversion in more earthly and mundane terms. For them, conversion is seen as rescue from bondage and a realigning of loyalties and priorities, both social and political, as well as cultural.

Quite obviously, a more precise set of working definitions is needed. There can be little doubt that "conversion" is a "soft" concept, and that it possesses multiple denotations and connotations. Yet, in its broadest, most basic and simple sense, "conversion" means nothing more than "to turn" some-

19. Ashgar Ali Engineer, "The Conversion Controversy," *The Hindu,* Wednesday, January 20, 1999.

20. P. Radhakrishnan, "The Conversion Bogey — I & II," *The Hindu,* Monday and Tuesday, January 25 and 26, 1999.

21. "Politics of Conversion," in *A Retrospect of Christianity in India* (www.hindubooks.org/), ch. 6: "Christians of India are converts or descendants of converts whose conversion had been secured during some period of history by force or fraud; conversion by persuasion is a rarity."

thing — anything — around. Turning from one direction to another, from a negative to a positive (as in turning from alternating current to direct current of electricity), is conversion in its most elemental form. But, as and when applied to human circumstances, the term can also be used in ways both numerous and complex, so that different definitions talk past each other and different perspectives are at odds. Different kinds of "turning" can also be measured for degrees of intensity: exclusive or inclusive, total or partial, radical or moderate, strong or weak. "Turning" of some entity can be viewed, either exclusively or partially, in theoretical, theological, philosophical, ideological, political, or sociological terms. "Turnings" of any entity can be viewed in terms of qualitative or quantitative distinctions. When viewed in doctrinal or emotional (psychological) or "spiritual" terms, conversion is understood to be a cognitive and volitional action, a commitment of free will based upon a "turning" of beliefs or convictions as to the verity of something or other, whether of a cosmic truth or of a mundane change or correction of perception. As such, a human "turning" of mind can be fully logical and rational and consistent, only partially so, or entirely erratic and irrational. Conversion can bring about (or consist of) a totalistic transformation: in worldviews, values, and behaviors. For those who deny or reject the possibility of free volition, conversion can be seen merely as an involuntary consequence of cumulative and predetermined influences, whether environmental and/or hereditary, which have brought about changed and different sets of perspectives. In theological or theistic terms, "conversion" is a miraculous and supernatural event, resulting from an act of divine grace by a Supreme Being (be this called Deva, Allah, Yahweh, or God). In social, political, or cultural terms, on the other hand, "conversion" can constitute not only a change of external identity or loyalty but also a challenge to the status quo and stability of previous loyalties, relationships, and the structures which bind institutions together. So seen, "turning" involves not only a repudiation of previous identity but also a taking on of new identity. This being so, altered relations can be gradual and slow or, sometimes, profound, radical, and revolutionary.

Mass movements of conversion have had their most spectacular and sweeping impact, quite predictably, among those communities in India which have been least "Hindu" — namely, least "Sanskritized." This has been most evident among the *adivāsis* (tribal peoples) and among the *dālits* (outcaste and untouchable peoples). While movements of this sort have spread, in more recent times, into the heavily Sanskritized "Cow Belt" — namely, into Bihar, Gujarat, Orissa, Punjab, and Uttar Pradesh — the earliest and most profoundly radical impacts of conversion have been felt in the deepest southeast (and southwest), initially in Tirunelveli and what was once southern

Travancore, and, later, in the farthest northeast of Nagaland, Mizoram, and other hill-jungled fringes of Assam. Radical movements have occurred, initially, within isolated localities and scarcely noticed pockets of territory, often in hills, jungles, and mountain frontiers, hidden among the despised and lost or "backward" peoples. It is in remote places and among the alienated that conversion movements have spread most dramatically. Gradually and then more rapidly, they have fanned out and grown until they covered the entire length and breadth of India. Interestingly, no genuine mass movement of conversion in India has ever occurred or succeeded which was not indigenously generated and led.[22]

Beginning in the sixteenth century, movements of conversion en masse occurred among coastal fisher folk along the Gulf of Mannar and in Malabar. These actions, by Paravas and the Mukkavars, were initiated by local leaders on behalf of their communities, and were at least partially sociopolitical in nature. One hundred and fifty years later, in 1799, a convert of Satyanathan named David Sundaranandam led a "mass movement" among the lowly Shānars (now elevated to Nadars), a community from which he came. Thousands of "soil slaves" whose hereditary occupation was toddy tapping turned to the new faith. Whole villages in Tirunelveli country became Christian, and goddess temples were turned into prayer-schools. Such actions incurred the wrath of their landholding overlords. Warlords *(palaiyakarans)* plundered, confined, and tortured Christians, destroying their chapel-schools and burning their books. Hundreds suffered the loss of everything they possessed. Many were stripped of their clothes and sent into the jungle to die. Some were martyred. Sundaranandam himself disappeared. Movements of mass conversion continued to break out in Tirunelveli, as also in Nagercoil, Kaniya Kumari, and Travancore, throughout the nineteenth century, with whole village communities often turning Christian. Refugees from persecution who fled their homes established "Villages of Refuge" — i.e., Mudulur, Megnanapuram, Dohnavur, Suviseshapuram, and Anandapuram. As numbers of converts doubled and tripled during each decade of the nineteenth century, schools brought literacy, and voluntary self-help societies formed to care for the helpless — the widows and orphans, the hungry and the sick. Colleges and seminaries and hospitals were built, and Tirunelveli Christians transformed an entire local culture, economy, and society.

Similar movements, while not as dramatic, have occurred within virtually

22. Even if theologically explained as the work of the Spirit of God in an individual's heart, and even when missionary agency was not evident as a catalyst or for logistic support, as in times of persecution.

every low caste (untouchable) community and every tribal people, especially during the past century. Among *dālits,* massive conversions among Paraiyars, Pulaiyars, Chakkiraiyars, Pallans, Mahars, Malas, Madigas, Adi Dravidas, and many other ethnic groups are noteworthy. In the north, massive conversions have occurred among the Bhangis and Chamars of Uttar Pradesh, Chuhras of Punjab, and Mahars of Maharashtra. To list them all, or to describe in detail specific and distinctive features of each response to the gospel, in terms either of "conversion" and/or "Christianization," is not possible within the compass of this essay. Yet, each has its own unique, and sometimes remarkable, story to tell; and, while not all have been studied, each is worthy of a separate history and each deserves deeper, more careful, and intensive investigation.[23]

Similarly, there is hardly an *adivāsi* people anywhere in the continent, from Kashmir to Kanya Kumari and from the Brahmaputra Gorge in Assam to the Dangs of Gujarat, which, in varying degrees, has not been profoundly influenced by the impact of some revolutionary conversion movement. Badagas, Coorgs, or Kotas of the south; Chenchus, Hill Reddis, Yanadis, and Yerukalas of Andhra; Khonds and Gonds, Rabhas and Santals, Kurkus and Mangs and Bhils, ethnic groups stretching across the jungle belts of Central India from Bengal and Orissa to Kathiawar and Kutch: these are but a few of the countless numbers of aboriginal peoples in remote places whose lives have been touched by conversion movements, led by converts who were trained by Christian missionaries. Among the most dramatic are transformations that have occurred among formerly "backward," "primitive," or "savage" aboriginals of the North East. Here, from small beginnings a century ago to amazingly rapid changes during the past fifty years, virtually all Khasis, Mizos, and Nagas, and similar "borderland" or "marginal" peoples, have been radically transformed. Once fierce headhunters, ceaselessly fighting each other or launching raids against hapless inhabitants of the Assam Valley, such peoples have become highly advanced, educated, and relatively well off. Such peoples had never previously, in any significant degree, had to encounter or respond to "Hinduization," "Sanskritization," and/or "Islamization." Glad to escape from prior conditions of fear and want, they quickly appropriated the benefits of literacy and modern education. Integrated into cohesive communities, relatively free from the social segmentation and domination of "Hindu" caste structures, they had enjoyed a relative degree of autonomy within their own self-governing villages. At the same time, they had resented and resisted what they saw as "Hindu" en-

---

23. For some stories, see Andrew Wingate, *The Church and Conversion: A Study of Recent Conversion to and from Christianity in the Tamil Area of South India* (Delhi, 1999 and 2001), a published Ph.D. dissertation (University of Birmingham, 1995).

croachments, especially by money-lending bankers and shopkeeper merchants from Assam. Since they have never been fully "nationalized" into "India," whether empire or nation, their lack of patriotism has disturbed the government of India. As a consequence, ever since 1947, they have had to struggle to maintain their autonomy and have done so against what they have perceived to be "Hindu" domination and "Indian" colonialism. Armed insurgency has continued, sporadically, for fifty years.[24]

IV

Globalization of the gospel in India during the twentieth century has brought increasing complication and concern. As numbers of Christians and of Christian communities in India have grown and as new movements have proliferated at an ever-accelerating rate, complexities of culture, doctrine, and style have also increased. Radical changes have brought forms and styles undreamed and unheard of in previous centuries. These changes, however they may be perceived, have been bound to cause concern among many ordinary Hindus. For the forces of Hindutva, conversion movements have provoked alarm and outrage. Some recent forms of globalization have, at the same time, challenged and undermined many of the most hallowed indigenous traditions in India, and have done so for Hindu and non-Hindu alike.

*   *   *

All along, globalization has been a process with two faces — one benign and one malignant. The benign face of the gospel in India has always been perceived as "Hindu." Not withstanding the universality of its message, where the Word has been made flesh in India, this flesh and clothing have been "Hindu" ("Native") in culture. That being granted, the gospel's expression in indigenous motifs, styles, and terms can be seen as especially manifest in four spheres: (1) in the contributions of noteworthy individual "Hindu Christians"; (2) in the rise of the indigenous church movement; (3) in the remarkable increase and numbers of churchless believers; (4) and in the indigenizing character of Indian Pentecostalism, the largest single movement of Christian awakening and conversion.

24. From 70 to 90 percent of Nagas are Christian. For a study of Naga conversion, see Richard M. Eaton, "Comparative History as World History: Religious Conversion in Modern India," *Journal of World History* 8.2 (Fall 1997): 243-71; a revised version can be found in his *Essays on Islam and Indian History* (New Delhi, 2000), pp. 45-75.

The story of heroic individual believers who have made remarkable contributions to India's culture is an old one, with instances going back centuries. Three or four, among many, may be cited as having been especially noteworthy — Vedanāyakam Sāstri, Sadhu Sundar Singh, Narayan Vaman Tilak, and Pandita Ramabai (Saraswati). Others could also be described, but these four serve to make the case because they have been so highly regarded among non-Christians of India, Hindus and Muslims alike.[25]

Vedanāyakam Sāstri of Thanjāvur (1773-1864), along with Serfojee Maharaja, was a disciple of Schwartz. He never abandoned his claim to high status as a Vellālar of noble birth, nor his reverence for classical or high Sangam (Tamil) culture. As an evangelical and an intellectual, he was both founder and fountainhead of modern Tamil literature and learning. In lyric Tamil verse, he described, in great detail and by name, the wonders of the universe and the wonders of God's grace; the wonders of what science revealed in stars of the sky; the beasts and birds of the field; the cities of America, Asia, and Europe; and the absurdities of inhuman and sinful behavior. Yet, when castigated by younger missionaries for observing caste customs, such as segregated seating and eating in church services, he remained adamant: What, he asked, entitled Europeans to make such judgments? Bishop Heber had remarked upon the hypocrisy of Americans and Europeans having servants or owning slaves in the West while, at the same time, condemning caste among Christians in India. One English missionary with the Society for the Propagation of the Gospel (SPG) even had "Tanjore Christians" of Vedanāyakam's congregation publicly flogged for refusing to abandon caste/class strictures within the church.[26]

"Sadhu" Sundar Singh was a Sikh who, in 1904, had a vision of Christ which totally changed his life. Where he had once publicly burned the Bible and denounced the Christian community, he turned to them and asked for baptism. Yet, he never accepted European modes of Christian thought, explaining: "Indians do need the Water of Life, but not the European cup." In due course, he became a wandering mendicant. As a "Christian sadhu," he devoted the remaining years of his short life to presenting the gospel among re-

---

25. These samples were selected arbitrarily; there are hosts of others, too many to recount. Similarly, an exemplary Islamic-Christian, the former Sunni 'alim, 'Imad ud-din, whose career has been studied by Dr. Avril A. Powell, makes a case no less arresting. See Powell, "'Pillar of a New Faith': Christianity in Late Nineteenth Century Punjab from the Perspective of a Convert from Islam," in R. E. Frykenberg, ed., Christians and Missionaries in India (Grand Rapids and London, 2003), pp. 223-55.

26. R. E. Frykenberg, "Conversion and Crises of Conscience under Company Raj in South India," in Marc Gaborieau and Alice Thorner, eds., Asie du Sud, Traditions et changements (Paris, 1979), pp. 311-21.

mote hill peoples. This he did in a *bhakti* or devotional idiom, adopting ecstatic modes of fervor and shunning stuffy sermons being preached in the
regular missionary churches of the Punjab.[27]

Narayan Vaman Tilak (1861-1919) was a Maratha (Chitpavan) Brahman.
He had already become a celebrated poet, novelist, and thinker when, through
reading the Bible, he became a convert. In so doing, however, he insisted upon
being baptized by an Indian rather than a foreigner. His life-long quest (or
parampara) was devoted to reconciling his "Hindu" cultural heritage and his
commitment to Christ. Widely respected, he dedicated himself to the emancipation of oppressed and marginalized peoples, especially non-Brahmans,
untouchables, and women. From the end of 1912 until his death, he was editor
of *Dnyānsdaya,* an eight-page Marathi weekly which was published by the
American Marathi Mission and which blended news with religious articles,
poems, and translations. As a consequence of his many years of scholarship
and writing, Tilak left an enormous corpus of writings — including some 700
hymns, many of which are still widely sung. He urgently appealed for Indian
Christians to shed their dependency upon the West and to eradicate all denominational divisions among their congregations. During his last years, he
too became a *bhakta* and *sunnyäsi* — giving up material possessions and institutional connections, but never renouncing his family and home.[28]

Pandita Ramabai Saraswati (1858-1922) was a Brahman who, because of her
phenomenal grasp of Sanskrit literature, had confounded the greatest pandits
of Varanasi and Calcutta with her great erudition and learning. When, after a
brief marriage, she became a widow with a yet to be born child, she became
disenchanted and militantly opposed to the harsh treatment of women, especially widows, within Hindu culture. Through the reading of Scripture and
works of Nehemiah Goreh, she became a Brahmo-Christian. Yet, despite baptism, she refused the discipline of Anglo-Catholic sisters who had brought her
from Pune to Britain. Fêted among high society women on the eastern sea-
board of America, she lectured and studied and traveled extensively in North
America from 1886 to 1888. Her publication, *The High-Caste Hindu Woman*
(1887), was an indictment of the Hindu treatment of women (a work which
brought her fame and lionization ever after). Her words were (and still re-

---

27. A. J. Appasamy, *Sunder Singh: A Biography* (Madras, 1985); C. F. Andrews, *Sadhu
Sundar Singh: A Personal Memoir* (London, 1934); and Sundar Singh, *Durr-i hikmat* (La-
hore, 1923).

28. Malcolm J. Nazareth, "Reverend Narayan Vaman Tilak: An Interreligious Explo-
ration," Ph.D. dissertation, Temple University, 1998; J. C. Winslow, *Narayan Vaman Tilak:
The Christian Poet of Maharashtra* (Calcutta, 1923, 1934); Lakshmibai Tilak, *I Follow After,
An Autobiography* (Madras, 1951, 1956).

main) persuasive in India because they were spoken from a deep knowledge of Sanskrit literature and from an inside understanding of Hindu tradition. Still, she remained dissatisfied with what she found in America. Turning away from high society elites and rationalist theologies, her restless quest for greater truth drove her ever westward and downward into the faith of the lowly. On the west coast, she moved into evangelicalism and, eventually, into the "holiness" culture of Pentecostalism. Returning to India, she devoted the rest of her life to building institutions for the rescuing and educating of "child" widows. At her famous orphanage, Mukti (Freedom, Liberation, Salvation), a mission which she had opened at Kedgaon in 1898, an Indian form of Pentecostal revival broke out in 1905. As her health declined, she increasingly gave herself to making a new Marathi translation of the Bible.[29]

Unlike African independent church movements, which have been thoroughly studied, relatively little is known about independent church movements in India. Yet, demonstrations of indigenous incarnation of gospel faith within authentic and genuine Hindu cultures are becoming increasingly significant. In contrast to forms of "foreign missionary" Christianity which are products of efforts originating in alien cultures and brought from abroad, this kind of phenomenon is much more extensive and influential, however little about it may yet be known in the West. Knowledge of such movements is scant. This is because so much of the source material still remains hidden, local, and confined to vernacular languages. Surveys have been and are currently being conducted, and regional consultations have been and are being held, to gather more information. Results are being published by R. E. Hedlund and O. L. Snaitang.[30]

Perhaps the single most sweeping conversion movement currently going on in India is Pentecostal. This development parallels similar revolutionizing developments in Africa, Latin America, and other parts of the world. There is little doubt about the dramatic visibility of this movement in India. Long processions of believers, clad in snow-white garments, often consisting of long tunics and saris, can be seen regularly in virtually every major urban area, especially in the biggest cities. Studies made or currently in progress seem to indicate that the Pentecostal movement in India attracts peoples from the lower strata of society and that it challenges the intellectually or doctrinally liberal ideologies and programs introduced by foreign missionar-

29. Padmini Sengupta, *Pandita Ramabai Saraswati* (Bombay and New York, 1970).
30. *Churches of Independent Origin: Little Traditions in Indian Christianity* (in progress). See R. E. Hedlund, ed., *Christianity in India: The Emergence of an Indigenous Community* (Delhi, 2000).

ies, especially by purveyors of "social gospel" agendas who for many years secularized and minimized Christo-centric devotional faith and worship. Rather, in impoverished segments of the Hindu world where there is an acute consciousness of clear, immediate, and present dangers from evil, fear, hunger, and illness, Indian Pentecostalism represents an emphasis upon healing and upon driving out the ghosts of evil and fear in the name of the Holy Spirit. This kind of piety and religiosity finds resonance within some forms of popular Hindu culture, where local demons *(pay)* have long held sway over the minds and hearts of poor peoples. Even though the movement has been especially strong in cities, it has remained far removed from centers of power and privilege. This kind of religious belief and conduct can also be understood as part of a wider cultural dynamic in which dominance and resistance to dominance are parts of a never-ending struggle for survival within the Hindu World.[31]

The fourth and final form of indigenizing under consideration here has several names — "nonbaptized believers," "churchless Christians," or "Christian Hindus" ("Hindu Christians"). While it is really a very old phenomenon, it seems to have become increasingly prevalent, especially during the past half century. Hinduizing, or Indianizing, the gospel has taken on new meanings. Its character depends upon provenence and prevalence — whether in high-caste and low-caste families — at opposite ends of the social spectrum. In either case, it represents an almost totally different kind of religio-cultural environment. Where this kind of phenomenon is found, at its very core, one can identify varieties of dual-identity that, in essence, are both sociological and theological in character. Many low-caste believers remain unbaptized and stay outside any church because of their economic, political, or social (family) circumstances. Significant numbers, even of baptized, church-attending, and church-belonging believers, coming from both high- and low-caste families, retain dual identities. This they do, keeping both Hindu and Christian names, lest they suffer the loss of "affirmative action" kinds of benefits (in schooling, health, welfare relief, etc.) provided by the government. High-caste believers, in contrast, remain unbaptized for cultural and social reasons: they do not want to abandon, or be abandoned by, their close kindred (spouses, parents, children) or their personal heritage; and they do not want to abandon styles of personal appearance, celebration, devotion, and worship. Indeed, when and where they see strange goings-on in churches — alien cus-

---

31. Lionel Caplan, *Class and Culture in Urban India* (Oxford, 1987); Michael Bergunder, *Die südindishe Pfingstbewegung im 20. Jahrhundert: Eine historische und systematische Untersuchung* (Halle, 1997); Paul Hiebert, personal conversation.

toms and rituals (music, etc.), petty quarrels, blatant corruption, venality, and struggles over church positions or properties, together with "bad" reputations of members in some churches — they do not want to be associated with churches.

Also, as a matter of personal preference in style and taste, many do not want to be associated with large and public congregational meetings and conventions. Like many Hindus, they prefer, instead, acts of personal piety. For many a Hindu who takes spiritual life seriously and has found personal peace (*shanti*) in the redeeming love, mercy, and power of God in Jesus Christ (*Isa Masih* or *Yesu Kristu*), as personal Lord and Savior, no need for either baptism or communion seems compelling. All one needs is to have one's own *ishta avatar*. Devotion to one's own *ishta devata*, with disciplined daily exercises and carefully and closely disciplined attention to prayer and scripture, is deemed sufficient. One need but make the gospel one's own personal path, one's own *ishta marg*, and one can find both personal and eternal salvation, satisfaction, and security. This is a pattern common for many a nonbaptized, non-churched believer.

Questions concerning the existence and vitality of personal (and family) faith in Christ outside of the institutionalized structures of church and denomination, especially questions about inner meaning and on matters of historical significance, abound and are manifold. Controversies may well match the debates that arose within the Jerusalem Church in the first century, or those that provoked the great councils, reformations, and schisms of later centuries. Differences — between the churches of the East and West, Greek and Latin, Catholic and Orthodox, Evangelical and Reformed — may possess all sorts of manifold cultural forms and norms. One thing seems certain: numbers of believers and converts outside formal Christian structures in India may be much larger than anyone might have anticipated. A survey of the city of Madras (now known as Chennai), conducted by Madras Christian College, found that the number of high-caste Hindu believers who are devoted to the gospel of Christ was equal to that of the entire population of non-Catholic Christians within the metropolitan area.[32]

*   *   *

32. Herbert E. Hoefer, *Churchless Christianity* (Madras, 1991); reviewed in H. L. Richard, "Christ-Followers in India Flourishing — but outside the Church," *Mission Frontiers* (March-April 1999): 32-35; to which Hoefer added "Follow-Up Reflections . . ." in *Mission Frontiers* (March-April 1999): 36-39. Cf. H. L. Richard, "A Survey of Protestant Evangelistic Efforts among High Caste Hindus in the 20th Century," *Missiology* 25.3, 4, 5 (1997), reprinted in *All Things to All Men* 8.2, 3, 4 (1998).

A second face of contemporary globalization of the gospel in India seems, at least to some in India, to be more malignant, if not spurious. In the name of creating a new, harmonious, and integrated world Christianity — perhaps even a single global culture by which Pentecostal tongues may override the confusions of Babel — local differences of culture are sometimes being overridden, and sometimes squelched. Whatever may be the catholicity of evangelicalism or the orthodoxy of faith, in form and style this kind of global homogenization is itself another kind of quintessentially ethnocentric and ethno-local dominance. This kind of globalization in India is tantamount to another form of Westernizing "cultural imperialism." In some of its more crass forms, it also calls for an Americanization of indigenous cultures. When globalizing the gospel in India becomes a gloss for Americanizing the gospel in India, strange and unpredictable consequences should hardly be surprising. Ironically, therefore, the very process of globalizing cultural values in the name of the gospel has tended to reduce the common universality of that gospel and to become, instead, the universalizing of a highly charged form of ethnocentric and ethno-local cultural hegemony. Universal components, norms, and styles become confused with forms of American/Western Christianity. Globalization of the gospel in India has sometimes tended, in short, to become a means for strengthening the growth and influence of particularistic forms of American Christianity in India at the expense of indigenous forms of Indian Christianity.

What has begun to become especially apparent, moreover, is the proliferation of various kinds of "democratized" popular religion that have been imported from America. Religious entrepreneurship and free enterprise, sometimes hard-selling and sometimes self-aggrandizing, along with other features of popular evangelicalism in the West, in all sorts of manifold forms, have mushroomed. This can be seen not only in mass-mailing technologies, fund-raising campaigns, and promotional gimmicks but also in a "dumbing down" of the very content and essence of the gospel itself. A sort of "McDonaldization" of the gospel, with fast-food varieties of a less wholesome "Gospel-Lite," in the place of more solid and wholesome doctrinal menus of gospel light, is being sold and made available to customers through private distributorships. A homogenization of the gospel message has occurred in certain places, so that local cultures are being overwhelmed and local variations obliterated for the sake of uniformity. Indian Christian leaders, missionaries, pastors, and scholars are being co-opted by enterprising "off-shore" and/or "overseas" agencies to return to India and "parrot back" the language, style, and vocabulary of "Gospel Globalization." This language, style, and vocabulary, in some ways, may even tend, inadvertently, to reflect the material and mono-cultural perspectives of a currently trendy multiculturalism, albeit in evangelical clothing.

To the degree that globalizing tendencies are being imported from abroad and set up by Christians in India, Indian Christians themselves are finding that their own perspectives and pronouncements are viewed as alien and hostile by the dominant elites in India. Even moderate Hindus, those who are thoughtful and who are not wedded to the doctrines of Hindutva, are able to see what has been happening. Such Hindus are able to see differences and make distinctions between a vocabulary that is discriminating and strives to make the gospel user-friendly and one which categorically demonizes every aspect of culture within the entire "Hindu World."

Summary and Conclusion

From the perspective of defenders and protagonists of Hindutva, as religious nationalists, the increasing volume and velocity of Christian conversions and the increasing volume of mass movements of conversion to Christianity are seen as alarming. They have long been seen as a "national" threat. Christians and Hindus talk past each other. Among their differences are conflicting definitions of "conversion" as a concept. Christians see conversion in theological terms: it has to do with the relationship between an individual soul (or even a group of souls) and a gracious, redeeming Savior God. Hindus see conversion in sociological and political terms: it has to do with an evil, "foreign," and "hidden" menace, some sinister attempt to undermine and destroy the very foundations of India's cultural and national unity. Conversions, therefore, are not just an affront to cultural and national pride. Nor are they simply a threat to the sanctity of "sacred birth" and "sacred earth" as enshrined in *Sanatana-dharma* and embodied in *Varnāshramadharma*. Such threats are seen as immediate, and pertaining to material and political security and well-being, and even to vested interests of ruling elites.

The sense of threat arising out of conversion movements, as this essay has attempted to show, cannot be understood without reference to broader historical perspectives. Several successive waves of globalization have brought increasing measures of the gospel to India. These can be traced back to the coming of Saint Thomas and the Malankara Nazaranis. They can also be traced back at least two, if not four, centuries to Xavier and Ziegenbalg and Carey. Most recently, these can be traced to extremely vital "nativistic" movements within this century, to the Dornakal Mission of Bishop Azariah, and to countless other missions launched within the past few decades. And finally,

Hindus in India have been confronted by a frontal assault from an American-izing cultural invasion.[33]

Thus, when Hindus read militant rhetoric printed in the newsletter of an organization run by and for Indian Christian missionaries, one can hardly be surprised at the results. Rhetoric, milder than that of Dr. Ralph Winter, came from Indian missionary leaders Dr. Alex P. Abraham and Rev. C. George. It fell into the "wrong" hands and, after being published by *The Times of India* (on January 21, 1999), went onto the HVK web, along with VHP commentary by Hindutva polemicists. Among words put into *Operation Agapē* were such expressions as "conquer," "enemy territories," and "crusade" in reference to a "conversion" agenda: for example, "The Lord helped us to conquer many new territories"; we have plans for a "big crusade"; and we are "facing strong op-position from enemies of the gospel." The VHP argued that such words as "conquer" indicated a desire to use force, that Christians "are out to conquer this country through conversions" and that such "battle plans" included "66 territories." Abraham and George responded with apologies, and claimed that the words used had been taken out of their "purely spiritual context . . . well understood by the people [they] were meant for," and that neither a "nominal Christian" nor a non-Christian could "be an enemy for those who belong to God's kingdom and believe in Jesus Christ."[34]

Every major mass movement during the past two centuries has led, invari-ably, to misunderstandings, and these, in turn, have eventually led to violent reactions in one form or another. What are perceived, in sociological and po-litical terms, as being "forced" conversions have been met by counter forces. Persecution and riot, with destruction of church buildings and killings of Christians, have occurred, sometimes sporadically and sometimes systemati-cally.[35] In modern times, such reactions can be traced from the 1799 killings

33. The flip side of this ethnocentric globalization, of course, is the spread in Amer-ica, Australia, Britain, Canada, and the West of Hindu missionaries (e.g., *acharyas*, gurus, *pandarams, sadhus,* swamis, and the like), with their mystic New Age converts, massive temples (e.g., in Pittsburgh, Aurora, and Wembley), and massive financial support by af-fluent Hindu Non-Resident Indians (Indians who live and work outside India) to Hindutva militants for "reconversion" *(shuddhi)* of *adivāsis* and *dālits* by such agencies as the VHP and Bajrang Dal. This "globalization in reverse" is equally noteworthy.

34. HVK Archives: "Christian newsletter adds fuel to row . . ." (February 1999): http://www.hvk.org/articles; and circular email message from Alex Abraham (January 20, 1999): Internet: agapeldh@usa.net.

35. Praveen Swami, "A Catalogue of Crimes," *Frontline* 16.3 (January 30–February 3, 1999), cover story; "Christian Persecution in India," *Christian Persecution Report*, Monday, December 21, 1998, http://www.erols.com/tferleman/new/dec/0212498.html; "A List [79] of Atrocities Committed against Christians across India in the Golden Year of Independence,

in Tirunelveli to the 1999 and 2002 killings in Bihar, Gujarat, and Orissa. Violence has increased after every mass movement and every major outbreak of conversions. That violence — such as the fiery slaying of Graham Stewart Staines and his two young sons — should fall upon gentle persons who are least implicated in disruptive events, upon those who exercise loving care for the helpless and downtrodden (e.g., lepers, orphans, etc.), and upon those whose closest loved ones rise up to bless and forgive their persecutors and killers can be seen as significant and not untypical features of recent conversion movements.[36] There are still important questions, however, for which answers are needed. Analysis may reveal more, for example, about whether some of the misunderstandings and violent reactions provoked by Christians in India could have been avoided or mitigated. Seen with special reference to the historical contexts of the gospel in India, it is important that new ways be found for Christians and Hindus to avoid "talking past" each other. People in India, as well as people in the world, can no longer afford to clothe the gospel's long-standing history within "Hindu" culture in ambiguity and ignorance, obfuscation and obscurity. Nor does demonizing rhetoric serve to increase the power of the gospel's witness within the "Hindu World."

August 15, 1997 to August 15, 1998, and Beyond," *Persecuted for Christ in India* (http://www.angelfire.com/indian christians/persecution.html: January 29, 1999).

36. *The Hindu,* January 28, 1999: "Mrs. Gladys Staines proved to be a true Christian when she said those who were responsible for the death of her husband should be forgiven as it was the will of God. She is an example of divinity in a human being. All Hindus should take note . . . of this great Christian woman."

CHAPTER SIX

"The Pacific Is No Longer a Mission Field?"
Conversion in the South Pacific
in the Twentieth Century

ALLAN K. DAVIDSON

Please, stop introducing more religious groups in the Pacific. The Pacific is no longer a mission field. . . .

We urge churches and national councils of churches in New Zealand, Australia, Europe and North America to have open discussions with the leaders of different religious movements who are responsible for sending and supporting these movements to divert their energies, money and time in order to share the gospel of love, unity and justice in your countries first so that you and they will understand more of the causes of our threatening forces in order to be struggling with us in our efforts of unity and solidarity.[1]

Leslie Boseto, a leader of the United Church of Papua New Guinea and the Solomon Islands, made this plea at a plenary session on the Pacific at the sixth Assembly of the World Council of Churches meeting in Vancouver in 1983.[2]

1. Leslie Boseto, "The Gift of Community," *International Review of Mission* 72.288 (1983): 582-83.

2. Leslie Boseto served two terms as the bishop of the Solomon Islands Region of the United Church of Papua New Guinea and the Solomon Islands and was also its moderator or national leader for eight years. The United Church brought together the churches that resulted from the work of the London Missionary Society (LMS), which commenced in Papua in 1871, and the Australasian Methodist Overseas Missions, which started work in

Underlying Boseto's appeal was his concern about what Charles Forman described as the challenges facing "a small number of long-established Christian denominations," which have until recently "made up the Christianity of Oceania," from "new missions, mostly of Pentecostal and conservative evangelical groups."[3] Manfred Ernst, in his 1994 study of "rapidly growing religious groups in the Pacific," concluded that "if the trend of change in religious affiliation over the last 30 years continues, about one third of the generation after next will worship in places other than those of today."[4] Boseto was concerned primarily with the challenges which these new missionary groups were bringing to the relationships between individuals and their communities and the nature of Pacific societies. Whether this new evangelism in the Pacific represents a negative or positive force depends very much on the perspective taken by those influenced by these challenges and the changes they bring.

Globalization and the Pacific

Anthony Giddens, in his 1999 Reith Lectures, *Runaway World,* contrasts the skeptics, who want to argue that globalization is not new but is an extension of nineteenth-century economic developments, with the radicals, who hold

> that not only is globalisation very real, but that its consequences can be felt everywhere. The global market-place, they say, is much more developed than even in the 1960s and 1970s and is indifferent to national borders. Nations have lost most of the sovereignty they once had, and politicians have lost most of their capability to influence events. . . . The era of the nation-state is over.[5]

Giddens, however, points out that much of this talk about globalization has been focused "solely in economic terms." In his view, "this is a mistake.

the New Guinea Islands area in 1875, the Papuan Islands in 1891, the Solomon Islands in 1902, and the Southern Highlands in 1950.

3. C. W. Forman, "Some Next Steps in the Study of Pacific Island Christianity," in John Barker, ed., *Christianity in Oceania: Ethnographic Perspective* (Lanham, Md., 1990), p. 29.

4. Manfred Ernst, *Winds of Change: Rapidly Growing Religious Groups in the Pacific* (Suva, 1994), p. 4.

5. Anthony Giddens, *Runaway World: How Globalisation Is Reshaping Our Lives,* based on the 1999 BBC Reith Lectures (London, 1999), p. 8.

Globalisation is political, technological and cultural as well as economic."[6] While some would want to include religion under the category of culture, it would seem that in discussing the impact of globalization we should take into account the religious dimension in its own right.

This religious dimension is very important to any understanding of the impact of globalization on the peoples of the Pacific. For most Pacific peoples Christianity is the religion which helps define their world, their culture, and their identity. Christianity is, for example, an integral part of *fa'a Samoa*, the world of the Samoans. A Samoan commentator writes about the way in which "the church is seen as the vehicle which sanctifies the Samoan culture. To the Samoan involved in everyday living, a basic premise is that all things come from God."[7]

In examining the concepts of globalization, conversion, and evangelicalism in the Pacific, it is important to place current trends within a broader historical context. There is a real sense, taking the more skeptical view of globalization, that what happened in the late twentieth century in the Pacific is an extension of what has gone before. At the same time the impact of mass communication and technology, the global economy, the undermining of traditional societies, and the challenges to institutional Christianity represent the radical edge of globalization that is threatening what Ratu Sir Kamisese Mara from Fiji defined at the United Nations in 1970 as "The Pacific Way," or Albert Wendt translated as *fa'a Pasifika*.[8] The tension between *fa'a Samoa*, the local, and *fa'a Pasifika*, the regional, now contends with the global way.

Exploring the Pacific

Pacific Islanders, particularly the Polynesian voyagers, played a significant role in expanding their own world through their discovery and settlement of the Pacific Islands. The noted Maori anthropologist, Te Rangi Hiroa (Sir Peter Buck), gave this a heroic quality through the title of his book, *Vikings of the Sunrise*.[9] The European discovery and mapping of the Pacific, starting from the mid-sixteenth-century voyage of Mendana, took over three centuries. The impositions of other worlds on the Pacific are still seen in names like New

6. Giddens, *Runaway World*, p. 10.

7. Feleti E. Ngan-Woo, *Faa Samoa: The World of Samoans* (Auckland, 1985), p. 31.

8. Ron Crocombe, *The Pacific Way: An Emerging Identity* (Suva, 1976), p. 1. See also Sione Tupouniua, Ron Crocombe, and Claire Slatter, *The Pacific Way: Social Issues in National Development* (Suva, 1975), and Ron Crocombe, *The South Pacific* (Suva, 2001).

9. Peter Buck, *Vikings of the Sunrise* (Christchurch, 1964; first U.S. ed., 1938).

Caledonia, New Britain, New Zealand, and the Cook Islands. There has been some recovery of a Pacific identity — for example, in what was the New Hebrides, now Vanuatu; the Gilbert Islands, now Kiribati; the Ellice Islands, now Tuvalu. Terms such as Polynesia, Melanesia, Micronesia, and Pacific Islanders have been used as defining categories by outsiders to try to understand something of the diversity of the peoples of the Pacific, but they do not necessarily represent the way in which the people see themselves. The Pacific Ocean covers approximately one-third of the surface of the earth, contains hundreds of islands from small coral atolls to large land areas like New Guinea. The peoples of the Pacific speak hundreds of different languages, each one representing distinctive cultural differences.

Naming and putting places on the map were important European ways of creating identity and gaining control over other people's space. This is seen in the use of "Pacific Rim." This term describes the Americas on one side and Asia on the other, enclosing what is sometimes referred to in geo-political speak as the "Pacific basin."[10] The preoccupation with the edge, rather than with the center, tends to define out of existence what the Australian novelist, Patrick White, described as those "gritty little lumps with the heads of tousled palms set in a leaden sea."[11]

People in the Pacific, since the process of European exploration, have had to contend with definitions imposed from outside. Epeli Hau'ofa, a Tongan sociologist, has challenged what he sees as the "derogatory and belittling views of indigenous culture." The son of a Tongan missionary to Papua, Hau'ofa points to "the wholesale condemnation by Christian missionaries of Oceanic cultures" and the way in which "in a number of Pacific societies people still divide their history into two parts: the era of darkness associated with savagery and barbarism; and the era of light and civilisation, ushered in by Christianity."[12] As a person from within the Pacific, Hau'ofa wants to reclaim the Pacific for the people of what he prefers to call Oceania. Instead of viewing the Pacific as "islands in a far sea" he describes Oceania as "a sea of islands," adopting "a more holistic perspective in which things are seen in the totality of their relationships."[13] The sea, in this view, rather than becoming a boundary becomes an extension of the land, part of the environment which sustains and nurtures life.

10. M. Hutchinson and O. Kalu, eds., *A Global Faith: Essays on Evangelicalism and Globalization* (Sydney, 1998), p. 261.

11. Quoted by Sir Paul Reeves, "Building a Global Perspective," *Anglican Observer at the UN* 1.3 (April 1994): 1.

12. Epeli Hau'ofa, "Our Sea of Islands," in *A New Oceania: Rediscovering Our Sea of Islands* (Suva, 1993), p. 3.

13. Hau'ofa, "Our Sea of Islands," p. 7.

Part of the problem with the term "globalization" is that it can almost mean what people want it to mean. Giddens refers to the way in which "most people think of globalisation as simply 'pulling away' power or influence from local communities and nations into the global arena."[14] That is something Pacific people have experienced as micro-states where extraction of timber, fish, copra, sugar, minerals, and other primary products has subjected them to the economic vulnerability of world market forces and the burden of debts arising from attempts at Western-style development. The impact of metropolitan defense strategies that involved nuclear testing by America, Britain, and most recently France in the Pacific environment gave rise to the antinuclear movement. A Pacific perspective of this is summed up in the poster by Francie Moss from Fiji, which showed parents with a child standing on a globe surmounted by a cross with three palm trees in front of the world. The man is holding a banner: "Nuclear Wastes Destroying Our Future." The wording on the poster reads, "'In the beginning God created the heavens and the earth' — In the end?"[15]

Environmental and ecological issues have a direct bearing on the future of the Pacific and its sea of islands. Global warming, which threatens as a destructive expression of globalization, with the melting of the ice caps and the rise in sea levels, challenges the very existence of low-lying coral atolls like Kiribati, Tuvalu, Tokelau, and Ontong Java. The sea that gives life could also take it away. The message of salvation, in this situation, has material, political, environmental, and global dimensions. For some in the Pacific it could well be an eschatological situation. As with the antinuclear message there is a question as to whether the gospel has good news for people for whom the land on which they live, from which they gain their very being, is faced with the prospect of being swallowed up by the sea.

Evangelizing the Pacific

The arrival of Christian missionaries in the Pacific at the end of the eighteenth century was a form of evangelistic globalization. The mandate given by the Great Commission, "To go therefore to all peoples," was taken up by the British Protestant missionary movement in the 1790s. The accomplishments of European explorers, notably for the Pacific, James Cook, were a catalyst in stimulating evangelicals to look beyond their own shores. The Lon-

14. Giddens, *Runaway World,* p. 13.
15. Sulian Siwatibau and B. David Williams, *A Call to a New Exodus: An Anti-Nuclear Primer for Pacific People* (Suva, 1982), p. 90.

don Missionary Society (LMS) within two years of its founding in 1795 had stationed missionaries in Tonga, Tahiti, and the Marquesas. Theology and geography undergirded Christian expansion although the lack of an adequate missiology often meant that the early missionaries learned by their mistakes.

It is said of John Wesley that he made England his parish, while his spiritual descendants and those of the eighteenth-century evangelical revivals through the missionary movement made the world their parish. John Williams, who combined evangelism and exploration in a unique way, which had profound implications for the expansion of Christianity in the Pacific, wrote in 1823 to the Directors of the LMS while arguing for a sailing vessel: "I cannot content myself within the narrow limits of a Single reef . . . to these isolated Islands a Ship must carry you."[16] Williams expanded the missionary world from his base at Raiatea, sailing westward to the Austral Islands, the Cook Islands, Samoa, and to the New Hebrides, where he was killed in 1839.

Through his use of "native agency" or Pacific Islander missionaries, Williams made an important contribution to the rapid spread and acceptance of Christianity within Polynesia with indigenous people using their related languages and the influence of Christianity on their own lives and people to effect changes in their neighboring islands. The hierarchical and chiefly nature of these societies resulted in "the doctrine of *cuius regio, eius religio* (as the King, so the religion)" having "universal, not just European application,"[17] with chiefs often having a significant influence on their followers. Alan Tippett has demonstrated the significance of the "people movements in Southern Polynesia" and the impact of power encounters in which the old gods were tested by the new God proclaimed by evangelical missionaries and their converts.[18] James Belich, drawing on the complex debate over the rapid conversion of Maori in New Zealand to Christianity in the 1830s through the agency of the Anglican Church Missionary Society and the Wesleyan Methodist Missionary Society, concluded that "the Maori religious conversion" is "better defined as the Maori incorporation of Christianity."[19]

16. John Williams to Directors of LMS, Raiatea, September 30, 1823, in John Davies, *The History of the Tahitian Mission, 1799-1830*, ed. C. W. Newbury (Cambridge, 1961), p. 342. See John Williams, *A Narrative of Missionary Enterprises in the South Sea Islands* (London, 1839); John Gutch, *Beyond the Reefs: The Life of John Williams, Missionary* (London, 1974).

17. K. R. Howe, *Where the Waves Fall: A New South Seas Islands History from First Settlement to Colonial Rule* (Sydney, 1984), p. 145.

18. Alan Tippett, *People Movements in Southern Polynesia: A Study in Church Growth* (Chicago, 1971).

19. James Belich, *Making Peoples: A History of New Zealanders from Polynesian Settlement to the End of the Nineteenth Century* (Auckland, 1996), p. 168.

This process of the incorporation of Christianity within the localized cultures of the Pacific resulted in the evangelical gospel, which proclaimed the need for individual salvation and repentance, often being taken over by people who gained their identity through their membership in what Maori described as the *whanau* (family), *hapu* (clan), and *iwi* (tribe). Evangelization, in terms of the general acceptance of Christianity by the people of the eastern and central Pacific, the area known as Polynesia, was largely completed by the end of the nineteenth century. The exact nature of this Christianity is open to debate for in a real sense the missionaries had to introduce their evangelical worldview in order to save Pacific people from the consequences of it. Ron and Marjorie Crocombe, in identifying the main LMS contribution to Rarotongan culture, concluded that it brought

> a religion which replaced a local, inward-looking one with a universal faith, much better adapted to their needs once they were in contact with a wider world. Some Christian teachings and practices introduced by the LMS remain key elements of Rarotongan culture and seem likely to endure despite modification.[20]

Pacific Christianity was influenced by the receptive cultures as much as it was by the missionaries who brought it. While there are clear examples of evangelical conversions along the lines expected by the missionaries, the influence of the collective identity and chiefly the leadership were dominant contributing factors in the emergence of a semi-Christendom model of Christianity in many island communities. There were exceptions, notably in New Zealand, where the swamping influence of European settlement after 1840 resulted in the emergence of new indigenous religious movements that combined something of the traditional rituals and beliefs with the new Christian and other influences. Maori did not necessarily reject Christianity, but many of them rejected missionary Christianity. The evangelical missionaries had little understanding of these movements and treated them as heterodox and aberrant and in the process contributed to their continuance.[21]

The evangelization of Melanesia was built on the successes in Polynesia, particularly with the use of Pacific Islander missionaries.[22] The LMS and

20. Ron and Marjorie Crocombe, "The London Missionary Society and Culture: Impacts on and from Rarotonga," *South Pacific Journal of Mission Studies* (August 1996): 10.

21. See, for example, Bronwyn Elsmore, *Like Them That Dream: The Maori and the Old Testament* (Auckland, 1985); and, *Mana from Heaven: A Century of Maori Prophets in New Zealand* (Auckland, 1989).

22. Doug Munro and Andrew Thornley, eds., *The Covenant Makers: Islander Mis-*

Methodists expanded westward from Polynesia and worked alongside Presbyterians in the New Hebrides (Vanuatu) and Lutherans in New Guinea. The Anglican Melanesian Mission in the New Hebrides and the Solomon Islands was not directly evangelical in its approach, emphasizing the redemption of the whole person and adopting a more positive attitude toward Melanesian culture than did its evangelical counterparts.[23] Arising out of the economic exploitation of Melanesian laborers in the sugar plantations of Queensland was the unique Queensland Kanaka Mission which became the South Sea Evangelical Mission (SSEM). Founded by Florence Young, a Brethren, the SSEM moved back to the Solomon Islands with returning laborers and established itself at the extreme edge of iconoclastic evangelicalism, condemning indigenous cultures and beliefs but at the same time promoting indigenous leadership.

The conversion of Melanesia presented new problems, notably much greater diversity than Polynesia with some 1,200 different languages and the consequent fragmentation of the society. The difficulty of making contact, of being understood, and of translating the Bible presented enormous challenges. Sociological patterns also differed, with many groups placing an emphasis on "big men" who gained their status through their own efforts, alongside some chiefly societies more like their Polynesian counterparts based on inheritance. Payback, based on revenge and retribution, had profound implications for missionary work as the Anglican Bishop, John Coleridge Patteson, found out to his cost. His death in 1871 was most likely the result of the people of Nukapu killing him in lieu of five young men taken from their island by labor traffickers. He was the wrong man, in the wrong place, at the wrong time.[24]

Missionaries in Melanesia were confronted with the principle of reciprocity so that regular attendance at church could be followed by the people demanding something back in return. The Melanesian approach to religion was pragmatic: "'Does it work? Is it effective? Will it bring abundant life?' The question, 'Is it true?' which may be very important to a Western Christian," as Darrell Whiteman notes, "is a cognitive entity separate from experience and thus not an important element in Melanesian religions."[25] This materialistic

sionaries in the Pacific (Suva, 1996). For further references see the bibliographies, pp. 12-16 and pp. 38-40.

23. David Hilliard, *God's Gentlemen: A History of the Melanesian Mission, 1849-1942* (St. Lucia, 1978).

24. G. W. Trompf, *Payback: The Logic of Retribution in Melanesian Religions* (Cambridge, 1994).

25. Darrell Whiteman, "Melanesian Religions: An Overview," in Ennio Mantovani, ed., *An Introduction to Melanesian Religions*, Point, vol. 6 (Goroka, 1984), p. 97.

approach to salvation found expression in the so-called "cargo cults" which attempted to gain material wealth by religious means using a combination of traditional and Christian rituals and beliefs.

The context in which missionaries undertook their work in Melanesia was often hostile, with personal safety under threat and with tropical diseases, notably malaria, resulting in illness and the death of many. Given the fragmentation of Melanesian society, extensive people movements were not possible on the scale experienced in Polynesia. The acceptance of Christianity, however, was still largely a community response. Ewan Stilwell in writing about conversion in Melanesia notes that "if the Westerner can say 'I think therefore I am,' or even more so today, 'I experience therefore I am,' the Melanesian would say, 'I have brothers therefore I am.' The interests of the community, the clan, are paramount."[26] In Melanesia the acceptance of Christianity was often associated with power encounters, the acquisition of the superior mana and status of the missionaries' God, the ending of fear and the bringing of peace. Christian Keysser, a Lutheran missionary, was particularly successful because of his recognition of the community nature of Melanesian societies. He took seriously the grafting of the Christian gospel into the lives of both individuals and their villages.[27] Whiteman similarly pointed to the way in which the Church of Melanesia, which came from the work of the Melanesian Mission, placed its "religious emphasis . . . on corporate groups such as the family and village community," noting that "in traditional Melanesian society, religion is a community activity and not just an individual experience." He contrasted this with the South Seas Evangelical Church, which came from the SSEM, and the way in which their emphasis on "individual conversion, with converts making cognitive decision, choosing Christ as their 'Personal savior' . . . could lead to atomization of the church with people desiring to go their own individual ways."[28]

Garry Trompf in evaluating the missionary impact in the Pacific concluded that,

> quite apart from one's ideological proclivities . . . the influence of Christianity on the local peoples of the southwest Pacific has been enormous. . . . Its widespread acceptance and the degree of its incorporation into local cultures are truly remarkable. The 1980 census of Papua New

26. Ewan Stilwell, "Towards a Melanesian Theology of Conversion," *Melanesian Journal of Theology* 9.1 (April 1993): 32.

27. Christian Keysser, *A People Reborn* (Pasadena, 1980).

28. Darrell Whiteman, *Melanesians and Missionaries: An Ethnohistorical Study of Social and Religious Change in the Southwest Pacific* (Pasadena, 1983), p. 335.

Guinea, for instance, showed that 96 percent of the country's inhabitants associated themselves with some Christian denomination or mission. Sheer nominalism taken into account, this betokens an extraordinary social transformation in a country where sizeable inland populations were barely touched by the outside world until after the Second World War.[29]

Evangelicals and Ecumenism

The LMS was born out of a form of ecumenical evangelicalism with its fundamental principle, agreed upon in 1796, declaring that it was their design "not to send Presbyterianism, Independency, Episcopacy, or any other form of Church order and Government . . . but the Glorious Gospel of the Blessed God to the Heathen."[30] Evangelicals practiced comity (with some exceptions such as in Samoa, where Methodists and LMS were caught up in rivalry, in the Pacific) throughout the nineteenth century and the first half of the twentieth century. The major Christian tension in the Pacific was between Catholics and Protestants. This rivalry was often intensified by the largely French influences on Catholic missions, while British influences were dominant in the Protestant missions. In most areas Protestants preceded Catholics and the Bible came before the flag. Missionaries were to form one side of the colonial triangle with the colonial powers and the economic interests represented by traders and planters the other two sides. The local people were often caught in the middle among these contending forces. The impact of colonialism on the Pacific was a form of globalization that had its sequel in the military impact experienced with sometimes devastating results in the Second World War when the western and central Pacific became the battleground of external powers.

The moves toward autonomy and independence in the Protestant mission churches in the Pacific after the Second World War usually anticipated nationhood and were achieved without great struggles.[31] Local churches often

29. Garry Trompf, "Geographical, Historical, and Intellectual Perspectives," in G. W. Trompf, ed., *The Gospel Is Not Western: Black Theologies from the Southwest Pacific* (Maryknoll, N.Y., 1987), p. 6.

30. John Garrett, *To Live Among the Stars: Christian Origins in Oceania* (Geneva and Suva, 1992), p. 10.

31. C. W. Forman, *The Island Churches of the South Pacific: Emergence in the Twentieth Century* (Maryknoll, N.Y., 1982), pp. 164-81; John Garrett, *Where Nets Were Cast: Christianity in Oceania Since World War II* (Suva and Geneva, 1997).

retained links with the missionary organizations which gave them birth, thereby retaining local and global dimensions. In the twentieth century, comity developed into ecumenism as is seen in the birth of the Pacific Conference of Churches in 1961, the Melanesian Council of Churches in 1964, and local councils such as the Solomon Islands Christian Association. Cooperation in theological education found expression in the establishment of Pacific Theological College in Suva in 1966 and the South Pacific, and the Melanesian Associations of Theological Schools in 1969.[32]

Given the concern of Leslie Boseto, with which this chapter began, there is a question as to how far the evangelical heritage remains part of the core identity of the churches which resulted from the missionary work of the Methodists, the LMS, and the Presbyterians, and how far it has been submerged within the identity of the churches which emerged from this work. Drawing on a conversation with Boseto in 1992, Ernst refers to the way in which "the United Church sees the New Religious Groups and especially the kind of theology they bring in as a real challenge to *ecumenism* and the Historic Mainline Churches."[33] The mainline churches have over time become the old-line churches. Whereas they represented challenge and change when they first arrived as missionary organizations in the Pacific, they have become identified with the voice of tradition through the way in which the gospel has been inculturated and institutionalized in Pacific societies. That is seen particularly in the semi-chiefly status given to ministers in some parts of the Pacific and the tension between a chief-king, a servant-priest, and a liberating-prophetic ministry.[34] The members of traditional churches are generous in their hospitality and the support they give to the church. The traditional churches play a significant role in giving stability to society through the sanctions that they give to social structures and cultural identity. Whether gospel and culture have become so identified that one cannot do without the other if they are to survive in their present form represents part of the challenge of globalization.

32. C. W. Forman, *The Voices of Many Waters: The Story of the Life and Ministry of the Pacific Conference of Churches in the Last 25 Years* (Fiji, 1986); Emiliana Afeaki, Ron Crocombe, and John McClaren, eds., *Religious Cooperation in the Pacific Islands* (Suva, 1983).

33. Ernst, *Winds of Change*, p. 121.

34. C. W. Forman, "The South Pacific Style in the Christian Ministry," *Missiology* 2 (1974): 421-35.

Conversion and Globalization in the Pacific

The forces of globalization, whether they are European exploration, evangelization, ecumenism, economic exploitation, or militarization, have had a profound impact on Pacific peoples. In identifying the radical dimensions of contemporary globalization, Giddens indicated how "in Western countries, not only public institutions but also everyday life are becoming opened up from the hold of tradition," while "other societies across the world that remained more traditional are becoming detraditionalised." By this he does not mean "that tradition disappears" but that "less and less . . . is it tradition lived in the traditional way."[35] In looking at the impact of the past upon the present, Giddens argued that "every context of detraditionalisation offers the possibility of greater freedom of action than existed before. . . . In tradition, the past structures the present through shared collective beliefs and sentiments."[36] The challenges of globalization, for what have become the traditional churches in the Pacific, have to do with their continuing identity, their relevance to the present and the future.

Giddens pointed out that "globalisation not only pulls upward, but also pushes downwards, creating new pressures for local autonomy." This is seen in "the revival of local cultural identities."[37] Tradition can be both reinforced by globalization and undermined. Joseph Bush described these tensions in Fiji where half the population are indigenous Fijians (with nearly 75 percent of them being Methodists) while 42 percent are "descendants of indentured labourers brought to Fiji [from India] by the British at the turn of the century," with the majority of them being Hindu.[38] He outlines the struggles within the Methodist Church over the two coups which took place in Fiji in 1987, the process of constitutional revision, and whether the Church should support a multicultural democratic country or one in which the indigenous Fijian and the Methodist Church are given privileges. Bush points to Fullerton's description of Fijian Methodism as a "sociological form of 'folk church,' intimately wed to the culture of the people." For Bush, the "historic intimacy between Christianity and the culture of indigenous Fijians has impelled the resurgence of a desire for Fijian Christendom despite secularising trends and the pluralistic character of the larger Fijian society."[39]

35. Giddens, *Runaway World*, p. 43.
36. Giddens, *Runaway World*, p. 47.
37. Giddens, *Runaway World*, p. 13.
38. Jospeh E. Bush, "Claiming a Christian State Where None Exists: Church and State in the Republic of Fiji," *Pacifica* 12 (February 1999): 55.
39. Bush, "Claiming a Christian State," p. 56.

Traditional social structures and loyalties that have been sanctioned and sanctified by the Church in the Pacific are coming under pressure from within and without. Ninety-five percent of television programs in Fiji, for example, have "overseas content and are beamed into Fiji homes from Western countries." It is claimed that Fijian chiefs, who have considerable status, "may not admit it openly but they cannot ignore the fact that their influence is on the wane. Its decline cannot be arrested, as Western culture has made deep inroads, changing the indigenous lifestyle."[40] The challenge facing the Methodist Church in Fiji is how to hold on to its understanding of *vanua,* land, from which Fijians gain their identity and nationalism, with the reality of living as part of a multicultural population coming under increasing global and secularizing forces. Within this milieu the rise of new religious movements presents new challenges.

New Religious Movements

Amnesty International reported in 1998 that in Samoa "five men were hog-tied and their home destroyed for conducting a non-Methodist service in their village." In defending what happened, "Methodist chiefs involved in the incident have said they were following customs which permit only Methodist worship in their village."[41] The close relationship between Christian and Samoan identity, the *fa'a Samoa* in this case, is reproduced throughout the Pacific. The monopoly, however, of the churches arising from the work of the LMS and Methodist, Presbyterian, Anglican, and Catholic missions has been challenged since the Second World War. In the Solomon Islands, for example, Ernst identifies eighteen religious groups as active. Of these, twelve had their origins in the Solomons after the Second World War, and nine of them emerged in the 1970s and 1980s.[42] While these groups are still relatively small, Ernst warns "that the process of massive change in religious affiliation has just started and in the years to come will reach the level seen in other parts of the region."[43] He has calculated, for example, that between 1966 and 1992 new religious groups grew in Tonga from 9.7 percent of the population to 29.5 percent, in Samoa from 8.9 percent to 18.6 percent, and in Fiji from 2.9 percent to

40. Rajendra Prasad, "Indians Get Date with Destiny," *New Zealand Herald,* May 18, 1999, A11.

41. "Samoans Hog-tied for non-Methodist Worship," *New Zealand Herald,* November 5, 1998, p. B3.

42. Ernst, *Winds of Change,* p. 125.

43. Ernst, *Winds of Change,* p. 126.

11.6 percent.[44] Tonga's Crown Prince Tupouto'a commented that "the kingdom's economy was getting worse and the only thing the country never ceases to produce was a surplus of religion," and he equated the many churches with "la-la land."[45]

Teeruro Ieuti, writing about the Kiribati Protestant Church (KPC), which originated from the work of the LMS, points to the way it "has experienced a considerable erosion of membership," with many of its members joining the Seventh Day Adventist Church, the Baha'i World Faith, the Church of Jesus Christ of Latter-day Saints, and Pentecostal groups such as the Church of God and Assemblies of God.[46] He identified four reasons why people have left the KPC.

1. *Finance.* New churches attracted considerable financial resources from overseas to build new institutions such as schools, while the KPC, which has been independent since 1968, has had to support itself from local people with limited incomes.

2. *Education.* The KPC has found it difficult to compete with churches which have large resources and provide students with opportunities to go overseas to undertake further study, giving them thereby a passport beyond the cash economy.

3. *Belief and Dogma.* Distinct teachings and a claim to having a unique and exclusive truth have attracted people from the KPC, which has not been as clear-cut in its beliefs and in its teaching.

4. *Dissatisfaction.* The dominance of the ministers in the KPC, its largely nonparticipatory style of worship, and the weakness of its pastoral ministry are advanced as reasons for dissatisfaction, which has led some to seek spiritual, psychological, and social identity in a new group.

These factors are found elsewhere in the Pacific where the traditional churches have seen Christian affiliation as an expression of cultural identity. Other factors can be added:

5. *Sociological changes.* The impact of urbanization and values external to the traditional society and the emergence of a new middle class and educated elite working for the government, in business, and in education have brought new levels of fragmentation as people lose touch with what previously gave them their identity. The sanctions of the village, the elders, and the Church no longer carry the weight they once did. A new identity is shaped for people

---

44. Ernst, *Winds of Change*, p. 5.

45. *New Zealand Herald*, June 9, 1999.

46. Teeruro Ieuti, "The Kiribati Protestant Church and the New Religious Movements 1860-1985," in C. W. Forman, ed., *Island Churches: Challenge and Change* (Suva, 1992), p. 72.

belonging to the new groups that both create new values and help people make sense of them.

6. *Personal experience.* The impact of Western styles of education, which often removes children from their traditional environment and emphasizes individual attainment, along with the influence of Western values through such things as television, undermines the sense of collective identity which is at the heart of traditional society and which the traditional churches have reinforced. Pentecostal and evangelical churches with their emphasis on personal experience and the work of the Holy Spirit in the life of the individual are particularly attractive to adolescents and young adults who are separated from their traditional influences. When people find "new life" through personal experience and then go back to their village and try to share it with others, the extreme reaction indicated in the Samoan example above represents the clash between traditional and conservative community values and new and radical individual experience.

7. *Emotional experience.* Influenced by the "pop culture" transmitted electronically into even remote villages, younger people are attracted to worship that is lively and contemporary in contrast to what seems boring in the traditional churches. Preaching which is authoritative and based on biblical certainty and music that is appealing result in people accepting new ways of being Christian that contrast with the traditional church.

8. *Spiritual power.* The emphasis on "signs and wonders," "the gifts of the Spirit," "the prosperity gospel," and spiritual and physical healing have considerable appeal in the Pacific. The pragmatic, pietistic, and emotional dimensions attract more interest than do the reflective, liberationist, and mystical approaches to religion.

In accounting for the appeal of new religious groups in the Pacific Islands, Ernst concluded that they seem to meet

> the very fundamental needs of individuals in rapidly changing societies. The New Religious Groups seem to live by what they believe with powerful conviction, devotion and commitment. The New Religious Groups also meet the people where they are, warmly, personally and directly. They pull the individual, at least on the surface, out of anonymity, promote participation, spontaneity and responsibility. Conversion is usually celebrated by rebaptism. . . . the respective NRGs really do appear to the convert as the embodiment of the Good News in a chaotic world.[47]

47. Ernst, *Winds of Change*, p. 248.

This individualism is part of the new expression of Christianity through-out the Pacific as people stand, sometimes in an uneasy relationship, with their traditional culture and identity. But this individualism finds a new expression of collectivity through membership in the new tribe that the new religious group comes to represent. Ernst emphasizes that these new religious groups are not a homogenous group throughout the Pacific but that they share overlapping ideological and theological characteristics. These include "a conformist passivity and a turning away from worldly matters" and a "conservative outlook on family issues and the opposition to labour unions, minimum wages and feminism."[48] This contrasts with the traditional churches which at the local, national, and regional levels both support and critique governments.

Boseto, in the quotation with which this chapter began, was concerned with the sending and supporting of new religious movements to the Pacific from outside the region. The origins of the new religious groups, however, are complex, and an understanding of globalization indicates that it is impossible to put up walls to prevent new movements from originating in the Pacific. While external sources of funding and missionary initiative lie behind some groups, others have originated with Pacific Islanders returning to their country as missionaries for these new religious groups, while others have arisen within Pacific communities as breakaway groups from traditional churches. There is a sense in which the new religious groups are the result of late-twentieth-century people movements in which indigenous initiative and leadership are sometimes present. Whereas the people movements of the nineteenth century were based on tribal affiliation, the current movements are often the result of new sociological factors. Whereas Islanders in the nineteenth century went from their homeland to another country and became missionaries, Islanders today often become evangelists among their own people. The global dimensions, however, are present in the way in which "what most of them have in common is their North American origins and the sharing (to different degrees) of views held by what is known as the New Christian Right."[49] Kevin Barr, writing about Fiji, refers to "the Americanization of Christianity" with the "coca-colaization of the world" being matched by the export from the United States of "new religions and religious groups . . . to Fiji and the Pacific."[50]

48. Ernst, *Winds of Change*, p. 272.
49. Ernst, *Winds of Change*, p. 271.
50. K. J. Barr, *Blessed Are the ~~Poor~~ Rich . . . Praise the Lord . . . An Examination of New Religious Groups in Fiji Today* (Suva, 1998), p. 4.

In his assessment of the impact of these groups on Pacific societies, Ernst concluded that "the clearest and most evident consequence . . . can be seen in that more and more families and villages are divided by different beliefs, which in general accelerates the deterioration of traditional lifestyles which are characterized by living, producing and sharing together."[51] In the nineteenth century, missionaries, particularly those from the evangelical spectrum, were often accused of destroying aspects of Pacific cultural identity and not distinguishing essentials from nonessentials in bringing the gospel to bear on people's way of being. It is ironic that new religious groups are now being accused of doing the same thing to the societies of which the traditional churches, which originated from this so-called destructive evangelization, are a part.

Emigration and Conversion

Emigration of Pacific Islanders to New Zealand, Australia, and the United States can be seen as part of the process of globalization that has a double dynamic affecting the place of origin and the place of residence. Remittances from migrant Pacific Islanders have been a significant source of overseas funds in the small Pacific economies relating the Pacific Rim to the center. Pacific Island churches have played an important part in helping the new migrants "sing the Lord's song in a strange land." The Church has been the place where language and culture have been valued in a way that the dominant culture of the host country has not allowed. As well as being a spiritual home away from home, the Church has become a social and cultural center, providing advice on housing, employment, and welfare. The tension between being from the old and becoming part of the new is seen in the way in which some of the Pacific Island churches in New Zealand, for example, are extensions of the churches of their home islands. In other cases they have joined the New Zealand denomination linked to their own, while in yet other cases they have established independent churches.[52]

A new challenge is emerging as the New Zealand–born children of the Pacific Islander migrants grow up "caught between cultures" and find that their loyalty to the faith of their fathers and mothers is under pressure.[53] Samoans

51. Ernst, *Winds of Change*, p. 274.

52. Betty K. Duncan, "Christianity: Pacific Island Traditions," in Peter Donovan, ed., *Religions of New Zealanders* (Palmerston North, 1990).

53. Jemaima Tiatia, *Caught Between Cultures: A New Zealand–Born Pacific Island Perspective* (Auckland, 1998).

who came to New Zealand, for example, "have moved from an open house with no walls to a private, nuclear and insular culture."[54] While the Pacific Island churches remain strong and vibrant, there are signs that the forces which have been identified as operating in the islands are also at work in New Zealand. The impact of education in English, the loss or diminution in the use of island languages, the pervasive influence of television and mass media, the attraction of sport, the dispersal of those who speak the same language throughout the community, the undermining of the sacredness of Sunday, unemployment, and social problems are some of the factors affecting the cohesiveness of migrant communities. There are tensions between traditional obligations such as contributing financial support to the Church and sending money home to relatives and newer obligations such as paying the mortgage and supporting the family.

Some New Zealand–born Pacific Islanders opt out of traditional churches and are attracted to Pentecostal groups with their "contemporary music, informality, and lack of liturgy or ritual." Feiloaiga Taule'ale'ausumai, a New Zealand–born Samoan woman and Presbyterian minister, comments:

> Not only does the Pentecostal/Charismatic Church affirm their individuality, it also assimilates their Samoanness into the melting pot of a cultureless, look-and-act-alike community of faith. The *fa'a Samoa* and the diverse relationships within it become discarded as a burden to one's individual and spiritual growth. In this way the individual is freed to make life decisions and choices for him- or herself, at the same time that they are alienated from their biological ties and responsibilities as well as their relationships with parents and extended family.[55]

The status and role of women in both the Church and traditional society are coming under pressure from both within and without the Pacific. The acceptance, for example, of ordained Pacific Island women in the New Zealand Presbyterian and Methodist ministry has challenged the traditional churches in the Pacific. Some churches are making tentative beginnings in this area while others are defending the status quo. As churches struggle with these changes, new religious groups ironically often reinforce the traditional attitudes toward the role of women in religious leadership.[56]

54. Feiloaiga Taule'ale'ausumai, "Pastoral Care: A Samoan Perspective," in P. Culbertson, ed., *Counselling Issues & South Pacific Communities* (Auckland, 1997), p. 226.

55. Taule'ale'ausumai, "Pastoral Care," p. 231.

56. C. W. Forman, "'Sing to the Lord a New Song': Women in the Churches of Occania," in Denise O'Brien and S. W. Tiffnay, eds., *Rethinking Women's Roles: Perspectives*

Conclusion

In responding to Ernst's study of new religious groups, Leslie Boseto drew attention to the poem by the Samoan, Fepai Kolia:

Lost Reality[57]

My sua[58] was presented.
It was peculiar.
One percent native culture.
Ninety nine percent alterations.
A tin of cola replaces a coconut.
A roll of cotton silk replaces tapa[59] cloth.
A plastic tray replaces a customary tray.
A tin of beef replaces a Samoan chicken.
A packet of biscuits replaces a bundle of taro.[60]
A case of herrings replaces a pig.
An ie laufala[61] replaces a fine mat.
Sua presentation
A symbol only
A mingle of cultures
A mess of ideologies
A lost reality.

For Boseto, "the reality is that our Pacific community is people based; we are a family and tribal community. . . . We are a real grass-roots-community of brothers and sisters. . . . We need an incarnate gospel which lives amongst us, not just a proclaimed gospel."[62] The issues of unity and solidarity have assumed a new significance for Boseto, whose ecumenical commitment was

---

from the Pacific (Berkeley, 1984). For the reflections of a number of Pacific women on theology and ministry see *Pacific Journal of Theology* 2.3 (1990): 33-55; 2.7 (1992): 3-48, 61-68, 74-75.

57. Leslie Boseto, "'Towards a Pacific Theology of Reality': A Grassroots Response to *Winds of Change*," *Pacific Journal of Theology* 2.12 (1994): 52.

58. "A *sua* is a donation given in recognition of an event which can be a visit, marriage or birth, etc." (Boseto, "'Towards a Pacific Theology of Reality,'" p. 52).

59. *Tapa* is a traditional cloth made from bark.

60. *Taro* is a root crop used as a staple in many parts of the Pacific.

61. A *ie laufala* is a mat of lesser quality than a fine mat (Boseto, "'Towards a Pacific Theology of Reality,'" p. 52).

62. Boseto, "'Towards a Pacific Theology of Reality,'" pp. 57-58.

recognized in his election as a president of the World Council of Churches. In retirement Boseto entered politics, and as Minister of Home Affairs in the Solomon Islands' government he took a leading part in bringing about peace and reconciliation in Bougainville. The legacy of economic exploitation and ecological destruction through a huge copper mine and colonial boundaries which did not take account of ethnic identity have contributed in Bougainville to a civil war which was fought for ten years with a blockade, including the banning of medical supplies by the Papua New Guinea government, and which led to the death of thousands.

The challenges facing Pacific Christians are many as globalization impacts on traditional life and institutions. The demands for missiological and theological reflection are urgent as people struggle with issues to do with their identity now and in the future. Bush pointed to the irony associated with the notable attempts by Sione 'Amanaki Havea, a Tongan church leader and theologian, to develop an authentically Pacific theological voice. Havea's "coconut theology," using the coconut as a symbol, brought together "life and healing, *kairos* and patience, evangelism, the virgin birth, and especially the Eucharist — the body and blood of Christ." Bush commented that while "Pacific Islanders may have been weaned on the coconut . . . they also now eat and drink packaged products purchased with money in urban supermarkets." The challenge is how to connect theology with "the socio-economic forces affecting the Pacific."[63]

A number of questions arise from this essay, pointing toward the need for much more detailed reflection and work on the themes of globalization and conversion in the Pacific by Pacific people.

1. What does conversion mean for the individual and the community to which they belong?
2. How is the liberation brought by the gospel to be incarnated in the life of individuals, churches, and countries?
3. What does salvation mean in the face of globalization and the threat of environmental and ecological catastrophes?
4. What does it mean to express your faith in your local context while being part of the *oikoumenē*?

63. Joseph Bush, "Is Social Relevance Relevant?" *Pacific Journal of Theology* 2.12 (1994): 44. See Sione 'Amanaki Havea, "Christianity in the Pacific Context," in *South Pacific Theology: Papers from the Consultation on Pacific Theology, Papua New Guinea, January 1986* (Oxford, 1987), pp. 11-15.

Throughout the history of Christianity in the Pacific there have been tensions between individual response and collective identity, individual conversion and people movements, the medium and the message, the evangelist and the evangelized, tradition and context, gospel and culture. Often the Church became caught up in false dualisms where it distinguished between alternatives, either/or, rather than accepting a both/and approach. The two poles of globalization advance the extremes, with the macro society at one end having a pervasive influence through technology, the control of capital, and the manipulation of mass communication, while at the other end the micro society digs in behind the ramparts of tradition and turns its back on the world around it.

Christian conversion has always had individual and community dimensions. Jesus called his first followers as individuals and they became the disciples. The body of Christ and the fruit on the vine are images that express both individuality and collectivity. The one is connected to the many, and the many are one through their unity with Christ. Pacific communities, churches, and new religious groups are challenged to hold together the growing sense of individual identity along with respect for traditions, ties of kinship, and the strong sense of community through which unity and solidarity can be affirmed.

SECTION III

CHAPTER SEVEN

Conversion and Social Change: A Review of the "Unfinished Task" in West Africa

JEHU J. HANCILES

In becoming Christian, every culture undergoes a transformation, a conversion. It must accept new elements and purge itself, and correct and even abandon certain traditional institutions. . . . On the other hand culture is not a static entity but rather something which is identified with human continuity which is itself in a state of continuous development. Thus the integration and adaptation of the Gospel message to the culture of a people, while not able to ignore the institutions of the past, must take account of the dynamism of evolution which is at work in every culture at every moment in its history.[1]

Understanding Conversion

In Christian Scriptures the original Greek and Hebrew terms translated *conversion* literally mean "to turn" or "return." However, as used in the English language, the concept is associated with such a range of religious experiences that definitions proliferate. Contextual variables, the element of the numinous, and (inescapably) conflicting expert opinion all make for ambiguity and nebulousness. What is termed "genuine conversion" also tends to vary considerably from one religious tradition to another, giving validity to the obser-

---

1. R. Laroche, "Some Traditional African Religions and Christianity," in C. G. Baëta, ed., *Christianity in Tropical Africa* (London, 1968), p. 300.

vation that ultimately "conversion is what a group or person *says* it is."[2] No less a scholar than Stephen Neill was sufficiently exasperated with the variations of meaning and controversy which the concept evoked to suggest that it might be well to avoid the word altogether![3]

Neill himself was at pains to argue that the defining element of conversion is *change:* "change in the structure of personality," or in the surrender of the human will, as the "Ego" is "displaced from the centre and replaced by the living God."[4] Neill's views were quite possibly influenced by the thinking of his close acquaintance, A. D. Nock, whose *Conversion, the Old and the New in Religion from Alexander the Great to Augustine of Hippo* (1933) was one of the most authoritative treatments of the subject at the time. Nock distinguished between "adhesion" and "conversion." In *adhesion,* he explained, the old spiritual home is not abandoned for a new one in a single movement; rather there is "an acceptance of new worships as useful supplements and not as substitutes." *Conversion,* on the other hand, involves "the reorientation of the soul of an individual, his deliberate turning from indifference or from an earlier form of piety to another, a turning which implies a consciousness that a great change is involved, that the old was wrong and the new is right."[5]

As helpful as these two definitions of conversion are, both writers lay themselves open to criticism by depicting conversion as essentially an *individual* and *psychological* (or "interior") experience. Perhaps due to an evangelical predilection, neither makes provision for "group" conversion, an approach considered more efficacious in contexts, like Africa, where "religion" is communally regulated, while the "interiorist bias" ignores both the significance of "context" and the variability of the phenomenon.[6] L. R. Rambo's *Understanding Religious Conversion* (1993) provides us with a contemporary and far more insightful treatment of the subject, and we shall use some of his arguments to provide orientation for the rest of the chapter.

2. Lewis R. Rambo, *Understanding Religious Conversion* (New Haven, 1993), pp. 3, 7.

3. Stephen Neill, *The Unfinished Task* (London, 1957), pp. 35-52.

4. Neill, *The Unfinished Task,* pp. 44, 46. This *change,* he added, "may be extremely gradual or it may in appearance at least be sudden. It may be marked by no crisis, or by a memorable crisis. It may take place at an identifiable moment or not. None of these differences is of great importance; what is all-important is that the change should genuinely have taken place."

5. A. D. Nock, *Conversion, the Old and the New in Religion from Alexander the Great to Augustine of Hippo* (Oxford, 1933), p. 7.

6. Useful criticisms are provided by Robert W. Hefner, ed., *Conversion to Christianity: Historical and Anthropological Perspectives on a Great Transformation* (Berkeley, 1993); Carole M. Cusack, "Towards a General Theory of Conversion," in L. Olson, ed., *Religious Change, Conversion and Culture* (Sydney, 1996), pp. 4-5.

Like Neill, Rambo identifies *change* as "the central meaning of conversion."[7] But he makes it clear that a variety of religious changes applies: "including simple change from the absence of a faith system to a faith commitment, from religious affiliation with one faith system to another, or from one orientation to another within a single faith system . . . , from a reliance on rote and ritual to a deeper conviction of God's presence . . . [or even] a radical shifting of gears that can take the spiritually lackadaisical to a new level of intensive concern, commitment, and involvement."

He also identifies five types of conversion:[8] (1) *apostasy* or *defection,* the repudiation of a religious tradition or its beliefs by previous members; (2) *intensification,* the revitalized commitment to a faith with which the convert has had previous affiliation, as when nominal members make a new commitment; (3) *affiliation,* the movement of an individual or group from no or minimal commitment to full involvement with an institution or community of faith; (4) *institutional transition,* the change of an individual or group from one community to another with a major tradition, as in switching from one Protestant denomination to another; and (5) *traditional transition,* the movement of an individual or group from one major religious tradition to another. This categorization helps to underscore the fact that conversion is a variable phenomenon experienced in a range of models.

Among the most debated questions about conversion is whether it is an *event* or a *process.* Again Rambo, not unlike Neill, is emphatic that the "overnight, all-in-an-instant wholesale transformation that is now and forever" exists mainly in popular mythology.[9] He asserts that "the process of conversion is a product of the interactions among the convert's aspirations, needs, and orientations, the nature of the group into which she or he is being converted, and the particular social matrix in which these processes are taking place.[10] He also proposes a *"process oriented,"* or sequential, model for the study of conversion whereby it is approached as "a series of elements that are interactive and cumulative over time."[11] He envisages a seven-stage sequence of processes:

7. Rambo, *Understanding Religious Conversion,* p. 2.

8. Rambo, *Understanding Religious Conversion,* pp. 13-14.

9. Rambo, *Understanding Religious Conversion,* p. 1. Neill also argued that even when non-Christians appear to have believed in Christ at the very first time of hearing him, "faith has in most cases followed only on a prolonged period of confrontation with Christ and the Gospel." He also saw this initial turning to Christ as only the first step in the process (*The Unfinished Task,* p. 46).

10. Rambo, *Understanding Religious Conversion,* p. 7.

11. Rambo, *Understanding Religious Conversion,* p. 17.

Stage 1	Stage 2	Stage 3	Stage 4	Stage 5	Stage 6	Stage 7
Context	*Crisis*	*Quest*	*Encounter*	*Interaction*	*Commitment*	*Consequences*

In this model, *context* forms not only the initial stage but also the milieu for the other stages. Also, a resequencing is possible, whereby, for instance, *encounter* (with the conversion agent) could precipitate *crisis* and *quest* rather than stem from either.

In relation to the African experience, Rambo's model helps us to treat conversion as "a dynamic, multifaceted process of transformation," and even to conceptualize a sequence of conversion and *reconversion* within the same spiritual journey, as fresh challenges or new realities cause spiritual maps to be reconfigured, recolored, or even abandoned and replaced. It also emphasizes that "context" — that is, the external sociocultural milieu and environmental variables which influence the process — is as significant as "internal" motivations, experiences, and aspirations. The religious matrix is particularly critical since conversion, rather than constituting a clean break from the past, often involves a reconstitution and reinterpretation of previous beliefs, symbols, and ritual to form a new dynamic which enables the convert to meet new challenges. Equally relevant is the argument that some form of "crisis," be it religious, cultural, psychological, or political, usually precedes conversion; and thus, while situations subject to rapid social change provide many catalysts for conversion, the process of conversion slows down markedly in contexts served by well-organized religions underpinned by political and economic stability.

The African Experience

In 1971, Robin Horton published a stimulating article on African conversion which sparked considerable debate.[12] Horton observed that the typical traditional (pre-Islamic, pre-Christian) African cosmology comprises a lower tier of lesser spirits primarily concerned with the local community and its environment (the *microcosm*) and an upper tier occupied by a supreme being primarily concerned with the world as a whole (the *macrocosm*). This multiplicity of spiritual agencies, he argued, does not mean that traditional cosmologies represent a lesser degree of coherence and rationality than world religions. For instance, the Yoruba cosmology operates as a well-articulated system. Horton then put forward the controversial thesis that even if con-

12. R. Horton, "African Conversion," *Africa* 41.2 (April 1971): 85-108.

fronted with elements of modernity, *without* the presence of Islam or Christianity, traditional religions had an inherent capacity to develop the monotheistic cosmology and ritual normally associated with acceptance of those two world religions.[13] He conjectured that the impact of the modern situation — notably the development of commerce and nation-states, dramatic improvements in communications with accompanying economic and political developments — would "lure a great many people away from their microcosms and set them down in a wider world." For these and others left inside the weakening boundaries, there could be only one explanation for their predicament: namely, that

> the lesser spirits (underpinners of the microcosms) are in retreat, and that the supreme being (underpinner of the macrocosm) is taking over direct control of the everyday world. Hence they come to regard the lesser spirits as irrelevant or downright evil. Hence, too, they develop a far more elaborate theory of the supreme being and his ways of working in the world, and a battery of new ritual techniques for approaching him and directing his influence.

In essence, therefore, the beliefs and practices of Islam and Christianity were accepted only "where they happen to coincide with responses of the traditional cosmology to other, non-missionary, factors of the modern situation." Islam and Christianity were little more than "catalysts," "stimulators and accelerators of changes which were 'in the air' anyway."

Horton was quick to state that this conclusion "sounds extreme and does in fact contain an element of caricature," but his thesis met with critical response. One of the earliest was Humphrey J. Fisher's "Conversion Reconsidered," published in the same journal.[14] Fisher argued that the assumptions underpinning Horton's arguments — that adherents of African traditional faiths would interpret and respond to changes in their society in a particular way — had no sound historical basis. After all, in some African societies, like the Nuer and Dinka, the cult of the supreme being was highly developed prior to the advent of Islam or Christianity, while societies which had long been exposed to the modernizing effects of international trade (in northern and central Ghana, for instance) gave no evidence of having developed an elaborate

---

13. Cf. Horton, "African Conversion," pp. 102-3. This conclusion formed part of what he called a "thought experiment."

14. H. J. Fisher, "Conversion Reconsidered: Some Historical Aspects of Religious Conversion in Black Africa," *Africa* 43.1 (January 1973): 27-40.

cult of the supreme being. Fisher was convinced, in fact, that the evidence points the other way: that among people "whose transference from microcosm to macrocosm has been particularly dramatic, it is the spirit cults, rather than awareness of the one God that flourishes."[15]

More recently, Robert Hefner has faulted Horton's model for an overemphasis on the "boundedness of traditional communities."[16] He points out that many religious systems in premodern Africa transcended ethnic and territorial boundaries, in contrast to the closed microscopic worlds projected in Horton's thesis. We might also add that Horton does not successfully account for the persistence of the African cosmological worldview alongside Christian missionary doctrine well into the process of modernization.

But, for all its manifest weakness, Horton's model provides significant insights into the development of African Christianity in the twentieth century. He helps us to appreciate that in a situation where the microcosm suffers profound disturbance, access to the benefits and advantages of the wider social order provides significant motivation for conversion and a necessary impetus for the restructuring of indigenous religion.[17] In this regard, Christianity benefited not only from its association with modernization and technological advancement but also from a global image which contrasted sharply with the localized framework of African religions. And at no other time was the limitation of the traditional cosmologies more acutely felt and exposed than in the course of the twentieth century.

The New Era of Colonialism

The partitioning of Africa in the 1890s by aggressively competitive European powers had incalculable consequences for the future of the continent, not least for its religious development. Included in this colonial revolution were the new demarcation of frontiers, the establishment of a new economy epitomized by enforced taxation, and the imposition of European languages pursuant to new systems of education and political administration. All this por-

---

15. Fisher, "Conversion Reconsidered," p. 32. Here, Fisher cites the case of the "recaptives" in early-nineteenth-century Sierra Leone as an example of the tenacity with which old habits and beliefs persisted among African peoples who had experienced the searing experience of slavery.

16. Hefner, *Conversion to Christianity,* pp. 3-46, esp. pp. 20ff. Current scholarship, he explained, demonstrates the error "of automatically identifying traditional religions with closed microcosmic worlds."

17. Horton, "African Conversion," pp. 102-3. Hefner makes a similar point.

tended radical transformation and massive social change.[18] Traditional societies, particularly in the African hinterland, were caught up in profound crises as centuries-old structures, geared to the ethos, needs, and survival of small-scale communities, proved utterly inadequate in the face of the colonial juggernaut. Their "world" expanded rapidly and uncontrollably with technological developments that also brought unprecedented levels of interaction between African societies and the rest of the Christian world.[19] The nature of the encounter and the social upheaval which accompanied it swung the odds heavily in favor of Christian conversion.

In many areas the religious systems underpinning societal existence suffered acute paralysis as the social boundaries to which they were intrinsically linked dissolved. Virtually every modern development had religious ramifications: growth in commerce and industry produced new communities and people movements which severely disrupted the old microcosms; population congestion facilitated the spread of diseases that often defied traditional medicine and magic, further undermining the religious fabric; and infrastructure developments (the building of railways, bridges, dams, tarmac roads, etc.) radically changed the environment that had been the domicile of spirits and objects of worship. Never was the vast technological superiority of the Western world, with which Christianity was associated, so manifest; whether or not European occupation was preceded by military defeat, the old "gods" had manifestly failed. In the midst of such profound dilemmas the power of the invaders and the possibilities they offered stood out clearly. There was widespread readiness to embrace the new religion. Since the advent of colonial rule also induced a dramatic increase in the number and quality of missionaries,[20] Christian expansion reached unprecedented levels.

18. Cf. A. Hastings, *The Church in Africa, 1450-1950* (Oxford, 1994), p. 401; P. Curtin et al., eds., *African History,* 2nd ed. (London, 1995), p. 464.

19. Medical advancement led to the discovery that the regular administration of quinine acted as a prophylactic against the deadly malaria, and, at the turn of the century, it was ascertained that mosquitoes were the infective vector. In West Africa, where the mosquito (under anonymity of course) had long discouraged large-scale European presence, the situation changed rapidly — "heat and flies" hardly presented the same challenge. Advances in iron metallurgy not only enhanced firearms technology (which accentuated the disparity between the powerful and the powerless) but also produced significant developments in the construction of railways and ships. Radio telegraphy transformed communications, while the invention of the bicycle (in 1876) significantly altered the scope and nature of European missionary service.

20. Cf. Hastings, *The Church in Africa,* p. 419; Roland Oliver, *The African Experience* (London, 1993), p. 207. In most of the southern two-thirds of Africa, notes Oliver, "missionaries were thicker upon the ground than colonial officials."

Motives for conversion were complex, but it cannot be emphasized too strongly that for many Africans conversion to Christianity became a way of coping with innumerable crises and dilemmas, a means of adapting to rapid change as radically disrupted microcosms signaled inevitable transition to a wider, more complex world. In truth, potential converts were confronted with two obvious choices: Christianity or Islam — two religions linked into a wider universe and able to provide "keys to meaning and a means to adjustment when a people's traditional lore is no longer able to do so."[21]

Islam, with a longer history in West Africa, had gained significant footholds in the interior and boasted competent administrative bureaucracies useful to the new invading powers. For this, among other reasons, colonial administrators were very tolerant of Islam and even sought to preserve predominantly Muslim areas from Christian missionary activity.[22] But Christianity had the edge. It was the faith of the conquerors, and Christian nations were clearly superior in military power, technological resources, and knowledge.[23] Medical services, for instance, became a valuable instrument of evangelization, and disease epidemics invariably produced a flood of conversions.[24] However great the reluctance to abandon the old gods was, the pull of social progress and the benefits of modern science were greater — if only to keep up with one's rivals, as the following Igbo prayer indicates:

> Our great ancestors, we greet you. The world is changing with us. What used to be the norm when you were here on earth no longer obtains. Civilisation, Christianity and travelling are forcing us to adjust ourselves to the new way of life. Our neighbouring villages which were inferior to us in battle, trade and farming are now growing in strength because they have taken to the new ways. . . . Very soon, but God forbid,

21. Andrew Walls, *The Missionary Movement in Christian History* (Maryknoll, N.Y., 1996), p. 132.

22. Cf. Oliver, *The African Experience*, p. 202.

23. Cf. Hastings, *The Church in Africa*, p. 405. T. O. Beidelman also comments that "the force of weapons, skill in manufacturing medicine and textiles, and the widespread literacy all implied somehow to be part and parcel of the same cultural package, even though in many areas these secular forces had worked to undermine religious faith. Missionaries were keen to present most aspects of European life as integrally related, as though the kind of minds that theologised about sin and salvation were necessarily those which could develop vaccines, lead conquering troops, or organise a productive textile mill" ("Social Theory and the Study of Christian Missions in Africa," *Africa* 44.3 [July 1974]: 235-48).

24. Cf. Felix K. Ekechi, "The Medical Factor in Christian Conversion in Africa: Observations from South-Eastern Nigeria," *Missiology* 21.3 (1993): 289-309.

they will become our master if we pay no heed to the changing situation and the new ideas which we feel are not entirely bad.[25]

The Conversion Process

The chief means of Christian expansion was Western education. From the early days European missionaries had recognized that education provided the most effective means of converting Africans; throughout West Africa the association between church and school was integral to evangelization. European empire building increased the need for educated Africans (to serve as petty officials, clerks, and skilled artisans in the cumbersome colonial structure), and this in turn generated a heavy demand for schools. Since Christian missions controlled all paths to literacy, the conversion situation was greatly transformed. Villages competed for the privilege of having a mission school and chiefs hitherto indifferent to Western learning clamored for the missionary. In western Nigeria, the Sudan Interior Mission's official policy of opposition to the "school approach" caused it to lose many of its converts to other missions. Eventually, in 1930 (after two decades of persevering but despairing labor), SIM opened its first school. Over the next two decades its converts multiplied from a few hundred to 6,000.[26] The mission school guaranteed a modicum of social advancement and ensured participation in the modernization process. As a tool of conversion it was exploited to the fullest by denominational groups locked in boisterous competition for the soul of Africa. "Bush schools" — organs of mass literacy of the most elementary kind — multiplied all over the West African landscape as the century progressed. To these were added high schools and colleges, built and maintained at considerable expense by various missions.[27] By the mid-century Africans with Christian education would increasingly monopolize employment in the modern sector of the developing colonial economies, laying the foundation for Christian dominance in the postcolonial period.

No useful purpose can be served here by revisiting the complex debate

25. Cited in Cyril C. Okorocha, "Religious Conversion in Africa: Its Missiological Implications," *Mission Studies* 9.18 (1992): 168-80.

26. Cf. Peter B. Clarke, *West Africa and Christianity* (London, 1986), p. 105.

27. Seminaries provided advanced training for African clergy; prestigious boarding schools (such as the CMS Grammar School in Sierra Leone, Mfantsepim and Achimota in Ghana, and King's College in Lagos) catered to the children (both male and female) of the African middle class; primary and secondary schools produced a steady stream of teachers and laid the foundation for entry into learned professions.

about the impact of Western education on Africa. Our concern lies with the implications for African conversion. The school approach to conversion had manifest defects. While it was demonstrative of the fact that the potential convert's aspirations and needs are critical to the conversion process, "classroom religion" made conversion particularly susceptible to secular motives.[28] In many instances the desire for Western education was simply that, a desire for Western education (and the benefits it conveyed) without a corresponding readiness for religious change. Unconsciously, literacy became a prerequisite for conversion, so that the process depended less on personal faith than on the ability to memorize and recite a set of doctrines and creeds,[29] with the appropriate behavior modification.

Schools, even "bush schools," required considerable investment of time and money, and societies with a viable local economy benefited most. Also, the almost exclusive focus on the young — considered more pliant and open to the intellectual approach — skewed the process of expansion and subverted traditional authority structures. Perhaps most significantly, Christianity became inextricably linked with Western culture, so that the Church often existed as an exotic addition to the religious environment, without effective anchorage in the religious culture. John V. Taylor expressed it quite forcefully:

> It is bad enough that religious pictures, films and film-strips should have almost universally shown a white Christ, child of a white mother, master of white disciples; that he should be worshipped almost exclusively with European music set to translations of European hymns, sung by clergy and people wearing European dress in buildings of an archaic European style; that the form of worship should bear almost no resemblance to traditional African ritual nor the content of the prayers to contemporary African life; that the organisational structure of the Church and its method of reaching decisions should be modelled ever more closely on Western concepts rather than deviating from them. But in the last resort these are all merely outward forms that could easily give place to others. They are serious because they are symptoms. They

28. Ogbu Kalu, *The Embattled Gods: Christianisation of Igboland, 1841-1991* (London, 1996), p. 115, records, for instance, that when Chief Onyeama of Eke in Igboland discovered that the school in his compound was being taught in the vernacular "he knew he had invited the wrong group," since he wanted his people to learn English and deal with the colonial officers. The chief took immediate steps to remedy the situation.

29. Cf. Teresa Okure, "Conversion, Commitment: An African Perspective," *Mission Studies* 10.1-2 (1993): 109-33.

persist because they are the school uniform of classroom religion reflecting a world-view that is fundamentally European.[30]

To suggest, however, that the encounter between gospel and traditional culture was less than wholesome at this stage is not to devalue the legacy of the Western missionary movement. Certainly the process of conversion was well under way, progressing steadily, transforming societies. If we accept that conversion is a "multifaceted process of transformation," it is possible to argue that whatever the imperfections of the first encounter, a process is set in motion, which is readily responsive to new stimuli. Furthermore, the Christian Scriptures made available in the vernacular have time and time again proved to be a self-propagating, spiritual-organic force, and once introduced into a context, however imperfectly, and appropriated by a particular people, the Scriptures enable Christianity to advance and gain adherents (Acts 12:24), out-distancing the best efforts of the missionary. Denominational rivalry and improved organizational structures meant that, by the mid-twentieth century, there were few societies on the continent "without at least one set of missionaries living in their midst, learning the local language, reducing it to writing, standardising the dialects, producing translations of the scriptures and educational and catechetical materials for the schools."[31] It is also important to add that despite the prominence of the European missionary in missionary historiography, African agents, serving as catechists, schoolmasters, and interpreters, formed the main vanguard of the Christian advance.[32] This was particularly so as the cutting edge of mission shifted from the "mission station" to the school and village.

Because new ideas and concepts can be absorbed only via the categories of the old, converts to a new religion appropriate the new system within the thought forms and religious experiences with which they are already attuned. On the basis of studies among the Igbo of Nigeria, Cyril Okorocha argues that at least two vital aspects of the "African religiousness" influenced conversion to Christianity: namely, "pragmatism" (a religious system must have practical value) and "power-centredness" (a religion is "useful and worthy of profession only if it embodies and imparts *power*").[33] Thus African conver-

---

30. John V. Taylor, *The Primal Vision* (Philadelphia, 1963), pp. 21-22.

31. Oliver, *The African Experience*, p. 207.

32. Cf. Oliver, *The African Experience*, p. 210; Hastings, *The Church in Africa*, pp. 437-38. For a comparison of the European and African element in Christian expansion, see Ogbu Kalu, "Colour and Conversion: The White Missionary Factor in the Christianisation of Igboland, 1867-1967," *Missiology* 18.1 (January 1990): 61-74.

33. "Power" in this case must be understood as a mysterious force — a form of *mana* — which accounts for success, progress, or achievement in real life.

sion to Christianity was informed less by secular motives than a religious rationale. In Okorocha's words, it was a "conscious and rational movement . . . in the direction of power."[34] But since, as Okorocha himself affirms, religion permeates all aspects of life in African society, the distinction between secular and religious motives is purely academic. It is also arguable whether the acceptance of a "greater" power necessarily implies the abandonment of other objects of power — local spirits, divinities, ancestors — which invested the weakened microcosm with form and meaning. Rather, there may be a *reordering* of these powers so that, although the relationship between man and the supreme being is transformed, the lesser powers continue to exist in one form or another, and exercise an influence contingent to the perceived limitations of the greater power.

From this point of view, the mission-by-education model might have precipitated a spiritual crisis, a new "quest for belonging."[35] Western education is informed by a scientific rationality which interpolates a dichotomy between the spiritual and the temporal, and missionary Christianity became a "daylight religion of reason and reasonableness set over against the darkness of superstition."[36] Consequently, vital dimensions of the African spiritual universe — to which *power* is crucially applied — remained outside the scope of the Christian faith and, by implication, outside the cognizance of the Christian God. The denigration of African culture completed the image of Christianity as an alien force; even for the most well-meaning convert, the new faith was essentially divorced from the exigencies of daily life. This discontinuity created spiritual vacuums and a dislocation of identity. It also introduced pervasive tensions between the local and the global, presenting the new Christian societies with the challenge of liberating the Christian message from the possessive clutches of a powerful dominant culture while, at the same time, adjusting to the massive irreversible legacy of its global dimensions. The emergence of Prophet-Healing movements was in part a response to this challenge and to the spiritual void created by a classroom religion.

A Third Way

As early as the late nineteenth century, African Christian reaction to white racial hegemony — typified in the European missionary apparatus and colonial

34. Okorocha, "Religious Conversion in Africa," p. 171.
35. This would amount to a resequencing of Rambo's model.
36. Taylor, *The Primal Vision*, p. 20.

expansion — had stimulated the rise of *Ethiopianism:* a movement of religious nationalism which, *inter alia,* affirmed the African cultural heritage, defended African capability, and called for ecclesiastical autonomy. From its beginnings in the Sierra Leone colony, Ethiopianism spread throughout the West African region, stimulating cultural revolt and spawning numerous African Church movements.[37] These movements signified deep dissatisfaction with a form of Christianity modeled on the ethos and value system of foreign agents. Under their impetus, African forms were introduced into church liturgy, polity, and organizational structures by the turn of the century. Initially, Ethiopianism was mainly championed by leading African intellectuals in church and society, but as its ideals spread it frequently transformed into a popular movement — in part because some of its advocates countenanced polygamy (that incubus of European missionary enterprise in West Africa).

Ethiopianism provided the seed-plot for the emergence of Prophet-Healing movements in West Africa. In the Niger Delta (southern Nigeria) a popular Ethiopian revolt produced the creation of the Niger Delta Pastorate in the 1890s. Not quite twenty years later a Niger Delta Christian, Garrick Sokari Braide (ca. 1882-1918), baptized in 1910 after a laborious and lengthy process of instruction, became a lay preacher. After a visionary experience (about 1912) Braide embarked on an extraordinary evangelistic campaign in the Delta.[38] Some of his pronouncements reflected Ethiopian rhetoric, and at least one colonial official condemned his movement as resurgent Ethiopianism.[39] In a radical departure from the conversion-by-catechism approach of the established Church, Braide simply demanded that his hearers destroy fetishes and idols, confess their sins, and be baptized. Acts of healing and miracles gave tremendous force to his message, and the strict regulatory observances imposed on converts provided a meaningful ritual alternative to traditional forms.[40] His ministry produced revival and mass conversions (sometimes of whole villages), severely stretching the resources of the local churches.[41]

37. For a treatment, see J. Hanciles, *Euthanasia of a Mission: African Church Authority in a Colonial Context* (Westport, Conn., 2002).

38. For a detailed treatment of the Garrick Braide movement see G. O. M. Tasie, *Christian Missionary Enterprise in the Niger Delta, 1864-1918* (Leiden, 1978), ch. 5.

39. Tasie, *Christian Missionary Enterprise in the Niger Delta,* p. 189. Percy A. Talbot, the district officer for Degema, railed against the Braide movement as "essentially one of Ethiopianism, of blacks against whites."

40. These included abstinence from alcohol and magic, prescribed times of prayer, ceremonial observance of the Sabbath, and indigenized liturgy.

41. Tasie, *Christian Missionary Enterprise in the Niger Delta,* pp. 183ff. The number of "inquirers" in Niger Delta churches increased from little more than 300 in 1909 to 2,933 by

Some 1,300 miles to the west, another prophet movement founded by William Wadé Harris (1860-1929) was having an even greater impact. Harris, a native of Liberia, was converted at a revival in 1881 and subsequently became assistant teacher and catechist in the Episcopal Church. In the early 1900s he befriended Edward Blyden, a leading Ethiopianist and ardent African nationalist, through whose influence he was drawn into political activism. His activities led to imprisonment in 1909. While in prison, Harris's life was transformed by a visitation from the Archangel Gabriel, and, after his release in 1910, he embarked on an extensive Prophet-Healing ministry. Barefoot, dressed in a white robe, equipped with nothing but a Bible (King James Version), a staff, and water for baptism, Harris traversed the length of the Liberian coast. He later extended his ministry to the Ivory Coast, the Gold Coast, and Sierra Leone. In a campaign accompanied by healing and other remarkable signs, he demanded the destruction of fetishes, attacked traditional religion and preached repentance. The response was extraordinary. Waves of mass conversions transformed the countryside, including areas where European missionaries had labored for years without much result. Over 100,000 Africans are said to have been baptized in eighteen months.[42]

The similarities between the Braide and Harris movements are strikingly obvious. Apart from a divine commissioning, both modeled themselves on Elijah (the Bible's most confrontational prophet), emphasized the reading of the Word, and tolerated polygamy. Though it agitated Church authorities, the acceptance of polygamy no doubt contributed to their remarkable impact. But the main reason for their success lies elsewhere. Both prophets preached a simple message accompanied by a "power encounter" in the form of healing and miracles, which rendered the old idols useless and disposable. The Christian God thus staked effective claim to the entire spiritual universe. The fact that conversion was typified by decisive action — the throwing away of fetishes and idols — and was followed almost immediately by baptism also maximized the results of the encounter. The Braide movement lasted only until the late 1930s,[43] but there are Harris Churches today in the Ivory Coast, Liberia, and Ghana.

1912; in some provinces there were so many to baptize that church services lasted well into the evening.

42. David A. Shenk, "William Wadé Harris, ca. 1860–1929: God Made His Soul a Soul of Fire," in G. Anderson et al., eds., *Mission Legacies* (Maryknoll, N.Y., 1996), pp. 155-65.

43. Conflict with the established church over matters of discipline, the rise of fraudulent prophets, and opposition from a government concerned as much about the unlawful destruction of idols as the decline in liquor sales, all contributed to the demise of the movement and Braide's imprisonment in 1916. His supporters later constituted themselves into the Christ Army Church.

The Harris and Braide movements are only two examples of a phenomenon that became a prominent feature on the African religious landscape. Prophet-Healing movements addressed crucial aspects of the African religious need neglected by mission Christianity — notably healing and the fear fetish — and had remarkable grassroots appeal. Independent prophets and prophetesses, including not a few charlatans, multiplied throughout the region, but many ministries were short-lived. More enduring and extensive than most was the *Aladura* (a Yoruba word meaning "prayer people") movement which emerged in western Nigeria between 1918 and 1930 and briefly affiliated itself with Faith Tabernacle (a Pentecostal church) in Philadelphia. Its most powerful offshoot, the *Church of the Lord,* founded by a young Anglican teacher in 1930, quickly transcended ethnic and national boundaries, growing from three congregations in 1931 to seventy-two branches (in Ghana, Ivory Coast, Liberia, Sierra Leone, and Guinea) by 1961.[44]

Shenk rightly identifies *prophetism* as "a kind of third way between traditional religion and mission-planted churches."[45] Initially, the explosive impact of these movements filled mission churches to the bursting point; but the routinization of charisma, or the development of organizational structures, led many, like the *Aladura,* to constitute themselves into independent churches somewhat in competition with their older counterparts. Undoubtedly, theirs is a vibrant and popular form of African Christianity and such is their appeal that every African Christian is a potential member. But it is possible to exaggerate how much the African Independent Church movement (their churches are commonly referred to as AICs) has contributed to the expansion of Christianity in West Africa. A significant percentage of their adherents are drawn from, and often remain members of, the mainline churches; significantly, they have grown fastest in urban centers, where the immigrant sector is largest. The extent to which mainline churches have contributed to their success is often overlooked in the relevant literature.

As products of Evangelical enterprise, mainline churches in Africa uphold basic Evangelical doctrine with varying degrees of consciousness and conformity. Certainly up to the 1960s, their average member unquestioningly upheld the authority of Scripture and the tenets of the Apostles' Creed. Many were steeped in the Christian Scriptures and could quote choice passages from memory; and whether they attended church regularly or not, few would

---

44. The two most important works on the *Aladura* remain H. W. Turner, *African Independent Churches: The Church of the Lord (Aladura)*, 2 vols. (Oxford, 1967) and J. D. Y. Peel, *Aladura: A Religious Movement among the Yoruba* (London, 1968).

45. Shenk, "William Wadé Harris," p. 162.

have hesitated to affirm Jesus as Lord and Savior (in fact if not by dint of personal experience). It is possible to argue that it was the existence of this sedimentation of convictions that made the dynamic Pentecostal spirituality of the AICs such a desirable alternative (or supplement) to what was perceived as the antiquated ecclesiology and fossilized forms of ministry in the mainline denominations. For many, the transition from one institution to the other represented an attempt to achieve congruence between private spiritual needs and official church allegiances. Whether conversion represented a clean break or not, many items of furniture — notably "hymns" — made the crossover. But the AICs themselves began to lose momentum and membership as the evolving sociopolitical context produced new spiritual needs.

The Third Wave

Since the 1970s "a new Pentecostal wave," which differs significantly from earlier manifestations within the African Independent Church movement, has become increasingly evident.[46] Variously described as neo-Pentecostal, Pentecostal, or Charismatic, the new wave has complex fluid dimensions and a variety of organizational forms (embracing churches, para-church movements, and independent ministries). Central elements include the "Faith (or Prosperity) Gospel," intensive use of media production, pronounced emphasis on evangelism and ministries of deliverance, strong "mission" ties with North American Pentecostalism, and a self-conscious international or global image. The new Pentecostal/Charismatic movements have precipitated a great shift in the frontier of Christian expansion. Their emergence is also a function of sociopolitical developments, for the closing decades of the twentieth century witnessed a degree of social change that is comparable in its impact and repercussions to the colonial encounter.

The factors responsible for the current African crisis are complex and varied, comprising an interlocking grid of internal and external agents. While it is outside our scope to fully unravel its dimensions, a brief outline of the current sociopolitical matrix is indispensable for a proper understanding of recent developments within African Christianity.

In the wider context, Africa now has the worst statistics on the planet with regard to population increase, living standards, and violence. Infrastructural collapse, retarded economic growth, environmental degradation, and a high

---

46. Cf. Paul Gifford, *African Christianity: Its Public Role* (Bloomington, Ind., 1998), pp. 31-56.

incidence of deadly diseases are all active agents in a calculus of unmitigated hardship. The United Nations Human Development Report of 2001 (which rated 162 countries on the basis of life expectancy, adult literacy, daily calories supply, access to safe water, and under-five mortality) indicates that Africa is home to the 28 least developed countries in the world.[47] Six of the bottom ten are in West Africa. The outlook is grimmer still when the massive political and social turbulence afflicting many areas — a litany of inexplicable carnage, lawlessness, bloody civil war, social catastrophe, tidal waves of displaced refugees, and dysfunctional political leadership — is taken into account. "Three decades of independence from colonial rule," lamented G. Ayittey in 1992, "have produced nothing but economic misery and disintegration, political chaos, and institutional and social decay."[48]

West Africa's socioeconomic situation is somewhat a microcosm of the whole. The region boasts the greatest cluster of Lilliputian states (cartological constructs really!) and suffers from a corresponding political fragility. Few West African states are viable as autonomous entities, and in the postcolonial period many have failed to achieve or sustain genuine national unity or statehood. In his widely debated article, "The Coming Anarchy" (1994), Robert Kaplan painted, with wide brush strokes, an utterly gloomy picture of the region's immediate future:

> West Africa is becoming the symbol of world-wide demographic, environmental, and societal stress, in which criminal anarchy emerges as the real "strategic" danger. Disease, overpopulation, unprovoked crime, scarcity of resources, refugee migrations, the increasing erosion of nation-states and international borders, and the empowerment of private armies, security firms, and the international drug cartels are now most tellingly demonstrated through a West African prism. . . .[49]

Kaplan's prognosis is evocative of a Malthusian doomsday scenario. It is therefore somewhat ironic that Nigeria, with a population greater than the

---

47. I depended on internet access for this information — http://www.undp.org/hdro/oc17.htm; also of relevance is an article by S. Rasheed and E. Chole, "Human Development: An African Perspective," Occasional Paper no. 17, Human Development Report Office.

48. G.-N. Ayittey, *Africa Betrayed* (London, 1994), p. 8. This work was first published in the United States in 1992.

49. Robert D. Kaplan, "The Coming Anarchy," *The Atlantic Monthly* (February 1994): 44-76. He would expand on his views in his later work, *The Ends of the Earth: A Journey to the Frontiers of Anarchy* (New York, 1996).

rest of the region put together,[50] is seen by many analysts as the region's only "hope."[51] This dependence on a country which, despite an oil-rich status and a promising return to democratic government in early 1999, has yet to address and surmount immense internal problems of its own, sums up the West African predicament.

But while this state of affairs generates palpable "afro-pessimism" and fuels saturnine premonitions, it has provided the Church with a ripe harvest. By the closing decades of the twentieth century, Christianity had successfully transformed itself from a religion identified with Western culture and hegemony into a popular African religious movement that provides ample spiritual resources in an age of profound anxiety and uncertainty. The AICs played a significant role in this process; but once the Church became a fact and factor in the subcontinent, the principal concerns which stimulated the rise of AICs — including use of African forms in worship and liturgy, opposition to European control, incorporation of a rich cultural heritage, and the effective dethroning of pre-Christian gods — lost their cogency. This is not to infer discontinuity between older and newer movements. But new sociopolitical developments and accompanying economic change required new responses and a further reshaping of spiritual maps. The new Pentecostal/charismatic movements have flourished in so far as they have readily adapted to the new context. We only have space to assess their impact briefly.

Most conspicuous among the defining elements of the new movements is the Faith (also described as "Full" or "Prosperity") Gospel model formulated in the entrepreneurial climate of American media evangelism.[52] This model teaches that since Christ, through his death, has gained victory over sin, sickness, and poverty, every true believer (by applying simple scriptural principles) can achieve personal wealth and success, an approach which Ruth Marshall-Fratani aptly describes as "morally controlled material-

50. Nigeria accounts for 108 million of the region's estimated population of 210 million.

51. To be sure, Nigeria has been the prime mover behind important initiatives for political stability and economic advancement, and the 21st annual summit of the Economic Community of West African States (ECOWAS) in October 1998 devoted much of its time to panegyric affirmation of Nigeria's pivotal role in resolving regional conflict (conspicuously within the multinational Ecomog intervention force). Cf. "Nigeria and ECOWAS Special Report," *West Africa*, October 19–November 1, 1998, pp. 753-58.

52. For details, see Gifford, *African Christianity,* pp. 39-44, 84-86; also, Rosalind Hackett, "Pentecostal Appropriation of Media Technologies in Nigeria and Ghana," *Journal of Religion in Africa* 28.3 (1998): 258-77. Gifford goes as far as to describe them as "Faith Gospel Churches."

ism."[53] In a climate characterized by severe economic hardship and despair, the promise of health, success, wealth, and victory over adverse socioeconomic circumstances has stimulated widespread response. The emphasis on individual success and ambition appeals to young and old alike, but conversion is highest among the better-educated youth and upwardly mobile. Certainly it is the interests, aspirations, and concerns of this group that the "new breed" churches primarily address. In Nigeria, for instance, the origins of the new wave have been traced to a Pentecostal revival among university students already involved in relatively newer organizations like the Student Christian Movement and the International Fellowship of Evangelical Students.[54]

The convert becomes a member of a new dynamic community and gains access to networks that transcend local, ethnic, or class boundaries and extend beyond the national to the global. Marshall-Fratani observes that "even if the particular mission or ministry to which a believer belongs is small, it carries with it the sense of belonging to a global movement and access, if not immediately to financial or technological support, to resources such as literature and ideas."[55] These new "forms of identification and community formation" meet vital needs in a context characterized by rapid social change, strained social relationships, urban crisis, and problematic national identity.

Individual conversion also necessitates the construction of a new identity. The convert is "born again" and expected to make a complete break from the past and enter a new life with new material and spiritual possibilities. Family, friends, and neighbors often become casualties in this identity reconstruction, in which the new "other" — all who are not "born again" — are regarded as potential instruments of the evil forces which seek to reclaim the convert or hinder the fruits of conversion. For similar reasons, traditional religious practices (the ancestral cult in particular) are viewed negatively and often demonized. Younger (and often well-educated) converts are also likely to view cultural beliefs and practices as antithetical to the new, progressive, and modernizing spiritual principles they have embraced.

Even so, the new spiritual quest is informed by distinctly African religious categories and thought forms. Healing, prosperity, and success are secured in the face of a host of evil spirits and demonic forces that often work through

---

53. Ruth Marshall-Fratani, "Mediating the Global and Local in Nigerian Pentecostalism," *Journal of Religion in Africa* 28.3 (1998): 278-315.

54. Cf. Matthews A. Ojo, "The Charismatic Movement in Nigeria Today," *International Bulletin of Missionary Research* 19.3 (July 1995): 114-18.

55. Marshall-Fratani, "Mediating the Global and Local," p. 284.

human agents. "Deliverance" ministries have gained increasing prominence with the perception that demonic activities are behind practically every imaginable form of misfortune. Moreover, the rather jaundiced view of the African cultural heritage is often held in precarious tension with strong pride in African identity and an instinctive defensiveness about African capability. Surely, strains of Ethiopianism persist in the view that white [mis-]interpretations of the biblical narrative obscure the black element and represent yet another form of oppression.[56]

Extensive use of media production as a tool of evangelism is also a hallmark of the new Pentecostal/charismatic movements. The mountain of print, audio, and video media that has accompanied their growth is circulated and distributed regionally and beyond, effectively dissolving boundaries (congregational, institutional, ethnic, national, etc.). De-localizing the message in this manner also transforms the conversion situation by rendering the number of potential converts illimitable. It further creates among members "a new mode of imagining the self and community in terms of transnational identity."[57] At a time when much of the continent is still homeless within the growing "global village" (a product of multimedia technology and the rapacious expansion of multinational companies), this globalizing prospect increases the appeal of the new churches. Many have cultivated worldwide links — primarily with North American Pentecostal groups. Their commitment to modernization and their ability to connect converts to "the modern world of commodities, media and financial flows" also help to account for their impact.[58] From another perspective, increasing domination of the media has also allowed the new movements to insert themselves into the public space, filling a void created by dysfunctional political systems and considerable public disenchantment.[59]

---

56. A recent book by Mensa Otabil, founder of one of the largest Faith Gospel churches in Ghana (International Central Gospel Church), is titled *Beyond the Rivers of Ethiopia: A Biblical Revelation on God's Purposes for the Black Race* (Accra, 1992); briefly reviewed in Gifford, *African Christianity*, pp. 82ff.

57. Marshall-Fratani, "Mediating the Global and Local," p. 299.

58. Marshall-Fratani, "Mediating the Global and Local," p. 299.

59. As Western governments have wound down official links with African nations, those links are now predominantly mediated through Western NGOs (Non-Governmental Organizations), which have proliferated and gained considerable dominance in the sociopolitical arena as African governments have collapsed and retreated in the face of unmanageable crises. Gifford argues that the (predominantly North American) missionaries who have flooded into Africa in connection with the new Pentecostal/Charismatic wave have often had an effect on the Christian landscape just as substantial as that of the NGOs on the sociopolitical terrain. Cf. Gifford, *African Christianity*, pp. 10-11, 44-45.

It is also worth mentioning that the impact of the new Pentecostal/charismatic movements on mainline churches has been considerable. The new explosion started as *renewal* movements with a loose nondenominational structure comprising Bible study groups and weekday fellowships that provided a potent spiritual supplement to the vapid staple of mainline denominations. Inevitably, the new movements eventually developed their own churches,[60] and their adherents have remained sharply critical of the older churches (including the AICs). But groups like the Full Gospel Businessmen's Fellowship International, also part of the new wave, direct their evangelistic efforts principally at mainline church members, who are "saved" and/or "baptized in the Spirit" over an expensive breakfast rather than at a revival meeting. Occupying prominent positions in the mainline churches, many such converts are reluctant to leave, so the pattern of overlapping local Christian networks and plural representation continues.

Essentially, the African Christian landscape remains a very fluid one. It is intriguing to note, for instance, that though the new Pentecostal wave is indigenous in orientation and direction, the intensification of a Western missionary presence — preponderantly in the area of theological education — represents a reversal of trends within older AICs and even older mainline churches. This underlines the need to resist an approach that views these manifestations of African Christianity as rigid self-contained categories or emphasizes one at the expense of the other. It may be more helpful to view them as functional elements of the whole — the whole being the African Christian experience.

Facing a New Century

In the course of a century marked by massive and recurrent social change, the Church in Africa has emerged as one of Africa's most powerful institutions. The continent has transformed from a "mission field," which boasted the smallest number of Christians of any continent (with the exception of Oceania),[61] into an area "experiencing the fastest church growth of any re-

60. Cf. Ojo, "The Charismatic Movement in Nigeria Today," p. 115.

61. Cf. D. B. Barrett, "Annual Statistical Table on Global Mission," *International Bulletin of Missionary Research* 23 (January 1999): 24-25. Significantly, not a single African was present at the first World Missionary Conference in Edinburgh (1910), where non-Western representation was limited to "a symbolic handful of Indian, Chinese, and Japanese Christians" (A. F. Walls, "African Christianity in the History of Religions," *Studies in World Christianity* 2.2 [1996]: 183-203).

gion" in the world.[62] From just under 9 million in 1900, the number of African Christians is now estimated at over 333 million; and, if current projections are accurate, this number will almost double by 2025, by which time there will be more Christians in Africa than in any other continent in the world except Latin America.[63] This phenomenal growth raises urgent questions about the global and historical significance of African Christianity, questions which invite in-depth study. Professor Walls' declaration over a decade ago that "what happens within the African Churches in the next generation will determine the whole shape of church history for centuries to come" plainly sets the tenor for any meaningful appraisal.[64]

But perceptions based solely on abstract statistical accounts can be misleading. Applying empirical methods to the study of Christian movements has great missiological value, but the picture becomes oversimplified when undue weight is placed on mathematical summations. The "head-count" approach is liable to overlook the considerable mobility and overlapping of members and converts among the various new and "old" movements. Most importantly, a preoccupation with the grand narrative of continental accessions obscures the equally significant instances of setback, failure, or stunted growth at the regional or national level. African Christianity has faltered as well as flourished; both dimensions are crucial for a meaningful appraisal. The West African story with which we are primarily concerned is an important case in point. A close scrutiny of this region reveals a religious landscape that fits uneasily into the broader picture:[65] Islam is predominant, and primal religion retains a more significant hold than is generally allowed.[66] Much of West Africa is *not Christian*. Professing Christians constitute a clear majority in only five of its eighteen nation-states (Ghana, Togo, Gabon, Cameroon, and Equatorial Guinea) — the corresponding number for Islam is eight (see the table on p. 179). Islam, to be sure, has had a continuous presence in West Africa for almost a millennium,[67]

---

62. Cf. J. A. Siewert and E. G. Valdez, eds., *Mission Handbook* (Monrovia, Calif., 1997), p. 34.

63. Barrett, "Annual Statistical Table on Global Mission," *International Bulletin of Missionary Research* 27:1 (January 2003): 24-25.

64. Walls, "African Christianity," p. 186.

65. Ogbu Kalu is one of the few African scholars who have drawn attention to this trend. See "Jesus Christ, Where Are You? Themes in West African Church Historiography at the Edge of the 21st Century," paper presented at the Global Historiography Consultation, Fuller Theological Seminary, Pasadena, Calif., April 1998.

66. The statistical data used here is derived from M. Shaw, *The Kingdom of God in Africa: A Short History of African Christianity* (Grand Rapids, 1996), p. 306. It is not without minor inaccuracies, but it serves our purposes.

67. Lamin Sanneh attests that one of the earliest indications of conversion to Islam

Country	% Traditional Religion	% Christian	% Muslim	Total Population
Benin	55.0	28.0	17.0	3,900,000
Burkina-Faso	35.0	15.0	50.0	6,900,000
Cameroon	36.0	43.0	20.0	10,100,000
Chad	20.0	35.0	45.0	5,000,000
Equatorial Guinea	6.0	93.0	1.0	400,000
Gambia	10.0	2.0	85.0	700,000
Ghana	35.0	49.0	16.0	12,200,000
Guinea-Bissau	49.0	11.0	40.0	6,000,000
Ivory Coast	39.0	35.0	26.0	10,000,000
Liberia	39.0	37.0	23.0	1,500,000
Mali	15.0	3.0	82.0	8,200,000
Mauritania	0.1	0.5	99.0	1,900,000
Niger	10.0	0.5	90.0	6,500,000
Nigeria	8.0	47.0	45.0	100,000,000
Senegal	2.0	6.0	92.0	6,500,000
Sierra Leone	49.0	11.0	40.0	3,100,000
Togo	36.0	43.0	21.0	3,000,000

while the most effective Christian penetration dates only to the nineteenth century. Powerful Islamic strongholds to the north of the region have acted as a check on the Christianization process. This is set to continue since resurgent Islam, like new African Christian movements, is a missionizing and modernizing (if anti-Western) force.[68]

The tardiness of Christian expansion is perhaps best illustrated by the state of affairs in Sierra Leone, a country that has the distinction of representing the first successful Christian settlement in the region and is home to the first African Church in sub-Saharan Africa. After over two centuries of sustained Christian presence and witness, this small state of about 4.5 million people, once considered a beacon of light in a "benighted" continent, is only 9-10 percent Christian — the corresponding figures for Islam and indigenous

in the region is provided by a written record dated 1067. See *Piety and Power: Muslims and Christians in West Africa* (Maryknoll, N.Y., 1996), p. 12.

68. The standoff between Christianity and Islam is most evident in Nigeria, where the new Pentecostal/Charismatic movement has adopted an aggressive missionary stance toward Muslims. See Ogbu Kalu, "The Vine and Brambles: Christianity, State and Development in Nigeria, 1900-1994," *Studia Historiae Ecclesiasticae* 22.2 (December 1996): 88-113.

religions are 41 percent and 49 percent, respectively. A "Target 2000 Church Survey" conducted by the Evangelical Fellowship of Sierra Leone in 1992 revealed that only 6.7 percent of the population in the greater Freetown area (the most Christianized area in the country) attend church regularly.[69] Moreover, it would appear that, with the exception of Benin, no other country in West Africa (or on the continent, for that matter) has a higher percentage of adherents to primal religion.

A strong case can be made to support the view that Christianity often exerts a greater influence on society and social institutions than mathematical percentages suggest. But the point at issue is that unless balanced with an informed assessment of local or regional realities a global perspective can be misleading.[70] The West African Christian landscape continues to transform and develop new features in response to the evolving sociopolitical context. Yet, one must resist facile prognostications. Lesslie Newbigin warned that "the same acids of modernity are bound to have the same effects on the third world as they have had in Europe."[71] Alarmingly maybe, the continent's emergence as a major heartland of Christianity coincides with its economic marginalization in the global arena, thus creating a situation where the strongest and most vibrant centers of Christianity lack the resources for global missionary enterprise. But, despite current sociopolitical dilemmas, Africa could conceivably enter the stream of globalization more fully as the new century progresses. This, too, will bring extensive social change and require fresh Christian responses, as each successive generation is won afresh in the ongoing task of conversion and reconversion. For Christians that task, as Stephen Neill's memorable phrase puts it, "is an unfinished task, and always will be."[72]

69. "*Target 2000* Evangelistic and Church Survey," conducted by the Evangelical Fellowship of Sierra Leone (Freetown, 1992).

70. As Vinoth Ramachandra observes in a not dissimilar context, "Knowing that 30 percent of Koreans are now Christians, while the corresponding figure in India is only 2 percent, doesn't tell me very much about what God is doing in either country" ("The Honour of Listening: Indispensable for Mission," *Evangelical Mission Quarterly* 30 [October 1994]: 404-9.

71. Lesslie Newbigin, *A Word in Season: Perspectives on Christian World Missions* (Grand Rapids, 1994), p. 185.

72. Neill, *The Unfinished Task*, p. 7.

CHAPTER EIGHT

African Initiated Churches in Southern Africa: Protest Movements or Mission Churches?

MARTHINUS L. DANEEL

Introduction

This essay attempts an interpretative profile of the main currents of develop-ment in the African Initiated (or Independent) Churches, known as AICs, in the course of the twentieth century. In the past, AICs have been categorized as protest movements, yet I would argue that they find their primary identity to-day as mission churches and have successfully developed contextual mission models. The essay will explore how AICs work out their sense of mission through innovative and liberative patterns of church life, and particularly through the sacramental and environmental motives for mission that are prominent features of AIC life. The material presented here is largely based on the self-interpretation of AIC members and on many years of my own partici-pation in and observation of AIC worship and ceremonial life. Having always focused on the phenomenon in its local manifestations in Zimbabwe and, to a lesser extent, in South Africa, and having faced the complexities of formulat-ing adequate and fair generalizations even for a single church, I am wary of continent-wide generalizations. Hence, my analysis focuses on the AICs in southern Africa and, more specifically, on the movements in Zimbabwe.[1] Be-

1. My approach reflects the conviction that we need more in-depth case studies of an interdisciplinary nature (historical, socio-anthropological, phenomenological, and theological) if we are fairly and accurately to assess the diverse identities of the AICs as they relate to African Christianity, the world Church, and globalizing processes.

fore moving on to examine the nature of AICs as mission churches in detail, I want to make a few observations on their historical background, thus setting them briefly into context.

General Context of the AICs

Broadly speaking, AICs can be classified into three distinct groups. The "Ethiopian type," or nonprophetic churches, lay no claim to special manifestations of the Holy Spirit, and their patterns of worship resemble those of the Western mission churches from which they originated. The "Spirit type" churches — mainly Zionist and Apostolic movements — share a special emphasis on the work of the Holy Spirit, manifested by speaking in tongues, prophetic activities, and faith healing. In Zimbabwe, these churches refer to themselves as *maKereke oMweya* ("churches of the Spirit"); hence my preference for the designation "Spirit type," as distinct from Pentecostal churches. The so-called "messianic church" emerges as a third category when a Spirit-type leader achieves such prominence that he/she usurps Christ's mediating function, either wholly or in part. In reality, few AIC leaders present themselves as substitute Black Christ figures. Those who do develop messianic traits are more appropriately characterized as "iconic leaders"[2] insofar as their leadership positively mirrors and concretizes the person of Christ in the African context for their followers.[3]

AICs vary in size from a single family or extended family unit with only a few members to mass movements of iconic leaders that, in some instances, count several million adherents. Growth rates for AICs throughout the twentieth century have been steady. Based on the growth rate indicated in David Barrett's 1968 assessment,[4] the total current number of AICs continent-wide could well range between seven and eight thousand. The continued growth of AICs contrasts sharply with a decline in the growth of the major Western-

2. B. G. M. Sundkler, *Zulu Zion and Some Swazi Zionists* (London, 1976), pp. 309-10; M. L. Daneel, *Quest for Belonging: Introduction to a Study of Independent Churches* (Gweru, Zimbabwe, 1987), p. 187.

3. In South Africa the best-known iconic leaders are Isaiah Shembe of the Nazarene Baptist Church and Enginas Lekganyane of the Zion Christian Church; in Zimbabwe, Samuel Mutendi, founder of an autonomous branch of the Zion Christian Church, and Johane Maranke of the African Apostolic Church of Johane Maranke. The leadership of these churches has already become the responsibility of the second and third generation male descendants of the deceased founder-leaders.

4. D. B. Barrett, *Schism and Renewal in Africa: An Analysis of Six Thousand Contemporary Religious Movements* (Nairobi, 1968), pp. 78-79.

oriented "mission churches." The 1991 official South African census estimated that fully 46 percent of black South Africans belonged to AICs, while only 33 percent belonged to the so-called "mission" or "mainline" churches, that is, the Dutch Reformed, Roman Catholic, Anglican, Methodist, Lutheran, and other churches which count additional white membership in South Africa and abroad.[5] Earlier surveys in Zimbabwe showed approximately 50 percent of African Christians belonging to AICs.[6] These figures are certainly not representative of all southern African countries, but they would seem to be indicative of a trend of sustained growth in the AIC movement. Despite the preponderance of males as founders and senior office-bearers in these churches, women comprise up to 80 percent of their total adult membership. The Manyano or Ruwadzano women's associations are well known for their family care, Bible study, and evangelistic campaigns. Individual women often achieve prominence in AIC ranks as prophetesses and healers, and there are also a number of women who have founded their own AICs.[7]

Historical Roots and Ecclesial Interconnections

AICs interpret the historical roots of their movements along two basic lines: demonstrating a direct link with the Bible and the early Christian church as the authenticating source of their existence, and defining their roots in the more recent traditions of Christian history (both in Africa and abroad) in relation to the local mainline mission churches responsible for the introduction of Christianity into their part of the world. Intense denominational rivalry and a lengthy initial phase of nonrecognition of the AICs by the Western mission churches aggravated the need in AIC ranks for a form of genuine, independent, religious legitimation. Theirs was, and remains, a quest for an authentic African mythical charter establishing original closeness and ecclesial descent directly from Christ and the Bible without reference to the apostolic successions claimed in Western churches.

The concern for a mythical charter can be gauged from the significance

5. A. Anderson, *Tumelo: The Faith of African Pentecostals in South Africa* (Pretoria, 1993), pp. 7-8.

6. M. L. Daneel, *Old and New in Southern Shona Independent Churches*, vol. 2: *Church Growth: Causative Factors and Recruitment Techniques* (The Hague and Paris, 1974), p. 40.

7. These include Ma Nku's St. John's Apostolic Faith Mission in Gauteng, Mai Chaza's City of God movement in Zimbabwe, and the churches of Alice Lenshina in Zambia and Miriam Ragot and Gaudencia Aoku in Kenya.

attributed to church names. In a sense the church's name *is* its charter, its historical positioning. The different types of AICs attempt to establish this name-charter link in different ways. Ethiopian-type AICs seek to link themselves with the early Christian church via the church of Ethiopia, hence the popularity of names like "First Ethiopian Church." The Bible text cited as the basis for this name is Psalm 68:31: "Ethiopia shall soon stretch out her hands to God." The "correct interpretation" of this text validates the argument that the Ethiopian church is the oldest and therefore the most authentic on the continent.[8] The 1935 Italo-Abyssinian War gave momentum to the spread of an Ethiopian mythology in South Africa and neighboring countries. According to Sundkler, "the Abyssinian ideology of the Ethiopians . . . is in essence an attempt to give the Independent Church an ancient Apostolic succession and a charter, linking their Church with the Bible."[9] Linked with rising African nationalist aspirations, the Ethiopian ideology certainly added to the attraction of AIC movements as they claimed autonomous leadership and patterns of inculturation for themselves.

Spirit-type churches, by contrast, establish the immediacy of the presence of the Holy Spirit and/or of Christ and his apostles through the use of names such as "Zion," "Apostolic," "Moriah," "African Zionist," or "African Apostolic." Church headquarters named "New Jerusalem," "Zion City," "Holy City," "City of God," etc. illustrate a direct identification with the holy places in Scripture and the need to replicate God's presence as portrayed in the Bible for the African situation. One of the favored texts used by Zionist leaders to assert God's presence in the "holy cities" is Revelation 14:1: ". . . there was the Lamb standing on Mt. Zion; with him were 144,000 people who have his name and his Father's name written on their foreheads." In the Jerusalem or Mt. Zion of Africa, the presence of Christ and his kingdom is mirrored in the iconic leader, surrounded by his/her followers as described in Revelation 14. Sundlker speaks of

> a more or less holy competition between the [Zionist] leaders for acquiring the most truly Biblical name possible for their Churches. The name gives status to the church . . . they secure for their Church a supernatural bond with those holy guarantees and they signify a charter showing the spiritual strength of the church.[10]

8. See M. L. Daneel, *Old and New in Southern Shona Independent Churches*, vol. 1: *Background and Rise of the Major Movements* (The Hague and Paris, 1971) and M. Aquina, "The People of the Spirit: An Independent Church in Rhodesia," *Africa* 37.2.

9. B. G. M. Sundkler, *Bantu Prophets in South Africa* (London, 1961), pp. 57-58.

10. Sundkler, *Bantu Prophets in South Africa*, p. 59.

One need only consider the life histories of the Zionist forerunners in Zimbabwe to gauge the importance of a Bible-based charter as a key factor in the rapid expansion of Zionism.[11]

Whether, ultimately, an AIC charter evolves from an emphasis on identification with and reenactment of portions of Scripture, or the rewriting and interpretation of aspects of church history, or a combination of both, the mythical immediacy and authenticating link with the historic Christ and his disciples remain of prime importance. Through ritual enactment and repeated proclamation, divine affirmation of the charter becomes entrenched and obtains canonical value for the church. In the context of inter-ecclesial competition and earlier rejection of AICs by the "mainline" churches, a biblically sanctioned charter also provides a measure of leadership autonomy and spiritual independence which places the integrity and freedom of innovative religious expression beyond dispute.

The second line of AICs' interpretation of their historical roots — self-definition in relation to more recent Christian history and local mainline mission churches — is, perhaps, more complex. Does the preoccupation of AICs with their mythological roots override their recognition of their historical roots in the "mainline" mission churches to the extent that this rootedness is relativized or trivialized? Did the schisms in the early history of some AICs cause such a radical severance of ties with the mission churches that they eliminated further interaction and continuing influence of the originating "mother" churches? How do the Spirit-type churches, in particular, relate to the worldwide Pentecostal movement?

There is a school of thought which classifies Spirit-type AICs[12] as "African Pentecostals" or "Pentecostal-type"[13] churches, emphasizing particularly the influence of the Christian Catholic Apostolic Church in Zion (CCACZ) of

11. Prior to their recruitment in South Africa both Bishop Samuel Mutendi and Bishop Andreas Shoko were deeply impressed by the Sotho Zionists' adherence to a so-called "proper biblical name." To them it evidently was a significant discovery that the name "Dutch Reformed Church" — the name of the mission church responsible for their earliest encounter with Christianity and for their education — could not be found in the Bible. See Daneel, *Old and New in Southern Shona Independent Churches*, vol. 1, p. 345.

12. Spirit-type churches may constitute up to 80 percent of all AICs in southern Africa. See G. C. Oosthuizen, *Religion, Intergroup Relations, and Social Change in South Africa* (New York, 1988); Allan Anderson, *Bazalwane: African Pentecostals in South Africa* (Pretoria, 1992), p. 21.

13. See, for example, Anderson, *Bazalwane;* Sundkler, *Bantu Prophets in South Africa* and *Zulu Zion and Some Swazi Zionists;* W. J. Hollenweger, *The Pentecostals* (London, 1972); and Harvey Cox, *Fire from Heaven: The Rise of Pentecostal Spirituality and the Reshaping of Religion in the Twentieth Century* (London, 1996).

Dowie, Illinois, and the Azusa Street revival.[14] Allan Anderson classifies South African Pentecostals into three categories: (1) the "Pentecostal mission churches" which originate from the predominantly white Pentecostal missions; (2) the younger Pentecostal or charismatic churches, founded and governed by blacks, referred to as "independent African Pentecostal churches"; and (3) the "indigenous Pentecostal-type churches," that is, the Spirit-type AICs, which constitute the vast majority of "African Pentecostals."[15] He argues that these churches share common historical, liturgical, and theological roots. Despite some striking differences, he contends that they "all have a marked emphasis on the working of the Holy Spirit in the church with supernatural 'gifts of the Spirit', especially healing, exorcism, speaking in tongues and prophesying. . . ."[16] For Anderson, these factors distinguish them from other Christian groups and justify their inclusion under one generic category of "African Pentecostal churches." Because of similarities in worship between classical Western Pentecostals and African Spirit-type churches, it appears that the latter are subtly appropriated through a superficial classificatory exercise. In this manner, "Pentecostal" membership and growth figures are inflated far beyond the impact that the missionary activity of the Western "Pentecostal mission churches" and "independent African Pentecostal churches" could ever have had. Given the emphasis on the historical roots of the South African Zionists in the American Holiness movement and in Pentecostal and CCACZ activities during the early 1900s, Anderson's statistical analysis[17] can easily give the misleading impression that the massive growth of the "AIC Pentecostals" is due somehow to Western-related Pentecostal fervor and influence rather than to the impact of the declining "mainline mission churches." However, in my view, this position overlooks the massive impact on African society and AIC growth of the "mainline mission churches." Although these churches in southern Africa are clearly on the wane, they have, nevertheless, profoundly molded the AICs — historically, spiritually, and theologically — in the course of the twentieth century, a fact obscured by the autonomous nature of AICs and by the suggestion of a direct "Pentecostal connection." The Zimbabwean AICs[18] bear out this point quite clearly. Sev-

14. Sundkler, *Bantu Prophets in South Africa*, p. 48; *Zulu Zion and Some Swazi Zionists*, pp. 13-67.

15. Anderson, *Tumelo*, p. 5.

16. Anderson, *Tumelo*, pp. 5-6.

17. Anderson, *Tumelo*, pp. 5-15.

18. The Pentecostal roots of Zionism in South Africa have received little acclaim among Zimbabwean Zionists or Apostles. The Zionists of Masvingo Province acknowledge no connection with the Pentecostals other than the ecumenical ties recently devel-

eral indicators point to a negligible connection between the local Spirit-type and Pentecostal churches.

First, since the middle 1960s I have frequently heard both *Ndaza* Zionist and Zion Christian Church (ZCC) preachers refer during their sermons to the Dutch Reformed Church as *vaDutchi ndimai nababa vedu* (our spiritual fathers and mothers).[19] Such sermons signal an awareness of existential rootedness and spiritual nurturing in the mission church to which most of the Zionists have had some form of allegiance over the years.[20] This observation does not detract from the conflicts, schisms, and individual defections from the mission churches in the past. Complaints about the racist or superior attitudes of the white missionaries, or, in the case of the *VaPostori*, about the neglect in the Methodist church of the manifestations of the Holy Spirit, were frequently vented in the Spirit-type churches concerned. Yet, as in any close interpersonal relationship, rootedness can include the contradictory attitudes of resentment, frustration, and even antagonism, on the one hand, and appreciation, affinity, and a sense of belonging, on the other.

Second, the dynamic of sustained interaction between the Dutch Reformed Church and AICs in the Masvingo Province was largely determined by the educational system. From the beginning of the 1900s until Zimbabwean Independence in 1980 the DRC controlled a vast number of rural schools throughout the region, at its peak managing more than six hundred schools. Consequently, the vast majority of first generation AIC members received their basic theological orientation in Reformed schools where they received regular religious instruction and catechetical training, irrespective of whether they attained full church membership or not. Even in the event of secession or individual defection from the DRC mission church, the

---

oped with them through the auspices of "Fambidzano" (see M. L. Daneel, *Fambidzano: Ecumenical Movement of Zimbabwean Independent Churches* [Gweru, Zimbabwe, 1989]). Moreover, despite distinct Pentecostal traits in worship and beliefs, none of the Shona Spirit-type churches deliberately characterize themselves as Pentecostal.

19. This, normally, in the context of an appeal to fellow Zionists for improved spirituality and Christian discipleship. Reference to the DRC — now called the Reformed Church of Zimbabwe — invariably included anecdotes on the life of the saintly Rev. Andrew Louw, founder of the church's mission at Morgenster, or the lives of influential missionaries, such as the well-known Dr. Tommy Steyn, Revs. Henry and George Murray, and their wives.

20. A similar trend was noticeable in the discussions I had with the *vaPostori* of Johane Maranke in the Mutare area in the east of Zimbabwe. Some Apostles proudly claimed that they were actually *maWisiri* (Wesleyans, i.e., Methodists) — the mission church to which many of them, including their founder, Johane Maranke, and the nuclear leadership of the church had formerly belonged.

ongoing attendance of thousands of AIC children and grandchildren in DRC schools contributed toward sustained interaction and reciprocal ties.[21] Thus autonomous AIC leadership did not entail complete isolation or independence of the budding new movements from the originating mission church.

Third, this religio-educational interface between mission church and AICs left its imprint on the latter. Whatever Pentecostal traits emerged in the Spirit-type churches, their theological foundation and premises remain distinctly Calvinist-Protestant, with an emphasis on the sinful nature of humans, redemption solely through the grace and blood of Christ, the necessity of personal faith, and definite conversion as a condition for personal salvation. Self-interpretation and inculturation within the AICs have of course contributed toward internal change. The development of Zionist and Apostolic holy cities, for instance, has its own biblical and African flavor. But the parallels between the models of these church headquarters and the Reformed mission stations — as staging posts for missionary campaigns, as seats of power where church councils exact discipline, and, in the case of the ZCC, as centers of control over schools and faith-healing hospitals — are striking and illustrate the deeply imbedded influence of the Protestant heritage. Small wonder, then, that Bishop Mutendi traced the roots of African Zionism not through classical or world Pentecostalism but through the Reformed and Catholic traditions, back to what he considered to be the original "Zion Church."

Fourth, compelling evidence of lasting DRC influence in the Spirit-type churches is to be found in an emergent AIC theology of religions at Zionist and Apostolic healing centers. Both church traditions share an explicit interest in and preoccupation with African cosmology, unlike the local Pentecostal churches, whose faith-healing praxis is not undergirded by penetrative interaction with African traditional religion. In terms of carrying the gospel message into the inner world of African religion and incarnating it at the deepest levels of religious experience, the Spirit-type AICs have in fact moved far ahead of the DRC and most other mainline mission churches. Nevertheless, the Reformed roots are in evidence in the emergent AIC *theologia religionum* in the sympathetic but confrontative dialogue of prophetic healers with their patients about ancestral demands as the cause of certain ailments, in the radical rejection of any form of *kupira mudzimu* (ancestral veneration) within the

21. A random sample survey on the correlation between AIC membership and education that I conducted in the Gutu district during the 1960s indicated that no less than 83 percent of the educated AIC adults had attended DRC-directed schools. Daneel, *Old and New in Southern Shona Independent Churches*, vol. 2, p. 37.

church, and in the insistence on deliberate Christianizing transformation of all traditional rituals to be inculturatively incorporated into the church.

Fifth, it is noteworthy that the DRC-related AICs seek recognition from the "mother mission church." Despite past conflicts and disaffection, AIC leaders have sought — both overtly and, in some respects, unwittingly — appreciative reciprocation from the DRC. They desired the Mission's acceptance of their dignity and their innovative and evangelistic initiatives as church leaders, and full affirmation of their status as fellow disciples in Christ. Unfortunately, they were often rebuffed by DRC officials, both black and white, and treated as Separatist offenders who posed a threat to the mission church, or as wayward and syncretistic sects who had moved to the periphery of Christianity.

The historic roots and ecclesial interconnections of the Shona AICs reveal that they have essentially three interlinked sets of historical interpretation regarding their origin and, by implication, their relatedness to other churches. Psychologically, their mythological roots in the early Christian church by way of a biblical charter are probably the most gratifying. Divine sanction liberates the AICs from the judgmentalism of mission churches and from the complex history of Western Christendom. Insofar as Pentecostal roots are recognized by the Spirit-type churches, they trace them back to the founding African church fathers rather than to classical Pentecostalism. They do not see the latter as a bridge to world Pentecostalism, nor do they want to be classified as Pentecostals in the world church. Instead, their more immediate roots in the mainline mission churches — paradoxically in relation to their mythological roots — appear to function more directly at the existential level of church life. Historically, and in terms of their theological foundations, it may therefore be correct to interpret the AICs as a self-made and fully Africanized branch of Western Protestantism, regionally reflecting Reformed, Methodist, Anglican, or Lutheran characteristics in accordance with the earlier or still prevailing dominant mission church influence in the region. Similar trends are likely where AICs have emerged as a result of schism in or defections from the Roman Catholic Church, although comparatively few AICs have emerged from within the Roman Catholic tradition.[22] The Pentecostal traits found in the Spirit-type churches can hardly be seen simply as the fruit of the missionary endeavor of Western Pentecostal churches. Despite obvious parallels in worship and emphasis on the centrality of the Holy Spirit, the de-

---

22. For a full discussion of the reasons why the Roman Catholic Church has suffered less from schisms and defections than the Pentecostal churches, see my *Quest for Belonging,* pp. 87-97.

velopment of Zionist and Apostolic prophetic healing and related Spirit-led inculturated ministries suggest that these have evolved more directly from internal and independent Bible interpretation in relation to African needs and worldviews rather than from sustained nurturing or directives by Pentecostal missions.

How representative are the Shona AICs as a case study for southern Africa? I would argue that my provisional findings apply to most Zimbabwean AICs. The two Spirit-type churches which I have studied intensively — the Maranke Apostles and the ZCC — are the largest AICs in Zimbabwe. Taken together with the other indigenous churches in the central and southeastern regions of Zimbabwe, they include millions of adherents, a significant cross-section of the Spirit-type churches in southern Africa. Because I am wary of sweeping generalizations about this phenomenon in Zimbabwe alone, at most I can surmise, on the basis of periodic contacts with AIC leaders in the Gauteng region,[23] that some of my observations may also be relevant in South Africa. It is my impression that here, too, the connection with classical Pentecostalism is incidental rather than primary.[24] As AICs increasingly participate in local and global ecumenical movements, they will find their own niche and craft their own typologies in the context of the world Church.

Protest Movements or Liberation Movements?

Although the protest theory of the origination and rise of the AICs predominates in the early literature, I would argue that the designation "liberation movements" is a more appropriate term. Protest theorists contend that racial segregation and colonialism's oppressive sociopolitical conditions provided the impetus for religious Independentism. While theorists in the field do not sharply distinguish between sociopolitical and religious protest, their differences in emphasis allow for such differentiation even though it must be conceded at the outset that the close identification of Christianity with colonial rule renders a radical compartmentalization of political and religious factors impossible.

---

23. Notably Bishops Ngada, Ntongana, Mofokeng, and Dr. Lydia August, among others.

24. Bishop Ngada, for instance, prefers to call Spirit-type churches in the ecumenical movement he had founded the "African Spiritual Churches" as opposed to "African Pentecostal Churches."

Sociopolitical Protest

Sundkler, for many years the leading authority on South African AICs, argued that Separatism was the result of the color bar within the Christian Church. AIC membership and growth were directly related to racism and the tightening squeeze on Africans through land legislation.[25] Others have related the phenomenon of AIC growth to the need for political expression,[26] the reaction of the colonized to the colonizers,[27] or the "simple correlation between the appearance of the cults and the absence of political representation."[28] Thus, AICs, generally referred to then as the Independent Churches, were portrayed as movements of political protest.

More recently, Jean Comaroff has developed an extensive "ritual protest thesis." Her analysis of Zionist dance in South Africa as an example of a "ritual of reconstruction" identifies the objects of protest, namely, the neocolonial marketplace and the apartheid state.[29] In modern South Africa, she contends, it is obvious that

> within the "safe" and legitimate world of ritual action, a composite show of defiance is being acted out. Men demonstrate the threat of their physical strength . . . [their] boots beat out a tattoo of resistance and resolve. While there is seldom overt reference to the diffuse coercion of the neo-colonial marketplace, or to the more concentrated oppressions of the apartheid state, the identity of evil is unmistakable.[30]

In his assessment of Comaroff's protest theory Craig Scandrett-Leatherman makes two observations:

> First the common semantic of the word "protest" suggests a conscious object against which a person or group resists or rebels, but the acquies-

25. Sundkler, *Bantu Prophets in South Africa*, p. 37.

26. E. Andersson, *Messianic Popular Movements in the Lower Congo*, Studia Ethnographica Upsaliensia, no. 14 (Uppsala, 1958), passim.

27. G. Balandier, "Messianismes et nationalismes en Afrique Noir," in *Cahiers Internationaux de Sociologie* (Paris, 1953), pp. 41-65.

28. L. Mair, "Independent Religious Movements in Three Continents," *Comparative Studies in Society and History* 1 (1963): 181.

29. J. Comaroff, *Body of Power, Spirit of Resistance: The Culture and History of Southern African People* (Chicago, 1985), p. 164.

30. Comaroff, *Body of Power, Spirit of Resistance*, p. 248; C. Scandrett-Leatherman, "The Signifying Politics of Black Religion: Reconstructing African American Home and Dignity in a Chicago Storefront Church," M.A. thesis, University of Chicago, 1999, p. 12.

cent words, tones and work-ethics of Zionists make it difficult to interpret their ritual in this way. The second problem is that the protest thesis
does not account for the ritualists' exegesis, rather it imposes an academic or state politics foci, a metropolitan perspective on African rituals by "requiring" that the focus of rituals must somehow be on the gov-
ernmental state in the form of a protest or acquiescence.[31]

This criticism is based to some extent on J. P. Kiernan's observations that
Zionist rituals focus on the purity of the person and the power of God and
that the arena of power in this movement is not the outside world but the
kingdom of Zion.[32] Zionist rituals, according to Kiernan, appropriate symbols of power not so much as a means of cultural resistance to the state, as
Comaroff infers, but as a way of establishing an identity distinct from the im-
moral life associated with African townships.[33]

Although Kiernan's critique of protest theory is valuable, it is also somewhat one-sided as he attributes his insights to the "urban experience" and to
the literature since 1975 on urban AICs. "Religious independence," he claims,
"is now viewed less as a negative reaction [a form of protest or withdrawal]
on the part of the powerless to intolerable deprivation and more as a positive
and potentially rewarding response to the demands of an urban environment."[34] Kiernan contends that the weakness of the protest theory as all-
embracing explanation is exposed when its relevance is reviewed in relation
to the ritual and observance of the African Independent Churches.[35] What he
fails to take into account (by focusing on urban AICs and the literature from
1975 on) is the *rural* AIC experience.[36] At most, the insights on AIC causation
derived from urban studies corroborate and augment what has already been
observed and substantially documented for AICs in their rural manifestation.

Recognition of the limitations of the protest theory does not require one
to characterize AIC movements either as politically inactive or as supportive

31. Scandrett-Leatherman, "The Signifying Politics of Black Religion," pp. 20-21.
32. J. P. Kiernan, *The Production and Management of Therapeutic Power in Zionist
Churches within a Zulu City* (Lewiston, 1996), pp. 88, 101.
33. For this brief and admittedly incomplete discussion of the Comaroff thesis, I am
indebted to Scandrett-Leatherman for his discerning exposition on this subject in his unpublished "The Signifying Politics of Black Religion."
34. Kiernan, *Production and Management*, p. 7.
35. Kiernan, *Production and Management*, p. 18.
36. My critique of protest theory, unlike Kiernan's, derives from a predominantly
rural AIC experience. See Daneel, *Old and New in Southern Shona Independent Churches*,
vol. 2.

of the political powers of the day. Although some would classify the Zionists as politically acquiescent,[37] neither political protest theory nor the acquiescence hypothesis does full justice to the variety of factors determining the life and growth of southern African AICs. My objection to these socio-anthropological theories is their categorical or exclusive application. Such a narrow focus on political orientation in the AICs invariably distorts the overall picture at the expense of significant religious, theological, and related factors.

Religious Protest

Theologians who employ protest theory tend to shift the focus from political to more specifically religious protest. AIC growth is thus largely attributed to African Christians' *negative* responses to the flaws and limitations of Western churches. David Barrett, a leading exponent of this viewpoint, characterizes religious independency as a reaction to missions, the root cause of which is "a failure in sensitivity, the failure of missions at one small point to demonstrate consistently the fullness of the biblical concept of love and sensitive understanding toward others as equals, the failure to study or understand African society, religion, and psychology in any depth. . . ."[38] Prominent historians and missiologists[39] hold similar views even while acknowledging the interplay of other causative factors.[40] The focus, however, is on the inadequacies of foreign missions (e.g., poor communications, lack of dialogue, ignorance of indigenous beliefs and customs, racist attitudes, divisions caused by Western denominationalism, etc.) as the prime factor contributing to AIC growth.

Religious protest theories are fundamentally flawed in that they reflect an overriding preoccupation with the limitations of foreign missions at the expense of examining what really motivates the AICs. One seeks in vain for an explanation of AIC growth and outreach in terms of the movement's own innovative mission strategies. Instead, the basic assumption that AICs origi-

---

37. See, e.g., R. P. Werbner, "The Argument about Images: From Zion to the Wilderness in African Churches," in W. M. J. Van Binsbergen and M. Schoffeleers, eds., *Theoretical Explorations in African Religions* (Boston, 1985), pp. 268-72; W. M. J. Van Binsbergen, *Religious Change in Zambia: Exploratory Studies* (London, 1981), pp. 55-59; M. Schoffeleers, "Black and African Theology in Southern Africa: A Controversy Re-examined," *Journal of Religion in Africa* 18.2 (1998): 113-14.

38. Barrett, *Schism and Renewal in Africa*, p. 56.

39. E.g., Adrian Hastings, David Bosch, and G. C. Oosthuizen.

40. Daneel, *Quest for Belonging*, p. 71.

nated within Western-oriented mission churches is unmistakable. Such assumptions often include interpretations of the AICs as "sheep-stealers" or "Separatists" who derive their primary expansion from schisms or individual defections from mission churches. My research findings on the Shona AICs lead me to argue that protest was peripheral to sustained AIC growth.[41] Much more important is the response of AIC missionaries to their own understanding of the gospel challenge.

Liberationist Trends

Rather than categorizing AICs as political protest movements or — by contrast — as politically acquiescent, we should perhaps regard them as liberation movements. AIC leaders on the whole do not refer to their churches as "liberation movements," nor are they generally aware of Latin American liberation theology or familiar with the literature on South African black theology. Nevertheless, liberationist features are in evidence in the histories of the AICs. Unlike black theology with its combination of academically sophisticated sociopolitical analysis and theological reflection, which crystallizes into a written theology and conferences dominated by the theme of liberation, AICs enact their own brand of liberation, unobtrusively yet forcefully at the grassroots of African society. Here, liberation belongs to the very being of the church — every form of ecclesiastic articulation expresses some form of independence from Western encroachment or control. The value of this implicit liberation theology for an emergent African theology is generally underrated because AIC leaders keep a low profile in national events and the news media. Theirs is an unwritten, heterogeneous theology in which liberation is often more an intuitively lived reality than an explicit theme of sermons or planned programs of action. Nevertheless, distinct trends of liberative action, some of which coincide with discernible periods of national history in the countries of Africa, are in evidence. We will look briefly at four trends.

Religio-cultural Liberation

In the early history of AICs their exodus from Western missionary institutions permitted a new experience of determining their own religious identity and exploring scriptural truths in a liberated atmosphere of song, dance, and sermons improvised to suit the occasion. Thus organizational emancipation led

41. Daneel, *Old and New in Southern Shona Independent Churches,* vol. 2.

to liturgical indigenization and transformation. This process, insofar as it included a reevaluation of indigenous culture and religion, led to numerous church rites informed by local African worldviews. The Shona AICs, for instance, replaced the traditional *kugadzira* (ancestral home-bringing ceremony) with a Christian *runyaradzo* (consolation ceremony); they replaced the traditional *mukwerere* rain rituals and oracular ceremonies of the Mwari cult with Christian rain requests during *ungano yembeu* (seed conferences), and the healing practices of the traditional *nganga* (doctor-diviner) with a host of symbolically appropriate faith-healing practices.[42] Faith-healing practices in the Spirit-type churches clearly reflect that religio-cultural liberation is not just a reaction to Western mission control and medical science, accompanied by an uncritical affirmation of indigenous rituals and customs. The healing rites of Zionist and Apostolic prophets represent pastoral and psychological liberation for people threatened by destructive forces, including spiritual powers. This pastoral-psychological approach of the prophet-healer communicates the Christian message of salvation at the core of the African conceptual and experiential world. As such it constitutes the essence of healing, the single most effective recruitment mechanism of the entire movement.

Socioeconomic Liberation

The AICs are all well adapted to southern Africa's rural conditions. Extensive leadership structures and well worked out church responsibilities for office-bearers and lay members enable people who have little political say or social standing to improve their social status. Church ceremonies, where members appear in their dignified robes or uniforms bearing their leadership monograms, provide opportunity for the proud assertion of a new identity. Spontaneous worship, song, and dance enhance a sense of control over the problems of peasant existence. Thus church life, in all its absorbing and colorful variations, liberates participants from the blight of social obscurity and drudgery.

In a rural subsistence economy AICs represent economic progress and communicate the good news of freedom from economic impotence and fatalism in the face of poverty and restricted farming conditions. This message is conveyed through identification with the poor and concerted application of modern farming methods, resulting in improved cash crops. In Zimbabwe the Spirit-type leaders in particular qualified as master farmers and acquired farms in the erstwhile "Native Purchase Areas." Through a combination of improved farming and business enterprise they became examples of a degree

42. Daneel, *Old and New in Southern Shona Independent Churches*, vol. 2, passim.

of economic prosperity. The ZCC links the entire rural agricultural economy with religion in a holistic fashion. In Zion City, Bishop Mutendi introduced a mutual aid system. He prayed for rain just before the planting season and blessed the seed to be sown by his followers throughout the country. ZCC congregations reciprocated by bringing part of their harvest to Zion City, where it is used to feed orphans, the poor, and the sick, or as relief for church members in drought-stricken areas, thus honoring the traditional principle of reciprocity. Farming is stimulated and improved by extending it beyond the narrow family context to the God-given, mystically protected context of the church. Consequently, efficient farming methods and good harvests are interpreted as signs of divine blessing and become the subject of witness in ZCC sermons. Although the agriculture-based mutual aid systems of the ZCC and other AICs are not unqualified success stories, the improved ability of participant subsistence farmers to cope during crises and to start afresh with confidence communicates something of the uniqueness of a God whose love and mercy will not let one go.[43]

In recent years AIC ecumenical movements such as Fambidzano and the Association of African Earthkeeping Churches (AAEC) have succeeded in soliciting considerable amounts of development funds from donor agencies abroad to enable rural communities to engage in development projects.[44] The ZIRRCON[45] Women's Desk currently empowers eighty Women's Clubs, composed of both traditionalist representatives of AZTREC (Association of Zimbabwean Traditionalist Ecologists) and leading AIC women of the AAEC, to engage in a wide range of income-generating and ecological projects.[46] Despite the disadvantage of creating a degree of dependence of foreign support, these ecumenically orchestrated economic initiatives serve as a major contribution in the struggle of ruralists against poverty.

In the urban situation the AICs emerge as "reorientation centers" — communities offering security and a chance of social integration in a harsh, re-

---

43. M. L. Daneel, "Communication and Liberation in African Independent Churches," *Missionalia* 11.2 (1983): 74-75.

44. Fambidzano's erection of a large number of community development centers at AIC headquarters for purposes of vocational training, agricultural advancement, clothes manufacturing, food, oil and soap production, as well as the construction of water schemes in deprived villages signals the determination of AIC leaders to grapple with modernizing processes of economic advancement. See Daneel, *Fambidzano*, ch. 8.

45. ZIRRCON is the Zimbabwean Institute of Religious Research and Ecological Conservation.

46. M. L. Daneel, *African Earthkeepers*, vol. 1: *Interfaith Mission in Earth-care* (Pretoria, 1998), ch. 3; *African Earthkeepers*, vol. 2: *Environmental Mission and Liberation in Christian Perspective*, African Initiatives in Christian Mission 3 (Pretoria, 1999), ch. 6.

lentlessly competitive world where stabilizing kinship codes and tribal mores no longer function effectively. Martin West, in his Soweto-based study, provides a representative picture of the value of urban AICs in their encounter with the complexities of urbanization.[47]

Kiernan's excellent study of Zionists in KwaMashu, near Durban, reveals similar trends. The Zionists themselves are poorer than poor. Yet, they manage to organize their "bands" (i.e., congregations) as welfare organizations based on the principle of self-help, providing an "insurance system" whereby their members, through regular contributions to the church, receive the necessary financial aid for the conduct of their socially significant ceremonies: birth, marriages, and deaths. As in Soweto, the Durban Zionist churches function as protective institutions in hostile surroundings, dealing with the mystical threats of sorcery accusations, providing security and group cohesion through the invocation of the liberating power of the Holy Spirit.[48]

The overall image that emerges from West's and Kiernan's studies is one of urban churches that actualize a theology of fellowship and economic stability among the poor by way of new social structures and behavioral codes. This provides support to members in stressful situations marked by economic deprivation, alienation, and isolation. Material and spiritual frames of reference, adapted to the industrial environment, give meaning, hope, and a sense of liberation from an otherwise disorienting and emotionally debilitating urban existence.

Political Liberation

The sermons and catechesis of mission churches throughout southern Africa in all likelihood created an impression among Africans of a God who was concerned about individual morals and salvation rather than one who was directly involved in the daily activities of rural life. In this situation the prophetic AIC leaders transformed the image of a *deus remotus* into one of direct divine involvement in tribal and national politics. Here one can cite the sensitive leadership of outstanding prophetic figures such as Shembe and Lekganyane senior in South Africa,[49] Mutendi and Maranke in Zimba-

---

47. M. West, *Bishops and Prophets in a Black City: African Independent Churches in Soweto Johannesburg* (Cape Town, 1975), p. 195. A few of the outstanding features of urban AICs include: (1) brotherhood and social interaction, (2) protection, and (3) information and assistance.

48. Kiernan, *Production and Management*, ch. 4.

49. Sundkler, *Buntu Prophets in South Africa*, p. 278; *Zulu Zion and Some Swazi Zionists*, pp. 161-97.

bwe,[50] and Kimbangu in Zaire.[51] Because of their close contact with chiefs and tribal elders, they were aware of the problems of local administration and therefore presented a relevant gospel message at this level.

Mutendi's appeal among tribal leaders in Zimbabwe derived largely from his courageous resistance to colonial rule in the educational and religious spheres, for which he was arrested and detained on several occasions. His Zion City symbolized not only the Christian kingdom but also the ancient Rozvi dynasty, evoking the by-gone glory of Shona nationhood. Thus his popular title, "man of God," had both religious and political connotations.[52] Mutendi introduced the gospel message into tribal politics by having his Zionist prophets appointed as advisors to the tribal courts of affiliated chiefs. In this way, guidance through revelations of the Holy Spirit, as experienced by Zionists, could directly influence the customary judiciary and various facets of local government, especially regarding boundary disputes. Aware of the conflicts chiefs and headmen had to face — torn between the disparate demands of colonial administration and local tribespeople — the "man of God" sought to provide frustrated tribal elders with a spiritual anchorage which could help them function optimally, in a situation which constantly reflected their impotence in relation to white overlords.

In this context the Zionist message of liberation evolved. It did not promise easy solutions or revolutionary changes that could bring sudden freedom from bondage. Instead, the Zionist support system enabled chiefs and headmen to cope by liberating them from the fears and anxiety that often beset them. As Christ did not constitute a Messianic order which would satisfy Jewish nationalistic aspirations, Mutendi did not promise another Rozvi confederation or Zionist empire which would overthrow white rule. But he did set an example to the chiefs of how one could realistically co-operate with the rulers without loss of dignity, and how to resist unjust legislation or actions even if such resistance rarely brought about the desired results. In a sense, Zion City became for the chiefs a "halfway house" between colonial rule and radical African nationalistic factions — a protective refuge where the chiefs and headmen could participate in the subtle resistance of their people to foreign influence without entirely jeopardizing their positions in relation to the European administration on whom they depended.[53]

50. Daneel, *Old and New in Southern Shona Independent Churches,* vol. 1, p. 285.
51. M.-L. Martin, *Kimbangu — an African Prophet and His Church* (Oxford, 1975).
52. Daneel, *Old and New in Southern Shona Independent Churches,* vol. 1, p. 386.
53. One of the most striking instances of Mutendi's resistance to colonial rule occurred in 1965 when the bishop supported the local Rozvi chief's opposition to the district commissioner's arbitrary ruling on a well-publicized Rozvi-Duma boundary dispute. The

While Zimbabwean AICs on the whole maintained a low profile in national politics for pragmatic reasons of self-preservation, this does not imply political acquiescence. Black nationalist sentiments were regularly expressed in sermons and church activities, including themes of racial equality, the dignity of the black race, and the competence of Africans to rule themselves. The main AIC contribution to political liberation lay in providing religious justification for the liberation struggle, by adducing the necessary scriptural affirmation. In this sense the AICs were the religious vanguard of black nationalism.[54] The AICs on the subcontinent have certainly not generally been politically acquiescent or supportive of oppressive rule.[55] A study of the history of AICs will compel African theologians, who have hitherto tended to see these churches' merits as limited to the indigenization or inculturation of church praxis, to accord greater recognition to the distinctive socioeconomic and political contribution of AICs to the independence of African states.

---

ruling jeopardized the ZCC holy city by placing it under the direct jurisdiction of a hostile Duma chief. When the Rozvi appeal failed, Mutendi took the initiative in launching a supreme court suit against the local district commissioner, the provincial commissioner, and the minister of the interior. He lost the court case, but for both the Rozvi people and the ZCC the entire episode had a tremendous psychological value. In this struggle, liberation meant that the "man of God" would brook no compromise in that, at the risk of losing his holy city — the pride and joy of his followers throughout the country — he would oppose the colonial regime. God's protection in this instance did not spell the retention of Zion City. Instead, it became manifest in the courage of an already aged bishop, who led his followers and a large number of Rozvi tribespeople in a massive exodus from Bikita district to a distant home in northern Gokwe. There they built a new Zion City, and the ZCC flourished anew. Through his role in these events as an African Moses figure, Bishop Mutendi wrote a chapter of resistance or liberation history in the annals of ZCC, thus providing, on the eve of *chimurenga* (Zimbabwe's liberation struggle), a precedent for the active participation of his church in the bush war that was to culminate in independence.

54. Examples of this include the following: Bishop Matthew Zvimba, founder of the Shiri Chena Church, who displayed his black nationalist colors at the beginning of the century by declaring the traditional religious martyrs of the first *chimurenga* (the 1896 rebellion) saints in his church; Bishop Mutendi, whose entire public career (1925-76) in Zimbabwe promoted essentially nonviolent black resistance against colonial rule, provided an ideological model, through his holy city, of a black-ruled state, and facilitated the socioeconomic welfare of thousands of followers; and the African Apostolic Church of Johane Maranke (AACJM), which expressed aggressive anti-white sentiments on the assumption that whites had killed Christ, withheld the message of the church of the Holy Spirit from Africans, and oppressed the "house of Ham" (the African race).

55. The role of AICs in the liberation history of Zimbabwe, as enacted in the bush war, remains to be written.

Environmental Liberation

Throughout the 1990s a large contingent of Zimbabwean AICs engaged in a wide-ranging ministry of environmental liberation, popularly referred to as the "War of the Trees." In many ways they pioneered a fully inculturated African eco-theology, which includes new patterns of close interaction and dialogue with traditionalists, new interpretations of Christology, and the proclamation of a salvation which extends to all of creation.

Two features of the AICs' commitment to the environmental liberation struggle need to be mentioned here. First, the entire movement stands fully in the tradition of Zimbabwe's liberation history. The traditionalist counterparts of the AIC earthkeepers, namely, the spirit mediums and Mwari cultists of AZTREC, include many who were active in the *chimurenga* war front. Likewise, quite a number of affiliated AAEC prophetic leaders actively supported the guerrillas. The green fighters, therefore — be they traditionalists operating on behalf of the guardian ancestors of the land or Christians responding to the call of Christ the Earthkeeper — draw on a rich liberationist heritage in their mobilization of grassroots communities for environmental reform, and they interpret their struggle as a direct extension of the war that led to independence.

Second, the AAEC's earthkeeping drive blends with the attempts of AICs in recent years to engage in the socioeconomic uplifting of their people. The "war" against poverty and the "war" against uncontrolled environmental devastation go hand in hand. In both instances AICs are increasingly involved in the planning and implementation of modern projects which require technical skill, interaction with donor agencies, the development of accountable financial control systems, the conscientization of rural communities through workshops, the control and monitoring of nurseries and wood lots, and so forth. Significantly, much of this is achieved without a loss of religious identity and with a growing awareness that AICs are part of the world Church and valued members of the global village. The quest for liberation in all its diverse manifestations seems to enrich, rather than distract from or distort, church life. A healthy dialectic among liberative impulses, conversion, and spiritual growth apparently prevails. The church remains the church — calling its members to repentance, preaching the gospel, administering the sacraments, and reaching out into the world in mission — despite and also because of the specific liberationist concerns which hold sway during particular historical periods.[56]

56. During the period of crisis in 1965 when Bishop Mutendi opposed the government's ruling on the Rozvi-Duma boundary dispute (see note 53), I observed that the church's annual program of paschal celebrations followed by missionary campaigns was

Missionary Churches

Although few observers have applied the term "mission church" to the AICs,[57] they have developed such a wide range of inculturated mission models that they undoubtedly qualify as African mission churches, served by their own African missionaries. Judged by Henry Venn's three-selves criteria for church planting, the AICs on the whole are fully self-governing, self-supporting, and self-propagating.[58] In their enactment of local grassroots theologies they can also be said to be self-theologizing. They may lag behind the mission-founded African churches — called mainline "younger" or "daughter" churches — in terms of institutional development, theological education, and access to Western resources, but they certainly are more autonomous, self-reliant, and capable of coping with the often scant resources at their disposal than their Western-related counterparts.

AIC mission praxis frequently remains hidden in the growth histories of these churches. A variety of mission models are enacted daily at the grassroots of African society, though they are never written up and appropriated in theoretical shape by specialized missiologists to be implemented by some church council or board. Instead, these models are diffuse and integral to holistic patterns of church life, escaping exact definition yet manifesting distinct contours where AIC leaders and fellow believers proclaim and live the gospel. This is particularly evident in the missionary impetus derived in the Spirit-type churches from the sacrament of Holy Communion. I shall pay special attention to three variations of the Eucharist-related mission model in a brief overview of only a few of the most outstanding features of AIC missions. Illustrations will be drawn mainly from the two largest AICs in Zimbabwe: the ZCC (Zion Christian Church) and the AACJM (African Apostolic Church of Johane Maranke), popularly referred to as the *vaPostori* (the Apostles).

---

maintained and intensified. ZCC sermons of the time had a special focus on the urgency of conversion against the backdrop of God's judgment and Christ's cross and resurrection. Reference to Mutendi's plight and the possible loss of Zion City, if anything, served to deepen the Zionists' understanding of a suffering Christ.

57. "Mission church" has been so widely used in Africa to refer to Western "mainline" churches that AIC leaders themselves seldom use it in order to maintain their own unique identity; nor do they refer to those in their midst engaged in evangelistic outreach as "missionaries."

58. For a discussion of Venn's three-selves formula, see J. Verkuyl, *Contemporary Missiology: An Introduction* (Grand Rapids, 1978), pp. 52-53; Max Warren, ed., *To Apply the Gospel: Selections from the Writings of Henry Venn* (Grand Rapids, 1971); and P. Beyerhaus, *Die Selbständigkeit der jungen Kirche als Missionarisches Problem* (Wuppertal, 1959), pp. 39-41.

The Sacrament as "Launching Pad" for Missionary Endeavor

Many of the Spirit-type churches in Zimbabwe, including the *Ndaza* Zionists, have built their mission campaigns around their annual paschal celebrations in which the Eucharist is the climactic flash point, sending off bands of office-bearers to preach, convert, and baptize people. In particular the ZCC and the *vaPostori* excel in fusing the sacramental peak of these celebrations — called "Paseka" by the Zionists and "Pendi" (Pentecost) by the Apostles — with the church's response to Christ's "Great Commission."

During massive ZCC meetings at Zion City, preceding the Eucharist, the late Bishop Mutendi would preach repeatedly about Christ's classic mission command as found in Matthew 28:19. As Christ urged his disciples, the Zionist "man of God" would confront his thousands of followers with the command: "Go ye forth and make disciples of all nations!" In response, the church councilors planned and prayed daily for the forthcoming missionary campaign, based on the mobilization of the entire church.

Bishop Mutendi seldom dwelt on the actual meaning of the words "all nations," save to imply that a rich harvest of new converts was expected. Neither did he describe precisely the objects of missionary endeavor. His references in his sermons to his own perseverance on preaching tours were intended to inspire his followers to overcome opposition. In addition, he rebuked those who evaded the mission task by comparing them to the Israelites' hardening of heart (Rom. 11:25). Mutendi also closely identified his own work with that of Jesus Christ. In the convictions and life-long commitment of the Zionist leader, the claim of Jesus Christ that "all power in heaven and on earth are given to me" (Matt. 28:18) — those powers on which the Great Commission rests — takes concrete, appealing, Zionist shape. The iconic leadership of the "man of God" is most strikingly illustrated in the calling of his entire church to mission. God becomes compellingly visible in the black face, the hands, the feet, the message of his emissary.

ZCC women feature prominently in such campaigns, engaging in Bible instruction, healing activities, and witness sermons in surrounding villages, drawing large crowds to the weekend rallies where conversion and baptism take place. Meanwhile, the home congregation at Zion City engages in daily intercession for the campaign, until all the team leaders have returned to report on the state of the congregations they have visited and the recruitment of new members.

Similarly, the annual Pentecost celebration of the AACJM, held near Mt. Nyengwe in the Maranke communal lands, serves to encourage the Apostles to mission. Preoccupation with Maranke's life[59] during Pentecost sermons stimulates in the ranks of his followers a renewed commitment to the church's missionary mandate. Focusing on the apostolic leader as icon of Christ is tantamount to considering both the head and the body of the entire church. And as the founder-leader was nothing but an itinerant missionary, proclaiming and living the good news, the entire church is exhorted to be similarly engaged, to cross boundaries in mission.

For seventeen days, as the masses of Apostles — up to 100,000 members — prepare themselves for the Eucharist, the community of believers, that is, the *kereke*, is cleansed through fasting and prayer, preaching, choir song, confession of sin, and a concerted drive by the prophets to rid participants of all indwelling evil spirits. In this way the believers' communal witness to the world, through renewal by the Holy Spirit, is considered to be strengthened. As the "Pentecost" progresses toward its Eucharistic climax, Maranke increasingly features as the true emissary, the Apostle of Africa, sent by Christ to bring deliverance to the neglected and oppressed house of Ham. This "house" — the African race — is now carrying out Christ's commission because the houses of Shem and Japheth, the whites, proved themselves incapable of faithful missionary service. In their greed for the riches of Africa they had dropped the banner of the Holy Spirit, only for it to be picked up by the Apostles of Africa.

Like the Zionist Eucharist, the Apostolic sacrament ceremony, which lasts a full day and night, is a massive statement of missionary resolve. The late Maranke's missionary life, which mirrors a pilgrim discipleship in Christ, is sacramentally grafted onto the church's existence. Consequently, a ripple effect of Apostolic witness and recruitment is achieved all over Zimbabwe and surrounding countries as the *vaPostori* return to their home districts. In this case, reports of campaigns and conversions are not made back at the church headquarters as the Zionists do but to their senior regional office-bearers, to suit the Apostles' somewhat decentralized form of church organization. Church growth and the creation of new Sabbath (i.e., congregational) centers are confirmed and assessed during regional *Pendi* festivities, when Maranke's living representatives and heads of the church visit the districts to participate and give guidance to local church life. In the principal leaders' itinerant lifestyle and deliberate rejection of any attempt to develop a holy city, Maranke's

---

59. Maranke did not build a "holy city" as Mutendi did, but spent the thirty years of his working life in evangelizing travel, much of it on foot, throughout Zimbabwe, Mozambique, Malawi, Northern Transvaal, and Congo, converting, baptizing, healing, and organizing thousands of followers into new Apostolic congregations.

singular determination to imitate the ministry of Christ and that of the New Testament Apostles remains in evidence.

The link between sacrament and mission annually expressed in the two churches surveyed is less the result of theological reflection than of an intuitive understanding of the dialectic between compassionate spirituality and Christian witness, with growth in the body of believers as a result.[60] As missionaries, the strength and influence of both Mutendi and Maranke lay in their leading by example and sharing their commitment to Christ's commission with their followers. At the very point of inviting their followers to the communion table they were challenging them to share the salvific good news not only among themselves but also with the wider family of humankind. The black iconic leader, as Christ incarnate, was handing his followers earth-bound symbols of internal bondedness in community and external outreach. In Bishop Mutendi's case, the same hands that handed out the sacramental elements would, in the aftermath of the paschal Eucharist, be laid on the heads and bodies of thousands of departing Zionist missionaries to bless their coming missionary campaign across the country and beyond its borders. Here rests Africa's communal response to Christ's great commission.

That both leaders, dead but represented by the leadership of their offspring, are considered by their followers to maintain the impetus of the missionary drive and growth of their churches — mainly through inspiring dreams and visions — is further indication of Africa's religious genius at

60. A theological evaluation of this type of mission model should take the following points into consideration:

First, both AIC leaders have succeeded in forging a direct link between the Eucharist and the Great Commission.

Second, the *Christology* undergirding this model is contextually African and subject to some limitations. Unevenness in church praxis and belief systems is the hallmark not only of the AICs but also of the world Church, and should stimulate ongoing theological reflection, interaction, improvement, and growth.

Third, the Eucharistic sacrament qualifies and repeatedly affirms the very nature of the church as missionary. Ecclesial definitions were not uppermost in the minds of men like Mutendi and Maranke. But they shared and lived the conviction that the churches they had founded were essentially part of the *missio Dei*. Because of such conviction and their own life-styles as itinerant missionaries, the churches they led became "pilgrim churches."

Fourth, the desire to mediate salvation continues to play a central role in the ZCC's and AACJM's mission, as it did in the history of Christian missions worldwide. As Jerald Gort (J. Gort, "Heil, onheil en bemiddeling," in *Oecumenische inleiding*, pp. 203-18, quoted in David J. Bosch, *Transforming Mission: Paradigm Shifts in Theology of Mission* [New York, 1991], p. 393) correctly observes, the "soteriogical motif" may indeed be termed the "throbbing heart of missiology" since it concerns the "deepest and most fundamental question of humanity."

work in contextualizing the missionary nature of the church. In this instance the Christian cloud of witnesses (Hebrews 12) of deceased missionary leaders provides new content to the traditional bondedness of the living with their ancestors. The ongoing interpretation and implementation of mission from within the Eucharistic context continue to be informed by the life histories, experience, and mission strategies established by these deceased emissaries of God. The inspirational value of the exemplary lives of these outstanding African missionaries in itself begs historical recording, not only for the sake of the local African church but also for the world Church.

While I cannot describe in detail here the wide-ranging effects of Zionist and Apostolic witnessing and recruitment activities triggered by sacramental celebration,[61] it is important to note that a unique feature of this mission model is that it actuates the *entire* church in outreach and service. Whatever the eschatological balance or imbalance in the soteriology of the two churches concerned, the evidence points to an exceedingly rich legacy in mission history and a contextually enacted, if unsystematized, theology of mission. There is no doubt that there are in this legacy important building stones for an original and long overdue African missiology.

Ecumenical Sacrament and Witness

The tradition of a mission-activating Eucharist was extended and given new content in the context of the AICC (African Independent Church Conference), popularly called Fambidzano (lit., "co-operative of churches"), the first ecumenical movement of substance among the Zimbabwean AICs, founded in 1972.[62] Fambidzano, which at its peak had a membership of some ninety churches, selected as its core-message the text of John 17:21 23, where Christ prays that his disciples be united so that the world can "see" and "believe" that he (Christ) has been sent by his Father. To the AICs concerned, this text called for church unity as condition for effective missionary witness. Their newly found reconciliatory ecumenism spelled a joint enterprise in theological training[63] and also a message of good news and hope through the implementation of community development programs to combat poverty and lack of economic opportunity.[64] In the weekend meetings of regional member

61. See M. L. Daneel, "Missionary Outreach in African Independent Churches," *Missionalia* 8.3, passim.
62. Daneel, *Fambidzano.*
63. Daneel, *Fambidzano*, chs. 5-7.
64. Daneel, *Fambidzano*, chs. 8-9.

churches, joint paschal celebrations eventually caused the former exclusively conducted Eucharist of each church to be given a broader ecumenical base. Although such Eucharists did not ensue in united missionary action of the same magnitude or duration as that of the ZCC or the *vaPostori*, they remained the vehicles of missionary outreach. Fambidzano's ecumenical paschal sermons, for instance, tended to trigger conversions and baptisms. Thus, the direct result of sacramental celebrations was baptismal ceremonies during which the leaders of participant churches would enter the "waters of Jordan" (any dam or river suited for the occasion) together to baptize converts according to the church of their choice.

Fambidzano's Eucharist-in-mission reflected the tendency, much like the Eastern Orthodox churches, to celebrate rather than formulate church unity. Saayman's observation about Orthodox ecumenism that "experience of the given unity [in Eucharistic communion] is much more important than theologizing about unity" also applies to the Fambidzano experience.[65] That the Eucharist could serve as a platform for ecumenical mission was quite remarkable, considering the exclusivist and opposing doctrinal traditions of the Spirit- and Ethiopian-type churches. In the pre-Fambidzano period, each camp had serious reservations about the Christian nature of the other. Quite apart from exposure to Fambidzano's more regular ecumenical programs in joint theological training, annual general conferences, women's work, etc., it was the dedication and persistence of regional leaders which was required to bridge the deep-seated attitudes of prejudice and distrust between churches before the ecumenical celebration of sacraments became a reality. The late Bishop Matthew Forridge of the Gutu district, Theological Education by Extension graduate, and one of the rotating presidents of Fambidzano, was such a man.

As successor to Bishop Makuti, who had broken away from Mutendi's ZCC in 1947,[66] Forridge developed a brand of ZCC Zionism which was less dominated by a personality cult and therefore ecumenically more flexible than Mutendi's church. Yet it took him years to establish regular patterns of ecumenical endeavor in the eastern chiefdoms of Gutu where he regularly operated. He propagated the essential link between ecumenism and mission with great fervor until he eventually succeeded in drawing the widest possible cross-section of Mission (Dutch Reformed, Full Gospel, Methodist, Church of Christ, etc.) and Independent Churches into a regular program of joint paschal celebrations. Forridge's success in persuading large numbers of *vaPostori* to participate — the church with arguably the strongest anti-

---

65. W. A. Saayman, *Unity and Mission* (Pretoria, 1984), p. 9.
66. Daneel, *Old and New in Southern Shona Independent Churches*, vol. 1, p. 300.

ecumenical bias in Zimbabwe — underscores the far-reaching ecumenical impact of his ministry.

Concerned with the witness character of *Paseka* against the background of ZCC mission strategy and Fambidzano's interpretation of John 17, Bishop Forridge molded his ecumenical Eucharist into a ceremony which combined internal reorientation, cleansing, and spiritual uplifting in the church's visible unification as the body of Christ, with the outbound witnessing movement of the church into the world. In other words the paschal event itself, instead of forming the launching pad of missionary work still to be conducted elsewhere in the country, became mission and witness to the world. Preparatory sermons for sacramental celebration increasingly combined calls for confessions of sin, inner cleansing, and conversion. Ecumenism in this context engendered a spirit of ecclesial altruism whereby the focus shifted from a specific church benefiting from ecumenical recruitment to the more broadly conceived salvific dispensation wrought by Christ incarnate.

Representatives of Fambidzano-participant churches do not single out missionary or recruitment strategies as subjects of extensive proclamation or debate.[67] Yet, the undercurrent of awareness that unity in Christ incorporates the Church's witness to the world is unmistakable. At no point does concern for inner sanctity as a condition for sacramental union or insistence on individual conversion result in calls for the distancing of the Church from the world. The entire event serves as a powerful statement about God's mission to the world and a call to all humans to repent.

Ecological Eucharist and Widened Perceptions of Mission

Our third variation of sacrament-inspired mission concerns yet another ecumenical Eucharist, one which serves the earthkeeping drive of the Shona AICs and which affirms the two sacramental traditions discussed above. In recent years a tree-planting Eucharist has been developed in the context of the AAEC. Popularly referred to as the *maporesanyika* (lit., "earth-healing") ceremony, this Eucharist unites the attempts of AICs to make a worthwhile contribution in Zimbabwe's environmental liberation struggle, or "War of the Trees." The AAEC currently counts some 150 member churches representing an estimated two million adherents in Zimbabwe — mainly prophetic movements of the Zionist type, but also including the AACJM. As an earthkeeping contingent

---

67. See my analysis of the main features of the Fambidzano-inspired paschal sacrament in Daneel, *Fambidzano*, pp. 127-46.

they form the Christian counterpart of AZTREC, a traditionalist movement in which chiefs and spirit mediums play significant ecological roles at the behest of the senior guardian ancestors of the land *(varidzi venyika)* and the ancient high-god cult at the Matopo hills. Together, the two sister organizations belong to the financially empowering agency, ZIRRCON, which today represents the largest nongovernmental organization for environmental reform at the rural grassroots in Zimbabwe.[68] Through AZTREC and the AAEC, peasant communities are mobilized on a massive scale to establish their own wood lots near stable water points, and a great variety of trees are planted for commercial, religious, aesthetic, and ecologically protective purposes.

Unlike the ZCC practice where the Eucharist is the flash point of missionary mobilization within the confines of a single church, followed up by a geographically wide-reaching campaign of evangelistic work and membership recruitment, the AAEC tree-planting Eucharist is in itself the witnessing event, the proclamation of good news to all creation. The sacrament integrates the healing of earth and humans as witness of Christ's good news to the world. It is enacted in nature and in the presence of non-Christian fellow fighters (AZTREC) in the War of the Trees. The traditionalist earthkeepers do not partake of the bread and wine but they assimilate the message, observe the sacrament, and assist with tree planting. The classic mission command of Matthew 28:19 is assumed rather than featured as a central theme of proclamation. Not that ecological endeavor in any way supersedes the call for repentance, conversion, human salvation, and church formation — the essential missionary dynamic of all prophetic AICs. But the mission mandate here is derived from the healing ministry of Christ and related to the believer's stewardship in service to all creation, as required by God in the creation story of Genesis, and highlighted repeatedly with reference to Colossians 1:17: "in Christ all things hold together." In sermons delivered during these Eucharists, Christ emerges as the healer of all creation and his disciples as fellow earth healers. Hence, the popular designation of these Eucharistic events as *maporesanyika* (healing the earth) ceremonies; the Christian counterpart of AZTREC's ancestral tree-planting rituals, called *mafukidzanyika* (clothing the earth).

A sermon by Bishop Wapendama, leader of the Signs of the Apostles Church, demonstrates how the tree-planting Eucharist constitutes and empowers earth-healing missions:

68. Some seven million trees have already been planted in more than 2,000 wood lots. Ten nurseries in various districts in the Masvingo Province each cultivate between 50,000 and 100,000 seedlings per year. ZIRRCON and its sister organizations cultivate larger numbers of indigenous tree seedlings than any other institution in Zimbabwe.

Mwari [God] saw the devastation of the land. So He called His envoys [ZIRRCON/AAEC leaders] to shoulder the task of delivering the earth. . . . Together with you, we, the Apostles, are now the deliverers of the stricken land. . . . We, the deliverers were sent by Mwari on a divine mission. . . . Deliverance, Mwari says, lies in the trees. Jesus said: "I leave you, my followers, to complete my work!" And that task is the one of healing! We, the followers of Jesus, have to continue with his healing ministry. . . . So, let us all fight, clothing, healing the earth with trees! . . . It is our task to strengthen this mission with our numbers of people. If all of us work with enthusiasm we shall clothe and heal the entire land with trees and drive off affliction [the evil of destruction]. I believe we can change it!

By delivering this message in the context of an ecumenical holy communion, Wapendama implies that where the union between Christ and his disciples (cutting across denominational boundaries) is sacramentally confirmed, the mission of earth healing integral to it is visibly acknowledged and revitalized. God certainly takes the initiative to deliver and restore the ravaged earth, but the responsibility to deliver the stricken earth from its malady here and now lies with the Christian body of believers, that is, the Church.[69] Wapendama's insights hint at Africa's understanding of the Church's comprehensive missionary task in its world, not as a privileged community of mere soul savers but in terms of Bishop Anastasios of Androussa's vision that "the whole world, not only humankind but the entire universe, has been called to share in the restoration that was accomplished by the redeeming work of Christ."[70]

The good news of salvation at the heart of the AIC proclamation of the gospel has always included concern for the individual human being and for the community of believers. The call for conversion at no point excluded soul salvation and the promise of eternal life for believers in heaven, yet one of the major characteristics of AIC eschatology has also been an emphasis on the realization of salvation here and now, in the black holy cities or in the quality of life experienced in communities where the men or women of God mirror divine grace in the context of Africa. Consequently salvation to many in the AIC world connotes primarily healing and liberation: healing of the entire body and spirit of the individual human being and of destructive interhuman

---

69. J. Carmody, *Ecology and Religion: Toward a New Christian Theology of Nature* (New York, 1983), p. 78.

70. Quoted in D. E. Messer, *A Conspiracy of Goodness: Contemporary Images of Christian Mission* (Nashville, 1992), pp. 69-70.

relations; and liberation from such oppressive forces as white missionary tutelage, poverty, and political powerlessness, unto justice and a renewal of human dignity.

The AAEC's tree-planting Eucharist functions as a vehicle for the proclamation and realization of just this kind of comprehensive "good news." It is conducted as an integral part of the church's struggle for justice and is in essence the sacrament of the War of the Trees, directly linked to the country's and the AIC's history of liberation through the presence of church leaders and traditionalists who played prominent roles during the *chimurenga* struggle. The presence of these leading figures evokes a sense of destiny and reminds the green fighters of how Mwari, the God of all creation, dealt with different forms of oppression through the passage of time in their own country. The combination of *chimurenga* experience and holistic views about the interaction of human beings and nature contributes to a potent message of God's mysterious and protective presence in all of life and creation. It emphasizes, moreover, the restoration of justice through the just War of the Trees.

Good news is sacramentally proclaimed by incorporating earth's inanimate members — the trees, water, and soil — as ritual participants in the sacred communion between Christ and his disciples. By virtually standing in embrace with trees at the communion table, earthkeeping communicants are admitting to God that they are incomplete as individuals, that their humanity is informed and qualified by and in nature, and that in such "widening" of the concept of communion they are not interfering with, but recognizing, Christ's lordship over all the earth (Matt. 28:18) by paying such respect to all "members" of creation as was originally required by the Creator God. This is the AIC way of replacing exploitative perceptions of human dominion over nature with a service of humble stewardship. The earth is liberated by the acknowledgement of its ability to retaliate as a *ngozi* (vengeful spirit) does when abused, by the address of trees as "brothers" and "sisters" in a kind of dialogue which recognizes the value and dignity of the tree and allows it to respond in the liturgy, and by the request to the soil to receive and protect the seedlings entrusted to it.

The tree-planting Eucharist signals much more than the liberation of nature through the greening of a barren countryside. It repeatedly underscores the empowerment of the poor and marginalized people of two-thirds of the world to make a contribution that will be of such significance that it captures, for once, the imagination of the nation and the recognition of the government. It also incorporates quality of being for the earthkeepers, *their* liberation from obscurity in a remote part of Zimbabwe, *their* overcoming of marginality and futility as news media repeatedly report on their work, and *their* liberation from the hopelessness of poverty as salaried nursery keepers; budding wood lots and small-scale income-generating projects at least revive some hope for a better future. Hence, the good news of engagement in a sacramental service to nature is that the dehumanizing shackles of decades of colonial rule and the desecration of nature caused largely by disproportionate land apportionment are both shaken off in the quest for holistic healing for all life on earth.

There can be little doubt that the soteriology at the basis of this mission model contains a widened perspective of healing and liberation in comparison with the first two models. Salvation is still basically human salvation. God's free gift of grace still requires the human response of conversion and spiritual growth. But integral to this interaction between Savior and humanity is the salvation of all creation, not merely as a new dispensation ushered in by God but as a challenge to his people, a challenge made meaningful through the empowerment of the poor.

The healing ministry of Christ is still focal in the church's mission, but it now includes, more deliberately than before, the holistic deliverance and salvation of all of Mwari's stricken land. This extended perception of salvation obtains clarity to the extent that the church realizes its role as keeper of creation in a mission that mobilizes its entire membership as active agents instead of only a number of specialized evangelizing missionaries. In such healing of creation there is a new dimension of liberation in the church itself, liberation from an overriding preoccupation with the human condition. In healing the earth, by reaching out beyond the physical and mental ailments of human beings, by setting internal leadership and interchurch conflicts aside for a higher God-given purpose, the earthkeeping church, the earthkeeper himself or herself, is healed of self-serving indulgent isolation. In such liberation to earth service the Apostolate of the church obtains prominence and meaning.[71]

There is endless variation in the AAEC's tree-planting sermons that bear out the strong theological undercurrent of understanding earth care as *missio Dei* and therefore as the mission of God's Church. Rev. Davidson Tawoneichi of the Evangelical Ministry of Christ Church, for instance, preached that:

> Earthkeeping is part of the body of Christ. It is so because we as humans are part of His body and the trees are part of us; they are essential for us

---

71. For more detailed discussion of the missiological implications of ZIRRCON's work, see M. L. Daneel, "Earthkeeping in Missiological Perspective: An African Challenge," *Mission Studies* 13 (1996): 25-26.

to breathe, to live. So, trees, too, are part of Christ's body. Our destruction of nature is an offense against the body of Christ . . . it hurts Christ's body. Therefore the church should heal the wounded body of Christ. . . .

This view complements Bishop Wapendama's assertion that mission is an extension of Christ's healing ministry. Only, in this instance, Christ's body is understood as itself being afflicted by the abuse of nature, underscoring the growing tendency in AAEC tree-planting Eucharists to view Christ's body in both its ecclesiastic and its cosmic dimensions. First, through partaking in the elements of the sacrament the earthkeepers witness to their unity in Christ's body, the Church, and derive from it strength, compassion, and commitment for their environmental struggle. Second, they subsequently set out on their healing mission of tree planting to restore the cosmically wounded body of Christ.

How then does the green mission affect the life and shape of the earthkeeping church? The most convincing sign of adjustment is noticeable in the shift of the healing focus at church headquarters. Although the AICs do not have elaborate ecclesiologies,[72] a predominant image of the church, springing from the comprehensive healing ministries of the Spirit-type churches in particular, is as a "hospital," an institution of compassion and protection. The black "Jerusalems" are still healing colonies where the afflicted, the marginalized, and the poor can feel at home. But the concept *hospitara* is visibly expanded insofar as dedicated earthkeeping prophets are expanding their colonies into "environmental hospitals" to accommodate the wounded earth. The "patient" in this instance is the denuded land. The "dispensary" becomes the nursery where the correct "medicine" for the patient, in terms of a wide assortment of indigenous, exotic, and fruit trees, is cultivated. The entire church community now becomes the healer-agent under the guidance of the church's principal earth-healer and the "high-command" of the War of the Trees, at the ZIRRCON/AAEC operational headquarters in Masvingo town. Consistent aftercare in new wood lots provides proof of the church's commitment in mission; the wood lot itself becomes the focus of witnessing sermons and the source of inspiration for an expanding ministry, as the testimonies of healed human patients in the past

72. The AICs' accommodation of kinship mores and tribal codes of conduct has caused observers to characterize them, perhaps somewhat misleadingly, as "tribal churches" or "ecclesiastical tribes." Sundkler, *Bantu Prophets in South Africa*, pp. 310-23; G. C. Oosthuizen, *Post-Christianity in Africa: A Theological and Anthropological Study* (London, 1968), p. 82.

contributed both to a reaffirmation of belief in God's healing powers and to the church's recruitment of new members. Far from interfering with the church's worship and pastoral work, the earth-healing ministry appears to provide new impetus and direction to church life, as well as numerical church growth.

In addition, within the context of the AAEC a new generation of iconic church leaders, environmental missionaries whose evangelical drive includes good news for all creation, is emerging, replacing prominent first-generation AIC leaders like Bishop Mutendi (ZCC) and Johane Maranke (AACJM). Now, instead of a single leader giving substance to the presence of the biblical Messiah in Africa's rural society through the mediation of rain and good crops for peasants, faith-healing, education, and sociopolitical involvement, revolving around a single "holy city," the mode of operation is shifted to an entire group of "Jerusalems" helping to establish the grace and salvation implicit in Christ's presence in the Creator's neglected and abused garden. Thereby the entire *oikos* is declared God's "holy city." The AAEC missionaries see themselves as mediating the power of Christ (Matt. 28:18) through persistent presence in village life where the masses of people, who all want to participate, are empowered to share a new dominion of service. The "mediation" thus facilitated by the earthkeeping icons through tree planting may be seen by some evangelicals as obscuring Christ's lordship or savior-hood; the AICs see it as unveiling and illuminating dimensions of the mystery of divine presence in nature which may have gone unnoticed by both believers and nonbelievers.

Finally, the AAEC's afforestation programs have stimulated a need for *new ethical codes.* There is little hesitation among leading earthkeepers that green church laws should be drafted and that stringent church discipline should be applied if such laws are trespassed. Bishop Farawo has propagated a process of church councils trying tree-fellers and punishing wanton offenders through extra duties of tree planting and aftercare to compensate for the damage done. Bishop Chimhangwa urges prompt earthkeeping legislation to reinforce the gospel message of the earth's salvation and to set the parameters for the church's ecological mission. He considers many people still to be ignorant of the "gospel of the trees," as a result of which "the threat of the destructive axe must be repelled." Seen as an institution with legislative and disciplinary powers, the church — in the Earthkeeper's view — also becomes the vehicle of uncompromising struggle as it discerns and opposes evil forces that feed on mindless exploitation of the limited resources of the earth. In this mission the church is at risk, willing to be controversial, to suffer and sacrifice whatever discipleship in this realm requires.

Other Mission Models

Next to their sacrament-related mission activities the AICs have also developed a variety of other mission models. I mention but two of these in passing to emphasize the innovative nature of these churches, especially in their inculturated designs of missionary outreach.

The healing ministries of the Spirit-type churches arguably represent the most potent recruitment device in church growth. In a survey of Shona Zionist and Apostolic motivation for becoming church members, the majority of respondents singled out the healing treatment of prophetic healers, experienced by themselves or witnessed in the lives of others, as the major attraction which drew them into the AIC fold.[73] Healing is part of the daily routine at prophetic church headquarters, and it features prominently during all church services. Thus the diagnostic and therapeutic work of the prophetic healers — which clearly illustrate the paradigm of Christ in Africa as the *healing nganga*[74] — remain prominent in all of church life. Not only do the afflicted seeking treatment feel psychologically well catered for time-wise, but they also appreciate prophetic healing techniques because of their resemblance to traditional *nganga* healing praxis. The main similarity is that the prophet, like the *nganga*, ascribes virtually all forms of affliction or misfortune to neglected ancestral spirits, alien spirits, evil powers such as wizardry, and the like. However, the prophet explicitly states that his/her extraperception comes from the Holy Spirit and not from the divinatory means used by the *nganga*. Moreover, the prophet insists that the spirits causing illness or misfortune have no legitimate claim to the embattled patient. Therapy therefore does not consist of traditional sacrificial rites of the appeasement of spirits or the use of medicine, but of the exorcism of threatening spirits and a wide range of protective symbolic actions in the name of the triune Christian God, thereby manifesting the liberating and protective power of the Holy Spirit. The prophet as personification of Christ's healing ministry extends the *nganga* tradition but at the same time radically transforms and Christianizes it.

In the encounter between healer and afflicted individual or community, African cosmology is consistently dealt with at the existential level. AIC heal-

73. Daneel, *Old and New in Southern Shona Independent Churches,* vol. 2, ch. 3.

74. For a discussion of Christ as a healer in the African setting and the role of the traditional healer, the *nganga,* as paradigm for an indigenous Christology, see M. L. Daneel, *Christian Theology of Africa* (Pretoria, 1988), pp. 127-30; M. Schoffeleers, "Christ as the Medicine-Man and the Medicine-Man as Christ: A Tentative History of African Christological Thought," *Man and Life* 8.1-2 (1982).

ers appear to establish more realistic, penetrative, and appealing patterns of dialogue and therapy in the ongoing interface between Christianity and African religion than foreign missions have succeeded in doing. Therefore, in addition to AIC healing evolving as a singularly important vehicle for propagating and enacting the Christian gospel in the African world of poverty and suffering, it also provides a consistent platform for the development of a unique "theology of religions." This grassroots theology, which reaches into the inner recesses of African life and sense of being, is in my view the most outstanding contribution of AICs toward an African theology of missions.

The other mission model concerns recent developments in both mission-founded churches and African Initiated Churches in the Eastern regions of Zimbabwe. In the aftermath of the liberation struggle the churches of Manicaland have appropriated the traditional *pungwe* (night vigil) and turned it into a singularly powerful vehicle of evangelism, community bonding, church growth, and theological debate. In traditional religion the *pungwe* featured as a pivotal nocturnal event of spiritual encounter between family and/or clan members and their ancestors for the purpose of safeguarding the well-being of the living and the living dead. During *chimurenga* the guerrillas popularized the *pungwe* as all-night rallies of lectures, songs, and communication with the ancestors. In this manner they succeeded, alongside the spirit mediums, in mobilizing and uniting peasant society in their quest for the reclamation of the lost lands at the behest of the senior ancestral *varidzi venyika* (guardians of the land). In his publication, *Transfigured Night,* Presler provides us with lucid descriptions of fascinating innovations in Christianized *pungwe* ceremonies.[75] Methodists, Anglicans, and Presbyterians have crafted their night vigils into revivalist, evangelistic, ecumenical, and female emancipatory events. Ecstatic manifestations in sermons, song, and dance feature at the same time of darkness when spirit possession climaxes in the traditional *pungwe.*

AICs, in turn, have developed their own distinct *pungwe* patterns of spiritual growth and missionary outreach. The Maranke Apostles proclaim with their fire-walk the imminent judgment of God and the urgency of conversion. The Pentecostal Apostolic Church of God, led by women, engages in elaborate night ceremonies of fasting, cleansing, and confession as they prepare for the exorcism of vengeful spirits. *Ndaza* Zionists proclaim the economically liberative presence of God in Zion through their colorful robe dances. The Jekenishen Church focuses on a sacred sleep, followed by spiri-

75. T. Presler, *Transfigured Night: Mission and Culture in Zimbabwe's Vigil Movement* (Pretoria, 1999).

tual inspirational dream narration, and the Unity of the African Apostolic Church arranges nocturnal pilgrimages up wilderness mountains. Presler succeeds in unraveling with great insight not only the rich tapestry of ritual life in the *pungwe* movement but also the extent to which African grassroots Christians, and the AICs in particular, are directing the process whereby the proclamation of the gospel good news and the expressions of worship take root in African cultures.

Conclusion

An essay of this nature probably leaves us with more questions than answers about the nature of the southern African AICs. With reference to the self-interpretation of these churches' historical roots and how they relate to classical Pentecostal and "mainline" mission or mission-founded churches, I have indicated the difficulties of arriving at correct and just typologies. Regional histories of AIC growth generally classify the Spirit-type churches as "Pentecostal," and in some respects this is misleading. Without attempting to minimize the missionary initiatives of the Pentecostal churches, it is true to say that the Zimbabwean AICs are more the fruit of mainline mission endeavor and have been more profoundly molded by these mission churches than by the classical Pentecostal movement.[76] In the final analysis, however, the typological preference of the AICs themselves should be key to the academic debate on issues of characterization and classification.

Because of liberationist trends in the history of the Shona AICs as well as their innovative church-planting initiatives, I have argued against interpreting them as movements of either political protest or acquiescence. "Liberation movements" appears to me to be a more appropriate qualification because the dimension of protest or resistance is recognized in its bearing on whatever unjust rule or restrictive living conditions are at stake, without being elevated to a one-sided explanatory theory which obscures rather than illuminates the richly varied existence of the AICs. Admittedly, the liberation theologies enacted by the AICs have thus far not received adequate consideration, and certainly warrant further enquiry.

The three variants of mission-activating Eucharists underscore the mis-

---

76. In the light of this reality I have in the past encouraged the Dutch Reformed missionaries to view their neighboring AICs — many of whom have their religious roots clearly imbedded in the Protestant tradition — not as competitors or wayward sects but as incultured extensions of the Christian family of churches, equally entitled to citizenship in God's kingdom as the Reformed Church itself.

sionary nature of the AICs. They challenge us to rethink missions in Africa in terms of creatively designed and inculturated mission models described in this chapter. It is fitting that the ecclesial ritual that, more than any other, symbolically articulates the essence of Christian good news, that is, salvation mediated in Christ's death and resurrection, should become the impulse and context for the church's ongoing outreach in the world.

Each of the three variants of mission-activating Eucharists also has a healing focus. In the first variant, the message is of healing and well-being in this existence. Through the healing hands of the "men of God," the New Testament ministry of Christ tending to specific individuals takes shape through identification and reenactment in the African context. Healing in the second variant is focused less on individual healing than on the mending of interchurch relations, on breaking the isolation and exclusivism of different church communities. Here the healed and united body of Christ becomes the condition for missionary witness. The ecumenically inspired missionary drive complements and enriches the outreach of single churches through a shift of focus which frees the salvific work of Christ from the kind of ecclesial introversion and self-promotion that seeks to identify the reign of God's kingdom with the performance of individual church leaders and their own denominations. The third variant's widened perception of healing stimulates a comprehensive understanding of the church and its mission. As keeper of creation the church now proclaims a message that not only includes soul salvation and physical well-being for humans but also the restoration of all creation. Consequently, conversion, for it to be genuine, implies earth-care, a mandate for *all* churches and *all* Christians. Because all things hold together in the risen Savior (Col. 1:17) the entire earth community is represented at the table of Holy Communion.

I have pointed out the significance of an authentic theology of religions developed by the Spirit-type churches in their ministry of healing. The earthkeeping Eucharist adds a new dimension to this theology in that the eco-mission on which it is based promotes essentially different patterns of interfaith dialogue. Complementary to the distinct Christian missionary witness of the tree-planting Eucharist described above, is a well-established praxis of reciprocation which allows for far-reaching and continuous dialogue between Christian and traditionalist earthkeeping partners. The majority of AAEC leaders and their followers, for example, attend AZTREC's ancestral and Shona high-god related ceremonies. They appear satisfied that united action in the war of the trees in no way exacts a price of religious compromise or syncretist acquiescence. Church bishops and ministers sit among traditionalist elders, even discuss ancestral directives as transmitted by the spirit mediums, contribute to the discussions on the planning of AZTREC projects, and help with the planting of trees in day-long land-clothing ceremonies. They only withdraw temporarily when the ancestors are being addressed and refrain from drinking sacrificial beer as witness to their Christian allegiance in similar fashion as the traditionalist chiefs who observe but do not participate at the table of Holy Communion of their Christian counterparts. Likewise key Zionist figures of the AAEC accompany delegations of chiefs and mediums during their annual 300 km trip to the cult shrines of Mwari in the Matopo hills, where the latest earthkeeping endeavor is discussed during oracular discourse with the traditional high-god. Here, too, a Christian presence is welcomed by cultists since it does not intrude offensively on the traditional world of veneration and worship. Christian abstention from the specific aspects of traditional ritual, which connote worship or sacrifice, is not generally experienced by the AZTREC chiefs and mediums as judgment or personal rejection, but as genuine and acceptable religious differentiation. Consequently, a mood of sharing and openness to ongoing dialogue prevails.[77]

Throughout this chapter, and in all my work on AICs, my central hypothesis has been that their outreach and growth result from Africanized missionary strategies and practice. As missionizing institutions in their own right, the AICs have contextualized the gospel message, its ceremonial expression, and its holistic application in African society. What has drawn millions of people into these churches is an understandable and persuasive existential involvement in enactment of the Christian good news. Here lies the great challenge for an extended future development of African missiology, for the "reinvention of Christianity" or the experience of Christianity "with the African soul" for which Ela calls.[78]

---

77. The question arises as to whether the far-reaching processes of inter-religious exchange and identification in eco-mission do not unavoidably expose Christian participants to syncretist compromise at the expense of a Christ-centered focus on conversion. To date, the answer would seem to be no. See Daneel, *African Earthkeepers*, vol. 2, p. 272.

78. J. M. Ela, *African Cry* (Maryknoll, N.Y., 1986), p. 120.

SECTION IV

CHAPTER NINE

Contours of Latin American Pentecostalism

PAUL FRESTON

Latin American Pentecostalism: An Expanding Field of Study

Latin American Pentecostalism has grown from humble beginnings to become a mass phenomenon and is now attracting increasing academic scrutiny. This essay seeks to present the main characteristics of Latin American Pentecostalism. This will involve: an examination of continent-wide statistical data; an analysis of its social composition; investigation of the causes and effects of its segmentation; an evaluation of attempted typologies; and an accounting for regional diversity of denominational composition and national origin. Further, some key controversies will be surveyed, including: the extent of foreign influence; explanations for growth; the contrasting fortunes of Pentecostal churches and Roman Catholic Base Communities; the role of the media; implications for women and for indigenous peoples; economic effects and political role; and the aptness of characterizing Latin American Pentecostalism as "Protestant."

In recent years, academic interest in Latin American religion, previously focused on progressive Catholicism, has turned to the *evangélicos* (as all Latin American Protestants are usually called) and especially to their largest and fastest-growing sector, the Pentecostals. The region has become a laboratory for studying the emerging mass Protestantism of the Third World. Brazil, for example, now has the second largest community of practicing Protestants in the world: size, growth, and independence produce new phenomena, not reducible to North American or European models.

Latin American Pentecostalism, especially Brazilian and Chilean, first attracted scholarly attention in the 1960s. By the late 1980s, attention had switched to Central America where, in some countries, Protestantism had grown enormously and was overtaking Brazil and Chile in proportional terms. Even other large, previously resistant countries (Mexico, Colombia, and Argentina) began to show growth and to interest researchers. It became possible to talk of a regional phenomenon, and academic studies on "Protestantism in Latin America" multiplied.

Most works have come from American scholars, the best being of recent vintage.[1] But a high percentage of the most influential authors are European: Léonard, Willems, Lalive D'Epinay of a generation ago, Bastian and Martin more recently.[2] Within Latin America, the reigning sociological paradigms of modernization and dependency for a long time have marginalized the theme of religion in general.[3] The same was true of Brazil.[4] Even so, with its large churches and sizeable social-scientific community, Brazil stands out for the depth of scholarship on its own Protestantism (Fernandes, Alves, Rolim, Mendonça, Souza, Mariz, Novaes). A qualitative advance now seems to be under way in Brazilian and Argentine studies of Pentecostalism. The almost total lack of Argentine academic interest until the early 1990s is now busily being rectified (Frigerio, Wynarczyk, Semán).[5] The other country with a strong tradition in the social sciences, Mexico, with its secularist tradition and more restricted Protestantism, has made a smaller contribution. From the rest of the region, recent studies by Chilean researchers are useful (Chacón and Lagos, Fontaine and Bayer).

As for contributions by Latin American Pentecostals themselves, Brazil

---

1. David Stoll, *Is Latin America Turning Protestant?* (Berkeley, 1990); Virginia Garrard-Burnett, "Conclusion: Is This Latin America's Reformation?" in V. Garrard-Burnett and D. Stoll, eds., *Rethinking Protestantism in Latin America* (Philadelphia, 1993), pp. 199-210; Elizabeth Brusco, "The Reformation of Machismo: Asceticism and Masculinity among Colombian Evangelicals," in Garrard-Burnett and Stoll, *Rethinking Protestantism in Latin America,* pp. 143-58; John Burdick, *Looking for God in Brazil* (Berkeley, 1993).

2. Émile Léonard, *O Protestantismo Brasileiro* (São Paulo, 1963); Emílio Willems, *Followers of the New Faith: Culture Change and the Rise of Protestantism in Brazil and Chile* (Nashville, 1967); Christian Lalive D'Epinay, *Religion, dynamique social et dépendence: les mouvements Protestants en Argentine et au Chili* (Paris, 1975); Jean-Pierre Bastian, *Historia del Protestantismo in América Latina* (Mexico City, 1990); David Martin, *Tongues of Fire: The Explosion of Protestantism in Latin America* (Oxford, 1990).

3. Cristián Parker, "Perspectiva crítica sobre la sociología de la religión en América Latina," in A. Frigerio, ed., *Ciencias sociales y religión en el Cono Sur* (Buenos Aires, 1993), pp. 123-50.

4. Cecília Mariz, "La enseñanza y la investigación en la sociología de la religión en Brasil,' in Frigerio, *Ciencias sociales y religión,* pp. 72-85.

5. Hilario Wynarczyk, "Las aproximaciones a la sociología del campo evangélico in la Argentina," in Frigerio, *Ciencias sociales y religión,* pp. 61-71.

has some poor denominational histories (commissioned by church leaders for edification) of the Assemblies of God (AG) and the Church of the Four-Square Gospel.[6] Zavala (AG-Peru) and Gaxiola (Apostolic Church–Mexico) are better. But the best works by Pentecostals are Saracco's doctoral thesis on Argentina and Sepúlveda's articles on Chile.[7]

The lack of academic histories of large parts of Latin American Pentecostalism has hindered the sociology of the phenomenon. As Joachim Wach says, without the work of the historian of religion the sociologist is helpless.[8] The fine synchronic studies do not allow us to capture the dynamic evolution. This negligence may perhaps reflect a belittling: since Pentecostals are not *historicals* (as non-Pentecostal Protestants are usually called), they must have no history! With regard to Brazil, at least, innovation in the sociology of Pentecostalism has been largely restricted to the micro level. There has been little study of the evolution of the large Pentecostal churches and their institutional relationship to society. Despite excellent synchronic studies, we lack information on the large churches as *dynamically evolving institutions*.

It is true that historical research on Pentecostalism is not easy. Some groups have virtually no written sources; others, like the AG-Brazil, have many biographies of leaders, useful for the study of a church structured around an oligarchy of *caciques* (headmen). But domestically produced sources must be used with care. The official memory of an organization always reflects the demands of some segment within the group itself. In addition, Pentecostalism has a tense relationship with history. Taking its name from the descent of the Holy Spirit at Pentecost, it sees itself as a return to origins. Thus, domestic histories concentrate on the (epic) origins of the denomination, which are seen as a recovery of the first Pentecost; later events are reduced virtually to geographical expansion. There is little idea of development, since all is contained in the original event. And most, though not all, Pentecostals do not accept that their religious phenomena are rooted in actions analyzable by the social sciences. Despite the Christian principle of incarnation, the official organ of the AG-Brazil declares that Pentecostalism "is

6. Emílio Conde, *Histórica das Assembléias de Deus no Brasil* (Rio de Janeiro, 1960); Alcebíades Vasconcelos, *Sinopse histórica das Assembléias de Deus no Brasil* (Manaus, 1983); Abraão Almeida et al., *História das Assembléias de Deus no Brasil* (Rio de Janeiro, 1982); Júlio Rosa, *O Evangelho Quadrangular no Brasil* (n.p., 1978).

7. Norberto Saracco, "Argentine Pentecostalism: Its History and Theology," Ph.D. dissertation, University of Birmingham, 1989; Juan Sepúlveda, "Pentecostalismo y democracia: una interpretación de sus relaciones," in *Democracia y evangelio* (Santiago, 1988), pp. 229-50.

8. Joachim Wach, *Sociology of Religion* (Chicago, 1944).

a movement of the Holy Spirit and, consequently, immune to the natural factors which condition human societies."[9] Texts for edification stress heroism and exceptional events, neglecting the normal and mundane with which sociology is concerned. We need to read between the lines and put the feet of the docetic heroes back on the ground.

A Brief History of Pentecostalism

Pentecostalism's early arrival in Latin America is hardly surprising given the proximity of Los Angeles, the birthplace of Pentecostalism, to the Mexican border. A movement largely composed of blacks, immigrants, and the poor in general, there were Mexicans present at the famous meetings on Azusa Street, Los Angeles, in 1906.[10] Key factors in the rapid international expansion were the many American missionaries in contact with events at home and the many immigrants in the United States in contact with their homelands and with countrymen elsewhere. Chile, Mexico, and Brazil, respectively, are examples of these three routes.

In 1907, an American Methodist missionary in Chile, informed of the novelty by friends in the United States and missionaries elsewhere, began to teach Pentecostal doctrine. Although the intention was not to create new institutions, his followers were expelled from the Methodist Church two years later and founded a denomination which later became the Pentecostal Methodist Church, now Chile's largest Protestant group. The year 1909 also saw the first Pentecostal conversions in Argentina through Luigi Francescon, an Italian artisan living in Chicago and an evangelist of the Italian diaspora. No church resulted immediately from his work (the Christian Assembly of Argentina dates its foundation from 1916). In Brazil, however, Francescon inaugurated in 1910 the Christian Congregation among Italians in São Paulo. In the early 1910s beginnings were made in Central America (mostly by independent U.S. or Canadian missionaries) and in Mexico (partly by returning emigrants). A start was made in Peru in 1919 by the American Assemblies of God, and in Venezuela by an independent missionary, but on the whole the remaining South American republics were slow off the mark. The last country to witness the effective start of a Pentecostal church was Ecuador in 1956.

The initial fortunes were modest everywhere. The words of Troeltsch about Christian *sects* in general seemed to be vindicated: "[They] do not wish

9. *Mensageiro da paz,* April 1985, p. 5.
10. Manuel Gaxiola-Gaxiola, *La serpiente y la paloma* (Pasadena, 1970), p. 157.

to be popular churches. . . . They maintain they possess the absolute truth of the gospel, but claim this truth is far beyond the spiritual grasp of the masses and the State."[11] In the 1950s, the first signs appeared that this might not hold true in some parts of Latin America; by the 1980s, Pentecostalism seemed to be within the spiritual grasp of ever-larger masses in almost every country, and in a few a new relationship was also being forged with the State.

Before moving on to discuss the characteristics and controversies of Latin American Pentecostalism, we should emphasize two aspects of what we are talking about. Pentecostalism is a form of Protestantism but different in key ways from historical (non-Pentecostal) Protestantism. As we shall see, both these aspects have important consequences in Latin America.

Pentecostalism is *Protestant*. In Latin America, it is the popular (i.e., mass lower-class) version of Protestantism. David Martin locates it in the history of Protestant dissent.[12] This dissent comes in three waves, Calvinist, Methodist, and Pentecostal, at ever lower levels in the societal status system and accompanied by greater emotionalism. Pentecostalism expands where Methodism and Calvinism hardly penetrated: the Catholic societies of Europe and Latin America, and areas dominated by Lutheran state churches.

The genealogy of Pentecostalism goes back to the Methodist doctrine of a second work of grace distinct from salvation. In the nineteenth century, the holiness movement in the English-speaking world democratized the concept: instead of a long search, an instant experience available for all called the "baptism in the Holy Spirit." This movement, besides penetrating many denominations, produced a separatist fringe of small holiness groups, and it was among these that Pentecostalism was born. The turn of the century provoked the expectation that the imminent end of the world would be preceded by a revival of glossolalia (speaking in tongues). The doctrinal synthesis that enabled Pentecostalism to arise as a distinct movement was achieved by 1900: tongues were evidence of baptism in the Holy Spirit. But the spark of worldwide Pentecostalism was ignited by a black waiter born as a slave, W. J. Seymour.

In 1906, Seymour was invited to preach in Los Angeles by the female pastor of a black holiness church. Glossolalia was a success there, and Seymour rented a warehouse for his "Apostolic Faith Mission." The novelty and the favorable location (Los Angeles, besides being one of the strongholds of the Holiness movement, was the fastest-growing city in the country, with many

11. Ernst Troeltsch, *The Social Teaching of the Christian Churches*, vol. 2 (London, 1931), p. 998.

12. David Martin, *The Dilemmas of Contemporary Religion* (Oxford, 1978), pp. 9-11.

ethnic minorities and a frontier ethos) soon attracted whites, but the initial leadership of blacks and women was pronounced. White pastors from the South came to be ministered to by black leaders. But this unusual situation did not last. The Pentecostal movement, originally conceived as a renewal of the churches, soon solidified in independent groups separated by doctrinal differences. In each segment, racial separation occurred within a decade. The whites ordained in the (predominantly black) Church of God in Christ left to found the (almost exclusively white) Assemblies of God in 1914.[13]

The novelty in Pentecostalism was not speaking in tongues itself but the doctrine that gave it theological and liturgical centrality. Its Protestant emphasis on a coherent doctrinal system, a law-governed cosmos and subordination of charismatic phenomena to biblical revelation, separates it from religions such as Umbanda which compete for the Latin American masses.[14] As we shall see, its Protestant nature makes it a qualitatively new religious phenomenon in Latin America, affecting its relationship with cultural and intellectual currents.

Pentecostalism, however, is also a *distinct form of Protestantism.* In Hollenweger's definition, it embraces all those who profess at least two religious crisis experiences: rebirth and the "baptism of the Holy Spirit."[15] Whereas conservative evangelicalism stresses the correct grammar of belief, Pentecostalism stresses the experience of the gifts of the Spirit.[16] Most Pentecostals in Latin America are fundamentalists in an unreflective way. They agree with fundamentalist beliefs such as biblical inerrancy when explained; but what really matters is not whether the biblical miracles happened as told, but whether the same miracles happen today. Their naïve fundamentalism is functional for growth. As Steve Bruce says, "fundamentalism is a democratic philosophy, a critique of the intellectual hierarchy of society and of theologians as elitist defenders of a new priestcraft."[17]

Sociologically, Latin American Pentecostalism is organized in a large number of *conversionist sects* that emphasize emotional involvement and devote large resources to evangelism.[18] According to Mendonça and Velasques,

13. Robert Mapes Anderson, *Vision of the Disinherited: The Making of American Pentecostalism* (New York, 1979), p. 189.

14. Peter Fry and Gary Howe, "Duas respostas à aflição: Umbanda e Pentecostalismo," *Debate e crítica* 6 (1975).

15. Walter Hollenweger, *The Pentecostals* (London, 1972), p. xxi.

16. Martin, *Tongues of Fire*, p. 52.

17. Steve Bruce, *God Save Ulster! The Religion and Politic of Paisleyism* (Oxford, 1989), p. 23.

18. Bryan Wilson, *Religious Sects: A Sociological Study* (London, 1970), pp. 41-42.

it unites Protestant rationalism and popular Catholic mysticism.[19] Martin sees it as a combination of black spirituality and white religious enthusiasm, operating in both preliterate and postliterate modes and provoking a discharge of guilt and disease and a charge of power leading to a many-sided "betterment" of life.[20]

Latin American Pentecostalism: The Main Contours

Continent-wide Statistical Data

There is need for great caution with statistics of Pentecostalism (and Protestantism in general) in Latin America. If the source is an official census, there may still be reasons in some areas for not declaring oneself Protestant. Almost always, the internal distinctions of the Protestant world are a challenge to census takers. In 1980, Brazil distinguished for the first time between "traditionals" and "Pentecostals," but the list of churches to be placed in each category never catches up with the formation of new denominations. The biggest problem with censuses, however, is that of frontiers. Among the popular classes of Latin America, plural religious practice is considered a positive value, linked to the preservation of personal autonomy.[21] Although Protestantism tries to break with this institutionally uncommitted tradition, proselytism always guarantees a certain number of unaffiliated attenders. The ideal of exclusive practice is to a great extent obeyed by members, but evangelism blurs the borders because the process of affiliation may be slow. Since people have religions and not vice-versa, religious identity may include comings and goings. For instance, a survey in Costa Rica showed nearly the same number of ex-*evangélicos* as current ones.[22]

Statistics produced by the churches themselves are rarely to be trusted since bureaucratic procedures in general are not the strong point of popular *sects*, and since numbers can influence prestige, access to financing, and, in some countries, political clout. An example is the AG-Brazil. The Foreign Missions Board of the AG-United States publishes statistics of all countries where it has missionaries. According to the data for 1990, the United States

---

19. Antônio Gouvêa Mendonça and Prócoro Velasques Filho, *Introdução ao Protestantismo no Brasil* (São Paulo, 1990), p. 238.

20. Martin, *Tongues of Fire*, p. 6.

21. Carmen Cinira Macedo, *Tempo de Gênesis* (São Paulo, 1986), p. 125.

22. Jorge Gómez, *El crecimiento y la deserción en la iglesia evangélica costarricense* (San José, Costa Rica, 1996).

had two million Assemblies members; no foreign country came near this except for Brazil, which had over 14 million. Not even their American brethren could hide their disbelief: "The Brazilian numbers, as sent by the national church . . . are difficult to verify independently."

One can make a conservative estimate of about 45 to 50 million *Protestants* in Latin America, just over 10 percent of the population. A key imponderable in this figure is Brazil. With 40 percent of the land mass and a third of the population, it probably has half of the region's Protestants (well down from the two-thirds of the 1920s).[23] The 1991 census placed Protestants at 9.1 percent, although a 1988 survey by the census-taking agency had estimated 10.8 percent. The 2000 census can reasonably be expected to show some 15 percent (or about 25 million) Protestants.

The number of *Pentecostals* in Latin America is probably around 30 million, or 60 percent of all Protestants. The degree of Pentecostalization of each country's Protestantism is far from uniform, varying from perhaps 30 percent in some Andean countries to almost 80 percent in Chile. Central America's Pentecostals grew from only 2.3 percent of Protestants in 1936 to 37 percent in 1965,[24] to over half by the 1980s.[25] Brazil is again determinant: in 1980, historical Protestants were still a slight majority, but today Pentecostals probably represent between 60 percent and two-thirds of Brazilian Protestants.

We thus have a general picture. Brazil has by far the largest Protestant community in absolute terms (15 percent of the population), of which some two-thirds are Pentecostals. The other country that has a long-standing Protestant population is Chile: 15-20 percent of the population, perhaps three-quarters of which is Pentecostal. High growth in these countries goes back to the 1950s and continues to be impressive. But some parts of Central America took off from low levels in the 1970s and may now have overtaken Chile and Brazil in relative terms. Guatemala leads with anywhere from 20 percent to 30 percent of the population as Protestant; about three-quarters of the Protestants are Pentecostal. El Salvador's Protestant community, virtually nonexistent in 1940 and only 7 percent in 1978,[26] grew meteorically

---

23. Ronald Frase, "A Sociological Analysis of the Development of Brazilian Protestantism: A Study in Social Change," Ph.D. dissertation, Princeton Theological Seminary, 1975).

24. Wilton Nelson, *Protestantism in Central America* (Grand Rapids, 1984), p. 59.

25. Martin, *Tongues of Fire*, p. 52.

26. Kenneth Coleman et al., "Protestantism in El Salvador: Conventional Wisdom versus the Survey Evidence," in Garrard-Burnett and Stoll, *Rethinking Protestantism in Latin America*, p. 112.

thereafter, reaching between 12 percent and 22 percent of the population by the late 1980s;[27] about two-thirds of the Protestants are Pentecostal.[28] Nicaragua's Protestant population grew from some 5 percent to over 15 percent of the total population under the Sandinista government. In fact, there may be a positive correlation between relatively democratic left-wing governments and Protestant growth; Santiago went from 5.5 percent to 8 percent Protestant in Allende's three years in office, a faster growth rate than at any other time.[29] This fact is inconvenient both for unreconstructed left-wing analysts who insist on seeing Pentecostalism as pathological and for those Pentecostal leaders who call for a right-wing vote because the left will persecute the *evangélicos*.

Other parts of Central America have had more modest success, and proportions of Pentecostals would seem to be lower. A hitherto very resistant country, Colombia now seems to be developing a Protestant community; also growing rapidly in recent years are the communities in Mexico (3 percent Protestant in the early 1980s, of which 75 percent were Pentecostal)[30] and Argentina. The Andean countries are also growing from moderate starts. Bolivia, 3 percent Protestant in 1975,[31] has reached 11 percent; Pentecostals were only 10 percent of Protestants in 1967.[32] There, as in Peru, Adventists have traditionally predominated. The weakest Protestant communities are those of highly secularized Uruguay and Venezuela (0.5 percent in 1982; Caracas, 1.6 percent more recently).[33]

Some comparative data give an idea of the relative importance of Latin American Protestantism, in proportional and absolute terms. In the English-speaking world, the most instructive comparison is not with the *nominally* Protestant population. A 1978 U.S. survey distinguished "evangelicals" (22 percent of the population) and "liberal Protestants" (35 percent).[34] Since the overwhelming majority of Brazil's Protestants would be classified as "evangelicals" (perhaps 12 percent of the population), the point of comparison is

27. Carlos Benjamin Lara, "Iglesias evangélicas y conflicto político en el Salvador," *Cristianismo y sociedad* 103 (1990): 108; Reed Elliot Nelson, "Organizational Homogeneity, Growth and Conflict in Brazilian Protestanism," *Sociological Analysis* 48.4 (1988): 319-27.

28. W. Nelson, *Protestantism in Central America*, p. 74.

29. Humberto Lagos, *Crisis de la esperanza: religión y autoritarismo en Chili* (Santiago, 1988), p. 280.

30. Jean-Pierre Bastian, *Protestantismo y sociedad en México* (Mexico City, 1983), p. 221.

31. Mortimer Arias, "El Protestantismo," *Presencia*, June 8, 1975, p. 189.

32. Arias, "El Protestantismo," p. 184.

33. Martin, *Tongues of Fire*, p. 84.

34. James Hunter, *American Evangelicalism* (New Brunswick, N.J., 1983), p. 49.

with the 22 percent figure for American evangelicals. Thus, the percentage of Brazilian evangelical Protestants is slightly more than half the size of the evangelical Protestant population in the U.S. In a 1984 U.S. survey, 39 percent of all Protestants (approximately 22 percent of the total U.S. population) claimed to have gone to church the previous week.[35] If Brazil is 15 percent Protestant, of which 76.9 percent claim weekly practice and 16.5 percent monthly practice, more than 12 percent of the total population attend a Protestant church every week.

In Great Britain, on the other hand, only 11 percent of the total population (including Catholics) attends a church in an average week. The total membership of the Christian churches in Britain is no more than 7 million; one Brazilian church on its own (the AG) has as many. The Methodist Church in England, for all its historical significance, has only 430,000 members; half a dozen Pentecostal groups in Brazil surpass it easily. In Europe as a whole, Protestant attendance at church is a mere 5 percent.[36] Only some peripheral regions of Europe (Scotland, Northern Ireland, Wales, parts of Norway) have a higher percentage of church attendance than Brazil.

The trend seems set for the foreseeable future.

Protestant Growth in Brazil

	Population (% growth per decade)	Protestants (% growth per decade)
1940-50	26	62
1950-60	35	62
1960-70	33	70
1970-80	28	64
1980-90	21?	116?

Sources: Censuses; PNAD (IBGE), 1988.

While the Brazilian demographic curve reaches a peak in the 1950s and 1960s and then falls, Protestant growth accelerates. The same is true of Chile,[37] although not, it seems, of Guatemala.[38]

35. Steve Bruce, *A House Divided: Protestantism, Schism and Secularization* (London, 1990), p. 178.

36. David Martin, *A General Theory of Secularization* (Oxford, 1978), p. 152.

37. "Luz de las encuestas de opinión pública," *Estudios públicos* 44 (1991): 91.

38. James Grenfell, "The Participation of Protestants in Politics in Guatemala," M.Phil. thesis, Oxford University, 1995.

For three major South American cities we possess interesting (and seemingly trustworthy) surveys: Greater Rio de Janeiro, Buenos Aires (Federal Capital only), and Greater Lima.

The Lima survey of 1993 discovered 959 churches, comprising a Protestant community of 3.22 percent of the population. The census of 1981 had shown 3.6 percent of "non-Catholic Christians" in Lima. A large part of the difference is made up of Adventists, a group usually included in surveys of Protestants but omitted in the 1993 Lima data. The Assemblies of God constitute about 20 percent of non-Adventist Protestants; all Pentecostals come to 42 percent. The relatively strong presence of "holiness" churches (the milieu in which Pentecostalism started) such as the Christian and Missionary Alliance, as well as the strong Adventist presence among the Indians, may account for the relatively low Pentecostalization of Peru's Protestantism. About a third of non-Adventist Protestants in Lima speak Quechua.

The Buenos Aires survey (1992) calculated a Protestant community of about 150,000, or 5 percent of the population, distributed among 262 churches. From 9 churches in 1900, to 39 in 1930, 78 in 1960, and 131 in 1980, the 1980s saw rapid growth, especially after the return to democracy in 1983. Two-thirds of Protestant members are Pentecostals. One can presume (from other countries) that a survey including Greater Buenos Aires outside the Federal Capital would show a somewhat higher percentage of Protestants in the population and a greater Pentecostalization of Protestantism.

The Greater Rio survey (1992), the most complete and professional of the three, focuses on institutions and not membership. It arrives at a total of 3,477 churches. Between 1990 and 1992, an average of one new church was registered per weekday in the state of Rio. This contrasts with less than two new spiritist centers per week (either Kardecist or Umbanda) and only one new Catholic parish in three years. Of course, the juridical structure of Catholicism does not require the registration of new communities linked to an existing parish. Even so, a Catholic diocese in Greater Rio which has a register of all its local communities permits an illuminating comparison: there are, in that area, over twice as many Protestant places of worship as Catholic, and in the very poorest districts the ratio rises to almost seven to one.

Protestant growth is "an option of the poor," as Fernandes puts it, in a provocative reference to the less successful Catholic "option *for* the poor." The needier the district is, the higher the percentage of Protestants: according to the 1988 survey, nearly 20 percent of the population in the poorest areas of greater Rio were Protestant, versus 6 percent in the rich South Zone of the city. Fernandes concludes that Protestantism is an "option" because it results from conversion, and "of the poor" because it grows more quickly (though not exclusively) among them and through "institutional means which are equally 'poor.'"[39]

In denominational terms, 61 percent of churches in Greater Rio are Pentecostal, a percentage that increases daily: 91 percent of new churches (1990-92) are Pentecostal. Of the fifty-two largest denominations in Greater Rio, thirty-seven are of Brazilian origin (virtually all Pentecostal), and nearly all the rest have long been autonomous. "The denominational dynamic . . . has been 'Brazilianized.' It no longer makes sense to think of Protestantism as a 'foreign religion.'"[40] We can add that, in Brazil as a whole, no newly arrived foreign church has established a significant presence in over forty years. Protestant (and especially Pentecostal) religion is a *national, popular,* and *rapidly expanding* phenomenon. As Fernandes concludes, "it is perhaps the most important movement for changing mentalities in contemporary Brazilian society, above all among the poorest urban sectors."[41]

Segmentation of Latin American Pentecostalism

Latin American Pentecostalism is also extremely segmented, and there are hundreds of independent groups. If, in the Catholic world, all roads lead to Rome, in the world of Latin American Pentecostalism, many roads end where they begin: in a Rio shanty or a Guatemalan village. This segmentation is functional for expansion, stimulating social flexibility, competition, and localized supply.

Pentecostalism shares Protestantism's basic doctrinal tendency to schism: rejecting institutional unity centered on the papacy, it establishes the Bible as the sole theoretical source of authoritative knowledge. Organizational devices to maintain unity largely fail because they are not legitimated by any core doctrine.[42] But if doctrine permits the principle of segmentation, the actual rate is dependent largely on other factors. Not all types of Protestantism split as much, and the same type may split more in some social contexts than in others.

Organizations get the leaders who are psychologically and ideologically suited to the style of the organization. . . . Independent Protestant

39. Rubem César Fernandes, *Censo institucional evangélico CIN 1992: primeiros comentários* (Rio de Janeiro, 1992), p. 14.
40. Fernandes, *Censo institucional evangélico CIN 1992*, p. 19.
41. Fernandes, *Censo institucional evangélico CIN 1992*, p. 25.
42. Bruce, *A House Divided*, pp. 228-29.

churches are formed around dynamic leaders who select themselves (or more precisely, feel that God has selected them) and hence whose self-image is considerably more positive than that of most other people.[43]

They are thus good entrepreneurs but bad collaborators. The type is obviously relevant to Latin America: the leader who left the Pentecostal Methodist Church, who criticized the authoritarianism and life-long nomination of the bishop and the lack of an organized treasury, has since followed these very same practices in his own Pentecostal Church of Chile.[44] But not all types of Pentecostalism are equally subject to schism. Nelson elaborates on a typology of three organizational models used in Brazilian Protestantism: the bureaucratic (legal), the clientelistic (patrimonial), and the kinship (patriarchal).[45] All use metaphors rooted in Brazilian culture. The bureaucratic model, imported from the United States by American missions, is characteristic of the historical churches. Its consequences (slow growth, internecine struggles, doctrinal homogeneity) reflect the workings of this model in Brazilian society: limited to the middle class; privatized for nepotistic ends and manipulated in power struggles; and linked to a legal tradition with a fixation for orthodoxy. The clientelistic model, which characterizes most Pentecostal churches, is more socially accessible (demanding little administrative knowledge) and allows rapid growth, but also stimulates schisms (such as the many which punctuate the history of the Assemblies of God). The kinship model, restricted to the Christian Congregation, is based on the patriarchalism of Italian immigrants and rejects all bureaucracy and paid clergy. Lacking the entrepreneurial spirit of the clientelistic model, it grows more slowly but makes splits virtually unknown.

Protestant segmentation in Latin America began with the transplant of foreign denominations by missionaries and immigrants. In many parts of the region, it found a cultural echo in a tradition of independent lay Catholic brotherhoods and African or indigenous cults. The growth of Pentecostalism in separate (nonhistorical) denominations reflected a social factor: "the increase in social distance between classes is a major factor in the development of different emphases within the same . . . religious tradition."[46] In addition, as a religion of the *word* rather than the *rite*, Protestantism is especially prone to divide into socially homogeneous units. Today, in the vast number of Pen-

---

43. Steve Bruce, *No Pope of Rome: Militant Protestantism in Modern Scotland* (Edinburgh, 1985), pp. 204-5.

44. D'Epinay, *Religion, dynamique social et dépendance*, p. 187.

45. Nelson, "Organizational Homogeneity," pp. 319-27.

46. Bruce, *A House Divided*, p. 97.

tecostal groups, we see the pluralist model gaining ground in a context that is favorable socially (rapid urbanization breaking up old unities), juridically (legal facilities for founding a new religious group), and culturally (widespread social acceptance of the possibility of religious conversion).

If social differentiation and cultural models of leadership favor segmentation, the *sect's* difficulty in updating itself causes "waves" of Pentecostal institutional creations which renew their relationships to culture. New groups have freedom to adapt because they do not carry decades of tradition. The idea of waves emphasizes the versatility of Pentecostalism, but also the way each church carries the marks of the era in which it was born.[47]

Pentecostalism's segmentation does not mean there is no attempt at transdenominational unity. Although very few Latin American Pentecostal churches are affiliated to the World Council of Churches (two smaller Chilean churches joined in 1961; Brazil for Christ joined in 1968 and left in 1986), many participate in national evangelical bodies such as CONEP (Concilio Nacional Evangélico del Perú [National Evangelical Council of Peru]) in Peru, or in trans-Pentecostal bodies such as the recently formed CIP (Confederación de Iglesias Pentecostales [Confederation of Pentecostal Churches]), FIPA (Federación de Iglesias Pentecostales Autónomas [Federation of Autonomous Pentecostal Churches]), and CIPRA (Confederación de Iglesias Pentecostales de la República Argentina [Confederation of Pentecostal Churches of the Argentine Republic]) in Argentina. In Brazil, two attempts at unified Protestant organs, CEB (Confederação Evangélica do Brasil [Evangelical Confederation of Brazil]) in 1987 and CNPB (Conselho Nacional de Pastores do Brasil [National Council of Pastors of Brazil]) in 1993, have been largely Pentecostal initiatives, stimulated by political considerations.

Typologies of Latin American Pentecostalism

Increasing segmentation has posed a severe challenge to typologies. In addition to the theological and political criteria used in typologies of Latin American Catholicism, Protestantism requires (usually cross-cutting) institutional factors to be taken into account. The latter may use a series of criteria, such as the ideal types of *sect-denomination-church,* mode of transplant to Latin America, length of existence, theological distinctives, social origin of members, or range of action (local or national).

Perhaps the most sophisticated typology of Latin American Protestantism

47. Bryan Wilson, *Sociology of Religion* (Oxford, 1982), p. 106.

is D'Epinay's for Argentina and Chile, which is based on sociological type in the country of origin *(sect, established sect, denomination* or *ecclesia)* and mode of transplant to Latin America (through missionaries or immigrants, to immigrants or to the whole population).[48] The interesting typology which results from these structural and historical variables is, however, of limited use to us. For one thing, there is the problem of the classification of churches founded in Latin America, much more numerous in many countries today than in the Southern Cone of twenty-five years ago. In addition, D'Epinay retains as the historical variable the mode of transplant of the group from which the new church separated.[49] But, with successive schisms, the original heritage becomes very diluted. Where, for example, should we classify the greatest Pentecostal phenomenon of recent years, the (Brazilian) Universal Church of the Kingdom of God, a 1977 schism of the New Life Church, which itself separated from the Assemblies of God in 1960, which in turn began with a Baptist splinter group in 1911? However, the most severe limitation of D'Epinay's typology is that it places all the Pentecostal churches in a single category. Historical Protestantism, born in Europe, is correctly seen as a diversified field, but Pentecostalism, largely Latin American, is not.

Some recent Brazilian sociologists have tried to nuance the Pentecostal world. José Bittencourt uses country of origin and age as criteria.[50] He distinguishes between "classical Pentecostalism" (of American missionary origin), "autonomous Pentecostalism" ("dissident denominations . . . and/or those formed around strong leaders") and "charismatics" (Pentecostalizing schisms from the historical churches). This raises difficulties. The two main churches of "classical Pentecostalism" are said to be the Assemblies of God (which is actually of Swedish and not American provenance) and the Christian Congregation (basically a national church founded among Italian immigrants). In the list of "autonomous Pentecostal churches" we find the Four-Square, the only large Pentecostal church in Brazil of truly American origin.

Another recent typology is Antônio Mendonça's.[51] Although very suggestive for historical Protestantism, it also presents problems with regard to Pentecostals. The latter are divided between "classical" (AG, Christian Congrega-

---

48. D'Epinay, *Religion, dynamique social et dépendance.*

49. D'Epinay, *Religion, dynamique social et dépendance,* p. 117.

50. José Bittencourt Filho, *O Pentecostalismo autônomo: um remédio amorgo* (Rio de Janeiro, 1991), p. 12.

51. Antônio Gouvêa Mendonça, "Um panorama do Protestantismo Brasileiro atual," in L. Landim, ed., *Sinais dos tempos: tradições religiosas no Brasil* (Rio de Janeiro, 1989), pp. 43-44.

tion, Four-Square, Brazil for Christ) and "divine healing" (God Is Love and "numerous others"). Those absent are the Universal Church, the charismatic splits from the historical churches, and the new charismatic "communities." Mendonça's division of Pentecostalism is different from Bittencourt's: instead of "autonomous" churches, he talks of "divine healing agencies." The latter are not really churches since "they do not have a fixed body of members."[52] The largest is supposedly God Is Love, which "does not demand any commitment from people" and offers miracles "as an end in themselves and not as a route."[53] In fact, nothing could be further from the truth: God Is Love has the most highly developed casuistry and system of discipline for members of any Pentecostal church in Brazil.

The concept of "divine healing" draws on Durkheim's distinction between religion and magic: the latter creates a clientele and not a community. It was introduced into the discussion of Brazilian Pentecostalism by Duglas Monteiro in reference to the hypertrophy of healing (at the cost of doctrinal instruction) and a fluctuating clientele.[54] It is totally inappropriate for understanding the Universal Church of the Kingdom of God. The "clientele" model has limited utility. Only a small religious enterprise can be economically viable as long as it depends on a fluctuating clientele. Beyond a certain level (both God Is Love and the Universal Church work in over a dozen countries), a solid community of members is essential. Besides, the offer of (paid) services is not an exclusive characteristic of minute *sects* but is also practiced by large territorial *churches*. What is called "divine healing" is merely an initial stage of accumulation, to be superseded, in successful cases, by a stable community receiving doctrinal instruction.

Carlos Brandão divides the religious field of a small town in the interior of São Paulo vertically (Catholicism, Protestantism, and "mediumship religions") and horizontally (social class).[55] For him, competition in the Protestant camp is now not so much between historicals and Pentecostals as between "the stable churches of traditional Pentecostalism [or 'mediating churches,' on the border between the erudite and the popular] and the small sects of popular Pentecostalism."[56] The former he defines as nationwide agencies with "roots in other worlds and other social classes." The latter, the

52. Mendonça, "Um panorama do Protestantismo Brasileiro atual," p. 72.
53. Mendonça, "Um panorama do Protestantismo Brasileiro atual," p. 80.
54. Duglas Teixeira Monteiro, "Igrejas, seitas e agências: aspectos de um ecumenismo popular," in E. Valle and J. Queiroz, eds., *A cultura do povo* (São Paulo, 1979), pp. 81-111.
55. Carlos Rodriques Brandão, *Os deuses do povo* (São Paulo, 1986).
56. Brandão, *Os deuses do povo,* p. 110.

really "popular" groups, are no more than local or regional. The very lowest social ranks only *participate* in the former, whereas they *rule* in the latter. As the main groups grow, they institutionalize and seek respectability by reclassifying their members along unacknowledged class lines. This leaves space "below," which the small groups soon fill.

We thus have three suggested typologies of Brazilian Pentecostalism:

Bittencourt	Mendonça	Brandão
Classical	Classical	Mediating churches
versus	*versus*	*versus*
Autonomous	Divine Healing	Small local sects

The suggestions do not agree on which criteria should determine internal distinctions in Pentecostalism or on which churches should be placed in each category. The Pentecostal explosion in Latin America remains a typological challenge.

Regional Diversity in Denominational Composition

Many discussions refer to newer churches in Latin America as "neo-Pentecostal." But there is an important variation in usage. In Brazil, "neo-Pentecostal" refers primarily to churches such as the Universal Church which have a mainly lower-class appeal.[57] But the history of lower-class Brazilian Pentecostalism can be seen as successive *waves* of institutional creation, each wave updating its relationship to culture.[58] In this light, "neo-Pentecostalism" is merely the latest wave in the dynamic history of Pentecostalism, rather than a separate category. Recent Argentine literature has used the concept of neo-Pentecostalism in studies of leaders such as Hector Giménez,[59] but emphasizes their comparatively greater acceptance by the middle classes and by the

---

57. Ricardo Mariano, "Neopentecostalismo: os pentecostais estão mundando," M.A. thesis, University of São Paulo, 1995.

58. Paul Freston, "Protestantes e política no Brasil: da constituinte ao impeachment," Ph.D. dissertation, University of Campinas, Brazil, 1993; "Breve história do Pentecostalismo Brasileiro: 1. A Assembléia de Deus," in A. Antoniazzi et al., *Nem anjos nem demônios: interpretacões sociológicas do Pentecostalismo* (Petrópolis, 1994), pp. 67-99; "Pentecostalism in Brazil: A Brief History," *Religion* 25 (1995): 119-33.

59. Alejandro Frigerio, "Estudios recientes sobre el Pentecostalismo en el Cono Sur: problemas y perspectivas," in A. Frigerio, ed., *El Pentecostalismo en la Argentina* (Buenos Aires, 1994), pp. 10-28.

Protestant establishment. In Central America, neo-Pentecostal refers to middle-class and elite charismatic churches. Despite theological and methodological similarities (choreographed services influenced by television, extensive use of the media, emphasis on health and wealth, acceptance of the material benefits of modernity instead of ascetic rejection), they are very different social phenomena. The Central American literature makes a clear *sociological* distinction between neo-Pentecostalism and traditional Pentecostalism: the former are privileged city-dwellers; the latter are small-town merchants, peasants, and artisans.[60]

Guatemalan neo-Pentecostalism took off in the 1970s and represented the first significant Protestant presence in the middle and higher reaches of society. Dennis Smith traces its origin to rejection of Vatican II Catholic reforms: "By 1976 a significant group of socially prominent Catholic professionals . . . had begun to explore other religious options."[61] The Catholic charismatic alternative was blocked by the hierarchy. Some people therefore turned to Protestantism. At the same time, the 1976 earthquake had stimulated the arrival of new independent charismatic groups from the United States, among them the Church of the Word (Verbo), which soon recruited future president Ríos Montt. The model was soon copied by members of the Guatemalan elite, such as the former lawyer from a prominent family who founded El Shaddai, the church of former president Jorge Serrano.

Guatemala, probably the most Protestant country of Latin America, gives us a pioneer example of what can happen when Protestantism, besides reaching a certain numerical level, begins to be practiced by significant numbers of the elite. According to David Stoll, Protestants are no more than 5 percent of the elite,[62] but a dozen or so elite churches (with an upper- and middle-class membership) have achieved unusual prominence. The Protestant elite is best represented among owners of "modern" businesses importing technology, and least among the old elite of coffee planters whose requirements for labor control helped create the death squads. The combination of a certain elite presence, a vast popular base, and a weak State is transforming Protestantism into a new source of political and cultural hegemony. Class location makes neo-Pentecostals receptive to the American religious right and its vision of dominion in which believers take power and remold society from above. In a

60. Dennis Smith, "Coming of Age: A Reflection on Pentecostals, Politics and Popular Religion in Guatemala," *Pneuma* 13.2 (fall 1991): 136.

61. Smith, "Coming of Age," p. 134.

62. David Stoll, "'Jesus Is Lord of Guatemala': Evangelical Reform in a Death-Squad State," in Martin Marty and J. Scott Appleby, eds., *Accounting for Fundamentalisms* (Chicago, 1994), p. 108.

poor and war-ridden country, the State's weakness has led it to cooperate with the Protestants, especially the neo-Pentecostals, in educational and social programs.[63]

This situation contrasts with Brazil. There, charismatic schisms from the historical churches occurred in the 1960s and early 1970s. Later, a plethora of new independent charismatic communities sprang up, some of which are grouped together in networks. They are now the main focus of conversion to Protestantism in the middle and upper classes, and also attract some upwardly mobile Pentecostals. However, they do not have the same importance as in Central America; Brazilian Protestantism is very different, with a large and old historical middle class. Middle- and upper-class charismatic religion is not as central for the Protestant field, and even less so for its politics, unlike Central America.

Despite the prominence of elite churches in Guatemala, Pentecostal religion is generally associated with the Latin American poor. But, in a continent where the poor are the vast majority, that is not saying very much. Is it possible to be more specific about the social composition of Latin American Pentecostalism?

If we look at the metro area of Rio de Janeiro, only 16.27 percent of the general population earn less than two minimum salaries,[64] while 19.34 percent of Protestants are in that category. At the top end of the scale (over twenty minimum salaries) the relationship is reversed (9.18 percent of the general population versus only 5.30 percent of Protestants). Educational differences are even more marked: Protestants are over-represented among those with less than one year of schooling (13.28 percent versus an average of 9.64 percent) and very under-represented among those who have completed secondary education (only 6.49 percent against 12.02 percent of the general population). With regard to color, 47.74 percent of Protestants are nonwhite, as opposed to only 40.18 percent of the whole population. Thus, although the correlation between religious differences and social class is not very pronounced in Brazil, Protestantism is the preeminent religion of the poor and, even more so, of the less educated. It is also well represented among blacks and mestizos. Data from El Salvador, where rapid Protestant growth is very recent, paint a similar picture:

63. S. Rose and Q. Schultze, "The Evangelical Awakening in Guatemala: Fundamentalist Impact on Education and Media," in Martin Marty and J. Scott Appleby, eds., *Fundamentalisms and Society* (Chicago, 1993), pp. 415-51.

64. Information taken from "Religion and Social Class in the Metropolitan Area of Rio de Janeiro (in percentages)," in Rubem César Fernandes, "O governo das almas," in *Nem anjos nem demônios*, ed. A. Antoniazzi et al., p. 174 (based on PNAD 1988). One minimum salary equals approximately U.S. $70.

evangélicos are poorer and have a lower educational level and occupational status than practicing and nonpracticing Catholics.[65]

Beyond this, however, the data are contradictory. Coleman et al. contrast Protestant recruitment among the lower strata with Catholic Base Community recruitment in the well-established *barrios*.[66] Roger Lancaster notes that the Pentecostal explosion in Sandinista Nicaragua was associated with dire urban poverty in the poorest and newest *barrios* of Managua. In these areas, the percentage of Protestants is double the national average, and they are usually the poorest in these *barrios,* being associated with female-headed households and with recent or persistent illness.[67] On the other hand, many authors say Pentecostals may be associated with low-paying and low-status jobs or with unstable employment, but they are not mainly from the marginalized and very poorest sectors.[68] The true picture can be established only by more empirical research.

In occupational terms, we also have conflicting pictures. Lalive D'Epinay says Pentecostals in Santiago are disproportionately from the most marginalized of the poor: those without fixed employment or professional training. Pentecostalism is relatively strong in the coal-mining areas around Concepción, where low pay and high unemployment reign, and weak in the higher-paying copper-mining zones of the north.[69] Fontaine and Bayer confirm the picture: 77 percent of *evangélicos* are self-employed, against 38 percent of Catholics.[70] In the big Mexican cities, "the Protestant sects and the unions are not competitors; the former recruit in the marginalized sectors with a home-based strategy, whereas the latter recruit in the workplace among the organized working-class."[71] In poor municipalities of Greater Rio, Rolim discovered a pronounced sectorial imbalance in Pentecostal employment: 59.9 percent in services (against only 9 percent for the whole population of the area), and only 19.9 percent in industry (compared to 55.8 percent).[72] This means greater dependence and insecurity. On the periphery of

65. Coleman et al., "Protestantism in El Salvador."

66. Coleman et al., "Protestantism in El Salvador," p. 116.

67. Roger Lancaster, *Thanks to God and the Revolution* (New York, 1988), pp. 101-4.

68. David Martin, "Chile: What the Polls Show," mimeo, 1991; Hans Tennekes, *El movimiento Pentecostal en la sociedad Chilena* (Iquique, 1985), p. 87; Judith Hoffnagel, "The Believers: Pentecostalism in a Brazilian City," Ph.D. dissertation, Indiana University, 1978, pp. 49, 61.

69. Christian Lalive D'Epinay, *O refúgio das massas* (Rio de Janeiro, 1970), pp. 86-87.

70. Arturo Fontaine Talavera and Harald Bayer, "Retrato del movimiento evangélico a la luz de las encuestas de opinión pública," *Estudios públicos* 44 (1991): 90.

71. Bastian, *Protestantismo y sociedad en México,* p. 225.

72. Francisco Cartaxo Rolim, *Pentecostais no Brasil* (Petrópolis, 1985), p. 171.

Santiago, on the other hand, Tennekes found no significant differences between Pentecostals and non-Pentecostals in terms of employment.[73]

In short, the detailed social composition of Pentecostalism seems to vary from place to place and from church to church. Although there is no research locating Brazil's large churches on the social scale, there are clear differences between, for example, the Four-Square (modest prosperity) and God Is Love (extreme poverty). The social composition of churches also varies over time: the AG-Brazil has gone through a very evident process of upward social mobility in recent years. The appeal of Pentecostalism is not univocal, and marginal differences in liturgy and message can meet subtly different social demands.

The social composition of the founders of Latin America's major Pentecostal groups includes proletarians such as the Swedish foundryman Daniel Berg (AG-Brazil), the construction worker Manoel de Mello (Brazil for Christ) and the coalminer Victor Mora (National Wesleyan Church — Chile); independent artisans such as Luigi Francescon (Christian Congregation — Brazil) and the barbers and shoemakers of the Apostolic Church–Mexico; and lower-middle-class white-collar workers such as Edir Macedo (Universal Church — Brazil) and many of the missionaries from North America and Scandinavia. Rare are the founders of higher social origin, like the Methodist missionary Willis Hoover, a nonpracticing doctor who sparked the Chilean schism of 1909.

In many countries, Pentecostalism is largely a rural phenomenon. In El Salvador, it dates from the 1910s but reached the capital city only in 1956. In Bolivia, Protestants are 17 percent of the rural population but only 9 percent of the urban. The center of Mexican Protestantism, previously northern, has shifted to the rural south since 1940. "This ruralization of Protestantism occurs in the states where hunger and the subsistence economy predominate, and where seasonal migration is part of the family economy."[74] AG-Brazil has a strong rural base, still reflected in the origin of many leaders. The Christian Congregation is overwhelmingly rural and small-town: in the interior of São Paulo State the Congregation had 2,058 temples in 1991, compared to only 848 in Greater São Paulo (with half the state population). On the other hand, Brazilian Pentecostalism is now predominantly urban: the churches founded since the 1950s have been increasingly city-based, culminating in the Universal Church of the Kingdom of God, which has virtually no rural presence.

Latin American Pentecostalism shows considerable regional diversity in

73. Tennekes, *El movimiento Pentecostal en la sociedad Chilena*, pp. 29-30.
74. Bastian, *Protestantismo y sociedad en México*, p. 224.

denominational composition and degree of nationalization. Brazil is almost unique in having a broad range of long-established historical churches, often fairly strong, some of which bred movements for autonomy as early as the late nineteenth century. The subsequent historical/Pentecostal divide does not, therefore, correspond to a missionary/nationalist one. In Chile, on the other hand, historical Protestants never made a serious impact. The peasants were very dependent and the upper class was firmly allied to the Catholic Church,[75] making Chilean society far less permeable to religious dissent. In Brazil, historical churches managed to cut across class lines; in Chile, Protestantism has been more of a lower-class phenomenon, and therefore more Pentecostal.[76]

The Pentecostal schism in the Methodist Church of Chile marked the break between missionaries and nationals, between a foreign mentality and local sensitivity to the extraordinary, and between middle-class cultural forms and the popular classes.[77] Although the first Pentecostal Church was led by the missionary Willis Hoover, he broke with his mission under pressure from his Pentecostal flock. The new movement did not at all depend on him.

Chilean Pentecostalism is thus accentuatedly national in origin, a fact of which its leaders are proud.[78] Although foreign groups are present (Swedish autonomous AG, 1937; AG-USA, 1942; Four-Square, 1945; Church of God, 1950), they are all small.[79] Chilean Pentecostalism consists principally of the two churches into which the original schismatic National Methodist Church of 1909 split in 1932: the Pentecostal Methodist (IMP) and the Pentecostal Evangelical (IEP); and subsequent smaller divisions from these, such as the Apostolic Pentecostal Church, the Pentecostal Church of Chile, and the Mission Pentecostal Church (the latter two being members of the World Council of Churches). The Chilean Pentecostal field seems less susceptible to phenomena such as the Brazilian Universal Church or Central American "neo-Pentecostalism."

The Chilean trajectory is thus unique: its Protestantism is more accentuatedly Pentecostal, and its Pentecostalism more clearly national, than anywhere else in Latin America. Distance from the United States and absence of large immigrant groups doubtless helped in this. Chilean Pentecostalism is also characterized by very vertical and centralized structures, even compared

---

75. Willems, *Followers of the New Faith*, p. 62.
76. Willems, *Followers of the New Faith*, pp. 253-54.
77. D'Epinay, *O refúgio das massas*, p. 53.
78. Lagos, *Crisis de la esperanza*, pp. 53-54.
79. Willems, *Followers of the New Faith*, pp. 111-12.

to sister churches in other countries — the Methodist rather than Baptist or holiness origin being an important factor in this.

Neighboring Peru presents a very different picture in almost every respect. There, Pentecostalism is a minority sector within Protestantism and really took off only in the 1970s.[80] The Pentecostal field is dominated by the Assemblies of God. The latter resulted from American missionary work, and its history is punctuated by nationalist conflicts.

Peruvian Protestantism has been characterized by a fairly high degree of interdenominational collaboration. The first AG missionaries (1919) occupied the part of the country assigned to them by a Committee of Cooperation, the northern Sierra, where linguistic difficulties and religious intolerance limited expansion.[81] In 1937, the Springfield, Missouri headquarters of the Assemblies of God–USA sent a representative with "the express intention of organizing and centralizing authority. . . . The nascent ecclesiastical organization would be similar to that of the AG-USA."[82] The first board of directors was composed exclusively of missionaries and soon affiliated with the newly formed Evangelical Council of Peru. Peruvians effectively took over leadership only after a nationalist military regime came to power in 1968. But the American link was still operative. In the late 1970s, many leaders emigrated to the United States.[83] Conflicts between missionaries and nationals were endemic, leading to numerous nationalist schisms, in contrast to the absence of such schisms in the Swedish-influenced Brazilian AG.

El Salvador differs from the Chilean and Peruvian cases. About 60 percent of its large Protestant community is Pentecostal, divided between two large traditional churches (AG and Church of God) and a plethora of neo-Pentecostal groups of American or Guatemalan origin.[84] It was totally rural until recently, a possible factor in its far weaker political presence than in Guatemala. Missionaries from the United States have been important in its urbanization and arrival in the middle class and the media.[85]

The story of its two main groups is illustrative of a pattern. The AG's origins in El Salvador go back to an independent Canadian missionary in the 1910s. The American church took over in 1930. The Church of God began in

80. Frans Kamsteeg, "Pastor y discípulo," in B. Boudewijnse et al., eds., *Algo más que ópio* (San José, Costa Rica, 1991), p. 97.

81. Rubén Zavala, *Historia de las Asambleas de Dios del Perú* (Lima, 1989), pp. 69-79.

82. Zavala, *Historia de las Asambleas de Dios del Perú*, p. 82.

83. Zavala, *Historia de las Asambleas de Dios del Perú*, p. 94.

84. Everett Wilson, "Sanguine Saints: Pentecostalism in El Salvador," *Church History* 52 (1983): 194.

85. Wilson, "Sanguine Saints," p. 197.

1940 by a similar process. This pattern, of groups started by independent missionaries or even by breakaway nationals later seeking affiliation with a U.S. denomination, is typical of areas where Protestantism was weak, and is unknown in Chile or Brazil. It is not just a case of the geographical proximity of Central America to the United States and the small size of its national societies; even Argentina has followed the model.

Argentine Pentecostalism began with the Christian Assembly among Italian immigrants, whose roots go back to Francescon's visit in 1909 but whose ecclesiastical organization dates from 1916.[86] However, for many decades, "Pentecostalism was more readily accepted in mainly Indian communities or amongst central or northern European immigrants. The greatest resistance was met where there were most first-generation descendants of Italian or Spanish immigrants . . . [who did not want to] risk foregoing that which made them sense that this new Catholic country was indeed their own."[87] As compared to Chile, slow growth in Argentina had a lot to do with Protestantism's identification with immigrants; compared to Brazil immigrants, Italian immigrants to Argentina did not regard local Catholicism as weak and foreign and did not supply many converts.[88] Only in the 1950s did Pentecostalism find an expression among the urban poor following the failure of Peronist populism, and it reached new heights after redemocratization in the early 1980s left the Catholic Church shaken by its association with militarism.[89] Ecclesiastical history (including the largest denomination, the Union of the Assemblies of God) is marked by the establishment of churches, either by independent missionaries in the early days or by breakaway nationals from the 1950s, and subsequent links with U.S. churches, subordinating freedom to security.[90]

The general picture, therefore, is that most Latin American Pentecostal churches (unlike their historical counterparts) were founded either by Latin Americans who broke with an existing Protestant denomination or by independent missionaries, and only rarely by a foreign Pentecostal denomination. In some countries, independent groups would subsequently seek American links; in other countries, this was unknown, and groups founded from abroad tended quickly to achieve autonomy.

86. Saracco, "Argentine Pentecostalism," p. 45.
87. Saracco, "Argentine Pentecostalism," p. 69.
88. Martin, *Tongues of Fire*, p. 75.
89. Saracco, "Argentine Pentecostalism," p. 140.
90. Saracco, "Argentine Pentecostalism," p. 141.

Latin American Pentecostalism: Some of the Key Debates

In looking at current debates about Latin American Pentecostalism, it is necessary to bear in mind the history of academic work on Latin American Protestantism in general. In relation to the academic world, Brazil, as already mentioned, is the only country with significant production on Latin American Protestantism. For many years from the 1960s, this production was dominated by social scientists of Protestant origin. Due to severe theological and political crises in the historical churches, the sociologists of Protestantism were all "ex-pastors, ex-seminarians, ex-lay leaders."[91] Their work largely "emphasized the alienating character [of Protestantism]. . . . It was necessary to excite the 'revolutionary potential' of the people and delimit groups which hindered this aim."[92] Lalive D'Epinay's classic on Chilean Pentecostalism, *Haven of the Masses,* "was an important contribution to the schismatic literature of Protestant intellectuals . . . against their churches of origin."[93]

A new phase began in the late 1970s with more sympathetic anthropologists, usually without Protestant connections. They began to treat Pentecostalism positively compared to the social situation of the poor, rather than negatively compared to an intellectualist ideal of the social role of religion. As one anthropologist says, "among those interviewed [in the interior of the Brazilian northeast], the believers attracted my attention. . . . There was in them a restored dignity, despite the visible deterioration of their living conditions."[94]

Recently, an English social scientist has reflected critically on his own research experience among Brazilian Pentecostals. He says that what he experienced as Pentecostals' aggression was in fact a challenge to any assumption of superiority. "They placed me as an individual, without social, racial or cultural referent, but exclusively . . . as a 'soul' to be saved. . . . [Pentecostals are shocking because] they are not submissive. . . . The white male from a rich country was put on the defensive by . . . people who were poor, black and female."[95]

This new perspective is by no means general, however. There is a certain culturalist dislike of changes in the religious status quo; as a leading anthropologist remarked, "the Universal Church of the Kingdom of God is wiping

91. Rubem Alves, "A volta do sagrado (os caminhos da sociologia da regirião no Brasil)," *Religião e sociedade* 3 (1978): 134.

92. Ana Maria Leonardos, "O Protestantismo Brasileiro: três momentos de análise acadêmica," *Comunicações do ISER* 24 (1987): 15.

93. Rubem César Fernandes, "O debate entre sociólogos a propósito dos pentecostais," *Cadernos do ISER* 6 (1977): 49-50.

94. Regina Reyes Novaes, *Os escolhidos de Deus* (Rio de Janeiro, 1985), p. 7.

95. David Lehmann, *Struggle for the Spirit* (Cambridge, 1996), p. 11.

out the Umbanda *terreiros;* this is a tragedy." Or, in the words of a prominent sociologist at the University of São Paulo: "nobody likes the Pentecostals; I'm horrified at the idea Brazil might become a Pentecostal country." Only recently have the positive categories applied to new social movements in Latin America begun to be applied to the *evangélicos*.[96] The "neo-Pentecostals," accused of waging a religious war, have also been the victims of another type of religious war. As Cecília Mariz shows, social scientific criticisms betray a rationalist prejudice which devalues emotionalism in religion and rejects spending on the sacred.[97] The neo-Pentecostals are criticized precisely for those elements which link them, on the one hand, most closely to popular culture and, on the other hand, to the Catholic ecclesial model. While traditional Pentecostals (now treated with more respect in the literature) used to be criticized for their rigid morals, the neo-Pentecostals are now flailed for their flexible morality; and while the former were criticized for talking of salvation in another world, the latter are now attacked for emphasizing solutions to this-worldly problems.

Two factors are involved in the relationship between Pentecostalism and academia. First, Pentecostalism in Latin America is in an intellectually exposed position because, as a popular religion, it has few intellectuals of its own, and little contact with the intelligentsia. On the other hand, the Catholic Base Communities are linked to the Catholic institutional structure, and many studies of them have been done by pastoral activists. Intellectuals had an important role in systematizing Afro-Brazilian cults, and many social scientists (since Roger Bastide) have become personally involved in their practices. But no distinguished sociological work has been produced by a Brazilian Pentecostal, and no Brazilian social scientist has been initiated in Pentecostalism in order to understand it better!

Second, part of academia views Pentecostalism with dismay because it rejects the traditional Latin American model of the religious field and popularizes an alternative pluralist model. The latter is of mutually exclusive groups in competition, breaking not only with Brazil's nonexclusive tradition but also with its historic model of *hierarchical syncretism* which combines nonexclusive affiliation with acceptance of Catholic institutional hegemony. The difference was symbolized during the Pope's visit to Brazil in 1991. On the one hand, the Afro-Brazilian candomblé centers in Salvador stopped functioning

96. Matt Marostica, "La iglesia evangélica en la Argentina como nuevo movimiento social," *Sociedad y religión* 12 (June 1994): 3-16.

97. Cecília Mariz, "El debate en torno del Pentecostalismo autónomo en Brasil," *Sociedad y religión* 13 (1995): 21-32.

during the Pope's stay there. On the other hand, an Assemblies of God radio station refused to join the compulsory network formed to transmit the Pope's speech. Candomblé (the main form of Afro-Brazilian religion) is called a body without a head, because the head is in Catholicism. But Pentecostalism is a totally autonomous popular religiosity, the first mass religion in Brazil consciously to reject the institutional force field of the Catholic Church.

Among the academic and nonacademic debates provoked by Pentecostalism in Latin America are: Why does it grow? What effect does it have on indigenous peoples? Is it really Protestant? How does it affect economic attitudes? What is its political role? We shall now look briefly at these questions.

Explanations for Pentecostal Growth in Latin America

We cannot plunge straight into consideration of suggested reasons for the growth of Pentecostalism in Latin America without realizing that this question, far from being just a calm academic discussion, is a weapon in political, religious, and even commercial polemic. "Explanations" of Pentecostal growth can help to neutralize a rival force, stigmatizing it as illegitimate or pathological, or may reflect (un)conscious distaste for a phenomenon which has weak links with the academic community.

Catholic Analyses

Latin American Catholic analyses are, of course, profoundly influenced by ecumenical initiatives since Vatican II. Since the early 1980s, however, it has once again become acceptable for some Catholic leaders to show concern over Protestant growth, no longer by talking of "Protestants" in general but of the "sects." The latter are perceived as a threat to religious hegemony because they are autonomous groups that demand exclusive affiliation. A leading Catholic newspaper in Brazil (linked to the Vatican) talks of an "evangelical offensive" in Latin America, whose "impressive bellicosity" takes advantage of the "ignorance" of the people.[98] Another journal, linked to the Brazilian Bishops' Conference, says the "evangelical sects . . . almost always lead to a mystical view of the world, to a conformism and conservatism . . . which favour charlatanism."[99] These analyses reveal a static view of culture in which religions have people and not vice versa. "Sects" such as the AG are "move-

98. *Thirty Dias* (October 1990): 48-55.
99. *Jornal de opinião* (February 7-23, 1991).

ments rather than churches" and seduce converts by all sorts of means, affirmed the soon-to-be elected (1995) president of the Bishops' Conference.[100]

Seeing itself as the (most) legitimate religious institution in the region, much of the Catholic hierarchy tends to see the growth of "sects" as a failure in its own work. Selective imitation is proposed, including, most recently, greater episcopal approval of the Catholic charismatic renewal in Brazil. However, many such ideas were not new. "Much of the church had been labouring to implement them for decades, a circumstance that helps explain why many Catholics felt they needed a second reason, political in nature, to account for the multiplication of evangelicals."[101] The old conspiracy theory was resurrected: the "sects" grow thanks to politically motivated American money. In Brazil, this theory first appeared in the late nineteenth century, as the Vatican established greater power over Brazilian Catholicism (previously under the effective control of the Portuguese kings or Brazilian emperors). In the 1930s, the leading (conservative) archbishop viewed Protestant expansion as a plot by American millionaires.[102] In the mid-1980s, the Bishops' Conference (no longer conservative) was suspicious of CIA involvement. According to a 1991 Latin American report to the Vatican,

> the sects . . . are promoted by interests foreign to our own life. . . . Some
> governments also promote expansion . . . which gradually weakens the
> Catholic Church's power over the people. . . . The idea grows that there
> is no need to be Catholic . . . to maintain the greatness of national iden-
> tity.[103]

Even some (though by no means all) Catholic progressives adopt a conspiracy theory. The attraction to them of this elitist position would seem to be that Liberation Theology's project depends on the existence of latently Catholic masses mobilizing in the Base Communities. Pentecostal growth thus threatens the numerical base of liberationism.

In the polemic over the "sects," explanations always depreciate the people, as "victims" either of propagandist methods or of foreign money. Incapable of adapting a religion to their own needs, the people should be protected either by mother Church or the paternalist State. The "sects" only grow due to pathological situations, whether religious (Catholic pastoral de-

100. *Folha de São Paulo* (February 9, 1988).

101. Stoll, *Is Latin America Turning Protestant?* p. 34.

102. Scott Mainwaring, *Igreja Católica e política no Brasil: 1916-1985* (São Paulo, 1989), p. 60.

103. *L'Osservatore Romano* (April 21, 1991).

ficiencies) or social (poverty, anomie). They are never seen as signs of health in the social body.

Foreign Influence

The "invasion of the sects" theory obviously builds on empirical evidence. Latin American Protestantism has many foreign connections (whose presence is facilitated by Protestant institutional segmentation); the question is how important they are. Protestantism in certain countries is considerably more susceptible to foreign influence than in others. About 40 percent of Nicaraguan pastors were on the payroll of American anti-Sandinista organizations in 1983.[104] Personalist leaders of neo-Pentecostal churches in Guatemala seek orientation from mentors in the United States.[105] But Chilean Pentecostalism and Brazilian Pentecostalism are highly nationalized.

In terms of personnel and money, both Catholicism and historical Protestantism are, on the whole, far more foreign. Pentecostalism was in its infancy when it arrived in many parts of the region. Without great resources or established organizations, it did not create expensive institutions and relations of dependence. The Swedes who founded AG-Brazil, originating from a tiny and marginalized religious minority in a still poor country, were not institution builders. Subsequent U.S.-AG missionaries to Brazil have been few and uninfluential. The flow of benefits would seem to be mainly to, not from, the United States; the American church retains an almost symbolic presence because it helps fund-raising in the United States to say that they collaborate with the Brazilian AG, the largest in the world. The only major Pentecostal denomination in Brazil with a truly American origin is the Four-Square.

In much of the region, foreign presence is most noticeable in highly visible sectors such as the media, whose efficacy for growth is doubtful. In Brazil, on the other hand, the large media presence is totally national. Of the fifteen to twenty evangelical TV programs on the Rio–São Paulo channels, only one (an Adventist production) is foreign. Literature, however, is an area of greater foreign penetration: 70 percent of evangelical books published in Brazil in 1991 were translations.

Stoll for Spanish America and Fernandes for Brazil have made the most detailed analyses of the question.[106] The latter concludes that, despite the tri-

---

104. Stoll, *Is Latin America Turning Protestant?* p. 236.

105. Smith, "Coming of Age," p. 137.

106. Stoll, *Is Latin America Turning Protestant?*; Rubem César Fernandes, "As missões Protestantes em números," *Cadernos do ISER* 10 (1981): 27-84.

pling of the number of missionaries after the 1964 coup, mostly from "faith" missions whose "civilizing aspirations were exacerbated to the point of Manichaeism" by the fear of Communism, this has little to do with Protestant growth. Over a third of missionaries work with Indians, a mere 0.5 percent of the population. Most of the faith missions are anti-Pentecostal, and the Pentecostals make little use of foreign missionaries. Pentecostal success "casts an ironic shadow over the massive resources mobilized by the missionary enterprise: the churches which grow most owe little to international missions."[107]

Stoll focuses on the efforts of the New Christian Right in Central America. While speaking of the danger of evangelical missions being harnessed to U.S. militarism by the religious right, he stresses that the importance of foreign personnel, money, and TV programs is grossly exaggerated both by protagonists and antagonists. In addition, the efforts of the religious right in the 1980s were resisted not only by principled opponents but also, pragmatically, by many established conservative missions who feared a backlash. "Judging from where churches were growing rapidly, it seemed as if the recipe for success was for missionaries to leave."[108]

Political/Social/Economic Factors

This multiplication of autonomous popular religious groups is seen by many authors as a search for solace in a time of social crisis, and thus as a symptom of disease. But as Levine points out, one can equally well posit a model in which crises open up new creative opportunities.[109] The "sects" would thus be seen as a phenomenon of freedom, as they generally are in the historiography of the English Civil War. Rather than symptoms of disease (or even the disease itself), they would be signs of a vibrant civil society freeing itself from ancient restrictions.

Another version of the social pathology theory links Protestant growth to political repression. Bastian talks of Mexican Pentecostalism as "an expression of the innovative capacity on the part of the popular sectors when the political and economic fields are closed or under the iron control of the dominant classes."[110] In some cases, there is a basis for the connection. According to Stoll, "the reasons for the growth of Protestant churches in the western highlands [of Guatemala] did not have to be sought in Washington or in the North American

107. Fernandes, "As missões Protestantes em números," p. 81.
108. Stoll, *Is Latin America Turning Protestant?* p. 72.
109. Daniel Levine, "Protestants and Catholics in Latin America: A Family Portrait," mimeo, 1991.
110. Bastian, *Protestantismo y sociedad en México*, p. 208.

religious right . . . [but in] the cost of revolutionary strategy."[111] The extraordinarily rapid growth in Guatemala in the last thirty years would probably not have been possible without the twin factors of civil war and mass conversion of indigenous communities. However, this does not explain why people turned to this particular option (the supply side), nor why most people caught up in this situation did *not* convert (the micro level). Nor does it mean, of course, that Protestant growth is tied to the existence of such facilitating factors; only that it was capable of taking on this function in these unusual circumstances.

In Argentina, on the other hand, the moment of Pentecostal take-off was the redemocratization in 1983.[112] As mentioned above, Chilean and Nicaraguan Protestantism grew most rapidly precisely during nonrepressive left-wing governments. As for Brazil, Rolim suggests a link between repression and Pentecostal growth:

> Is it pure coincidence that an intensely sacred faith should arrive in Brazil at a time [the 1910s] when the urban workers were being shaken by another experience [anarchism and anarcho-syndicalism] producing workers' struggles? Was it exclusively religious motives which determined the Pentecostal leaders' arrival?[113]

Rolim also tries to date Pentecostalism's take-off from 1935, "when authoritarian measures began to weaken and stifle the workers' movements."[114] It is a repeat of E. P. Thompson's theory for Methodism in England (cycles of political activism, government repression, and retreat into religion), later questioned by Eric Hobsbawm, who suggested Methodism advanced concomitantly with radicalism.[115] The evidence also does not support Rolim. The founder of the Christian Congregation went first to Buenos Aires and then to São Paulo, following the route of the Italian diaspora in order of importance. The Swedes who founded the AG went first (following a prophecy) to the northern town of Belém. They then spent years evangelizing the hinterland of the Amazon delta, finally arriving in São Paulo nearly twenty years later; hardly an intelligent plan to save Brazil from an imminent proletarian revolution. As to the moment of Pentecostal take-off, the precarious statistics available point not to 1935 but to the late 1940s, a period of unprecedented democracy. The post-1985 redemocratization also seems to have witnessed unparalleled growth.

111. Stoll, "'Jesus Is Lord of Guatemala,'" p. 108.
112. Saracco, "Argentine Pentecostalism."
113. Rolim, *Pentecostais no Brasil*, p. 73.
114. Rolim, *Pentecostais no Brasil*, p. 80.
115. Michael Hill, *A Sociology of Religion* (London, 1973), pp. 192-97.

There would seem to be a better case for linking Pentecostal growth with economic crises. The "lost decade" of the 1980s (stagnation, mounting foreign debt, falling per capita income) saw an acceleration of Protestant growth in many countries. Economic desperation, and especially *impoverishment* (loss of access to services previously within reach) rather than poverty (which is endemic), are supposedly causing large numbers to seek solutions in miracle-working churches. The "health and wealth gospel" offers a "religion of results." In the context of "savage capitalism," it proclaims the "survival of the most faithful." The explanation is plausible. As in all such cases of simultaneity, however, there are other plausible possibilities, such as mere chronological coincidence, or the existence of a crucial third factor mediating the relationship (e.g., economic crisis accelerates the breakdown of certain social patterns which facilitates conversion). Or, finally, economic crisis may be a partial contributory factor without being a major determinant.

For D'Epinay, the contrasting cases of Argentina and Chile show that Pentecostal growth does not correspond to any socioeconomic typology. Instead, influenced by the dependency theory of the 1960s, he proposes the concept of a "field of possibilities": the crisis of the 1930s (import-substitution industrialization, migration to the towns) made mass sectarian Protestantism possible. In Argentina, however, Peronism preempted Pentecostalism. Socioeconomic destructuring is a necessary but not sufficient condition for large growth.[116]

The key concept in D'Epinay's argument is anomie, normative and existential disorientation caused by social and spatial uprootedness. The social structures of traditional society are said to be recreated in the *sect*. "Pentecostalism is a communitarian religious reply to the abandonment of large sectors of the population caused by the anomic character of a society in transition."[117] Should we conclude that Pentecostalism is a life-jacket which will be discarded later on? The data do not confirm this. Tennekes found that most Pentecostal migrants had arrived in Santiago long before.[118] In a large Brazilian city, Hoffnagel found that many were already Pentecostals before they migrated, that many others spent many years in the city before converting, and that only 5 percent of her sample had no friends or relatives in the city on arrival.[119] We can add that, since Brazil is now 70 percent urban, anomie caused by migration could today be no more than a secondary factor in

116. D'Epinay, *Religion, dynamique social et dépendence,* pp. 93-95.
117. D'Epinay, *O refúgio das massas,* p. 60.
118. Tennekes, *El movimiento Pentecostal,* p. 30.
119. Hoffnagel, "The Believers," pp. 40-41.

rapid Pentecostal growth. The rate of migration has diminished, while the rate of Pentecostal growth has increased.

Droogers talks of divergent and even opposed suggestions found in the literature and concludes that an eclectic approach allows us to see the latter as paradoxes resulting from partial explanations rather than as intractable contradictions.[120] Religion is ambivalent and offers different things to different people. This would seem to be a wise approach (although not yet an answer); Pentecostalism is very flexible, and there is unlikely to be a single grand reason for its success. An eclecticism based on the ambivalence of religion will need to take into account not only political and economic but also social, cultural, ethnic, and religious factors; not only the macro level (which social characteristics are favorable to conversion) but also the micro level (why some people with those characteristics convert but others do not); not only the appeal of Pentecostalism to men but also (and especially) to women; not only the demand side (why people are ready to convert) but also the supply side (what Pentecostals do to maximize their potential market). And it will need to ask not only why Pentecostalism grows so much, but why it does not grow more, and why some types grow more than others.

Not all these questions can be answered in our present stage of knowledge. At the macro level, social and cultural factors may be more important than political (repression) or economic (poverty) ones. Social autonomy has always been important for Protestantism's capacity to prize open the traditional unity of Catholicism and national and cultural identity in Latin America. Early growth was most notable in regions where small independent farms predominated. As Martin notes, Protestantism found a niche in the interstices of society, among those outside the downward thrust of power and also free from constraining horizontal ties.[121] More recently, with rapid urbanization, Protestant growth has reflected the expansion of pluralism and personal autonomy. As the old unities of faith and identity have weakened, it has become respectable to change religion. Protestantism, says Martin, is successful because it is sociologically advanced and theologically "backward": it separates faith from State power, corresponding to increasing social differentiation in Latin America; but at the same time it creates closed enclaves of the faithful in which social experiments can be carried out.[122]

120. André Droogers, "Visiones paradójicas sobre una religión paradójica: modelos explicativos del crecimiento del Pentecostalismo en Brasil y Chile," in B. Boudewijnse et al., eds., *Algo más que ópio: una lectura antropológica del Pentecostalismo Latinoamericano y Caribeño* (San José, Costa Rica, 1991), pp. 17-42.

121. Martin, *Tongues of Fire*, p. 79.

122. Martin, *Tongues of Fire*, p. 106.

In recent years, the demonstration effect of Protestant growth in parts of the region on the relatively weaker parts should not be discounted. This is strengthened by the sense of belonging to a cultural bloc (Latin America as the *patria grande*); the Catholic Church was an important element in this cultural unity, and its erosion also has regional repercussions.

In a few areas of the region, Protestantism arrived with foreign immigrants and came to be ethnically defined, handicapping its penetration among the national population. This is especially so for Argentina, and possibly for southern Brazil, where the growth of non-Lutheran Protestantism was slow until quite recently.

Another factor in slow growth in southern Brazil, as compared to the rest of the country, is the more European and Tridentine Catholicism in that region, a strong source of priestly vocations. This alerts us to another macrolevel factor: the constitution of the religious field is an important determinant of Pentecostal growth. "The optimum chances for Protestantism exist where the church has been drastically weakened and yet the culture has remained pervasively religious, as in Brazil, Chile and Guatemala."[123] Where, on the other hand, the Roman Catholic Church remains politically strong, as in Colombia, the going is tougher, and where there has been a comprehensive secularization of culture, as in Uruguay and Venezuela, Protestantism makes slow headway.

Proximity to Religious Tradition

Can we go beyond that? Rolim suggests most converts come from "atomized devotional Catholicism," that Catholicism which is linked neither to organized centers of pilgrimage nor to the parish structure. In a municipality of Greater Rio, 80 percent of all converts previously considered themselves Catholics, of whom 90 percent prayed to the saints but 80 percent never went to mass.[124] Hoffnagel says very few AG members claimed to have had past contact with Afro-Brazilian cults;[125] on the other hand, the Universal Church seems to recruit more extensively from regular or occasional attendees of such religions.

With regard to the Protestant field, immigrant Protestantism is not favorable to Pentecostal growth (strong minority identity between church and ethnicity); nor is a strong holiness tradition, as in some Andean countries (preempting some of Pentecostalism's attraction).

123. Martin, *Tongues of Fire*, p. 59.
124. Rolim, *Pentecostais no Brasil*, pp. 97, 160.
125. Hoffnagel, "The Believers," p. 46.

But the propensity of sectors of the population to convert is not the only component in Pentecostal growth. As Bruce says, macro-sociological analyses are always incomplete because the population with the characteristics favorable to conversion is always much greater than the number who actually join. To go further, we need the micro-sociology of personal relationships and social networks.[126] The processes of conversion to Latin American Pentecostalism have not been sufficiently studied. Related to this is the whole "supply" side of Pentecostal growth: the favorable components of Pentecostalism itself. As *conversionist sects,* Pentecostal churches are characterized by almost continuous proselytism, ideally involving the mobilization of every member (though lay initiative in evangelism is less pronounced in some newer groups such as the Universal Church). Less frequently mentioned but equally important is the effect of the growing religious market: competition stimulates constant innovation (subtle changes in message or style can assist penetration of hitherto resistant sectors of the population) and localized supply. The latter is vital, as the poor have little mobility and whatever religious option is available locally will corner the market.

All this presupposes, of course, the capacity to communicate to the Latin American poor. "The functionalist and Marxist accounts of revivals . . . are dogged by the same problem. . . . We cannot use function as purpose. . . . [We need to] consider the way in which people might see [for example] social stress as a stimulus to renewed religious activity."[127] Only already religious people tend to see solutions to their economic problems in religious activities. "There are very few religious revivals which involved people adopting an entirely new world-view."[128] Pentecostalism is not only *Christian* but also close to popular Latin American religiosity in many respects, tuned in to an inspirited world. Over time, it has come even closer, stressing the traditional Latin American concern for protection by the sacred more than the original (North American) theme of sanctification.[129]

This proximity to the religious tradition is stressed by the new vein of studies that try to account for Pentecostalism's success and the Catholic Base Communities' relative numerical weakness (a recent electoral poll in Brazil showed that 10 percent of the population was Pentecostal, and less than 2 percent, CEB members). Levine says the CEBs lose out to the Pentecostals because they lack institutional flexibility, their liberationist discourse is alien, and they have

---

126. Bruce, *God Save Ulster!* p. 247.
127. Bruce, *A House Divided,* p. 220.
128. Bruce, *A House Divided,* p. 220.
129. Rolim, *Pentecostais no Brasil,* p. 168.

deemphasized personal morality and healing in favor of politics, a culturally perilous activity for women, who are the majority of CEB members.[130] In Brazil, recent Catholic studies have talked of the conflict between progressive Catholic "pastoral rationalism" and the "popular symbolic universe," between the CEB "ethic of commitment" and the festive character of popular culture, which has led to CEB weakness among the marginalized masses.[131]

Brazilian anthropologist Cecília Mariz talks of similarities and differences.[132] Both CEBs and Pentecostalism value change in general, breaking with fatalism. Both develop a sense of dignity and the capacity to express oneself. Both represent a process of religious rationalization and motivate to deal with poverty. In the long run, she says (going against established wisdom), they will have similar consequences in changing the attitudes and behavior of the poor, despite their contrasting discourse. However, there are important differences. CEBs do not emerge spontaneously from the poor but from middle-class pastoral agents. Instead of "mission," their key concept is "consciousness raising." CEBs attract people who already have a sober lifestyle; Pentecostalism gives a sober lifestyle to those who do not have it. While Pentecostalism changes the values of popular religion, CEBs change its cognition. So, Pentecostals are doing better because their cognitive assumptions are closer to popular culture, and most leaders are from the same social origin, creating a more egalitarian cognitive relationship.

In a recent book, anthropologist John Burdick suggests four reasons for Pentecostalism's far greater numerical success than the CEBs in the Baixada Fluminense region of Greater Rio.[133] First, the CEB model has reinforced the association between the institutional Catholic Church and the relatively more stable, literate, and better-off segments of the working class, while Pentecostalism tends to accommodate the poor in general. Like traditional Catholicism, CEBs reject the idea of a rupture from worldly identities within the church. On the contrary, the demand to "connect faith and life" means that participants' worldly status tends to be on everyone's minds. In addition, anonymity is harder to achieve in a small group. Liberationist discourse encodes the values of literacy and articulateness. The poorest are thus reluctant to attend. Pentecostalism, on the other hand, creates what has been called a liminal state in which normal social relations are suspended. Condemnation of "vanity" in appearance, while restrictive, actually helps the poorest to es-

130. Levine, "Protestants and Catholics in Latin America," pp. 11-12.

131. Faustino Teixeira, et al., *CEBs: cidadania e modernidade* (São Paulo, 1993).

132. Cecília Mariz, "Religion and Coping with Poverty in Brazil," Ph.D. dissertation, Boston University, 1989.

133. John Burdick, *Looking for God in Brazil* (Berkeley, 1993).

cape competitiveness in dress. And, despite the centrality of the word, the Spirit is even more highly valued, enabling illiterate people to occupy leadership positions. In addition, while the CEBs demand a high level of commitment, Pentecostals do not actually base their identity in church attendance but on personal transformation and evangelistic effort. By tolerating a broad range of participatory levels, Pentecostalism allows people with heavy or inflexible work schedules (as well as young mothers) to remain upstanding members. We see, then, that the socially exclusive demands of the CEBs (time, snobbery, language, and "pastoral rationalism") swell the ranks of those disposed to convert to Pentecostalism.

Second, married women find it difficult to resolve domestic problems through progressive Catholicism. CEB discussion of such problems is rare, not only because liberationism emphasizes macro perspectives but also because neighborhood and kin relations make them gossip-prone. Women thus turn to Pentecostalism where they find the supportive atmosphere of a group recruited on the basis of suffering.

Third, unmarried youths find progressive Catholicism expects them to perform a difficult balancing act in relation to the pressures of urban popular youth culture. In the absence of a transformative discourse, youthful rivalries and status-rankings are transferred to the religious setting. But Pentecostalism permits a clear break with the culture of competitive sexuality and violence, and the forging of alternative, less pressured social networks.

Finally, CEBs fail to forge an effective counter-discourse to racism. Pentecostalism is much "darker" in membership and leadership. This does not mean it is a racial democracy, but it has provided a more positive practical context for black struggles for equality.

Mass Media and Gender Roles

What is the effect of the mass media on Protestant growth? In the United States, televangelism's evangelistic efficacy is very limited. According to Bruce, this is what we should expect from "diffusion of innovation" research. Television does not have a strong independent effect on behavior; it depends on reinforcement from factors such as personal relationships. The public reacts better to new information when it is mediated by acquaintances or reliable community leaders. When a product (such as a new religion) cannot be tested first, the plausibility of the medium is the plausibility of the message.[134]

134. Steve Bruce, *Pray TV: Televangelism in America* (London, 1990), pp. 117-25; Bruce, *A House Divided*, p. 221.

In the Brazilian case, the evangelical media (totally run by nationals) may be somewhat more effective evangelistically than in the United States. People are more religious, and more of them are converting to Protestantism anyway. Above all, the greater link between (some) programs and specific denominations probably reinforces the message with direct contact. Oro says that 46 percent of the members of the Universal Church that he researched had been attracted by radio and television.[135] But in many cases there were probably other factors in conversion, especially personal contacts. In short, we can admit greater evangelistic efficacy, but that does not mean the media have become basic to Pentecostal expansion in Brazil.

Since Protestantism grows in Latin America as part of the opening up of the region to religious pluralism — the creation of a floating mass without a strong social obligation to remain in the religion of their birth — Protestant identity is necessarily more precarious than the old Catholic one. Not only conversion but also religious nomadism is now acceptable. Protestant growth is thus inherently unstable.

A more detailed account of growth must also take note of what Pentecostalism offers for its considerable female membership. We must look beyond the patriarchal rhetoric to perceive Pentecostalism's "revalorization of the material, psychological and spiritual currency of the family and the individuals within it."[136] The advantages to poor women are financial, emotional, and physical. Elizabeth Brusco shows how Pentecostalism in Colombia helps women resocialize men away from the destructive patterns of *machismo*, even though (or, in fact, precisely because) it maintains the rhetoric of male control, reinforced by biblical language about headship.[137] A new male role totally opposed to machismo is offered, and the public-male/private-female boundary is redrawn. The private realm is placed at the center of both men's and women's aspirations. As an earlier study in Colombia had shown, the consumption priority of poor Catholics is a radio, whereas that of poor Pentecostals is a dining-room table.[138] Thus, not only is a new ideal of manhood promoted, but also a strategic alteration in consumption patterns. Male aspirations are redefined to coincide with those of their wives, centered on children and home. The novelty of this is illustrated by Caldeira's work on everyday life on the periphery of São Paulo:

135. Ari Pedro Oro, "Religiões Pentecostais e meios de comunicação de massa no sul do Brasil," *Revista eclesiástica Brasileira* 50.198 (1990): 329.

136. Garrard-Burnett, "Is This Latin America's Reformation?" p. 204.

137. Brusco, "The Reformation of Machismo," pp. 143-58.

138. Cornelia Butler Flora, *Pentecostalism in Colombia: Baptism by Fire and Spirit* (Cranbury, N.J., 1976), p. 221.

Life projects, always of social mobility, reveal clearly the different worldviews of men and women. . . . Women's dreams/projects are made much more for others [children, husband, home] than for themselves. . . . Men's projects are invariably formulated in the first person singular. . . . They speak also of wanting a better future for their children, but this is not an important point in their statements, and their wives are never mentioned.[139]

Pentecostalism's reconciliation of gender values is something middle-class feminism has not managed to achieve. Thus, it serves the practical interests of poor women in Latin America, even when it legitimizes male authority.[140]

If Pentecostalism's redefinition of gender roles is usually greater male integration into the private sphere, there is at least one large church that also to some extent promotes greater female integration into the public sphere. Over a third of the pastors of the Church of the Four-Square Gospel (which was of course founded by a Canadian woman) in Brazil are women; in many cases, the head pastor is the wife and the co-pastor is her husband. No historical church, however advanced its rhetoric, comes close to these numbers.

What Effect Does Pentecostalism Have on Indigenous Peoples?

In the Andean region and especially in southern Mexico and Central America, Protestantism has made great headway among indigenous peoples, often through virtual mass conversion. Maybe a third of Guatemalan Protestants are Indians. What is Protestantism's appeal to Indians, and is it harmful or beneficial for indigenous cultures?

Duncan Earle's portrayal of the success of Protestantism in highland Guatemala is typical of one line of interpretation.[141] Cashing in on the decline of community-wide authority and the increase in social discord, Protestantism exploits conflict as a source of recruitment, creating an ever more divided community and facilitating capitalist penetration, especially the commodifi-

139. Teresa Caldeira, *A política dos outros* (São Paulo, 1984), pp. 179-81.

140. Mónica Tarducci, "Pentecostalismo y relaciones de género: una revisión," in A. Frigerio, ed., *Nuevos movimientos religiosos y ciencias sociales (1)* (Buenos Aires, 1993), pp. 81-89; cf. Maria das Dores Campos Machado, "Adesão religiosa e seus efeitos na esfera privada — um estudo comparativo dos Carasmáticos e Pentecostais do Rio de Janiero," Ph.D. dissertation, IUPERJ Rio de Janeiro, 1994.

141. Duncan Earle, "Authority, Social Conflict and the Rise of Protestantism: Religious Conversion in a Mayan Village," *Social Compass* 39.3 (1992): 377-88.

cation of land. In the 1980s, the evangelical mayor of the community Earle studied accelerated transformation of communal land into private property and encouraged new employment for men in holiday bungalows for tourists. New male wealth is spent on clothing and drinking, but not on nutrition and children's education. "People go from worship and collective defence of their land to a pliant acceptance of its commodification and a desire to obtain a *patron* in this world to build and guard a vacation bungalow for [*sic*] in order to receive their own from a parallel *patron* in the sky after death," concludes Earle.

Earle portrays a community already undergoing differentiation and sees Protestantism as merely accelerating the breakup, without offering anything positive. Even its usual behavioral results (sobriety, more family-centered consumption) are reversed. Other analyses (especially a growing number of recent studies) have presented a rather different picture.

Sheldon Annis, for example, gives a more nuanced picture.[142] While recognizing that Protestantism reinforces individualist tendencies in detriment to communal identity, he says that what we now think of as Indianness is not so much a relic of a more glorious Mayan past but a cultural package that solidified Spanish control. According to Joanne Rapaport, the idea that evangelical missions obstruct the struggle of indigenous peoples to forge their own destinies according to their cultural particularities neglects the way Indian evangelicals filter missionary teaching according to their own interests.[143] She studies the Páez and Guambiano tribes of southern Colombia, where whole villages are Pentecostal. "They resoundingly reject the political orientation of national and foreign missionaries, and legitimate political activity oriented to self-determination."[144] After the Summer Institute of Linguistics had left, evangelical participation in land reclamation campaigns intensified. The Páez, while breaking with traditional ceremonies that legitimated their territory through worship of saints and drinking, developed evangelical alternatives. Two aspects were key in this indigenization of Pentecostal faith: the similarity of evangelical millenarianism to the tribe's traditional messianism, and Pentecostalism's reinforcement of ethnic identity by allowing a cult without nonindigenous intermediaries.

Southern Mexico has seen rapid Protestant growth in recent years, not least in Chiapas. In the last fifteen years, twenty thousand Chamula evangeli-

---

142. Sheldon Annis, *God and Production in a Guatemalan Town* (Austin, 1987).

143. Joanne Rapaport, "Las misiones Protestantes y la resistencia indígena en el sur de Columbia," *América Indígena* 44.1 (1984): 111-26.

144. Rapaport, "Las misiones Protestantes," p. 112.

cals have been expelled from their lands by *caciques* (headmen) for religious reasons. The relationship with the guerrilla movement that erupted in 1994 needs to be further elucidated. Certainly, the two phenomena have the same social root; whether Protestantism and guerrilla activity are adopted by different people, or by the same people simultaneously or in sequence, remains to be clarified. There are said to be Indian Protestants among the leadership of the *zapatistas*.

Jean-Pierre Bastian has studied southern Mexican indigenous Pentecostalism for some time. He sees it not as escapism but as defense of identity:

> With the penetration of capitalist structures into the countryside and the destructuring of traditional social relations, the caciques themselves broke the meaning of the traditional fiesta. It no longer serves to burn off excess or to renew the symbolic power of the people; it serves the political control of capitalist accumulation.[145]

Popular Catholicism is thus deflected from its reciprocal and redistributive functions. Conversion to Pentecostalism enables poor farmers to disentangle themselves from an exploitative system; they are then accused of destroying traditional community and culture. But, says Bastian:

> one must analyse the instrumentalization of the collective system by the caciques whose purpose is capital accumulation. Is it really true, as a cacique of Chiapas affirms, that they destroy "our culture because they no longer drink or get so ill, no longer fight so much or go to the faith-healer, no longer use candles or incense . . . and prefer to pray to solve their problems"?[146]

In short, indigenous Protestantism, as in *mestizo* society, has many faces. Its initial context is often the breakdown of old communities (though it does not usually provoke such breakdown). Its effect may be to deepen existing divisions or create new ones, or it may help to reconstitute community (although not in the old monolithic form: as Martin notes, Protestantism logically implies division, creating voluntary networks in place of inevitable ones).[147] As pluralism increases in the indigenous context, the role of Protestantism tends to be more integrative and less "destructive."

145. Bastian, *Protestantismo y sociedad en México*, p. 230.
146. Bastian, *Protestantismo y sociedad en México*, p. 238.
147. Martin, *Tongues of Fire*, p. 100.

Is Latin American Pentecostalism Really Protestant?

The growth of indigenous Pentecostalism in parts of the region has contributed to another debate: Is it satisfactory to call Latin American Pentecostalism Protestant? The discussion is hampered by the lack of a truly region-wide first-hand study of the phenomenon. Of the major comparative interpreters, Martin is the most ambitious and casts the broadest geographical net, but he uses only secondary sources. Stoll is limited virtually to Central America, and Bastian to Mexico and Central America. D'Epinay looked at the Southern Cone, and Willems, at Chile and Brazil, but both authors' research is now rather dated.

The present author cannot overcome the fieldwork limitation, but, in a small measure, may try to redress the balance. Some works on "Protestantism in Latin America" are really, at most, only about Spanish America. But there are actually more Portuguese-speaking Pentecostals than Spanish-speaking ones, and so no adequate interpretation can relegate Brazil to an appendix. While not necessarily typical (what would be a typical case?), Brazil is instructive because of its size, its distance from the United States, its longer Protestant history, and its relative independence from foreign control, giving it sufficient density for autochthonous processes which may emerge later in other parts of the region.

Martin emphasizes similarities between Latin American Protestantism (mostly Pentecostal) and earlier Protestant phenomena in Europe and North America.[148] He speaks of an "Anglo" pattern, cultural forms originated by the English-speaking peoples, which were loose, plural, and available for export: among them, a voluntary, fissile, and participatory form of evangelical religion. Martin structures his work around two large frames: the emergence of voluntarism, contingent on the breakdown of the organic unity of religion and national identity, and the four-hundred-year-old clash between the "Hispanic and Anglo-Saxon imperiums."[149] Martin is actually talking about models of social organization of religion, not about current religious geopolitics. The terminology is unfortunate, suggesting something intrinsically Anglo-Saxon about voluntaristic religion and intrinsically Hispanic about unitary religion. Although the "Anglo" model made its historical appearance in England, albeit with dress rehearsals elsewhere, especially Holland, it is now widespread.

As for Martin's analogy between English Methodism and Latin American

148. Martin, *Tongues of Fire.*
149. Martin, *Tongues of Fire,* pp. 9-13.

Pentecostalism, there are, of course, important differences in the religious context (Anglican versus Catholic), economic situation (Industrial Revolution versus the information revolution and dependency) and cultural ethos (skepticism versus an inspirited culture). Bastian, however, would go even further in emphasizing the discontinuity.[150] For him, Latin American Pentecostalism is a redeployment of rural forms of Catholicism without priests. "Instead of the Protestant principle of the universal priesthood of believers, are we not dealing with a model approaching the self-governing religious practices of 'confraternities' or a more diffuse version of millenarianism or messianism?"[151] Protestantism began in nineteenth-century Latin America within the culture of radical liberalism, and it served to inculcate democratic values and practices. But present-day Pentecostalism evolved from the religious and political culture of folk Catholicism, syncretic, corporatist, and politically passive. It is thus less an expression of the original Protestantism than a redeployment of popular religion:

> Latin American Protestant movements, with the exception of the transplanted churches of certain organizations arising from the historical denominations, are preponderantly syncretic. . . . One can even ask whether it is still possible to speak, as does Martin, of Protestant movements, i.e. of movements of religious, intellectual or moral reform.[152]

Instead of being a *sui generis* Protestantism, they are an ensemble of new non-Catholic movements, bricolage religions, and substitutionary Catholicisms.

There are several problems with Bastian's view. He gives a one-sided definition of historical Protestantism in Latin America (linked to the historically peculiar Mexican case) that emphasizes the contrasts with Pentecostalism. Ronald Frase on Brazilian Presbyterianism is a good antidote.[153] He defines Protestantism in terms not of its religious content but its relationship to social currents such as "modernity" and "anti-corporatism." One wonders whether, for Bastian, Protestantism has to have a European lineage, or whether there can be independent reformations of Catholic societies, *repeating* sixteenth-century Europe rather than adopting its institutional and cultural heritage. What could be said to make up a genuine non-Western expression of Protes-

150. Jean-Pierre Bastian, "Introduction," *Social Compass* 39.3 (1992): 323-26; cf. Jean-Pierre Bastian, "The Metamorphosis of Latin American Protestant Groups: A Sociohistorical Perspective," *Latin American Research Review* 28.2 (1993): 33-61.

151. Bastian, "Introduction," p. 326.

152. Bastian, "The Metamorphosis of Latin American Protestant Groups," p. 57.

153. Frase, "A Sociological Analysis of the Development of Brazilian Protestantism."

tantism? Is it possible to be "adapted" and "contextualized" (words which do not suggest illegitimacy) rather than "syncretized"? And to what extent has the principle of universal priesthood really been practiced in European Protestantism? Since Protestantism cannot always be recognized (as Catholicism can) by an institutional link, how can we avoid an elitist and static definition?

As we have said, Pentecostalism is the first totally autonomous mass popular religion in Latin America. There is no spiritual recognition of, or even social reverence toward, the Catholic hierarchy. Among popular Catholics and Umbandistas, the leaders of the erudite branches (parish priest, *kardecist* leader) are considered more respectable and, in certain ways, more legitimate;[154] and "leadership from the institutional church is now generally recognised as essential to the proper functioning" of the Base Communities.[155] Pentecostalism certainly does not have the same relationship to historical Protestantism. Leaders may not be democratic, but they are from the same social class as the participants. Although there may be syncretic elements (continuity with previous popular religion), it is not a syncretism that respects the dominant church or accepts plural affiliation. In any case, when the continuity with traditional religion is more formal than substantive, it is misleading to speak of syncretism.

The case of the Universal Church of the Kingdom of God is illustrative. Some Brazilian Protestants, including fellow Pentecostals, have labeled it syncretic, and it is true that it breaks with the symbolic poverty of Brazilian Protestantism in general. But although it makes ample use of symbols, there is no use of images in worship. It goes beyond Protestant dependence on audition, making ample use of the other senses. It also adapts the Catholic novena: specific periods of prayer, fasting, and attendance at services, with a view to obtaining a special grace. In its services, the spiritual entities of Umbanda are called upon to manifest themselves so that they may be expelled by the superior power of the Holy Spirit. In short, the Universal Church is an innovative updating of Pentecostalism's theological and liturgical possibilities.

How Does Pentecostalism Affect Economic Attitudes?

Does conversion to Pentecostalism have significant economic effects in Latin America? Peter Berger says it will lead to "the emergence of a solid bourgeoi-

---

154. Brandão, *Os deuses do povo*, p. 232.

155. W. E. Hewitt, "Religion and the Consolidation of Democracy in Brazil: The Role of the CEBs," *Sociological Analysis* 50.2 (1990): 150.

sie, with virtues conducive to the development of a democratic capitalism."[156] Is there any evidence for this? More modestly, is there evidence for any upward social mobility? Group ideology ("members [of the Assemblies of God] are preconditioned to believe they have experienced economic improvement")[157] should not be confused with reality.

Martin gives a cautiously positive answer.[158] Pentecostalism assembles a raft to which people lash themselves for safety. Initially, most of their energy is expended on constructing the raft. But what is the latent economic potential? How far will the sense of individual humanity, generated by the company of the faithful, be transmuted into economic initiative and new aspirations? Economic advancement depends on facilitating economic conditions. People advance by the margins available, pressing on their constraints rather than breaking out of them. What one can affirm is that economic advancement and evangelical religion often go together and appear to reinforce each other. Pentecostalism may console those who lose from social change, or it may select those who can make the most of the chances change offers. But capacities may take two or three generations to come to fruition, says Martin, recognizing that hard evidence is scarce. Without going as far as Berger, he suggests that Pentecostalism may be building a constituency well disposed to a capitalist form of development.

A recent study of El Salvador sees little evidence of upward mobility among Protestants but admits that massive Protestant growth is very recent and that civil war conditions are not favorable to advancement.[159] Annis suggests that in Guatemala there might be a positive relationship between Protestantism and economic advance, but Evans is more cautious.[160] Among the rural poor of northeastern Brazil, Novaes noted that the expectation of improvement is not accompanied by a new work ethic. Pentecostals expect to be compensated for their "testimony" (the "forced saving" of an ascetic lifestyle), but not for the quality and quantity of their work.[161] Mariz, studying a large city of northeastern Brazil, says Pentecostalism typically transforms a lumpen proletarian into a proletarian or a self-employed person.[162] It raises from misery to poverty (for example, through combating alcoholism), but no fur-

---

156. Cited in Martin, *Tongues of Fire*, p. ix.

157. Hoffnagel, "The Believers," p. 245.

158. Martin, *Tongues of Fire*.

159. Coleman et al., "Protestantism in El Salvador."

160. Timothy Evans, "Religious Conversion in Quetzaltenango, Guatemala," Ph.D. dissertation, University of Pittsburgh, 1990.

161. Novaes, *Os Escolhidos de Deus*, p. 111.

162. Mariz, "Religion and Coping with Poverty in Brazil."

ther than that. Even intergenerational occupational mobility in modern Brazil (a son who gets a white-collar job) does not necessarily mean social mobility. Pentecostalism is a tool for enduring poverty rather than for upward mobility. It changes attitudes to consumption rather than to work, offering a new plausibility for saving in an adverse context. The Brazilian Pentecostal ethic reinforces dominant capitalist values among people who have already embraced such values but have not been materially rewarded for them.

Thus, in reply to Berger, we can say that Latin American Pentecostalism does not have the classic Protestant work ethic, and it operates in a significantly different economic context. Evidence for upward mobility is scarce, and signs of a macro effect on Latin American economies even scarcer.

However, rapidly expanding Protestantism does offer internal economic opportunities. Pastors are often the main beneficiaries of conversion; Martin compares the pastorate to "an escalator to be walked on to and in a later generation stepped off."[163] More recently, and especially in Brazil's huge Protestant world, the consumption of various products and services has become large enough to attract entrepreneurs and sponsors.

In traditional Latin American Pentecostalism, the ideology of betterment (undoubtedly linked to Weber's dictum that ordinary men are attracted to religion by mundane expectations) coexists tensely with a religious "populism" which glories in God's choice of the poor and is suspicious of the spiritually deleterious effects of wealth. More recently, it has been released from this tension by the "health and wealth gospel," or Prosperity Theology, which has made inroads even into churches like the AG and is the main message of newer groups such as the Universal Church. This is a highly functional theology for church growth in a disputed market. A market situation means not only competition but also the collapse of monolithic structures of plausibility. Without the plausibility of the medieval church, the Universal Church cannot sell indulgences to commute so many years in purgatory; its promises must be more immediate and this-worldly.

But the Universal Church's recipe for prosperity is not just generous giving to the church; it also makes a fairly realistic analysis of economic opportunities in modern Brazil. As one sermon at the Universal Church in Campinas put it: "It's no good just giving an offering. You must quit your job and open a business, even if it's only selling popcorn in the street. As an employee you'll never get rich." Previous Pentecostal churches had valued self-employment only because it offered flexibility (the chance to give time to the

163. Martin, *Tongues of Fire*, p. 64.

church) and avoidance of spiritually damaging environments. Now, it is valued as a means to enrichment. Self-employment is just a stage on the way to becoming an employer: the Universal Church's publications contain practical suggestions on branches of business and the initial capital needed. Its message may reinforce the work ethic and petty entrepreneurial initiative in an adverse context. But, unlike the popular Puritanism of the "Protestant ethic," it separates wealth and salvation, thus lacking the psychological mechanism (anguish about eternal destiny) which supposedly impelled the Puritan in his rational search for prosperity.

The neo-Pentecostal groups are usually heavily criticized for their emphasis on giving to the church. On the other hand, Mariz says that, in popular mentality, giving is power.[164] Submission is symbolically reinforced by receiving. In Pentecostalism, the poor discover they are capable of giving and not just of receiving.

What Is Pentecostalism's Political Role?

Space is too short for an overview of Pentecostalism's relationship with politics. Here, I shall give a quick survey of the main cases so far of Protestant involvement in electoral politics.

In three countries of Latin America, Protestants have achieved a significant electoral and parliamentary presence: Guatemala since the early 1980s, Brazil since 1986, and Peru since 1990. Considerably behind in importance come Colombia, Nicaragua, El Salvador, and Venezuela. The phenomenon is far from uniform, but is affected by certain elements common to most of the region such as accelerated Protestant growth, the resurgence of democracy, economic crisis, and the erosion of the prestige of traditional political actors.

Between late 1989 and early 1991, Protestants played a significant role in electing three presidents: Collor (Brazil), Fujimori (Peru), and Serrano (Guatemala). The parallels are evident. The non-Protestants Collor and Fujimori both ignored the *evangélicos* once elected. All three carried out basically neoliberal policies. None of them were models of democratic government: Collor was impeached for corruption, Fujimori made an "auto-coup" and governed undemocratically, and Serrano, in attempting the same, was deposed.

However, there are important differences. In Peru, Pentecostals are less than a third of all Protestants, and elite charismatic communities are not prominent. The Protestant world is relatively united through CONEP. Protes-

164. Mariz, "El debate en torno del Pentecostalismo autónomo en Brasil."

tantism, only 7 percent of the population, is quite strongly indigenous; the Catholic Church is conservative; and the social context is of guerrilla warfare and acute impoverishment.

Hardly surprisingly, the abrupt entry of Protestants into politics in 1990 was very different from Brazil. There was a clear initiative from a secular political source, the Fujimori campaign. The main interest seems to have been access to the indigenous vote through the *evangélico* network. In the Andes and Central America, the extraordinary growth of indigenous Protestantism is a key factor in politics; in Brazil (0.2 percent indigenous) it is irrelevant. With their presence in areas where State, parties, and priests are conspicuous by their absence, Protestants are an alternative route to mass politics. In 1990, nineteen Protestants were elected to Congress, all but one on Fujimori's Cambio 90 ticket, mostly from historical churches, especially Baptists. There were very few Pentecostals, and none from the AG. The existence of CONEP was vital for a concerted Protestant action stimulated by secular politicians. Its role as intermediary was rewarded with the second vice-presidency for CONEP's president, a Baptist pastor. The fact that a pastor without any previous political participation could become second vice-president of the republic testifies to the much greater disintegration of public life in Peru than in Brazil. His complete marginalization by Fujimori, without any significant reaction, shows how dependent on outside forces was this precocious politicization of Peruvian Protestantism.

The Guatemalan case is also characterized by guerrilla warfare, an extremely fragile democracy, and a large indigenous population. But the Protestant field is very different. Guatemala may be 30 percent Protestant, but an estimated 80 percent of those are Pentecostals/charismatics. In addition, there is a completely different correlation of forces. The weakness of governments, the destruction of war, the proximity of the United States, and the smaller absolute scale of the problems mean that Protestants, mostly middle- and upper-class charismatics, have become key figures in social work and education, areas which the State has virtually handed over to them.

In 1990, Guatemala elected twenty-two Protestant national deputies, nearly 20 percent of the total, of whom about three-fifths were Pentecostals. Its two Protestant presidents, Ríos Montt (military dictator from 1982 to 1983) and Jorge Serrano (elected in 1991), were both politicians before conversion to charismatic churches in the 1970s. David Stoll claims that

> born-again religion has percolated upward into social strata habitually
> engaged in politics. . . . What brought the evangelical movement into
> politics was less pastoral activism [the Brazilian case] or North Ameri-

can influence [or solicitation of secular politicians, as in Peru] than the movement's extension upward in the class scale.[165]

Serrano's election does not appear to have been due especially to the Protestant vote; rather, it reflects Protestant penetration of the elite and the degree of social respectability it has acquired.

In Brazil, on the other hand, the political vanguard are the leaders of popular *sects* who have grown so far and so fast that they can start to think of appropriating the State for their own ends. In the 1986 elections, several leading Pentecostal churches chose official candidates in internal primaries, helping the Protestant caucus in Congress to rise from fourteen to thirty-three. This is not only different from Peru (where the involvement, mainly of historicals, was precocious and provoked by secular currents to permit access to the Indian vote) and from Guatemala (where elements of the elite in charismatic churches rearticulate the political participation they have always had); it is perhaps the first case in history in which *conversionist Christian sects* have had such a relationship to the State. In Catholic Europe, all Protestant groups remain small. In Protestant Europe, established churches limited the growth of *sects*, or else secularization and unfavorable electoral systems politically marginalized all religious groups. In the United States, all Protestant *sects* effectively became *denominations* in one or two generations,[166] a transformation facilitated by the lack of an established church, an expanding and egalitarian society in which *sects* could grow quickly in size and respectability, religious tolerance, and new immigrants who pushed the older ones up the social scale.[167] Brazil's sects grow quickly, but they do not conquer social and cultural respectability, there is still a semi-official church, and there is no economic expansion or immigration. Brazilian Protestant politics would therefore seem to have some historically unique features.

Conclusion

How much can Pentecostalism grow in Latin America? In the 1960s, D'Epinay said that, due to its specific social composition, Pentecostalism's potential clientele is large but not unlimited.[168] Today, especially in certain countries, we

165. Stoll, "'Jesus Is Lord of Guatemala,'" p. 107.
166. Richard H. Niebuhr, *The Social Sources of Denominationalism* (Cleveland, 1929).
167. B. Wilson, *Religious Sects*, p. 234.
168. D'Epinay, *O refúgio das massas*, p. 76.

must be more cautious. Pentecostalism begins to show versatility in crossing social boundaries and in "Pentecostalizing" the larger Protestant field. Martin prefers to talk of a religious limit: due to its aspect of protest, Pentecostal growth has a built-in decelerator, slowing down when there is little left about which to protest.[169] It should not, however, be seen Eurocentrically as a temporary efflorescence of voluntary religiosity to be succeeded by inevitable secularization. Whether Pentecostalism goes on growing or not, its relationship to society and politics is bound to evolve. A more stable membership would change the sociological nature of the churches and might produce a greater concern for social reform and more ideological and less corporatist political projects.

169. Martin, "Chile: What the Polls Show."

SECTION V

CHAPTER TEN

Evangelical Expansion in Global Society

DAVID MARTIN

The expansion of evangelical Christianity, and more especially of its potent Pentecostal mutation, is closely related to the emergence of a global society.[1] The essence of globalization is the increasing speed of movement as people, ideas, images, and capital take advantage of modern means of communication. As we all know, what began with road, canal, and railway is now communication by jet and Internet. The advertisement pages of newspapers are just one indication that the major social catalyst of mass tourism can take us to remotest Amazonia or Borneo. However, the consequences for religion on our planet are less obvious. In the early part of the twentieth century the extension of Methodist chapels in the surrounding area of Mexico City followed the line of the British-built railways. More recently, new roads out of Merida in the Yucatan and out of La Paz in Bolivia mark out the route of evangelical dissemination. Like any other kind of message, evangelical messages travel to the jungles of Irian on the Papuan border and to the remotest valleys of Nepal.

Whatever the complicated mesh of factors contributing to this process a major agent of change over the last half millennium has been the ability of capital to create an international economy. Wealth could not be constrained within the borders of the bureaucratic empires of France and Spain, and it went with the flow of the commercial empires of Holland, England, and the United States. All three of these Protestant North Atlantic powers abandoned the holism of their Catholic rivals, not only as a principle of social organiza-

---

1. It should be noted that this article was written in 1999. I have glancingly utilized Peter Beyer, *Religion and Globalization* (London and New Delhi, 1994).

tion but as a mode of social and philosophical understanding. At the same time, though to different degrees, all three countries were incubators of the voluntary principle in religion. That principle detached religion from polity, from State power, and from an anchorage in the territorial community. It also detached the work of the missionary from the work of soldier and trader. Of course, the detachment was bound to be partial, and in fact in the Anglo-American empires the Bible traveled in partial partnership with the sword. Nevertheless, the break was of world-historical significance. The British Empire did not become Anglican in the way Spain's Latin American Empire became assimilated to Latin Christendom. Indeed in some areas imperial administrators actively inhibited missionary activity.

A further consequence of the breakdown of holism and the establishment of the voluntary principle was the way Protestantism was able partially to absorb the Enlightenment and avoid the outright clash that tore apart Latin cultures, above all, France. The proximity of the established clergy to the secular intelligentsia also meant that Enlightenment could filter selectively into religion, creating versions of Christianity, such as Unitarianism, which act as a buffer zone. Clerical conservatives did not struggle with secularist liberals for control of the State, as happened all over Latin Europe and Latin America. The closest approximation was the mid-nineteenth-century tension between Protestant-dominated States and Catholic minorities in Germany, Switzerland, and Holland.

The period of modernization also saw a shift from hierarchy and ascribed status toward an increasing emphasis on merit and achievement and toward semi-autonomous class cultures. Within these cultures people were able to associate in terms of felt affinity rather than economic subordination. However, that had rather distinct consequences in the Protestant north of Europe, and in the societies of the North Atlantic. In such societies, and above all in the English-speaking world, the all-encompassing unity based on social and ecclesiastical hierarchy crumbled. It did so in three successive stages, beginning in the 1590s, accelerating from 1790 to 1850, and renewing the impulse again in the early 1900s. Very loosely these stages correspond to a movement toward a lay, popular, and enthusiastic Christianity, culminating in Pentecostal awakenings with a particularly powerful and influential eruption in Los Angeles in 1906. These awakenings were themselves harbingers of global society, and their spread corresponded to the movement of lay people around the globe, to South Africa, Norway, Sicily, Korea, or the Southern Cone of Latin America. No sooner converted than en route.

The people traveling around the globe with evangelical and Pentecostal messages were energetic and intelligent, of little education and authorized only by the Spirit.[2] The missionaries who preceded them as earlier messengers of a global faith had been only modestly educated, but they were at least authorized and prepared. In Pentecostalism, Christianity had generated an autonomous lay culture, once again composed, as in the New Testament, of "ignorant and unlearned men," and empowered by the Spirit with all that implies for good and ill in the exercise of personal authority. This was not a diaspora of liberal resource persons.

They represented the furthest extension of the voluntary principle not merely by being free of the State but also by being free to feed off the Bible raw and create whatever organization that seemed to imply. Not being weighed down by sponsorship of a social or ecclesiastical hierarchy or the relation of faith to territorial identity, they could treat the world as their parish. Frontiers meant little, whether they were the catchment areas established by missionary societies or the implicit catchment areas of long-established Christian civilization, such as Latin America.

Coming as they mostly did from the North Atlantic, they exploited the intimations of global society created by the spread of English in association with the British and American empires, and by extension Spanish, as a second metropolitan language. At the same time, they rapidly became indigenous or inspired indigenous associates, in part because of the remarkable resonance between their Spirit-filled religion and the spiritist layer of worldwide shamanism. So what began with minor hints of global religion, such as Moravians on the Atlantic coast of Nicaragua, Mennonites in Mexico, or Methodists in Sierra Leone, expanded until the world capital of Pentecostalism was not the City of Angels but São Paulo or Seoul. Evangelicals are not, of course, the only beneficiaries of modern communications. The neo-Buddhist Soka Gakkai is now established in Hawaii, in the area of Los Angeles, as well as in São Paulo. Furthermore, the empire can strike back as the spiritual conquistadores of La Luz del Mundo carry their messages to the United States and as the Brazilian Universal Church of the Kingdom of God makes converts in Portugal. Catholic and evangelical messengers from Brazil are now active in Mozambique, and Zimbabwean Pentecostals in London. Nor is this global mobility confined to transnational denominations. It is also exemplified in para-church organizations, such as Caritas, Adveniat, or the evangelical development agency "World Vision."[3] One might add here that

2. Grant Wacker, "Searching for Eden with a Satellite Dish: Primitivism, Pragmatism and the Pentecostal Character," in Richard Hughes, ed., *The Primitive Church in the Modern World* (Urbana and Chicago, 1995), pp. 139-66.

3. James Piscatori and Susanne Hoeber Rudolph, eds., *Transnational Religion and Fading States* (Boulder and Oxford, 1997).

although transnational denominations are competing in an open market and are prone to multiple schisms, nevertheless they also foster a kind of ecumenism in spirit, and often come together for mass meetings. Here they realize they count.

None of this means that the primordial relation of religion to local community and to territory is abolished, or that people no longer acquire their life-long religion at birth. Moreover, since the rise of nationalism over the past half millennium, religion has been closely bound up with ethnic identity, and the Church has been subordinate to the State. That subordination was as true of Hispanic Christianity as of Anglican Christianity. For Louis XIV *"L'Eglise c'est moi"* and eventually monarchical prerogatives passed to the nation, the people, and the national culture. Today Islam makes a point of being a complete system coextensive with society, and with ambitions to become the global faith. In Latin America the ecclesiastical elites still address the nation, and the Church educates the national elite. For that matter the base communities are predicated on the hegemonic idea.[4] In each locality the ties of faith are the links of the fiesta and godparenthood. All that implies that conversion to another faith involves opting out of the national identity and its historic culture. In Thailand and Burma the prestige of State, the elite, and the majority culture of the core areas of the nation are linked to Buddhism. Nor does globalization lead unambiguously to a relativization of such ties. The effect of missions is often to stimulate the receiving culture to renew its own boundaries and also to emulate the attractions of the new faith from within its own resources. The sense that a local religion which existed prior to global contact was normal and inevitable mutates into militancy and explicit exclusion of alternatives, as can be observed all over the Middle East, in the Indian subcontinent, and the Balkans. What had been coexistence in Albania or Lebanon becomes religio-ethnic cleansing.

However, this militant reaction to the onset of pluralism and competition on the part of the majority culture has interesting implications for transnational faiths. Just as majorities accentuate their cultural self-definition, so also do minorities. Under pressure from the majority and conscious of the global options open to them, they may adopt evangelical Christianity, with the result that the global becomes once again embodied in a particular territorial identity. Sectors of the Aymara in the Andes are a case in point. Hindus in Java, for example, coming under Muslim pressure, opted for Christianity.[5]

4. Anthony Gill, *Rendering Unto Caesar: The Catholic Church and the State in Latin America* (Chicago, 1998).

5. Robert Hefner, "Of Faith and Commitment: Christian Conversion in Muslim Java," in Robert Hefner, ed., *Conversion to Christianity* (Los Angeles and Oxford, 1993), pp. 99-128.

Some of the minority ethnic groups of the Russian Federation have reacted to Orthodox Christianity through self-conscious paganism, just as some African-Americans have opted for Islam. All over the world a new self-consciousness is engendered by global contact.[6] Minority peoples affirm difference, equality, and identity, in Thailand or Malaysia or Myanmar or wherever.

We have identified two obvious processes. One has to do with the emergence of voluntary religious associations, initially in the North Atlantic world and spreading in partial alignment with the English language and Anglo-American influence. The other has to do with the emergence of minority self-consciousness, which leaps over the pressure exercised by the local majority and links itself to evangelicalism as an expression of transnational modernity. Self-conscious identities breed their mirror images bolstered by difference, and evangelicalism is able to express that difference. Given that the United States is both the remaining superpower and an attractive expression of cultural modernity, evangelicalism enjoys an aura of association. Obviously, the adoption of evangelicalism (or Mormonism or the Jehovah's Witnesses) by minorities will run along the lines of fissure within that particular society, one sector developing in contradistinction to another.

One further tendency present in global society and relevant to evangelical expansion is a heightened sense of individuality as the self is released from the constraints of extended kin and the continuities of local community. The idea of conversion by a personal transaction is part of that individualization, because of its inwardness and its dependence on choice. It is a drama in the person through an incubation of experience generated by the Church, and then stabilized and molded by its collective disciplines. Plainly an established church, built into the community and sacralizing its mores, is always suspicious of the emotional transactions which give second birth to individual selves, whereas a transnational denomination may embrace them. However, what remains highly problematic is the different course of individualization in the developing world compared with its course in the developed world. In the developing world, evangelicalism (and other sources of inward personal transaction) manages to inhibit the fragmentations that so evidently follow from individualization in the developed world. In the United States, however, religious voluntary associations may inhibit individual fragmentation to

6. Svetlana Tchervonnaya, "The Revival of Animistic Religion in the Mari Republic," in Irena Borowik and Grzegorz Babinski, eds., *New Religious Phenomena in Central and Eastern Europe* (Krakow, 1997), pp. 369-78. Cf. Susanna Rostas and André Droogers, eds., *The Popular Use of Popular Religion in Latin America* (Amsterdam, 1993).

some extent, but the rate of divorce is the highest anywhere. The problem has to be flagged as needing more research.

Kinds of Faith Community

Before proceeding further one ought perhaps to indicate the core members of the evangelical family under consideration, and also their extensions. Clearly the historical core is the pietism of Northern Europe as active in the evangelical awakenings of Anglo-America and their revivalist variants. Then a further closely related awakening occurs in classical Pentecostalism through the mediation of Methodist holiness movements. That in turn generates or runs in parallel with the gospel of health and wealth and various free-floating charismatic movements both outside and crossing the borders of the historic churches in a kind of ecumenism in the spirit. In Latin America, for example, one encounters historic churches "in renewal." All kinds of combinations occur whereby Pentecostalism overlaps Afro-South American *cura divina* or global shamanism or religious contents semi-suppressed by colonial Christianity or varieties of Christian Zionism or Ethiopianism. Beyond that, and more or less distinct from evangelicalism, are semi-Judaic versions of Christianity such as Adventism, the New Israelites, the Mormons, and the Witnesses. Though these constitute separate genealogies, their trajectories of conversion intertwine with evangelical expansion while their American associations and the consequences of their ethos are somewhat similar. Indeed, the American associations are often more direct with Mormons and Witnesses than with Pentecostals.

Contrast: Developed and Developing World

Two further preliminary questions have to be explored which have links with the earlier point about the differing effects of individualization in the developing and the developed world. First, why is it that in the developed world evangelicals are the dominant partner, whereas in the rest of the world Pentecostals have increasingly become dominant, though not everywhere to the same extent? Second, why is it that within the developed world the degree of evangelical influence corresponds to a spectrum running from northern Europe through England to its peripheries, and thence through such English-speaking democracies as Canada and Australia to its apogee in the United States? That second question is relatively easy to answer since it corresponds to the space allowed for the institutional reproduction of subculture through the erosion of established, hierarchical, and centralized religious forms by disestablished, populist, and federal ones. In Canada, for example, there remain shadow establishments in French and in Anglo-Scottish Canada that have inhibited an evangelical expansion on the American scale, as well as switching the pattern of secularization since the sixties in a European rather than an American direction. Within the British Isles, each of the territorial peripheries has generated larger evangelical constituencies than England itself, and it is arguable that lines of connection run between these and the largest evangelical peripheries in the United States. In England itself it is not too difficult to see how the command posts of establishment in education and communications have switched from a vaguely religious ethos to a vaguely secularist one. Nevertheless, whether or not there is a cultural command economy, evangelicals constitute the liveliest sector across the North Atlantic spectrum.

Even if that analysis remains speculative, the question of Pentecostal dominance beyond the North Atlantic sphere is more puzzling, even if one takes into account the historical priority of evangelicalism in the North Atlantic area. After all, evangelicalism has been established for a long time in parts of the Anglo-Caribbean, and yet in contemporary Jamaica it has been eroded until Pentecostalism is arguably the established faith.[7] There are, of course, also those who believe a parallel erosion of Pentecostalism itself by neo-Pentecostalism is occurring in Brazil, Argentina, and parts of Asia and Africa. That is disputable, but it remains clear that in some countries, such as Zimbabwe, Pentecostalism runs at 10 percent of the population, and even in Korea it mounts a very strong challenge to an established evangelical tradition.

Perhaps the most promising line of explanation rests on the universal layer of spiritism outside the North Atlantic and continental European cultural sphere that resonates with the potent combination of black and white motifs in Pentecostalism. To that one might add a form of development outside the developed "West" that leaps through the global expansion of capitalism from the premodern to the postmodern. Of course, there are Western-influenced elites in many parts of the developing world, for example, Singapore, but the mass of the population has not passed through a modern developmental phase. That is as true of Latin America as elsewhere. The liberal elites absorbed a mixture of Anglo-American pragmatism and Latin European anti-clerical radicalism, especially the latter since they were after all Lat-

7. Diane J. Austin-Broos, *Jamaica Genesis: Religion and the Politics of Moral Order* (Chicago, 1997).

ins, but they did not follow up European success in spreading that metropolitan ideology downward to large sectors of the population. Those sectors still embraced an unstable mixture of Catholicism and pre-Columbian faiths. As far as Africa was concerned, the evangelical thrust, in partial cooperation with colonialism, achieved a very partial modernization, again largely confined to emerging elites. The Protestant penetration in Africa was as unstable as the Catholic penetration in Latin America. Thus, the masses both in Latin America and Africa were vulnerable to Pentecostalism. Asia was a different matter, perhaps best understood in terms of the vulnerability of areas or groups marginal to the dominant traditions. In this context the whole of Korea was vulnerable in relation to the dominance of Japan;[8] the Chinese minorities in different parts of Asia were also vulnerable, for example, in Malaysia and Singapore, as well as the peripheral peoples of Thailand, Burma, the Philippines, India, Malaysia, Indonesia, and even Nepal. Much depends on how far a folk tradition has been partially absorbed by a developed high tradition in association with the State and national solidarity. Where that has occurred, as in Buddhist Thailand and Burma, conversion is not very likely. On the other hand, where there is a folk tradition unabsorbed by a high tradition and without reinforcement from national solidarity, for example, Taoism in Singapore, then conversion can be quite rapid.

Western Europe

Western Europe represents the most secular group of cultures in the modern world, with the vines of faith twined around crumbling and centralized establishments and with exposure both to classical modernity and to an elite tradition of militant secularity capable of reproducing itself among the masses. The extension of the secular tilt in the western European heartlands beyond the French epicenter under the auspices of the European Economic Community has led to rapid secularization in Belgium and Spain. A further belt of post-Protestant secularity extends from Birmingham and Amsterdam to Berlin and Tallinn. Few footholds are available to Pentecostalism and evangelicalism except for the interstitial culture of the gypsies and the margins in Portugal and southern Italy. In Portugal the Brazilian "Universal Church" is now the second largest religious body; and, in Italy south of Ancona, Pentecostalism, as well as the Witnesses, has made significant inroads, per-

8. Mark Mullins and Richard Fox Young, eds., *Perspectives on Christianity in Korea and Japan* (Lampeter, Wales, 1995).

haps 1-2 percent of the population of the area.[9] Within the United Kingdom, Pentecostal and holiness movements have had their successes among the Caribbean population, reinforcing their original culture and offering protective solidarity, especially for women. Within Scandinavia there is a Pentecostal constituency of quite long-standing, taking over where the *inner mission* left off. However, the Social Democratic ethos is not conducive to expansion, though a notably successful "Faith Mission" operates in Uppsala.

Eastern Europe

Things are rather different in Eastern Europe where Turkish overlordship followed by Russian communist domination has reinforced ethno-religion. In Poland ethno-religion has been combined with high practice, though not obedience to Catholic norms, whereas in Serbia it is more a matter of identification, but in either case to adopt another faith is to desert the national tradition. Similar situations are found in Croatia, Slovakia, and Lithuania. However, in some cases religion was historically out of alignment with ethnic tradition and national solidarity, and so failed to reproduce itself under communist pressure, as, for example, in the Czech Republic, East Germany, and Estonia. So, in Poland, evangelicalism does not extend beyond about 0.1 percent and also makes few inroads into the areas of successful secularist indoctrination. That means that (gypsies apart) the main areas of vulnerability are at the junction of traditions, notably the multicultural march lands of Transylvania and the western Ukraine. In Transylvania, for example, German Baptists made some impact among Hungarians in the late nineteenth century, and there has been a rapid expansion among both Romanians and Hungarians since the seventies, accompanied by an even more rapid expansion of Pentecostalism and even some charismatic Calvinism.[10] Perhaps the evangelical constituency in Romania as a whole is 1-2 percent. The minority Protestant culture of Hungary and the uncertain Catholicism of Budapest also display a certain vulnerability to a faith mission, which appeals to some in the new middle classes, including new entrepreneurs.

9. Salvatore Cucchiari, "Between Shame and Sanctification: Patriarchy and Its Transformation in Sicilian Pentecostalism," *American Anthropologist* 4.17 (November 1990): 687-707.

10. David Martin, *Forbidden Revolutions* (London, 1996).

Latin America

In Western and Eastern Europe evangelical incursions have been minor. In Latin America by contrast, they have been major, varying between 4 and 30 percent, with an average for the whole continent of about 10 percent. Classical evangelicalism arrived in the nineteenth century, making a minor impact in the lower middle classes, and Pentecostalism arrived in the early twentieth, though the main expansion has been since the sixties. The classic incursion of Pentecostalism has been among the poor, but not the poorest, so that in some suburbs of Santiago the active evangelical population is about the same size as the active Catholic population. Two varieties are most in evidence here: the major denominations of the Methodist Pentecostal Church (or the Assemblies of God) and small groupings with exotic names often around a husband and wife, and honeycombing whole areas.

The situation in Latin America is one where the Catholic Church has been institutionally weakened either by State control as in Brazil or State hostility as in Guatemala, but this hostility or indifference has not been transmitted to the masses outside Cuba and Uruguay. This has assisted the intertwining of folk motifs with Catholicism, and it was this unstable combination that began to collapse in the sixties with the arrival of global communications and a global economy. Since that time competitive pluralism has become a norm and has linked together the fluidity of the premodern situation and of the postmodern. Pentecostalism and evangelical renewal have offered a new voice, a fresh space for the adoption of transforming disciplines that fast-forward the aspirations of millions as they move from countryside to mega-city. Also offered are a protective capsule for women and opportunity for the reformation of the family.[11]

However, there are other manifestations, appealing to somewhat different constituencies and directed toward a variety of spiritual needs. In the case of the Universal Church of the Kingdom of God one has a very rapidly expanding movement promoting "liberation," both of mind and body, and having a large black constituency.[12] It takes over cinemas or else erects large buildings open onto the street, into which people wander at any time, and its services have a format strongly resembling a television show. Its pastors are spiritual and material hustlers and offer miracles and "liberation" as the first induce-

11. David Martin, *Tongues of Fire* (Oxford, 1990), and Harvey Cox, *Fire from Heaven* (New York and Reading, Mass., 1994).
12. David Lehmann, *Struggle for the Spirit* (Cambridge, 1996). Cf. Andrew Chesnut, *Born Again in Brazil* (New Brunswick, N.J. and London, 1997).

ment to faith. The "Universal Church" is highly controversial, not least because it is heavily involved in radio and television to the point of being in rivalry with the vast conglomerate "Globo." Another source of controversy is its dramatic warfare against the gods of the spiritists: a case of fighting fire with fire, but also of the incorporation of Afro-Brazilian cultural resources.

In other cases one has free-floating charismatic groups. Some of them break away from the restrictive moral practices of the classical Pentecostals and often appeal to quite youthful middle-class and professional groups who have been involved in the drug culture. One of the largest of these is "Renascer" or "Born Again in Christ," which nightly fills an ex-cinema with the equivalent of spiritual "shows" and claims extensive success in the reclamation of young people from personal deterioration. This kind of charismatic Christianity, deploying all the appurtenances of modern technology in the style of the contemporary media, operates in contexts remote from the conventional church, whether it is a huge arena or in the basements of middle-class homes. In such homes one may have a couple of dozen charismatic-minded families meeting together to sing their songs, to meditate on Scripture under each other's guidance, and to share their everyday concerns.

These charismatic manifestations among the better off, dealing as much with stress and psychic and professional problems as bodily ills, are all over the Southern Cone, not only Brazil, but in Uruguay and — quite dramatically — in Argentina.[13] What we see here is the adaptability of mutations of the evangelical impulse to different social niches in a rapidly developing world. The global reach is indicated by the international connections and crisscrossing trails: from Nigeria to Atlanta to Manila to Bucharest to Seoul and to Buenos Aires. Nowhere in the world is there a clearer manifestation of the rapid take-off of middle-class charismatic and neo-Pentecostal Christianity and its ability to affect other denominations than Argentina.

Though evangelical churches arrived in Argentina well over a century ago, and Pentecostalism as early as 1906, the initial impact was slight, apart from modest gains in lower middle-class sectors by Baptists and Brethren. As everywhere else, this began to change in the fifties as Pentecostalism showed its capacity to "key in" to popular culture. But not until the eighties, with the crisis in political legitimacy, was there any dramatic movement. Pentecostals who had comprised 2 percent in the seventies comprised 5 percent by the

13. Hilario Wynarczyk and Pablo Semán, "Un análisis del campo evangélico y el Pentecostalismo en la Argentina," in Alejandro Frigerio, ed., *El Pentecostalismo en la Argentina* (Buenos Aires, 1994).

mid-nineties, and the members of the Assemblies of God numbered nearly half a million. In the eighties there were ten extra churches per year in Buenos Aires, and seventeen per year in the next decade. Evangelical churches in the capital exceeded Catholic churches in number, and if the participation of Catholics was some 5 percent of nominal adherents, then at least a quarter of the active Christian constituency was evangelical.

The character of this expansion contrasts with the classical Pentecostalism hitherto dominant elsewhere in South America. Centered in Bible Institutes and with many mega-churches, the emphasis is on spiritual warfare, exorcism, divine healing, charismatic gifts, and empowerment in everyday life and professional activity. Modern technology and contemporary popular culture are everywhere in evidence: Christian rock, musical events, videos, periodicals, new hymns, and a general atmosphere of perpetual motion and theatricality. Though there is some evangelical concern over accusations of financial and sexual misconduct, and thinly veiled eroticism, as well as about irrationality and a cheapening of the experience of salvation, nevertheless the same charismatic styles have penetrated the historic churches (as I discovered on attending an Anglican church in a comfortable suburb of Santiago), and there is a considerable amount of mutual cooperation. The smudging of boundaries and leakage of members aroused considerable concern at the 1998 Lambeth Conference of Anglican Bishops.

Also in Latin America one may find creative reformations of suppressed or despised cultural contents, as well as supportive spiritual depots for groups on the move. *La Luz del Mundo* is an extraordinary case since it also revives Judaic elements appropriate to peoplehood. In that respect it resembles the Mormons and the New Israelites of Peru. Members of *La Luz del Mundo* often travel backward and forward between Mexico and the United States, finding in their churches supply dumps and resting places for renewal among people of their own kind.[14] At their main base in Guadalajara they effectively run part of the city, creating a complex of schools and hospitals in an area which replicates the geography of Palestine around their vast temple, which holds many thousands. The group is run by an almost messianic figure, descended from the founder, and assembles emblems of its power, in such Ethiopian manifestations as the lions in its zoo and the flags of the nations missionized by the new "conquistadores" of the spirit. The light of the world not only flashes out to the rest of the city by laser beam but also descends annually through an aperture on to the head of the leader. This pre-Columbian remi-

14. Bobby Alexander, "A Pentecostal-Styled Mexican Mission in Dallas," unpublished.

niscence resonates with the way the temple architecture reflects Aztec models. Indeed, the group seems to have a considerable appeal for non-Hispanic peoples, rather as the Universal Church has for blacks.

In Latin America there are numerous instances of a reaction by ethnic minority groups to the increasing pressure of a Hispanic nationalism in terms of a new evangelical identity, sometimes reinforced by a symbolic association with the prestige of the United States. This means, other things being equal, that countries with large ethnic minorities could undergo extensive evangelical inundation. The Maya, the Mapuche, the Quechua, and numerous others are, so to speak, at risk, and all offer evidence of the effects. A paradigmatic example occurs among the Aymara of Bolivia as recently studied by Andrew Canessa.[15] The evidence of the tentacles of modernity is the relationship between good roads from the capital, La Paz, and the incidence of evangelical conversion, as well as the trail from the countryside to La Paz, marked by a migration of souls as well as bodies. The most interesting aspect of Canessa's study is the way the converted Aymara succeeded in reversing the stereotype of their ethnic character. In the Hispanic stereotype they were identified as lazy, undisciplined, backward, and given to intoxicants, whereas in their own revised estimate they were exemplary models of modernity in dress and habits. It also appears that once in La Paz, the Aymara found in their churches a space for their language, as well as opportunity for family discipline and mutual support among the women.

Asia

Similar manifestations can be found all over the Pacific Rim from Seoul to Manila and Hong Kong. According to the work of Michael Hill and his associates in Singapore, Christianity in a mixed Malay, Chinese, and Indian society is mainly Chinese, with a significant Indian minority, though in its charismatic form it shows a characteristic capacity to break down ethnic barriers.[16] Singapore after independence concentrated initially on economic advance but later turned to the moral dimension of nation building. In education,

15. Andrew Canessa, "The Politics of the Pacha: The Conflict of Values in a Bolivian Aymara Community," Ph.D. dissertation, University of London, 1993. Cf. Lesley Gill, "Like a Veil to Cover Them: Women and the Pentecostal Movement in La Paz," *American Ethnologist* 17.4 (1990): 718-21.

16. Michael Hill and Liam Kwen Fee, *The Politics of Nation Building and Citizenship in Singapore* (London, 1995), and Yong Mun Cheong, ed., *Asian Traditions and Modernization* (Singapore, 1992).

that stimulated some interest in Confucian ethics, believed to be conducive to order and an economic ethos. Malays as Muslims were suspected of disloyalty, and Christians, of social activism.

Then in the late eighties there emerged a dramatic shift among young, high-status, English-educated Chinese to charismatic Christianity, with some further interest in Buddhism or else secular irreligiosity. Young Chinese gravitate from the amorphous Taoism of the majority, so that about one in four of those in tertiary or university education are Christians. Protestant Christianity is viewed as modern and international and offers an orderly rational world, and also one in which there is opportunity for personal expression, musical catharsis, and close contact in a democratic atmosphere. Everything changes, and yet the charismatic churches establish continuity with the ancient spiritist tradition and its proffered mundane benefits. In the mainly Muslim context of (western) Malaysia, Michael Northcott argues that charismatic and Pentecostal churches offer the most significant challenge to the former mission churches.[17] Indifferent to liberal theology and the comparative analysis of religions, they combine Asian and Western cultural forms with a celebration of the spirit in everyday life and oral tradition in the mode of the New Testament. Charismatic Christianity is at home in the middle class of a modernizing society which is for the first time in reach of material goods, and yet it has a strong sense of the supernatural realized in renewed personal identities and moral reformation. In one direction a sense of crisis not unconnected with ethnic tensions is symbolized in millennial anticipation, while in another direction continuity with the past is assured by drawing on indigenous shamanism (while suspecting it elsewhere as demonic). This capacity to draw on shamanistic spiritism parallels the Korean experience. As in Singapore, there is some relation between social mobility and speaking English, and this fits in well with a gospel of health and prosperity. It also makes the movement open to an evident North American influence.

As has been noticed in urban South Africa and Latin America, the energies of charismatic Christianity cross ethnic lines, though some churches are distinctively Indian, such as the Pentecostal Church of Malaysia, while others have a majority Chinese membership. The Full Gospel Assemblies have a strong lay leadership, with a cell structure and frequent meetings in homes. Its members dress in smart, modern styles and deploy elements of television culture and popular music. However, the largest impact of charismatic Chris-

17. Michael Northcott, "A Survey of the Rise of Charismatic Christianity in Malaysia," *Asian Journal of Theology* 4.1 (1990): 266-78.

tianity is in fact within the Roman Catholic Church through parish-based renewal groups. The historic Protestant churches find themselves in more of a dilemma, uneasy about the theological trends but anxious not to be overtaken in numbers and influence.

Of course, it would be easy to multiply instances of this evangelical mutation in other parts of the aspiring sectors of the rapidly developing world, above all Korea, which is by now a society very extensively Christianized, but the objective is not to provide an exhaustive survey.

The next kind of expansion to be considered involves an appeal to groups at the ethnic margin of societies hitherto without distinct religious self-consciousness. It is, of course, modern global communication which helps arouse this consciousness. Interesting instances of this are in Nepal, Burma, and Thailand, and these run parallel to modest expansions in the major cities of the kind just discussed. In Nepal, Burma, and Thailand there is a strong religious identity espoused by the State and by a majority population infused with ethnic nationalism that inhibits conversion as involving loss of status and community membership. For the tribes at the geographical margin, therefore, the attraction of conversion includes an assertion of identity, equality, and difference.

Looking a little more closely at Nepal,[18] there are now a couple of hundred churches in Katmandu, run by Nepalese, and a perceived relation between Christianity, modernity, and global scope. Yet the areas of greatest success occur in the Tibeto-Burmese population in semi-autonomous valleys northwest of the capital. Lines of conversion run along the differences of lineage and may involve whole villages under local leadership, though where habitation is dispersed adhesion is individual or familial. Pastors tend to be hostile to the lamas, and there is dispute about the legitimacy of traditional sacred powers. The groups operating in this area are the Nepalese Christian Fellowship, Gospel for Asia, and Baptists of the New Life Mission Church, who have health and educational facilities.

In Thailand conversion has for a long time been largely confined to the hill tribes and border groups.[19] Traditionally Christians in Bangkok have tended to be Chinese or Vietnamese Catholics. And yet with the establishment of a Pentecostal Church in the capital in 1981, a Thai leadership emerged for the first time, and within five years the congregation had grown to five

18. Blandine Ripert, "Christianisme et Pouvoirs Locaux dans une vallée Tamang du Népal Central," *Archives de sciences sociales des religions* 99 (July-September 1997): 69-86.

19. Charles Keyes, "Why the Thai Are Not Christians: Buddhist and Christian Conversion in Thailand," in Hefner, *Conversion to Christianity,* pp. 259-84; and Philip Hughes, "The Assimilation of Christianity in Thai Culture," *Religion* 14 (1984): 313-36.

thousand, utilizing the cell structure pioneered in Korea. As in Korea (and elsewhere), elements of local culture have reemerged in Christian guise in spite of official repudiation, notably the Thai hierarchy of merit. Pentecostals are now 5 percent of all Protestant Christians; to what extent the characteristic Pentecostal dynamic has been reinforced by the crisis in political legitimacy is difficult to say. So we see here the coexistence of different patterns, at the center of the society and at the margin.

If we turn to India as discussed by Susan Bayley, we find that a large proportion of (south) Indian Christians now belong to activist churches which emphasize the gifts of the Spirit, including prayer, healing, exorcism, and prophecy.[20] They have charismatic leaders and promote corporate and individual discipline. At their heart are assemblies of lay people under lay leadership with little regard for established hierarchies. Women find the assemblies particularly attractive and enjoy the special opportunities they offer them. The professional and commercial middle classes are also attracted, both by the new churches and by parallel changes in the older Christian bodies, including Catholicism. The problem for the older bodies is their seeming relativistic and anodyne liberalism challenged by a very Indian reclamation of living presences and concrete powers, even though some idioms and organizational models come from elsewhere. As in Malaysia, communal tension plays a role, and the new movements mark out a terrain and defend a genuine if fragile Christian stake in the social order against a Hindu vocabulary of exclusion.

The imponderable element here is China, with about one sixth of the world's population. It is clear that evangelical Christianity has some appeal for the Chinese diaspora, and that there is a fairly easy transition to it from Chinese folk religiosity. Aside from the bodies granted official acceptance in the more repressive period of communist rule up to the eighties, an extensive underground Christianity developed in the form of conservative evangelical house churches. The main areas of expansion were in the southeastern coastal provinces and overlapped areas of long-established Christian activity. There was also rapid growth in the eighties in some inland rural provinces. This rapid growth has been termed "Christianity fever" and appears to involve some subsumption of folk practices. The main traditions are conservative in an Anglo-American mode, in keeping with the original missionary presence. As for the house church movement it was lay in inspiration, with many fe-

20. Susan Bayley, "Christians and Competing Fundamentalisms in South Indian Society," in Martin Marty and J. Scott Appleby, eds., *Accounting for Fundamentalisms* (Chicago, 1994).

male workers, and at least a sector of it offered healing, spiritual gifts, and exorcism. The influence of this sector is very evident in recent revivals along the Korean border. The view of "the world" without was apolitical, though the government displayed some unease after the crisis of June 1989. A middle-range estimate suggests that evangelical Christians are about 2 percent of the total Chinese population.[21]

Africa

In Africa we find variations on these themes. Nigeria is the largest nation in Africa, divided roughly half and half between Christians and Muslims, now semi-democratic but ruled until quite recently by a largely Muslim military establishment. Ruth Marshall regards Pentecostalism as creating autonomous space over against corruption, monopolies of power, State violence, and economic exploitation. Within this space is room for new practices that assist survival. She identifies two main niches that are clearly parallel to those observable in Latin America. One consists of denominational mission churches like the Assemblies of God and their indigenous counterparts. Within these enclaves narratives of conversion contrast helplessness with empowerment and invite believers into a world of equality and self-worth negating the hierarchies of wealth or age. Strong boundaries against "the world" and communal solidarity provide rudimentary social security and mutual assistance, and counseling is available on financial and marital matters.

The other main niche is a transdenominational charismatic movement, appealing to the young and mobile, with a strong base in the universities. Prosperity is treated as a mark of divine favor, and yet, at the same time, mere appetite is controlled by the rules and by norms of economic reliability and trust. There is a network of patrons and clients in the community, as well as private hospitals, kindergartens, and maternity wards. In such groups young women achieve by merit what might otherwise be gotten only by sexual favors, and they also have a chance to meet reliable, considerate spouses. Infidelity is treated according to a common standard for men and women, and marital disputes are adjudicated by the pastor. It also seems the choice of a partner crosses ethnic lines more frequently than elsewhere. There are in such groups a global consciousness and a capacity to exercise pressure, sometimes in the context of communal tensions. As is the case so often, the danger lies in

---

21. I have drawn *inter alia* on a paper circulated in 1991 by Alan Hunter and Chan Kim-Kwong, who also wrote *Chinese Christian Spirituality* (London, 1991).

concentrations of power and displays of success canceling the atmosphere of participation, as well as alliances between leaderships and politicians with doubtful records.[22]

The other African examples chosen are the Peki Ewe in Ghana, studied by Birgit Meyer, the Pentecostals in Zimbabwe, studied by David Maxwell, and Protestant groups in Zambia, studied by Paul Gifford. Birgit Meyer's work illustrates the relation between the oldest Evangelistic layer of German Pietism and contemporary Pentecostalism, as well as the way older cultural resources are reassembled inside a new format.[23] The original missionaries were — as so often — rather poorly educated men sent from their native Germany by upper-class sponsors. Though their pietism was not that far from African religion, they diabolized it. Conversion was initially infrequent, but by 1915 about a third of the Peki were Christians of various kinds. Motivations were related to a desire to achieve goods through faith, as well as health and educational advancement, though this was not what the missionaries actually preached. Many evaded missionary control and slid back into the old ways until the sixties, when a serious expansion of Pentecostalism began, with healings and vibrant services setting aside written orders and taken by untrained pastors. This was part of an undertone of protest against a religion based on rules that neglected the Spirit.

One major difference was that whereas the mission church envisaged a permanent shift to Christianity, Pentecostals maintained continuous warfare with the real powers of the old order. By projecting this contest in stories and media presentation they not only revived the healing practices and exorcisms of primitive Christianity but allowed believers to revisit the past safely armed by Christian prophylaxis. The older practice was incorporated in the new, including bodily movements and gestures. Once again this parallels the operation of Pentecostals in other contexts: the transplantation of the old within the new, without the kind of radical disenchantment that expels the whole world of the spirit. It is clear that Meyer rejects the idea of Pentecostalism as an alien import. Rather, she views it as providing a space for believers to negotiate modernity, especially as women strive for multiple adjustments within the family. Spiritual resources and communal support enable people to stand independently on their own two feet. Pentecostalism also allows hope for material betterment in a capitalist economy to burgeon without sell-

---

22. Ruth Marshall, "Power in the Name of Jesus," *Review of African Political Economy* 52 (November 1991): 21-37. Cf. Rosalind Hackett, ed., *New Religious Movements in Nigeria* (Lewiston, N.Y. and Lampeter, Wales, 1987).

23. Birgit Meyer, *Translating the Devil* (Edinburgh, 1999).

ing out to worldly seductions. As to the association of religion with betterment and "goods," it clearly resonated with traditional African motifs and needed little stimulus from elsewhere.

A somewhat different negotiation of modernity is analyzed by David Maxwell in the context of Zimbabwe, and his analyses show just how evangelical and Pentecostal Christianity enter into different niches in the social economy, in this case, for example, the search for independence on the part of young men and women.[24] As in Ghana, so in Zimbabwe, the Pentecostal churches make up a sizeable proportion of the population, maybe 10 percent. In other words the proportions reached in (non-Islamic) Africa match those in Latin America. Moreover, as far as timing goes, processes in the two continents mirror each other, with Africa about a decade behind. The two processes also have in common the multiplicity of sources, a two-way traffic with North America, and a history which begins earlier than is generally realized, as well as a great deal of creative indigenous invention bringing about a postmodern "bricolage." Maxwell also identifies an initial and rapid indigenization, followed by expansive transnational ambitions.

Though a fractious family, the Pentecostals coming to southern Africa saw themselves as harbingers of a worldwide movement, both transnational and moving across the boundaries of denomination. The initial awakenings were in 1908, about the same time as in Chile and Brazil. They reached Southern Rhodesia within the next decade, and by the 1920s Pentecostal movements had penetrated deep into the burgeoning urban centers, countering the personal social disintegrations of violence, promiscuity, alcoholism, gambling, and crime. They created, as they do now in Latin America, a counter-society based on work, self-discipline, the integrity of the family, and the mutuality of the church.

An interesting characteristic of Pentecostals was their indifference to the packaging of discrete territories by missionaries and to the "civilizing mission" the missionaries shared with the colonial administration. This offensiveness was compounded by their indifference to the invented tradition of the rulers who were a pillar of that administration. Maxwell comments that in southern as in central Africa, Pentecostals (like Witnesses) delegitimized chiefs by demonizing ancestor religion, provided young labor migrants anxious to retain their wages with legitimate reasons to break free from traditional commensality, and gave young women legitimate reasons to challenge

---

24. David Maxwell, "The Church and the Democratisation of Africa: The Case of Zimbabwe," in Paul Gifford, ed., *The Christian Churches and Africa's Democratization* (Leiden, 1995).

patriarchal authority.[25] In short these were poorly educated men and women behaving and speaking in modes outside colonial control, and so they were defined as on the margin of subversion. Here one observes the extent of the sociocultural changes that were initiated by the interaction of the local and global, black and white, in the first half of the twentieth century, and continued at an accelerated pace in the second half.

David Maxwell stresses the versatility of Pentecostalism sometimes poised against the partial cooption of historic denominations by the State in the form of Non-Governmental Organizations (NGOs), sometimes filling in gaps in the legitimation of doubtful regimes criticized by these denominations. It secures personal and collective buoyancy along the networks of labor migrating to the towns by undermining the moral ties and local gerontocracy and creating a new time and space within the church. It deploys modern media and music, creates self-reliance and "testifies" an economic culture into existence as it "sings away" poverty. Maxwell points also to the emergence of tension as an older and more populist Pentecostalism acknowledging suffering and the danger of riches, and valuing humility, meets a smoother Christianity susceptible to personality cults, display, greed, and opportunistic political alliances. At the leadership level it succumbs to bureaucracy and "authoritarianism."

An interesting example of the replication of Latin American (especially Brazilian) developments is provided in the tiny country of Cape Verde. Early incursions of Adventists and Nazarenes are now stalled as the field is disputed by "American" groups (Mormons, Witnesses), classical Pentecostals, and the Brazilian "Universal Church." The practices of the Universal Church chime well with Afro-Portuguese spirituality.

The object of the foregoing is not to provide an overall assessment of the global expansion of evangelical and especially Pentecostal Christianity but to outline some of the kinds of religious bodies and the kinds of social niches they occupy. I could have taken very different examples, comparing, for example, the successful alignment of evangelical and Pentecostal Christianity with Korean cultural identity with the resistance encountered in Japan. But whatever examples I took would illustrate an "awakening" to messages circulating around a world increasingly unified by modern communication, an engagement with capitalist transformations, the creation of voluntary transnational bodies operating across boundaries, and a mingling of motifs from the original North Atlantic heartlands of evangelical Christianity with indig-

25. Maxwell, "The Church and the Democratisation of Africa"; and David Maxwell, "Witches, Prophets, and Avenging Spirits," *Journal of Religion in Africa* 25.3 (1995): 309-39.

enous motifs and initiatives. In Latin America and Africa, as elsewhere, this mode of religiosity helps prize people out of old frameworks and reassembles old elements within a new format.

In summary form, evangelical Christianity, and by extension Pentecostalism, is a manifestation of modernity insofar as it is a voluntary association occupying a space within the cultural sphere and established across national borders. Within that space people who are on the move, geographically and socially, revise their moral selves and their domestic roles so as to reintegrate the family, and they also are accorded opportunity to participate and lead. The disciplines of the group generate solidarity and assist every kind of betterment, including material betterment, and that incidental link becomes explicit in the gospel of health and prosperity. This kind of Christianity manifests an ecumenism of the spirit while being organizationally fissiparous and cuts loose from Western professional theology as it enables lay people to feed at will on the biblical text. It is indifferent to the ideological maps of the Western secular intelligentsia and allows an eruption from below which unites the despised peripheries of the North Atlantic to the poor and the ethnically marginal groups of the South Atlantic and elsewhere. In doing so it shows some capacity to cross ethnic boundaries.

As a self generated vehicle of the aspiring poor it picks up contents within the universal shamanistic layer of spiritism overlaid by colonialism and integrates them into the frame of Holy Spirit Christianity. It is also well adapted to newly emerging middle classes, protecting them from psychic disintegrations and erecting zones of moral and professional integrity. In all its forms it has a special appeal to women, offering them opportunity for expression as well as havens of security and respect. It stands for the domestic table over against the street and the bar and the machismo culture of violence and indulgence. It is, arguably — with Catholicism, Islam, and Western secularity — one of the half dozen or so basic responses to the modern world. That, at least, is Peter Berger's view. Its global character is indicated by the symbol of the gift of a universal voice beyond the Babel of competing languages.

Put it another way: a particular kind of global transition is occurring engendered in the West by a fusion of black and white popular and populist religion which rejects the sponsorship and agenda of the post-Protestant and post-Catholic intelligentsias of sometime Christendom, along with their theological allies. It coincides with emergent self-consciousness in many different niches; it fuses ancient and postmodern; it operates across national and ethnic boundaries; and it keys in to local resources while framing them in a Christian format, mainly through indigenous carriers. It resonates least in areas of apathy left by collapsing establishments, especially where elite carriers of anti-clerical tradition have used centralized State power to erase the spiritual premise, as in France, (East) Germany, or Uruguay. It also makes little headway where there is a unity of State, society, and local community that drastically inhibits individual choice, for example, in Buddhist, Hindu, and above all Islamic contexts. Where it operates politically its stance depends on context, but in terms of a space for autonomous social learning and revision of social roles, and for institution building between State and individual, it is implicitly democratic as well as economically entrepreneurial.

Bibliography

Ackroyd, P. R., et al., eds. *Cambridge History of the Bible.* 3 vols. Cambridge, 1963-70.

Adeney, David H. *China: The Church's Long March.* Petuluma, CA, 1985.

Afealdi, Emiliana, Ron Crocombe, and John McClaren, eds. *Religious Cooperation in the Pacific Islands.* Suva, 1983.

Ajayi, J. F. Ade. *Christian Missions in Nigeria, 1841-1891: The Making of a New Elite.* Evanston, IL, 1969.

Almeida, Abraão, et al. *História das Assembléias de Deus no Brasil.* Rio de Janeiro, 1982.

Alves, Rubem. *Protestantismo a Repressão.* São Paulo, 1979.

————. "A Volta do Sagrado (Os Caminhos da Sociologia da Religião no Brasil)." *Religião a Sociedade* 3 (1978): 109-41.

Anderson, Robert Mapes. *Vision of the Disinherited: The Making of American Pentecostalism.* New York, 1979.

Annis, Sheldon. *God and Production in a Guatemalan Town.* Austin, 1987.

Antoniazzi, A., et al. *Nem Anjos Nem Demônios: Interpretações Sociológicas do Pentecostalismo.* Petrópolis, 1994.

Arias, Mortimer. "El Protestantismo." *Presencia* (8 June 1975): 181-89.

Arnold, Gottfried. *Historie und Beschreibung der mystischen Theologie oder geheimen Gottes Gelehrtheit wie auch derer alten and neuen Mysticorum.* Frankfurt, 1703.

————. *Verthädigung der mystischen Theologie.* (n.d.).

Austin-Broos, Diane J. *Jamaica Genesis: Religion and the Politics of Moral Order.* Chicago, 1997.

Ayandele, E. A. *The Missionary Impact on Modern Nigeria, 1842-1914: A Political and Social Analysis.* New York, 1966.

Ayittey, G. B. N. *Africa Betrayed*. London, 1994. This work was first published in the U.S. in 1992.

Baird, Robert. *The Progress and Prospects of Christianity in the United States of America; With Remarks on the Subject of Slavery in America; and on the Intercourse Between British and American Churches*. London, 1851(?).

Baker, Eric W. *A Herald of the Evangelical Revival*. London, 1948.

Barker, John. "Long God Yumi Stanap: Repositioning the Anthropology of Oceanic Christianity." Unpublished paper read at the Roundtable on Christianization in Oceania, École des hautes Études en Sciences Sociales, Paris, May 1999.

Barr, K. J. *Blessed Are the ~~Poor~~ Rich . . . Praise the Lord . . . An Examination of New Religious Groups in Fiji Today*. Suva, 1998.

Barrett, David. "Annual Statistical Table on Global Mission." *International Bulletin of Missionary Research* 23 (January 1999): 24-25.

———, et al. *Kenya Churches Handbook*. Kisumu, 1973.

———, ed. *World Christian Encyclopedia*. New York, 1982.

Bastian, Jean-Pierre. *Historia del Protestantismo en América Latina*. Mexico City, 1990.

———. "Introduction." *Social Compass* 39.3 (1992): 323-26.

———. "The Metamorphosis of Latin American Protestant Groups: A Sociohistorical Perspective." *Latin American Research Review* 28.2 (1993): 33-61.

———. *Protestantismo y Sociedad en México*. Mexico City, 1983.

Basu, Aparnu. *The Growth of Education and Political Development in India, 1898-1920*. Delhi, 1974.

Bayley, Susan. "Christians and Competing Fundamentalisms in South Indian Society." In *Accounting for Fundamentalisms: The Dynamic Character of Movements*, edited by Martin Marty and J. Scott Appleby, 726-69. Chicago, 1994.

Bays, Daniel H. *Christianity in China: From the Eighteenth Century to the Present*. Stanford, 1996.

Bebbington, D. W. *Evangelicalism in Modern Britain: A History from the 1730s to the 1980s*. London, 1989.

———. "Of This Train, England Is the Engine: British Evangelicalism and Globalization in the Long Nineteenth Century." In *A Global Faith: Essays on Evangelicalism and Globalization*, edited by Mark Hutchinson and Ogbu Kalu, 122-39. Sydney, 1998.

———. "Towards an Evangelical Identity." In *For Such a Time as This: Perspectives on Evangelicalism, Past, Present, and Future*, edited by Steve Brady and Harold Rowdon, 37-48. London, 1996.

Bediako, Kwame. *Christianity in Africa: The Renewal of a Non-Western Religion*. Edinburgh, 1995.

Behman, Jacob. *Memoirs of the Life of Jacob Behmen*. Northampton, 1780.

Beidelman, T. O. "Social Theory and the Study of Christian Missions in Africa." *Africa* 44.3 (July 1974): 235-48.

Belich, James. *Making Peoples: A History of New Zealanders from Polynesian Settlement to the End of the Nineteenth Century.* Auckland, 1996.

Bengel, J. A. *Erklärte Offenbarung.* 2nd ed. Stuttgart, 1746.

Benz, Ernst. *Die Christliche Kabbala: Ein Stiefkind der Theologie.* Zurich, 1958.

———. "Der Mensch and die Sympathie aller Dinge am Ende der Zeiten (nach Jakob Boehme und seiner Schule)." *Eranos-Jahrbuch* 24 (1955): 133-97.

———. *Die protestantische Thebais: Zur Nachwirkung Makarios des Ägypters im Protestantismus des 17. and 18. Jahrhunderts.* Wiesbaden, 1963.

Beyer, Peter. *Religion and Globalization.* London and Delhi, 1994.

Beyreuther, Erich. "Zinzendorf und das Judentum." Reprinted in *Zinzendorf Werke.* Bd. 2, XII. Reihe.

Bittencourt Filho, José. *O Pentecostalismo Autônomo: Um Remédio Amargo.* Rio de Janeiro, 1991.

Bose, Ashish, assisted by Mohan Singh Bista and Anita Haldar. *Population Profile of Religion in India: Districtwise Data from 1991 Census.* Delhi, 1997.

Boseto, Leslie. "The Gift of Community." *International Review of Mission* 72.288 (1983): 581-83.

———. "'Towards a Pacific Theology of Reality': A Grassroots Response to *Winds of Change.*" *Pacific Journal of Theology* 2.12 (1994): 53-61.

Brandão, Carlos Rodrigues. *Os Deuses do Povo.* São Paulo, 1986.

Brazier Green, J. *John Wesley and William Law.* London, 1945.

Brecht, M., and K. Deppermann, eds. *Geschichte des Pietismus.* 2 vols. Göttingen, 1995.

Brockington, John. *Hinduism and Christianity.* London, 1992.

Brown, Leslie. *The Indian Christians of St. Thomas.* Cambridge, 1982.

Bruce, Steve. *God Save Ulster! The Religion and Politics of Paisleyism.* Oxford, 1989.

———. *A House Divided: Protestantism, Schism and Secularization.* London, 1990.

———. *No Pope of Rome: Militant Protestantism in Modern Scotland.* Edinburgh, 1985.

———. *Pray TV: Televangelism in America.* London, 1990.

Brusco, Elizabeth. "The Reformation of Machismo: Asceticism and Masculinity among Colombian Evangelicals." In *Rethinking Protestantism in Latin America,* edited by V. Garrard-Burnett and D. Stoll, 143-58. Philadelphia, 1993.

Buck, Peter. *Vikings of the Sunrise.* Christchurch, 1964; first U.S. edition, 1938.

Burdick, John. *Looking for God in Brazil.* Berkeley, 1993.

Bush, Joseph E. "Claiming a Christian State Where None Exists: Church and State in the Republic of Fiji." *Pacifica* 12 (Feb. 1999): 55-68.

———. "Is Social Relevance Relevant?" *Pacific Journal of Theology* 2.12 (1994): 41-46.

Bush, Richard. *Religion in Communist China.* Nashville, 1970.

Buxton, Thomas Fowell. *The African Slave Trade and Its Remedy.* London, 1967; orig. 1840.

Caldeira, Teresa. *A Politica dos Outros.* São Paulo, 1984.

Calver, Clive. "The Rise and Fall of the Evangelical Alliance: 1835-1905." In *For Such a Time as This: Perspectives on Evangelicalism, Past, Present, and Future,* edited by Steve Brady and Harold Rowdon, 148-62. London, 1996.

Canessa, Andrew. "The Politics of the Pacha: The Conflict of Values in a Bolivian Aymara Community." Ph.D. thesis. University of London, 1993.

Carpenter, Joel A. *Revive Us Again: The Reawakening of American Fundamentalism.* New York, 1997.

Castillo, Ramón. "Elementos para una Historia del Pentecostalismo en Venezuela." In *Pentecostalismo y Liberación,* edited by C. Alvarez, 59-76. San José, Costa Rica, 1992.

César, Waldo. *Para uma Sociologia do Protestantismo Brasileiro.* Petrópolis, 1973.

Chan, Kim-Kwong. *Chinese Christian Spirituality.* London, 1991.

Chang, Jung. *Wild Swans: Three Daughters of China.* New York, 1991.

Chao, Jonathan. *The China Mission Handbook: A Portrait of China and Its Church.* Hong Kong, 1989.

————. "The Church in China Today: Officially Registered Churches and House Churches." In *Ershiyi shiji huaren fuyin shigong xin celue* (New strategies for Chinese evangelism in the twenty-first century), 135-37. Argyle, TX, 1998.

————. "Dalu jidujiao ri di quzhe jiqi qianzhan" (The origins and prospects of Christianity fever in Mainland China). *Ming Pao Monthly* [Hong Kong] (December 1994): 44-49.

————. *Zhongguo dui jidujiao di zhengce* (China's policy toward Christianity). Hong Kong, 1983.

Chen, Fong-ching, and Jin Guangtao. *From Youthful Manuscripts to River Elegy.* Hong Kong, 1997.

Cheong, Yong Mun, ed. *Asian Traditions and Modernization.* Singapore, 1992.

Chesnut, Andrew. *Born Again in Brazil.* New Brunswick, NJ, and London, 1997.

Choi, Jeung Man. "Historical Development of the Indigenization Movement in the Korean Protestant Church: With Special Reference to Bible Translation." D.Miss. diss., Fuller Theological Seminary, 1985.

Christian Education in Africa and the East. London, 1924.

Clarke, Peter B. *West Africa and Christianity.* London, 1986.

Coleman, Kenneth, et al. "Protestantism in El Salvador: Conventional Wisdom versus the Survey Evidence." In *Rethinking Protestantism in Latin America,* edited by V. Garrard-Burnett and D. Stoll, 111-42. Philadelphia, 1993.

Comaroff, Jean, and John L. Comaroff. *Of Revelation and Revolution,* vol. 1: *Christianity, Colonialism and Consciouness in South Africa.* Chicago, 1991.

Comaroff, John L., and Jean Comaroff. *Of Revelation and Revolution,* vol. 2: *The Dialectics of Modernity on a South African Frontier.* Chicago and London, 1997.

Conde, Emílio. *História das Assembléias de Deus no Brasil.* Rio de Janeiro, 1960.

Conference on Missions Held in 1860 at Liverpool. London, 1860.

Copley, Antony. *Religions in Conflict: Ideology, Cultural Contact and Conversion in Late Colonial India.* Oxford and New Delhi, 1997.

Cox, Harvey. *Fire from Heaven.* New York and Reading, MA, 1994.

————. "Jazz and Pentecostalism." *Archives de Sciences Sociales des Religions* 84 (Oct.-Dec. 1993): 181-87.

Crocombe, Ron. *The Pacific Way: An Emerging Identity.* Suva, 1976.

————, and Marjorie Crocombe. "The London Missionary Society and Culture: Impacts on and from Rarotonga." *South Pacific Journal of Mission Studies* (August 1996): 4-11.

Cucchiari, Salvatore. "Between Shame and Sanctification: Patriarchy and Its Transformation in Sicilian Pentecostalism." *American Anthropologist* 4.17 (Nov. 1990): 687-707.

Curtin, P., et al., eds. *African History.* London, 1991.

Cusack, Carole M. "Towards a General Theory of Conversion." In *Religious Change, Conversion and Culture,* edited by L. Olson, 1-21. Sydney, 1996.

Davidson, J. W. *The Logic of Millenial Thought: Eighteenth-Century New England.* New Haven, 1977.

Davies, John. *The History of the Tahitian Mission 1799-1830,* edited by C. W. Newbury. Cambridge, 1961.

De, Krishna Prasad. *Religious Freedom under the Indian Constitution.* Columbia, MO, and New Delhi, 1976.

De Jong, James A. *As the Waters Cover the Sea: Millennial Expectations in the Rise of Anglo-American Missions, 1640-1810.* Kampen, 1970.

De Kock, Leon. *Civilising Barbarians: Missionary Narrative and African Textual Response in Nineteenth-Century South Africa.* Johannesburg, 1996.

De Souza, Beatriz Muniz. *A Experiência da Salvação: Pentecostais em São Paulo.* São Paulo, 1969.

Deng Zhaoming (S. M. Dunn). *Chengshou yu cishou* (The torch and testimony in China). Hong Kong, 1998.

Dennis, James S., Harlan P. Beach, and Charles H. Fahs, eds. *World Atlas of Christian Missions.* New York, 1911.

D'Epinay, Christian Lalive. *O Refúgio das Massas.* Rio de Janeiro, 1970.

————. *Religion, Dynamique Social et Dépendence: les Mouvements Protestants en Argentine et au Chili.* Paris, 1975.

Downs, Frederick S. *History of Christianity in India,* vol. V, part 5: *North East India in the Nineteenth and Twentieth Centuries.* Bangalore, 1992.

Droogers, André. "Visiones Paradójicas sobre una Religión Paradójica: Modelos explicativos del crecimiento del pentecostalismo en Brasil y Chile." In *Algo Más que Ópio: una lectura antropológica del pentecostalismo latinoamericano y caribeño,* edited by B. Boudewijnse et al., 17-42. San José, Costa Rica, 1991.

Duncan, Betty K. "Christianity: Pacific Island Traditions." In *Religions of New Zealanders*, edited by Peter Donovan, 128-41. Palmerston North, 1990.

Duttenhofer, M. C. F. *Freymüthige Untersuchungen über Pietismus und Orthodoxie*. Halle, 1787.

Earle, Duncan. "Authority, Social Conflict and the Rise of Protestantism: Religious Conversion in a Mayan Village." *Social Compass* 39.3 (1992): 377-88.

Ecumenical Missionary Conference, New York, 1900. 2 vols. London and New York, 1900.

Edwards, Jonathan. *The Works of Jonathan Edwards*, edited by S. E. Dwight and E. Hickman, 2 vols. Edinburgh, reprint 1974.

Ekechi, Felix K. "The Medical Factor in Christian Conversion in Africa: Observations from South-Eastern Nigeria." *Missiology* 21.3 (1993): 289-309.

Elsmore, Bronwyn. *Like Them That Dream: The Maori and the Old Testament*. Tauranga, 1985.

———. *Mana from Heaven: A Century of Maori Prophets in New Zealand*. Tauranga, 1989.

Ernst, Manfred. *Winds of Change: Rapidly Growing Religious Groups in the Pacific*. Suva, 1994.

Evangelical Fellowship of Sierra Leone. "*Target 2000* Evangelistic and Church Survey." Freetown, 1992.

Evans, Timothy. "Religious Conversion in Quetzaltenango, Guatemala." Ph.D. thesis. University of Pittsburgh, 1990.

Evers, George. "Asia." In *The Encyclopedia of Christianity*, vol. 1. Grand Rapids, 1999.

The Exemplary Life of the Pious Lady Guion. Dublin, 1775.

"Faith and Statecraft: A Special Issue on Religion in World Affairs." *Orbis: A Journal of World Affairs* 42:2 (Spring 1998): 334.

Faivre, Antoine. *Eckartshausen et la Théosophie Chrétienne*. Paris, 1969.

Fernandes, Rubem César. "As Missões Protestantes em Números." *Cadernos do ISER 10* (1981): 27-84.

———. *Censo Institucional Evangelico CIN 1992: Primeiros Comentários*. Rio de Janeiro, 1992.

———."O Debate entre sociólogos a propósito dos pentecostais." *Cadernos do ISER 6* (1977): 49-60.

———. "O Governo das Almas." In *Nem Anjos Nem Demônios*, edited by A. Antoniazzi et al., 163-203. Petrópolis, 1994.

Fisher, Elizabeth. "'Prophesies and Revelations': German Cabbalists in Early Pennsylvania." *Pennsylvania Magazine for History and Biography* 109 (1985): 299-333.

Fisher, H. J. "Conversion Reconsidered: Some Historical Aspects of Religious Conversion in Black Africa." *Africa* 43.1 (January 1973): 27-40.

Fishman, Alvin Texas. *Culture Change and the Underprivileged: A Study of Madigas in South India under Christian Guidance*. Madras, 1941.

Flora, Cornelia Butler. *Pentecostalism in Colombia: Baptism by Fire and Spirit.* Cranbury, NJ, 1976.

Fontaine Talavera, Arturo, and Harald Bayer. "Retrato del Movimiento Evangélico a la Luz de las Encuestas de Opinión Pública." *Estudios Públicos* 44 (1991): 63-124.

Forman, C. W. *The Island Churches of the South Pacific: Emergence in the Twentieth Century.* Maryknoll, NY, 1982.

———. "'Sing to the Lord a New Song': Women in the Churches of Oceania." In *Rethinking Women's Roles: Perspectives from the Pacific,* edited by Denise O'Brien and S. W. Tiffnay, 153-72. Berkeley, 1984.

———. "Some Next Steps in the Study of Pacific Island Christianity." In *Christianity in Oceania: Ethnographic Perspective,* edited by John Barker, 25-31. Lanham, MD, 1990.

———. "The South Pacific Style in the Christian Ministry." *Missiology* 2 (1974): 421-35.

———. *The Voices of Many Waters: The Story of the Life and Ministry of the Pacific Conference of Churches in the Last 25 Years.* Fiji, 1986.

Forrester, Duncan B. *Caste and Christianity: Attitudes and Policies on Caste of Anglo-Saxon Protestant Missions in India.* London, 1980.

Frase, Ronald. "A Sociological Analysis of the Development of Brazilian Protestantism: A Study in Social Change." Ph.D. thesis. Princeton Theological Seminary, 1975.

Freston, Paul. "Breve História do Pentecostalismo Brasileiro: 1. A Assembléia de Deus." In *Nem Anjos Nem Demônios: Interpretações Sociológicas do Pentecostalismo,* edited by A. Antoniazzi et al., 67-99. Petrópolis, 1994.

———. "Breve História do Pentecostalismo Brasileiro: 2. Congregação Cristã, Quadrangular, Brasil para Cristo e Deus é Amor." In *Nem Anjos Nem Demônios: Interpretações Sociológicas do Pentecostalismo,* edited by A. Antoniazzi et al., 100-130. Petrópolis, 1994.

———. "Breve História do Pentecostalismo Brasileiro: 3. A Igreja Universal do Reino de Deus." In *Nem Anjos Nem Demônios: Interpretações Sociológicas do Pentecostalismo,* edited by A. Antoniazzi et al., 131-59. Petrópolis, 1994.

———. "Charismatic Evangelicals in Latin America: Mission and Politics on the Frontiers of Protestant Growth." In *Dynamics of the Charismatic Movement,* edited by S. Hunt, M. Hamilton, and T. Walter, 184-204. Basingstoke, 1997.

———. "Pentecostalism in Brazil: A Brief History." *Religion* 25 (1995): 119-33.

———. "Popular Protestants in Brazilian Politics: A Novel Turn in Sect-State Relations." *Social Compass* 41.4 (1994): 537-70.

———. "The Protestant Eruption into Modern Brazilian Politics." *Journal of Contemporary Religion* 11.2 (1996): 147-68.

———. "Protestantes e Política no Brasil: da Constituinte ao Impeachment." Ph.D. thesis. University of Campinas, 1993.

Frey, Sylvia R. *Water from the Rock: Black Resistance in a Revolutionary Age.* Princeton, 1991.

————, and Betty Wood. *Come Shouting to Zion: African American Protestantism in the American South and British Caribbean to 1830.* Chapel Hill, NC, and London, 1998.

Frigerio, Alejandro. "Estudios Recientes sobre el Pentecostalismo en el Cono Sur: Problemas y Perspectivas." In *El Pentecostalismo en la Argentina,* edited by A. Frigerio, 10-28. Buenos Aires, 1994.

Fry, Peter, and Gary Howe. "Duas Respostas à Aflição: Umbando e Pentecostalismo." *Debate e Crítica* 6 (1975): 75-94.

Frykenberg, R. E. [Robert Eric]. "India." In *A World History of Christianity,* edited by Adrian Hastings, 147-91. London, 1999.

————. "On the Study of Conversion Movements." *Indian Economic and Social History Review* 17.1 (1980): 121-37.

Gairdner, W. H. T. *"Edinburgh 1910": An Account and Interpretation of the World Missionary Conference.* Edinburgh and London, 1910.

Gao, Wangzhi. "Y. T. Wu: A Christian Leader under Communism." In *Christianity in China: From the Eighteenth Century to the Present,* edited by Daniel H. Bays, 338-52. Stanford, 1996.

Garrard-Burnett, Virginia. "Conclusion: Is This Latin America's Reformation?" In *Rethinking Protestantism in Latin America,* edited by V. Garrard-Burnett and D. Stoll, 199-210. Philadelphia, 1993.

Garrett, John. *To Live among the Stars: Christian Origins in Oceania.* Geneva and Suva, 1992.

————. *Where Nets Were Cast: Christianity in Oceania since World War II.* Suva and Geneva, 1997.

Gaxiola-Gaxiola, Manuel. *La Serpiente y la Paloma.* Pasadena, CA, 1970.

Giddens, Anthony. *Runaway World: How Globalisation Is Reshaping Our Lives.* Based on the 1999 BBC Reith Lectures. London, 1999.

Gifford, Paul. *African Christianity: Its Public Role.* London and Bloomington, IN, 1998.

Gill, Anthony. *Rendering Unto Caesar: The Catholic Church and the State in Latin America.* Chicago, 1998.

Gill, Lesley. "Like a Veil to Cover Them: Women and the Pentecostal Movement in La Paz." *American Pacha Ethnologist* 17.4 (1990): 718-21.

Goen, C. C. "Jonathan Edwards: A New Departure in Eschatology." *Church History* 28 (1959): 25-40.

Goodall, Norman. *A History of the London Missionary Society, 1895-1945.* London, 1954.

Goodhew, David. "Growth and Decline in South Africa's Churches, 1960-91." *Journal of Religion in Africa* 30.3 (2000): 344-69.

Gordon, Grant. *From Slavery to Freedom: The Life of David George, Pioneer Black*

Baptist Minister. Baptist Heritage in Atlantic Canada Series. Hantsport, NS, 1992.

Grenfell, James. "The Participation of Protestants in Politics in Guatemala." M.Phil. thesis. University of Oxford, 1995.

Groth, Friedhelm. *Die "Wiederbringung aller Dinge" im Wüttembergische Pietismus.* Göttingen, 1984.

Gutch, John. *Beyond the Reefs: The Life of John Williams, Missionary.* London, 1974.

Habermas, Jürgen. *The Structural Transformation of the Public Sphere: An Inquiry into a Category of Bourgeois Society.* Translated by Thomas Berger. Cambridge, 1989.

Hackett, Rosalind. "Pentecostal Appropriation of Media Technologies in Nigeria and Ghana." *Journal of Religion in Africa* 28.3 (1998): 258-77.

———, ed. *New Religious Movements in Nigeria.* Lewiston, NY, and Lampeter, 1987.

Hanciles, J. J. "Ethiopianism: Rough Diamond of African Christianity (a West African perspective)." *Studia Historiae Ecclesiasticae* 23.1-2 (December 1997): 75-104.

Harper, Susan Billington. *In the Shadow of the Mahatma: Bishop Y. S. Azariah and the Travails of Christianity in British India.* Grand Rapids, MI, and London, 2000.

Harrell, David Edwin. *Quest for a Christian America: The Disciples of Christ and American Society to 1866.* Nashville, 1966.

Hastings, Adrian. *The Church in Africa, 1450-1950.* Oxford, 1994.

———. *The Construction of Nationhood: Ethnicity, Religion and Nationalism.* Cambridge, 1997.

———. *A History of African Christianity, 1950-1975.* Cambridge, 1979.

Hatch, Nathan O. *The Democratization of American Christianity.* New Haven, 1989.

Hau'ofa, Epeli. "Our Sea of Islands." In *A New Oceania: Rediscovering Our Sea of Islands,* edited by Eric Waddell, Vijay Naidu, Epeli Hau'ofa, 2-16. Suva, 1993.

Havea, Sione 'Amanaki. "Christianity in the Pacific Context." In *South Pacific Theology: Papers from the Consultation on Pacific Theology, Papua New Guinea, January 1986,* 11-15. Oxford, 1987.

Haweis, Thomas. *An Impartial and Succinct History of the Rise, Declension and Revival of the Church of Christ.* 3 vols. London, 1800.

Haynes, Jeff, ed. *Religion, Globalization and Political Culture in the Third World.* New York, 1998.

Hefner, Robert W., ed. *Conversion to Christianity: Historical and Anthropological Perspectives on a Great Transformation.* Berkeley, Los Angeles, and Oxford, 1993.

Heimert, A. *Religion and the American Mind from the Great Awakening to the Revolution.* 2nd ed. Cambridge, MA, 1968.

Hewitt, Gordon. *The Problems of Success: A History of the Church Missionary Society, 1910-1942.* 2 vols. London, 1971.

Hewitt, W. E. "Religion and the Consolidation of Democracy in Brazil: The Role of the CEBs." *Sociological Analysis* 50.2 (1990): 139-52.

Hill, Michael. *A Sociology of Religion.* London, 1973.

————, and Liam Kwen Fee. *The Politics of Nation Building and Citizenship in Singapore.* London, 1995.

Hilliard, David. "Australasia and the Pacific." In *A World History of Christianity,* edited by Adrian Hastings, 508-35. London, 1999.

————. *God's Gentlemen: A History of the Melanesian Mission, 1849-1942.* St. Lucia, 1978.

Hirzel, M. *Lebensgeschichte als Verkündigung.* Göttingen, 1998.

Hoefer, Herbert E. *Churchless Christianity.* Madras, 1991.

Hoffnagel, Judith. "The Believers: Pentecostalism in a Brazilian City." Ph.D. thesis. Indiana University, 1978.

Hollenweger, Walter. *The Pentecostals.* London, 1972.

Honig, Emily. "Christianity, Feminism, and Communism: The Life and Times of Deng Yuzhi." In *Christianity in China: From the Eighteenth Century to the Present,* edited by Daniel H. Bays, 243-62. Stanford, 1996.

Horton, Richard. "African Conversion." *Africa* 41 (April 1971): 85-108.

Howe, K. R. *Where the Waves Fall: A New South Seas Islands History from First Settlement to Colonial Rule.* Sydney, 1984.

Hrangkhuma, F., and Sebastian C. H. Kim. *The Church in India: Its Mission Tomorrow.* New Delhi, 1996.

Hudson, D. Dennis. *Protestant Origins in India: Tamil Evangelical Christians, 1706-1835.* Grand Rapids, MI, and London, 2000.

Hughes, Philip. "The Assimilation of Christianity in Thai Culture." *Religion* 14 (1984): 313-36.

Hughes, Richard T. *Reviving the Ancient Faith: The Story of the Churches of Christ in America.* Grand Rapids, MI, 1996.

Hunter, Alan, and Kim-Kwong Chan. *Protestantism in Contemporary China.* Cambridge, 1993.

Hunter, James. *American Evangelicalism.* New Brunswick, NJ, 1983.

Hutchinson, Mark, and Ogbu Kalu, eds. *A Global Faith: Essays on Evangelicalism and Globalization.* Sydney, 1998.

Hutchinson, W. R., and Hartmut Lehmann, eds. *Many Are Chosen: Divine Election and Western Nationalism.* Minneapolis, 1994.

Ieuti, Teeruro. "The Kiribati Protestant Church and the New Religious Movements, 1860-1985." In *Island Churches: Challenge and Change,* edited by C. W. Forman, 67-109. Suva, 1992.

Ifemesia, C. C. "The 'Civilising' Mission of 1841: Aspects of an Episode in Anglo-Nigerian Relations." In *The History of Christianity in West Africa,* edited by Ogbu Kalu, 81-102. London, 1980.

Iliffe, John. *A Modern History of Tanganyika.* Cambridge, 1979.

Jameson, Fredric, and Masao Miyoshi, eds. *The Cultures of Globalization.* Durham, NC, 1999.

Jaykumar, Samuel. "A Critical and Comparative Study of the Relationship between Missionary Strategy, Dalit Consciousness, and Socio-economic Transformation in the Missionary Work by SPG among the Nadar and Paraiya Community of Tirunelveli District between 1830 and 1930." Ph.D. thesis. The Open University, 1997.

Jeal, Tim. *Livingstone.* New York, 1973.

Jeyaraj, Daniel. *Inkulturation in Tranquebar: Der Beitrag der frühen dänisch-halleschen Mission zum Werden einer indisch-einheimischen Kirche* (1706-1730). Erlangen, 1996.

Jones, Francis P. *The Church in Communist China: A Christian Appraisal.* New York, 1962.

————, ed. *Documents of the Three-self Patriotic Movement.* New York, 1963.

Jordan, David K. "The Glyphomancy Factor: Observations on Chinese Conversion." In *Conversion to Christianity: Historical and Anthropological Perspectives on a Great Transformation,* edited by Robert W. Hefner, 285-303. Berkeley, 1993.

Jordan, Philip D. *The Evangelical Alliance for the United States of America, 1847-1900: Ecumenism, Identity and the Religion of the Republic.* New York, 1982.

Kalu, Ogbu. "Colour and Conversion: The White Missionary Factor in the Christianisation of Igboland, 1867-1967." *Missiology* 18.1 (January 1990): 61-74.

————. *The Embattled Gods: Christianisation of Igboland, 1841-1991.* London, 1996.

————. "Jesus Christ, Where Are You? Themes in West African Church Historiography at the Edge of the 21st Century." Unpublished paper read at the Global Historiography Consultation, 1998.

————. "The Vine and Brambles: Christianity, State and Development in Nigeria, 1900-1994." *Studia Historiae Ecclesiasticae* 22.2 (December 1996): 88-113.

Kamsteeg, Frans. "Pastor y Discipulo." In *Algo Más Que Ópio,* edited by B. Boudewijnse et al., 95-113. San José, Costa Rica, 1991.

Kaplan, Robert D. "The Coming Anarchy." *The Atlantic Monthly* (February 1994): 44-76.

————. *The Ends of the Earth: A Journey to the Frontiers of Anarchy.* New York, 1996.

Karanja, John. "Athamaki for Kings: The Bible and Kikuyu Political Thought." NAMP Position Paper no. 41. Cambridge, 1997.

————. "The Role of Kikuyu Christians in Developing a Self-consciously African Anglicanism." In *The Church Mission Society and World Christianity, 1799-1999,* edited by Kevin Ward and Brian Stanley, 254-82. Grand Rapids, MI, Cambridge, and Richmond, 2000.

Karotemprel, Sabastian. *The Catholic Church in North-East India*. Shillong, 1993.

————. *The Impact of Christianity on the Tribes of North-East India*. Shillong, 1994.

Kessler, J. B. A., Jr. *Historia de la Evangelización en el Perú*. Lima, 1993.

————. *A Study of the Evangelical Alliance in Great Britain*. Goes, Netherlands, 1968.

————. *A Study of the Older Protestant Missions and Churches in Peru and Chile*. Goes, Netherlands, 1967.

Keyes, Charles. "Why the Thai Are Not Christians: Buddhist and Christian Conversion in Thailand." In *Conversion to Christianity: Historical and Anthropological Perspectives on a Great Transformation*, edited by Robert W. Hefner, 259-84. Berkeley, Los Angeles, and Oxford, 1993.

Keysser, Christian. *A People Reborn*. Pasadena, CA, 1980.

Kim, Hans-Martin. *Deutsche Spätaufklarung und Pietismus*. Göttingen, 1998.

Koepp, Wilhelm. *Johann Arndt: Eine Untersuchung über die Mystik im Luthertum*. Berlin, 1912.

Lagos, Humberto. *Crisis de la Esperanza: Religión y Autoritarismo en Chile*. Santiago, 1988.

La Iglesia Evangélica en Números: Resultados Estadísticos del Censo de Iglesias de Lima, Callao y Balnearios. Lima, 1993.

Lam, Joseph. *China: The Last Superpower*. Green Forest, AR, 1997.

Lam, Wing-hung. *Qu gao he gua: Zhao Zizhen di shengping ji shenxue* (The life and thought of Chao Tzu-chen). Hong Kong, 1994.

Lambert, Tony. *The Resurrection of the Chinese Church*. London, 1991.

Lamont, William M. *Richard Baxter and the Millennium*. London, 1979.

Lancaster, Roger. *Thanks to God and the Revolution*. New York, 1988.

Landau, Paul. "'Religion' and Christian Conversion in African History: A New Model." *Journal of Religious History* 23.1 (Feb. 1999): 8-30.

Lara, Carlos Benjamin. "Iglesias evangélicas y conflicto político en el Salvador." *Cristianismo y Sociedad* 103 (1990): 107-21.

Laroche, R. "Some Traditional African Religions and Christianity." In *Christianity in Tropical Africa*, edited by C. G. Baëta, 289-304. London, 1968.

Latourette, Kenneth Scott. "The Church on the Field." In *Interpretative Statistical Survey of the World Mission of the Christian Church*, edited by J. I. Parker. London, 1938.

————. *A History of the Expansion of Christianity*, vol. 5: *The Great Century in the Americas, Australia, and Africa*. New York, 1943.

————. *A History of the Expansion of Christianity*, vol. 6: *The Great Century in Northern Africa and Asia, 1800-1914*. New York, 1944.

————. *A History of the Expansion of Christianity*, vol. 7: *Advance through Storm, A.D. 1914 and after, with concluding generalizations*. New York, 1947.

Lawrence, Carl. *The Church in China: How It Survives and Prospers under Communism*. Minneapolis, 1985.

Lawson, Winston Arthur. *Religion and Race: African and European Roots in Conflict — A Jamaican Testament.* New York, 1996.

Lehmann, David. *Struggle for the Spirit.* Cambridge, 1996.

Lehmann, Hartmut. "'Absonderung' und 'Gemeinschaft' in frühen Pietismus." *Pietismus und Neuzeit* 4 (1977-78): 54-82.

————. *Pietismus und weltliche Ordnung in Württemberg.* Stuttgart, 1969.

————. *Protestantsche Weltsichten: Transformationen seit dem 17. Jahrhundert.* Göttingen, 1998.

Leonard, Emile. *O Protestantismo Brasileiro.* São Paulo, 1963.

Leonardos, Ana Maria. "O Protestantismo Brasileiro: três momentos de análise acadêmica." *Comunicações do ISER* 24 (1987): 15-24.

Leung, Beatrice, and John D. Young, eds. *Christianity in China: Foundations for Dialogue.* Hong Kong, 1993.

Leung, Philip Yuen-sang. "Mission History versus Church History: The Case of China Historiography." *Ching Feng* 40.3-4 (1997): 117-213.

Lewis, Donald M., ed. *Blackwell Dictionary of Evangelical Biography.* 2 vols. Oxford, 1995.

Liang, Jialun (Leung Ka-lun). *Gaige Kaifang yilai Zhongguo di nongcun jiaohui* (The Christian church in rural China since the reform era). Hong Kong, 1990.

————. *Wu Yaozong san lun* (Three essays on Wu Yaozong). Hong Kong, 1997.

Lockward, George. *El Protestantismo en Dominicana.* Santo Domingo, 1982.

London Conference of the Evangelical Alliance. *Report of the Proceedings of the Conference, Held at Freemasons' Hall, London, from August 19th to September 2nd Inclusive, 1846. Published by Order of the Conference.* London, 1847.

Ludden, David, ed. *Making India Hindu: Religion, Community, and the Politics of Democracy in India.* Delhi, Bombay, Calcutta, and Madras, 1996.

Lutz, Jessie G., and R. Ray Lutz. "Karl Gotzlaff's Approach to Indigenization: The Chinese Union." In *Christianity in China: From the Eighteenth Century to the Present,* edited by Daniel H. Bays, 269-91. Stanford, 1996.

Lyall, Leslie T. *God Reigns in China.* London, 1985.

Macedo, Carmen Cinira. *Tempo de Gênesis.* São Paulo, 1986.

McEvedy, Colin, and Richard Jones. *Atlas of World Population History.* New York, 1978.

Machado, Maria das Dores Campos. "Adesão Religiosa a Seus Efeitos na Esfera Privada — Um Estudo Comparativo dos Carismáticos a Pentecostais do Rio de Janeiro." Ph.D. thesis. IUPERJ, Rio de Janeiro, 1994.

McInnis, D. E. *Religion in China Today: Policy and Practice.* Maryknoll, NY, 1989.

Mainwaring, Scott. *Igreja Católica a Política no Brasil: 1916-1985.* São Paulo, 1989.

Mälzer, Gottfried. *Bengel und Zinzendorf.* Witten, 1968.

————. *Johann Albrecht Bengel: Leben und Werk.* Stuttgart, 1970.

Manickam, Sundararaj. *The Social Setting of Christian Conversion in South India.* Wiesbaden, 1971.

Mariano, Ricardo. "Neopentecostalismo: os pentecostais estão mudando." MA thesis. University of São Paulo, 1995.

Mariz, Cecilia. "El Debate en Torno del Pentecostalismo Autónomo en Brasil." *Sociedad y Religión* 13 (1995): 21-32.

———. "La Enseñanza y la Investigación en la Sociología de la Religión en Brasil." In *Ciencias Sociales y Religión en el Cono Sur,* edited by A. Frigerio, 72-85. Buenos Aires, 1993.

———. "Religião a Pobreza: uma comparação entre CEBs e igrejas Pentecostais." *Comunicações do ISER* 7.30 (1988): 10-19.

———. "Religion and Coping with Poverty in Brazil." Ph.D. thesis. Boston University, 1989.

Marostica, Matt. "La Iglesia Evangélica en la Argentina como Nuevo Movimiento Social." *Sociedad y Religión* 12 (June 1994): 3-16.

Marshall, Robert, and J. Thompson. *A Brief Historical Account of Sundry Things in the Doctrines and State of the Christian, or, as It is Historically Called, the Newlight Church.* Cincinnati, 1811.

Marshall, Ruth. "'Power in the Name of Jesus': Social Transformation and Pentecostalism in Western Nigeria 'Revisited.'" In *Legitimacy and the State in Twentieth-Century Africa: Essays in Honour of A. H. M. Kirk-Greene,* edited by Terence Ranger and Olufemi Vaughan, 213-46. Basingstoke and London, 1993.

Marshall-Fratani, Ruth. "Mediating the Global and Local in Nigerian Pentecostalism." *Journal of Religion in Africa* 28.3 (1998): 278-315.

Mar Thoma, Alexander (Metropolitan). *The Marthoma Church: Heritage and Mission.* Tiruvalla, 1985.

Martin, David. *The Dilemmas of Contemporary Religion.* Oxford, 1978.

———. *Forbidden Revolutions.* London, 1996.

———. *A General Theory of Secularization.* Oxford, 1978.

———. *Tongues of Fire: The Explosion of Protestantism in Latin America.* Oxford, 1990.

Marty, Martin E. "The Revival of Evangelicalism and Southern Religion." In *Varieties of Southern Evangelicalism,* edited by David E. Harrell Jr., 7-21. Macon, GA, 1981.

Mason, J. C. S. "The Role of the Moravian Church during the Missionary Awakening in England, 1760-1800." Ph.D. thesis. University of London, 1998.

Massie, J. W. *The Evangelical Alliance: Its Origin and Development, Containing Personal Notices of Its Distinguished Friends in Europe and America.* London, 1847.

Mather, Cotton. *Magnalia Christi Americana.* 2 vols. London, 1702; repr. Edinburgh, 1979.

Matthias, Markus. *Johann Wilhelm und Johanna Eleonora Petersen.* Göttingen, 1993.

Maxwell, David. "The Church and the Democratisation of Africa: The Case of

Zimbabwe." In *The Christian Churches and Africa's Democratization*, edited by Paul Gifford, 108-29. Leiden, 1995.

————. "Witches, Prophets, and Avenging Spirits." *Journal of Religion in Africa* 25.3 (1995): 309-39.

Mbiti, J. S. "Some African Concepts of Christology." In *Christ and the Younger Churches*, edited by G. F. Vicedom, 51-62. London, 1972.

Mendonça, Antônio Gouvêa. "Um Panorama do Protestantismo Brasileiro Atual." In *Sinais dos Tempos: Tradições Religiosas no Brasil*, edited by L. Landim, 37-86. Rio de Janeiro, 1989.

————, and Prócoro Velasques Filho. *Introdução ao Protestantismo no Brasil*. São Paulo, 1990.

Meyer, Birgit. "Translating the Devil." Ph.D. thesis. University of Amsterdam, 1995.

Middlekauf, Robert. *The Mathers: Three Generations of Puritan Intellectuals, 1596-1728*. New York, 1971.

Monteiro, Duglas Teixeira. "Igrejas, Seitas e Agências: Aspectos de um Ecumenismo Popular." In *A Cultura do Povo III*, edited by E. Valle and J. Queiroz, 81-111. São Paulo, 1979.

Mullins, Mark, and Richard Fox Young, eds. *Perspectives on Christianity in Korea and Japan*. Lampeter, 1995.

Munro, Doug, and Andrew Thornley. *The Covenant Makers: Islander Missionaries in the Pacific*. Suva, 1996.

Natarajan, Nalini. *The Missionary among the Khasis*. New Delhi, 1977.

Neill, Stephen. *The Unfinished Task*. London, 1957.

Nelson, Reed Elliot. "Organizational Homogeneity, Growth and Conflict in Brazilian Protestantism." *Sociological Analysis* 48.4 (1988): 319-27.

Nelson, Wilton. *Protestantism in Central America*. Grand Rapids, MI, 1984.

Newbigin, Leslie. *A Word in Season: Perspectives on Christian World Missions*. Grand Rapids, MI, 1994.

Ngan-Woo, Feleti E. *Faa Samoa: The World of Samoans*. Auckland, 1985.

Niebuhr, H. Richard. *The Social Sources of Denominationalism*. Cleveland, 1929.

Niño Chavarría, Adonis. "Breve Historia del Movimiento Pentecostal en Nicaragua." In *Pentecostalismo y Liberación*, edited by C. Alvarez, 47-57. San José, Costa Rica, 1992.

Nock, A. D. *Conversion: The Old and the New in Religion from Alexander the Great to Augustine of Hippo*. Oxford, 1933.

Nordmann, W. "Im Widerstreit von Mystik und Föderalismus." *Zeitschrift für Kirchengeschichte* 50 (1931).

Northcott, Michael. "A Survey of the Rise of Charismatic Christianity in Malaysia." *Asian Journal of Theology* 4.1 (1990): 266-78.

Novaes, Regina Reyes. *Os Escolhidos de Deus*. Rio de Janeiro, 1992.

Nurallah, Syed, and J. P. Naik. *A History of Education in India*. London, 1951.

Nuttall, G. F., ed. *Calendar of the Correspondence of Philip Doddridge.* No. 505. London, 1979.

O, Sek-Keun. *Der Volksglaube und das Christentum in Korea.* Munich, 1979.

Oddie, Geoffrey A. *Hindu and Christian in South-East India.* London, 1991.

―――. *Social Protest in India: British Protestant Missionaries and Social Reforms, 1830-1900.* Columbia, MO, and New Delhi, 1978.

―――, ed. *Religion in South Asia: Religious Conversion and Revival Movements in South Asia in Medieval and Modern Times.* Columbia, MO, and New Delhi, 1977.

―――, ed. *Religious Conversion Movements in South Asia: Continuities and Change, 1800-1900.* London, 1997.

Ojo, Matthews A. "The Charismatic Movement in Nigeria Today." *International Bulletin of Missionary Research* 19.3 (July 1995): 114-18.

Okorocha, Cyril C. *The Meaning of Religious Conversion in Africa: The Case of the Igbo of Nigeria.* Aldershot, 1987.

―――. "Religious Conversion in Africa: Its Missiological Implications." *Mission Studies* 9.18 (1992): 168-80.

Okure, Teresa. "Conversion, Commitment: An African Perspective." *Mission Studies* 10.12 (1993): 109-33.

Oliver, Roland. *The African Experience.* London, 1994.

―――. *The Missionary Factor in East Africa.* 2nd ed. London, 1965.

Orcibal, Jean. "The Theological Originality of John Wesley and Continental Spirituality." In *A History of the Methodist Church in Great Britain,* edited by R. Davies and G. Rupp, 1:81-111. 4 vols. London, 1965-88.

Oro, Ari Pedro. "Religiões Pentecostais e Meios de Comunicação de Massa no Sul do Brasil." *Revista Eclesiástica Brasileira* 50.198 (1990): 304-34.

Owandayo, M. O. "Bishop Samuel Ajayi Crowther (1810-1891)." In *Makers of the Church in Nigeria,* edited by J. A. Omoyajowo, 29-53. Lagos, 1995.

Page, Jesse. *The Black Bishop: Samuel Adjai Crowther.* London, 1908.

Paredes, Rubén. "Presencia Evangélica en Lima." In *El Evangelio en Platos de Barro,* edited by R. Paredes, 99-126. Lima, 1989.

Parker, Cristián. "Perspectiva Crítica sobre la Sociología de la Religión en América Latina." In *Ciencias Sociales y Religión en el Cono Sur,* edited by A. Frigerio, 123-50. Buenos Aires, 1993.

Peel, J. D. Y. *Aladura: A Religious Movement among the Yoruba.* London, 1968.

―――. "Engaging with Islam in Nineteenth-Century Yorubaland." NAMP Position Paper no. 27. Cambridge, 1997. Incorporated into J. D. Y. Peel, *Religious Encounter and the Making of the Yoruba.* Bloomington, IN, 2000.

―――. "For Who Hath Despised the Day of Small Things? Missionary Narratives and Historical Anthropology." *Comparative Studies in Society and History* 37.3 (July 1995): 581-607.

Peschke, Erhard. "Die Bedeutung der Mystik für die Bekehrung August Hermann Franckes." *Theologische Literaturzeitung* 91 (1966): 881-92; reprinted in *Zur neueren Pietismusforschung,* edited by M. Greschat, 294-316. Darmstadt, 1977.

Peterson, Derek. "Translating the Word: Dialogism and Debate in Two Gikuyu Dictionaries." *Journal of Religious History* 23.2 (Feb. 1999): 31-50.

Peuckert, Will-Erich. *Pansophie.* 3 vols. Berlin, 1956-73.

Phelps-Stokes Commission. *Education in Africa.* New York, 1922.

————. *Education in East Africa.* New York and London, n.d. [1925].

Pi Hugarte, Renzo. "Los Estudios sobre Religión en Uruguay." In *Ciencias Sociales y Religión en el Cono Sur,* edited by A. Frigerio, 93-122. Buenos Aires, 1993.

Piepmeier, Rainer. "Theologie des Lebens und Neuzeitprozesse: Fr. Chr. Oetinger." *Pietismus und Neuzeit* 5 (1979): 184-217.

Pirouet, M. Louise. "East African Christians and World War I." *Journal of African History* 19.1 (1978): 117-30.

Piscatori, James, and Susanne Hoeber Rudolph, eds. *Transnational Religion and Fading States.* Boulder, CO, and Oxford, 1997.

Plett, Rodolfo. *El Protestantismo en el Paraguay.* Asunción, 1987.

Poiret, P. *The Divine Oeconomy.* London, 1713.

Porter, Andrew. "'Cultural Imperialism' and Protestant Missionary Enterprise, 1780-1914." *Journal of Imperial and Commonwealth History* 25.3 (Sept. 1997): 367-91.

————. "Evangelicalism, Islam, and Millennial Expectation in the Nineteenth Century." NAMP Position Paper no. 76. Cambridge, 1998.

Prandi, Reginaldo, and Antônio Flávio Pierucci. "Religiões e Voto no Brasil: as eleições presidenciais de 1994." Unpublished paper read at the Annual Congress of the Associação Nacional de Pós-Graduação e Pesquisa em Ciências Sociais, 1994.

Pye-Smith, Charlie. *Rebels and Outcasts: A Journey through Christian India.* London and New York, 1997.

Quistorp, Heinrich. *Calvin's Doctrine of the Last Things.* London, 1955.

Ramachandra, Vinoth. "The Honour of Listening: Indispensable for Mission." *Evangelical Mission Quarterly* 30 (October 1994): 404-9.

Rambo, Lewis R. *Understanding Religious Conversion.* New Haven, 1993.

Ramos, Marcos Antonio. *Panorama del Protestantismo en Cuba.* Miami, 1986.

Ranger, Terence O. "Religious Movements and Politics in Sub-Saharan Africa." *African Studies Review* 29.2 (June 1986): 49-51.

Rapaport, Joanne. "Las Misiones protestantes y la resistencia indigena en el Sur de Colombia." *América Indígena* 44.1 (1984): 111-26.

Rawlyk, George A., ed. *Henry Alline: Selected Writings.* New York, 1987.

Raychaudhuri, Tapan. "British Rule in India: An Assessment." In *The Cambridge Illustrated History of the British Empire,* edited by P. J. Marshall, 357-69. Cambridge, 1996.

Reeve, Sir Paul. "Building a Global Perspective." *Anglican Observer at the UN* 1.3 (April 1994).

The Relations between the Younger and Older Churches: Report of the Jerusalem Meeting of the International Missionary Council March 24th–April 8th 1928. Vol. 3. London, 1928.

Ripert, Blandine. "Christianisme et Pouvoirs Locaux dans une vallée Tamang du Népal Central." *Archives de Sciences Sociales des Religions* 99 (July-Sept. 1997): 69-86.

Robert, Dana. "Shifting Southward: Global Christianity since 1945." *International Bulletin of Missionary Research* 24.2 (April 2000): 50-58.

Roberts, Bryan. "Protestant Groups and Coping with Urban Life in Guatemala City." *American Journal of Sociology* 73 (May 1968): 753-67.

Rolim, Francisco Cartaxo. *Pentecostais no Brasil.* Petrópolis, 1985.

Rosa, Julio. *O Evangelho Quadrangular no Brasil.* n.p., 1978.

Rose, S., and Q. Schultze. "The Evangelical Awakening in Guatemala: Fundamentalist Impact on Education and Media." In *Fundamentalisms and Society,* edited by Martin Marty and J. Scott Appleby, 415-51. Chicago, 1993.

Rostas, Susanna, and André Droogers, eds. *The Popular Use of Popular Religion in Latin America.* Amsterdam, 1993.

Rubinstein, Murray A. "Holy Spirit Taiwan: Pentecostal and Charismatic Christianity in the Republic of China." In *Christianity in China: From the Eighteenth Century to the Present,* edited by Daniel H. Bays, 353-66. Stanford, 1996.

Russell, Horace O. *The Missionary Outreach of the West Indian Church: Jamaican Baptist Missions to West Africa in the Nineteenth Century.* New York and Washington, 2000.

Sanneh, Lamin. "Gospel and Culture: Ramifying Effects of Scriptural Translation." In *Bible Translation and the Spread of the Church,* edited by Philip C. Stine, 1-23. Leiden, 1990.

―――. *Piety and Power: Muslims and Christians in West Africa.* Maryknoll, NY, 1996.

―――. *Translating the Message: The Missionary Impact on Culture.* Maryknoll, NY, 1989.

Saracco, Norberto. "Argentine Pentecostalism: Its History and Theology." Ph.D. thesis. University of Birmingham, 1989.

―――, ed. *Directorio y Censo Evangélico.* Buenos Aires, 1992.

Schering, Ernst. "Mystik als Erkenntnis: Motive und Aspekte der mystischen Theologie Fénelons." *Pietismus und Neuzeit* 5 (1979): 164-83.

Schmidt, Martin. "Die Biographie des französischen Grafen Gaston Jean-Baptiste de Renty (1611-1649) und ihre Aufnahme im 18. Jahrhundert." In *Wiedergeburt und neuer Mensch,* edited by Martin Schmidt, 390-439. Witten, 1969.

Schoeps, H. J. *Philosemitism im Barock: Religions- and geistesgeschichtliche Untersuchungen.* Tübingen, 1952.

Scholem, Gershom. *Alchemie und Kabbala: Ein Kapitel aus der Mystik.* Berlin, 1927.

————. *On the Kabbalah and Its Symbolism*. London, 1965.

Scott, Luis. *La Sal de la Tierra: Una Historia Socio-Política de los Evangélicos en la Ciudad de México (1964-1991)*. Mexico, 1991.

Sepúlveda, Juan. "Pentecostalismo y Democracia: una Interpretación de sus Relaciones." In *Democracia y Evangelio*, 229-50. Santiago, 1988.

Shaw, M. *The Kingdom of God in Africa: A Short History of African Christianity*. Grand Rapids, MI, 1996.

Shenk, David A. "William Wadé Harris, ca. 1860-1929: God Made His Soul a Soul of Fire." In *Mission Legacies*, edited by G. Anderson et al., 155-65. Maryknoll, NY, 1996.

Showalter, Nathan D. *The End of a Crusade: The Student Volunteer Movement for Foreign Missions and the Great War*. Lanham, MD, and London, 1998.

Siewert, J. A., and E. G. Valdez, eds. *Mission Handbook*. Monrovia, CA, 1997.

Siwatibau, Sulian, and B. David Williams. *A Call to a New Exodus: An Anti-Nuclear Primer for Pacific People*. Suva, 1982.

Smith, Dennis. "Coming of Age: A Reflection on Pentecostals, Politics and Popular Religion in Guatemala." *Pneuma* 13.2 (Fall 1991): 131-39.

Smith, George Adam. *Mohammedanism and Christianity: A Sermon Preached on September 30th, 1908, at the Autumn Session of the Baptist Missionary Society, Held in Bradford*. London, n.d.

Snaitang, O. L. *Christianity and Social Change in North-East India*. Shillong, 1993.

So, Ki Jong. "The Translation of the Bible into Korean: Its History and Significance." Ph.D. thesis. Drew University, 1993.

Soares, Luiz Eduardo. "A Guerra dos Pentecostais contra os Afro-Brasileiros: Dimensões Democráticas do Conflito Religioso no Brasil." *Comunicações do ISER* 44 (1993): 43-50.

Soares, Mariza. "Guerra Santa no País do Sincretismo." In *Sinais dos Tempos: Diversidade Religiosa no Brasil*, edited by L. Landim, 75-104. Rio de Janeiro, 1990.

Southey, R. *Life of Wesley*. 2 vols. London, 1925.

Spangenberg, A. G. *Apologetische Schluss-Schrift* (1752); reprinted in *Zinzendorf Werke*. Ergänzungsband 3. Hildesheim, 1964.

Stanley, Brian. *The Bible and the Flag: Protestant Missions and British Imperialism in the Nineteenth and Twentieth Centuries*. Leicester, 1990.

————. "Church, State, and the Hierarchy of 'Civilization': The Making of the Commission VII Report, 'Missions and Governments,' Edinburgh 1910." NAMP Position Paper no. 70. Cambridge, 1998.

————. *The History of the Baptist Missionary Society 1792-1992*. Edinburgh, 1992.

Statistical Atlas of Christian Missions. Edinburgh, 1910.

Stilwell, Ewan. "Towards a Melanesian Theology of Conversion." *Melanesian Journal of Theology* 9.1 (April 1993): 29-42.

Stock, Eugene. *The History of the Church Missionary Society*. 4 vols. London, 1899-1916.

Stoll, David. *Is Latin America Turning Protestant?* Berkeley, 1990.

———. "'Jesus Is Lord of Guatemala': Evangelical Reform in a Death-Squad State." In *Accounting for Fundamentalisms: The Dynamic Character of Movements,* edited by Martin Marty and J. Scott Appleby, 99-123. Chicago, 1994.

Stoudt, J. J. *Sunrise to Eternity: A Study in Jacob Boehme's Life and Thought.* Philadelphia, 1957.

Streiff, P. P. *Jean Guillaume de la Fléchère. Ein Beitrag zur Geschichte des Methodismus.* Frankfurt am Main, 1984.

Studdert-Kennedy, Gerald. *Providence and the Raj: Imperial Mission and Missionary Imperialism.* New Delhi, 1998.

Sundkler, Bengt. *The Christian Ministry in Africa.* Uppsala, 1960.

Tarducci, Mónica. "Pentecostalismo y Relaciones de Género: una Revisión." In *Nuevos Movimientos Religiosos y Ciencias Sociales (1),* edited by A. Frigerio, 81-96. Buenos Aires, 1993.

Tasie, G. O. M. *Christian Missionary Enterprise in the Niger Delta, 1864-1918.* Leiden, 1978.

Taule'aleausumai, Feiloaiga. "Pastoral Care: A Samoan Perspective." In *Counselling Issues and South Pacific Communities,* edited by P. Culbertson, 215-37. Palmerston North, 1997.

Taylor, John V. *The Primal Vision.* Philadelphia, 1963.

Tchervonnaya, Svetlana. "The Revival of Animistic Religion in the Mari El Republic." In *New Religious Phenomena in Central and Eastern Europe,* edited by Irena Borowik and Grzegorz Babinski, 369-78. Krakow, 1997.

Teixeira, Faustino, et al. *CEBs: Cidadania a Modernidade.* São Paulo, 1993.

Tennekes, Hans. *El Movimiento Pentecostal en la Sociedad Chilena.* Iquique, 1985.

Tiatia, Jemaima. *Caught Between Cultures: A New Zealand–Born Pacific Island Perspective.* Auckland, 1998.

Tiedemann, R. G. "China and Its Neighbours." In *A World History of Christianity,* edited by Adrian Hastings, 369-415. London, 1999.

Tiliander, Brör. *Christian and Hindu Terminology: A Study of Their Mutual Relations with Special Reference to the Tamil Area.* Uppsala, 1974.

Tippett, Alan. *People Movements in Southern Polynesia: A Study in Church Growth.* Chicago, 1971.

Troeltsch, Ernst. *The Social Teaching of the Christian Churches.* 2 vols. London, 1931.

Trompf, G. W. "Geographical, Historical, and Intellectual Perspectives." In *The Gospel Is Not Western: Black Theologies from the Southwest Pacific,* edited by G. W. Trompf, 3-15. Maryknoll, NY, 1987.

———. *Payback: The Logic of Retribution in Melanesian Religions.* Cambridge, 1994.

Tupouniua, Sione, Ron Crocombe, and Claire Slatter. *The Pacific Way: Social Issues in National Development.* Suva, 1975.

Turner, H. W. *African Independent Churches: The Church of the Lord (Aladura)*. 2 vols. Oxford, 1967.

Tyerman, L. *Life of the Rev. George Whitefield*. 2nd ed. 2 vols. London, 1890.

Underhill, Evelyn. *Mysticism: The Development of Humankind's Spiritual Consciousness*. 14th ed. London, 1995.

Uttendörfer, O. *Zinzendorf und die Mystik*. Berlin, 1950.

Van der Veer, Peter, ed. *Conversion to Modernities: The Globalization of Christianity*. New York and London, 1996.

Van Houten, Richard, and Jonathan Chao, eds. *Wise as Serpents, Harmless as Doves: Christians in China Tell Their Story*. Pasadena, CA, 1988.

Vasconcelos, Alcebíades. *Sinopse Histórica das Assembléias de Deus no Brasil*. Manaus, 1983.

Venn, John. *The Life and a Selection from the Letters of the Late Henry Venn*. Edited by H. Venn. London, 1834.

Village Education in India: The Report of a Commission on Inquiry. London, 1920.

Viscountess Knutsford (= M. J. Holland). *Life and Letters of Zachary Macaulay*. London, 1900.

Visvanathan, Susan. *The Christians of Kerala: History, Belief and Ritual among the Yakoba*. Madras, 1993.

Viswanathan, Gauri. *Outside the Fold; Conversion, Modernity, and Belief*. Princeton, 1998.

Wach, Joachim. *Sociology of Religion*. Chicago, 1944.

Wacker, Grant. "Searching for Eden with a Satellite Dish: Primitivism, Pragmatism and the Pentecostal Character." In *The Primitive Church in the Modern World*, edited by Richard Hughes, 139-66. Urbana and Chicago, 1995.

Wallman, Johannes. *Theologie und Frömmigkeit im Zeitalter des Barock*. Tübingen, 1995.

Walls, A. F. "African Christianity in the History of Religions." *Studies in World Christianity* 2.2 (1996): 183-203.

―――. *The Missionary Movement in Christian History: Studies in the Transmission of the Faith*. Maryknoll, NY, 1996.

―――. "Samuel Adjai (or Ajayi) Crowther." In *Biographical Dictionary of Christian Missions*, edited by Gerald H. Anderson, 160-61. New York, 1998.

―――. "Samuel Ajayi Crowther, 1807-1891: Foremost African Christian of the Nineteenth Century." In *Mission Legacies*, edited by Gerald H. Anderson et al., 132-39. Maryknoll, NY, 1994.

―――. "The Significance of Christianity in Africa." Friends of St. Colm's Public Lecture, 1989.

―――. "Thomas Fowell Buxton, 1786-1844: Missions and the Remedy for African Slavery." In *Mission Legacies*, edited by Gerald H. Anderson et al., 11-17. Maryknoll, NY, 1994.

―――. "The Translation Principle in Christian History." In *Bible Translation and the Spread of the Church*, edited by Philip C. Stine, 24-39. Leiden, 1990.

Wang, Changxin (Stephen C. H. Wang). *You Sishi nian* (Wang Mingdao: the last forty years). Scarborough, ONT, 1997.

Wang, Mingdao. *Wushi nian lai* (My fifty years). Hong Kong, 1950.

Wang, Xuezeng, ed. *Zongjiao wenti gailun* (Essays on religious issues). Chengdu, 1997.

Ward, Kevin. "Africa." In *A World History of Christianity*, edited by Adrian Hastings, 192-237. London, 1999.

———. "'Taking Stock': The Church Missionary Society and Its Historians." In *The Church Mission Society and World Christianity, 1799-1999*, edited by Kevin Ward and Brian Stanley, 15-42. Grand Rapids, MI, and London, 2000.

Ward, W. R. *Faith and Faction*. London, 1993.

———. "Mysticism and Revival: The Case of Gerhard Tersteegen." In *Revival and Religion since 1700: Essays for John Walsh*, edited by Jane Garnett and Colin Matthew, 41-58. London, 1993.

Webster, John C. B. *A History of the Dalit Christians in India*. San Francisco, 1992.

Wells, Kenneth M. *New God, New Nation: Protestants and Self-Reconstruction. Nationalism in Korea, 1896-1937*. Honolulu, 1991.

Wesley, John. *Explanatory Notes on the New Testament*. London, 1958.

———. *Letters of John Wesley*. Edited by J. Telford, 8 vols. London, 1931.

———. *Sermons*. 3 vols. London, 1872.

———. *Thoughts upon Jacob Behmen*. 1780. Reprinted in *Works of the Rev. John Wesley*. 3rd ed. 14 vols. London, 1830.

———. *Works of John Wesley (Bicentennial Edition)*. Vols. 22, 23. Journal and Diaries, edited by W. R. Ward and R. P. Heitzenrater. Nashville, 1995.

Whitefield, George. *George Whitefield's Journal*. Edinburgh, 1960.

———. *Letters of George Whitefield*. Edinburgh, repr. 1976.

———. *The Works of the Rev. George Whitefield*. 6 vols. London, 1771.

Whiteman, Darrell. "Melanesian Religions: An Overview." In *An Introduction to Melanesian Religions*, edited by Ennio Mantovani, 87-121. Point, vol. 6. Goroka, 1984.

———. *Melanesians and Missionaries: An Ethnohistorical Study of Social and Religious Change in the Southwest Pacific*. Pasadena, CA, 1983.

Whyte, Bob. *Unfinished Encounter: China and Christianity*. London, 1988.

Wickeri, Phillip. *Seeking the Common Ground: Protestants, the CCP and the United Front*. Marynoll, NY, 1989.

Willems, Emilio. *Followers of the New Faith: Culture Change and the Rise of Protestantism in Brazil and Chile*. Nashville, 1967.

Williams, C. Peter. *The Ideal of the Self-Governing Church: A Study in Victorian Missionary Strategy*. Leiden, 1990.

Williams, John. *A Narrative of Missionary Enterprises in the South Sea Islands*. London, 1839.

Wilson, Bryan. *Religion in Sociological Perspective*. Oxford, 1982.

———. *Religious Sects: A Sociological Study*. London, 1970.

Wilson, Everett. "Identity, Community, and Status: The Legacy of the Central American Pentecostal Pioneers." In *Earthen Vessels,* edited by Joel Carpenter and Wilbert Shenk, 133-51. Grand Rapids, MI, 1990.

————. "Sanguine Saints: Pentecostalism in El Salvador." *Church History* 52 (1983): 186-98.

Wilson, John F. "History, Redemption and the Millennium." In *Jonathan Edwards and the American Experience,* edited by Nathan O. Hatch and Harry S. Stout, 131-41. Oxford, 1988.

World Missionary Conference, 1910. Volume 1: *Carrying the Gospel to all the Non-Christian World.* Edinburgh and London, n.d.

————. Volume 2: *The Church in the Mission Field.* Edinburgh and London, n.d.

————. Volume 4: *The Missionary Message in Relation to Non-Christian Religions.* Edinburgh and London, n.d.

————. Volume 9: *The History and Records of the Conference.* Edinburgh and London, n.d.

Wu, Ying. "Idujiao zai dalu chengxiang di chuanbo yu fazhan" ("The spread and development of Christianity in the cities and villages in Mainland China"). *Ming Pao Monthly* [Hong Kong] (December 1994): 50-55.

Wynarczyk, Hilario. "Las aproximaciones a la sociología del campo evangélico en la Argentina." In *Ciencias Sociales y Religión en el Cono Sur,* edited by A. Frigerio, 61-71. Buenos Aires, 1993.

————, and Pablo Semán. "Un Análisis del campo evangélico y el Pentecostalismo en la Argentina." In *El Pentecostalismo en la Argentina,* edited by Alejandro Frigerio, 29-43. Buenos Aires, 1994.

————, Pablo Semán, and Mercedes De Majo. *Panorama Actual del Campo Evangélico en Argentina.* Buenos Aires, 1995.

Xing, Fuzeng (Ying Fuk Tsang), and Jialun Liang (Leung Ka Lun). *Wushi niandai sanzi yundong di yanjiu* (The three-self patriotic movement in the 1950s). Hong Kong, 1996.

Xinshiqi zongjiao gongzuo wenxian xuanbian (Selected documents on religious work in the new era). Beijing, 1995.

Yang, Zhouhuai. "Beijing jidujiao lishi he xianchuang tubiao" ("Graphic charts and tables on Beijing's Christian churches: past and present"). *Ming Pao Monthly* [Hong Kong] (December 1994): 56-57.

Young, Richard Fox. *Resistant Hinduism: Sanskrit Sources on Anti-Christian Apologetics in Early Nineteenth-Century India.* Vienna and Delhi, 1981.

————, and S. Jebanesan. *The Bible Trembled: The Hindu-Christian Controversies of Nineteenth-Century Ceylon.* Vienna, 1995.

Zavala, Rubén. *Historia de las Asambleas de Dios del Perú.* Lima, 1989.

Zhang, Richard X. Y. "The Origin of the 'Three Self.'" *Jian Dao* 5 (1996).

Zhang, Shengzuo, ed. *Zongjiao zhengce xuexi gangyao* (Principles of government's religious policy). Beijing, 1995.

Zimmerman, R. C. *Das Weltbild des jungen Goethe.* Munich, 1969.

Zhong, Min, and Kim-Kwong Chan. "The 'Apostolic Church': A Case Study of a House Church in Rural China." In *Christianity in China: Foundations for Dialogue,* edited by Beatrice Leung and John Young, 250-65. Hong Kong, 1993.

Ziegenbalg, Bartholomaeus. *The Propagation of the Gospel in the East.* Edited, with introductory notes, by A. W. Böhme, in "Preliminary Discourses Concerning the Character of Missions . . ." London, 1709, 1710, 1718.

Zub, Roberto. *Protestantismo y Elecciones en Nicaragua.* Managua, 1993.

Index